MISSION 376

The Stackpole Military History Series

THE AMERICAN CIVIL WAR
Cavalry Raids of the Civil War
Ghost, Thunderbolt, and Wizard
In the Lion's Mouth
Pickett's Charge
Witness to Gettysburg

WORLD WAR I
Doughboy War

WORLD WAR II
After D-Day
Airborne Combat
Armor Battles of the Waffen-SS,
    1943–45
Armoured Guardsmen
Army of the West
Arnhem 1944
Australian Commandos
The B-24 in China
Backwater War
The Battle of France
The Battle of Sicily
Battle of the Bulge, Vol. 1
Battle of the Bulge, Vol. 2
Beyond the Beachhead
Beyond Stalingrad
The Black Bull
Blitzkrieg Unleashed
Blossoming Silk against the
    Rising Sun
Bodenplatte
The Brandenburger Commandos
The Brigade
Bringing the Thunder
The Canadian Army and the
    Normandy Campaign
Coast Watching in World War II
Colossal Cracks
Condor
A Dangerous Assignment
D-Day Bombers
D-Day Deception
D-Day to Berlin
Decision in the Ukraine
Destination Normandy
Dive Bomber!
A Drop Too Many
Eagles of the Third Reich
The Early Battles of Eighth Army
Eastern Front Combat
Europe in Flames
Exit Rommel
The Face of Courage
Fist from the Sky
Flying American Combat Aircraft of
    World War II
For Europe
Forging the Thunderbolt
For the Homeland

Fortress France
The German Defeat in the East,
    1944–45
German Order of Battle, Vol. 1
German Order of Battle, Vol. 2
German Order of Battle, Vol. 3
The Germans in Normandy
Germany's Panzer Arm in
    World War II
GI Ingenuity
Goodwood
The Great Ships
Grenadiers
Guns against the Reich
Hitler's Nemesis
Hold the Westwall
Infantry Aces
In the Fire of the Eastern Front
Iron Arm
Iron Knights
Japanese Army Fighter Aces
JG 26 Luftwaffe Fighter Wing
    War Diary, Vol. 1
JG 26 Luftwaffe Fighter Wing
    War Diary, Vol. 2
Kampfgruppe Peiper at the Battle
    of the Bulge
The Key to the Bulge
Knight's Cross Panzers
Kursk
Luftwaffe Aces
Luftwaffe Fighter Ace
Luftwaffe Fighter-Bombers over
    Britain
Luftwaffe Fighters and Bombers
Massacre at Tobruk
Mechanized Juggernaut or Military
    Anachronism?
Messerschmitts over Sicily
Michael Wittmann, Vol. 1
Michael Wittmann, Vol. 2
Mission 376
Mountain Warriors
The Nazi Rocketeers
Night Flyer / Mosquito Pathfinder
No Holding Back
On the Canal
Operation Mercury
Packs On!
Panzer Aces
Panzer Aces II
Panzer Aces III
Panzer Commanders of the
    Western Front
Panzergrenadier Aces
Panzer Gunner
The Panzer Legions
Panzers in Normandy
Panzers in Winter
Panzer Wedge

The Path to Blitzkrieg
Penalty Strike
Poland Betrayed
Red Road from Stalingrad
Red Star under the Baltic
Retreat to the Reich
Rommel's Desert Commanders
Rommel's Desert War
Rommel's Lieutenants
The Savage Sky
Ship-Busters
The Siege of Küstrin
The Siegfried Line
A Soldier in the Cockpit
Soviet Blitzkrieg
Stalin's Keys to Victory
Surviving Bataan and Beyond
T-34 in Action
Tank Tactics
Tigers in the Mud
Triumphant Fox
The 12th SS, Vol. 1
The 12th SS, Vol. 2
Twilight of the Gods
Typhoon Attack
The War against Rommel's
    Supply Lines
War in the Aegean
War of the White Death
Winter Storm
Wolfpack Warriors
Zhukov at the Oder

THE COLD WAR / VIETNAM
Cyclops in the Jungle
Expendable Warriors
Fighting in Vietnam
Flying American Combat Aircraft:
    The Cold War
Here There Are Tigers
Land with No Sun
MiGs over North Vietnam
Phantom Reflections
Street without Joy
Through the Valley
Two One Pony

**WARS OF AFRICA AND THE
MIDDLE EAST**
Never-Ending Conflict
The Rhodesian War

GENERAL MILITARY HISTORY
Carriers in Combat
Cavalry from Hoof to Track
Desert Battles
Guerrilla Warfare
Ranger Dawn
Sieges
The Spartan Army

MISSION 376

Battle over the Reich, May 28, 1944

Ivo de Jong

STACKPOLE
BOOKS

Published in paperback in the United States in 2012 by
STACKPOLE BOOKS
5067 Ritter Road
Mechanicsburg, PA 17055
www.stackpolebooks.com

Cover design by Tracy Patterson

Printed in the United States of America

10 9 8 7 6 5 4 3 2 1

Library of Congress Cataloging-in-Publication Data

Jong, Ivo de, 1963–
    Mission 376 : battle over the Reich, May 28, 1944 / Ivo de Jong.
        p. cm. — (Stackpole military history series)
    "First published in Great Britain in 2003 by Hikoki Publications"—T.p. verso.
    Includes bibliographical references and index.
    ISBN 978-0-8117-1159-3 (pbk.)
    1. World War, 1939–1945—Aerial operations, American.   2. World War,
1939–1945—Campaigns—Germany.   3. United States. Army Air Forces. Air Force,
8th—History.   4. World War, 1939–1945—Regimental histories—United States.
I. Title.   II. Title: Mission three hundred seventy six.   III. Title: Mission three
seven six.   IV. Title: Mission three seventy six.
    D790.J667 2012
    940.54'213—dc23
                                                                          2012012224

Contents

Preface

It was a peaceful, quiet Sunday afternoon with fine spring weather in the village of Groenekan, near Utrecht in occupied Holland. Suddenly, barely missing a line of trees, a huge aircraft, accompanied by two fighters overhead, roars in the direction of the village. Several Dutchmen have a grandstand view of what is going to happen, including eighteen-year-old Willem de Jong. The pilots of the aircraft make a perfect belly-landing in a pasture, and after it has crossed several ditches, the aircraft comes to a stop and bursts into flames. Crewmembers jump out of the wrecked Flying Fortress, as it is now recognized by Willem de Jong, as he runs towards it. One of the crewmembers, badly wounded, is then carried by several Dutchmen to a barn, where he dies a few minutes later. The surviving crew are quickly taken prisoner by German troops, billeted in the nearby old fort Maartensdijk.

This was the story that was often told to me, when I grew up as the son of Willem de Jong. In the early 1980s, when I reached about the age my father had been during this incident, I became more and more interested in his story and, already fascinated by military history, decided to do my best to find out more about this particular Flying Fortress and its crew. After I established the date as 28 May 1944 and the Fortress as belonging to the 388th Bomb Group, I made my first efforts to get in contact with some crewmembers. With assistance of the 388th Bomb Group Association, I managed to find Clyde Waite, the former radio operator of the crew. His kind response to my first and very amateur letter of inquiry stirred an interest in me, which has finally led to this book.

What at first started with a family war story grew to an avid interest in the American Eighth Air Force and its mission of 28 May 1944 in particular. I learned that thirty-two bombers and fourteen fighters did not return to their respective bases that day and that numerous other events, worth recording, took place. But, of greater importance, no fewer than 107 American airmen died that day aboard their bombers or fighters, in a day's battle due to be forgotten. The mission on 28 May 1944 was planned to deal a large blow to the German oil and armament industry. It would, however, never get a place in history among the famous American air operations on dates such as 17 August and 14 October 1943, with missions to Schweinfurt and Regensburg, the 6 March 1944 mission to Berlin or the 11 January 1944 raid on Oschersleben. Missions like these have already been covered in some excellent books.

When I continued my research and letters from veterans kept coming in, I decided that their efforts and those of the 107 who died were worth recording for the generations to come. It became apparent to me that the air war over Europe was different than the impression that the books about those epic missions may give. The war in the air was a steady bloody battle of attrition between the USAAF—and RAF—and the *Luftwaffe*, day after day, month after month. And up to now, no book has been published describing just one of those many, many "ordinary" daylight strategic bombing missions. I felt it was important for future generations that there is such a book, covering in great detail the planning and actual execution of an ordinary strategic bombing mission. As my research progressed, I discovered that despite focussing on just "an ordinary mission," I was able to cover all possible aspects of daylight aerial warfare, not only bomber and fighter operations, but also air-sea rescue operations, escape and evasion attempts, and war crimes.

This book blends the stories and the emotions of the airmen into the overall picture of the execution of "an ordinary mission" and combines oral history with the barren facts from the archives and thus creates a detailed account of the events as they unfolded that day. I am well aware about the reservations that some famous historians have about the use of oral history, because of the distorted view that it may give. I have, however, taken the point of view that the reality of war can best be illuminated by the use of evidence, both oral and written, of those who have actually participated in battle. To address the criticism toward oral history as much as possible, I have carefully checked and balanced all stories, and where they differed from other sources, I have not hesitated to note this fact.

The reader will not find revolutionary thoughts or spectacular new insights in this book. It was not intended to be that way: I just wanted to give a balanced and detailed account of one of the many missions of the Eighth Air Force and to give this battle a personal touch by illustrating them with stories and pictures of the men who participated in it and sometimes lost their lives in it.

I sincerely hope that this book will be considered a lasting tribute to the 107 American airmen who died on this day and to the others who flew on this mission and have never been able to erase it from their minds.

CHAPTER 1

Strategy for Defeat

The crews of the 1,282 B-17s and B-24s that departed England around noon on 28 May 1944 most likely did not realize how much discussion had been taking place before they were finally assigned their targets for that day. An ordnance depot, an aircraft factory, and no fewer than five synthetic oil refineries were to be bombed. In addition to this main effort, experimental glide bombs were to be dropped on marshalling yards by another fifty-nine B-17s.

Looking at the selected targets, it is safe to say that this mission, only ten days prior to the invasion of Western Europe, was mainly a "strike at oil." And it was only for the second time in nearly two years of existence that the Eighth Air Force struck at oil refineries in Germany itself. The United States Strategic Bombing Survey established after the war that, by attacking these highly vulnerable oil refineries, the American air forces had achieved the greatest success in their strategic bombing campaign. It is therefore useful to explain why these targets were selected and attacked so relatively late in the war and also how the 28 May attack was to be executed. This is the topic of the next chapter.

Contrary to the policy adopted by the Royal Air Force, which had found out that unescorted bombers could not survive the *Luftwaffe* in daylight battles, the United States Army Air Forces went to war with the fundamental belief in the concept of the heavily armed bomber, executing daylight precision bombing missions on specific strategic targets.

Heavy bomber operations by the Eighth Air Force, based in England, commenced on 17 August 1942, with an attack on the rail yards at Rouen in France by a mere twelve B-17s. They continued with attacks on targets in France and the other occupied countries. Eighth Air Force senior commanders were strengthened in their belief in the heavy unescorted bombers, since their losses were relatively low and bombing results not too disappointing, in relation to the experience of the crews. *Luftwaffe* pilots seemed to be in awe of the many .50-caliber machine guns of the bombers and only occasionally succeeded in inflicting severe losses.

However, all this changed, as the *Luftwaffe* gained experience and the Americans started to attack targets deeper in Europe and into Germany

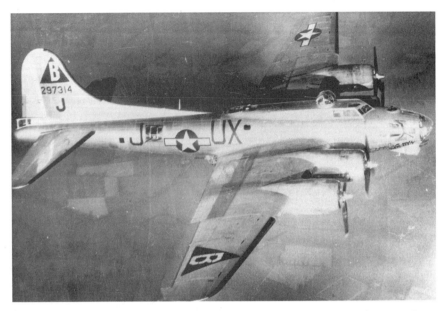

B-17G *Little John* (42-97314) was assigned to the 92nd Bomb Group on 7 May. It flew with the group to Ruhland on 28 May, but was heavily damaged the next day, during a mission to Cottbus. 1st Lt. Victor Trost then landed the aircraft in Sweden.
CATHERINE BROUSSEAU

itself without fighter escort along the entire route. The first bombing of a German target took place on 27 January 1943 when Wilhelmshaven was attacked. Losses increased, and the essence of this was clearly felt by the Allied Combined Chiefs of Staff, who approved of the "Pointblank" directive in May 1943. In this directive, targets were selected whose destruction would paralyze Germany's war effort and economy. Six target systems were proposed, comprising seventy-six precision targets to be destroyed. All targets were located within the range of the Eighth Air Force flying from England and the Fifteenth Air Force based in Italy. The proposed six target systems, judged vital for the major elements of the German military machine, were submarine construction yards and bases, the German aircraft industry, ball-bearing production, oil, synthetic rubber and tires, and finally military transport.

Since all targets selected for the 28 May 1944 attack came from three of these six target systems, it is worth noting what the appreciations of the Allied Chiefs of Staff regarding these targets were:

German aircraft industry
Depletion of the German Air Force will fatally weaken German capacity to resist our air and surface operations. Complete domination of the air is essential for our ultimate decisive effort.

Oil

The quantities of petroleum and synthetic oil products now available to the Germans are barely adequate to supply the lifeblood which is vital to the German war machine. The oil situation is made more critical by failure of the Germans to secure and retain the Russian supplies. If the Ploesti refineries, which process thirty-five percent of current refined oil products available to the Axis, are destroyed, and the synthetic oil plants in Germany, which process an additional thirteen percent, are also destroyed, the resulting disruption will have a disastrous effect upon the supply of finished oil products available to the Axis.

Military transport vehicles

Seven plants produce a large proportion of the military transport and armored vehicles. The precise proportion is unknown, but loss of these plants will directly strike at the German military strength.

But immediately after reviewing the merits of attacking these targets, the Chiefs of Staff had to admit: "The selection of these objectives is confirmed by the fact that the systems about which the Germans are most sensitive, and about which they have concentrated their defences, such as balloons, camouflage, anti-aircraft, searchlights, decoys and smoke, are aircraft factories, submarine construction yards, ball bearings and oil."

As we shall see, the strike force on 28 May would discover they were right. But prior to starting a major bombing campaign on targets such as oil refineries, a most important intermediate objective had to be met: "The Germans, recognizing the vulnerability of their vital industries, are rapidly increasing the strength of their fighter defences. The German fighter strength in Western Europe is being augmented. If the growth of this German fighter strength is not arrested quickly, it may become literally impossible to carry out the destruction planned and thus create the conditions necessary for ultimate decisive action by our combined forces on the continent."

On 22 June 1943, the Eighth Air Force carried out a raid on the synthetic rubber plant at Hüls in the Ruhr. The bombing stopped rubber production completely for a month and it was not restored until November of that year, for a loss of sixteen B-17s. In July, the B-24-equipped bomb groups of the Eighth flew to bases in North Africa to carry out a low-level bombing attack on the large Ploesti oil refineries in Rumania, on 1 August. Although losses were severe (a third of the attacking force was lost), much damage was inflicted on the target. It was a sign of things to come and several

German leaders expressed their anxiety about the German fuel situation, following this first attack.

Other units based in England bombed the ball-bearing factory at Schweinfurt and the Messerschmitt factory at Regensburg on 17 August. The air battles that ensued were among the greatest ever. No fewer than sixty Flying Fortresses did not return that day, most of them shot down by German fighters. It was a tough reminder of the intermediate objective that was identified by the Allied Chiefs of Staff. Then a raid on Stuttgart on 6 September and others on Bremen on 8 October, Gdynia/Anklam on 9 October, Münster on 10 October, and another on Schweinfurt on 14 October brought severe and almost unacceptable losses to the Americans. The original doctrine of bombers flying to their targets without fighter escort had to be abandoned.

At that time, fighter escort consisted of the American P-47 Thunderbolt and the British Spitfire. With these types, escort was only available to just inside the German border. After that, the bombers were on their own. However, experience had shown that for the bombers to be successful, fighter support during their entire mission was essential. The operational range of the available fighters, including the recently introduced twin-engine P-38 Lightning, was insufficient to accompany the bombers to their targets on the long missions as selected in the "Pointblank" directive. A new fighter, the P-51 Mustang, was put into service in late 1943, and the operational range of the Thunderbolt and Lightning was increased by adding larger droptanks. Gradually, the Eighth Air Force campaign resumed.

But not only increased fighter escort was to suppress the *Luftwaffe*. The attacks on factories producing its aircraft now received the highest priority. 11 January 1944 marked the resumption of the Eighth Air Force's strategic bombing campaign with a mission to Ochersleben. It culminated in attacks on major aircraft production centers during "Big Week" between 20 and 25 February. Another major shift in strategy was implemented in early January 1944. Until then, the available fighter escort was to stay with the bombers and let the *Luftwaffe* come up and fight. Therefore, they were on a permanent defensive posture, having to absorb the first blow. If the *Luftwaffe* chose not to attack, it had been a long trip for the fighters, but one that was largely in vain. This changed when James Doolittle, commander of the Eighth Air Force, ordered a major change in tactics. This decision was supported by Carl Spaatz, the commander of the Strategic Air Forces in Europe, who also had the Fifteenth Air Force in Italy under his command. The American fighters were now to take the initiative by attacking and pursuing the *Luftwaffe* and not necessarily near the bomber stream. Seeking out airfields and parked aircraft was encouraged. "Strafing," as it was called, was a highly successful way of depleting the *Luftwaffe*'s strength. At the same time, it was very dangerous, as the attackers were susceptible to small-caliber ground fire. Noteworthy is the fact that almost all great American aces—none of which were shot down by enemy fighters—fell victim to light flak when strafing. Francis Gabreski, John Godfrey, Gerald Johnson, and James Goodson—aces with twenty-eight, eighteen, eighteen, and fifteen air victories, respectively— are just a few of these many.

The bomber crews had mixed emotions about this change in fighter tactics, and many of them felt they were now used as bait for the *Luftwaffe*.

However, the relentless pursuit of the *Luftwaffe*, combined with the ever-increasing strength of the Eighth Air Force, both in fighters and bombers, brought the Americans virtual air superiority. On 28 May 1944, the Eighth Air Force had grown to thirty-six bomb groups (with four more becoming operational before D-Day) and fifteen fighter groups.

In early March 1944, a psychological turning point was reached. Berlin, the German capital and symbol of Hitler's reign, was bombed for the first time by the Eighth. Where the first mission on 4 March was hampered by bad weather, the second one, on 6 March, became a classic in air war history. It drew a fierce response, as no fewer than sixty-nine bombers did not return to England. Undaunted, two days later, the Eighth was over Berlin again, losing thirty-seven bombers, but the next mission, on 9 March, saw no appreciable enemy opposition. It was an important indicator of the blows that were dealt to *Luftwaffe* fighter and pilot strength.

B-24H *The Near-sighted Robin* (41-28851) of the 34th Bomb Group was flown to Lützkendorf by Lt. James C. Smith. The ship landed in Sweden with Lt. Giles Avriett at the controls on 24 August 1944. JAMES S. HOLLOWELL

In March, tensions ran high at the highest command levels. Spaatz wanted to use his American strategic bomber force in Europe (the Eighth Air Force in England and the Fifteenth Air Force in Italy) in the best possible way to support the coming invasion of France from England. He and his staff stuck to the Pointblank directive and now wanted to switch to the oil campaign. This was a compact and vital target system and its destruction would severely hamper German air and ground operations after D-Day. However, the Supreme Commander of the Allied Forces in Europe, Gen. Dwight Eisenhower, did receive other advice as well. Both Air Vice Marshal Trafford Leigh-Mallory, who was General Eisenhower's air component commander, and Air Chief Marshal Arthur Tedder, Eisenhower's deputy, advocated the so-called transportation plan. In this plan, all available bomber forces were to be employed for bombing the French and Belgian rail system and rendering it incapable of reinforcing and logistical support of the German forces in the invasion area. Although Spaatz argued that the oil campaign would have the benefit of being able to continue the attrition of the *Luftwaffe* at the same time, Eisenhower chose the transportation plan on 25 March. This offered easily measurable results and the effects of the oil plan, although logical, were difficult to assess with the existing Allied intelligence.

For several reasons, if only to prove the U.S. Army Air Force strategic doctrine of precision bombing during the oil campaign, Spaatz chose subterfuge. The Fifteenth Air Force was officially assigned the Ploesti rail yard as its target on 5 April, but, not surprisingly, most of its bombs fell in the adjoining oil refineries. This was repeated on 15 and 26 April. In April, the Eighth Air Force continued its battles with the *Luftwaffe*, but when the Germans were found to be remarkably absent during several major missions, fear grew that it was conserving its strength for the invasion that everybody knew would soon come.

Also in March the strategic bombing effort from England was distracted by another demand. The destruction of targets connected with the German V-weapons also became a priority.* Although these V-weapons had not yet been launched against England at that time, intelligence had discovered their existence and recognized their threat. In March, several smaller missions were flown to V-weapon sites in northern France, culminating in an almost 600-aircraft strike on 26 March. On 20 April, more than 800 bombers were dispatched to these sites and similar missions were flown on 27 April and 1 May.

In the meantime, Spaatz had taken issue with Eisenhower. The latter was distinctly unhappy about Spaatz's lack of progress in executing the trans-

---

* V-weapon comes from the German *Vergeltungswaffe*, or "revenge weapon." Best known are the V-1, the "flying bomb," and the V-2, a supersonic rocket.

portation plan. In fact, the Eighth Air Force had not yet bombed a single transportation target since the decision had been taken on 25 March. In the end, Eisenhower allowed Spaatz two days with "visual bombing weather" to prove his point with the oil campaign and test the *Luftwaffe* reaction. For his part, Spaatz promised more effort in the transportation plan and on 22 April, 800 bombers attacked the marshalling yards in Hamm, the largest rail yard in Germany.

Finding and striking the *Luftwaffe* on the ground was not easy for American fighter pilots. These Bf 109s of II./JG 27 are dispersed and camouflaged at the edge of a wooded area on an airfield in Germany. FRIEDRICH KELLER VIA JEAN LOUIS ROBA

Spaatz had to wait for three more weeks to get his first oil strike in visual conditions. This first mission was flown on 12 May. Almost 900 bombers and 735 fighters were dispatched to attack synthetic oil refineries at Merseburg, Lützkendorf, Brüx, Zeitz, and Böhlen. The German reaction, as predicted, was fierce. Both flak and fighters brought down forty-six bombers and seven fighters. The *Luftwaffe* struck hard at some bomb groups; one, the 96th, lost twelve, and the 452nd lost fourteen of its number. But huge columns of smoke gave firsthand evidence that the bombing had been successful, and thousands of tons of oil and their refineries had been destroyed or badly damaged. Both Brüx and Zeitz were put out of action, with Merseburg 60 percent and Böhlen 50 percent damaged. In his postwar memoirs, Albert Speer, the German minister of armaments, recalled this day as the one on which his nightmares became reality: "This day marked the end of the German armament." The Germans also took appropriate measures. Immediately after the 12 May attack, air defenses were expanded, camouflage and smoke covers improved. Even the highest headquarters were placed on alert. On 24 May, it was proposed to cut maneuvers and road movements of armored vehicles by 90 percent to conserve precious fuel.

In the meantime, the weather over the continent prevented the second oil strike. The next two weeks saw missions to satisfy everyone's needs. Strikes were made on V-weapon sites in France, industrial targets in Germany, marshalling yards in Belgium and France. Berlin received a visit from nearly 500 bombers on 19 May and a further 460 on 24 May, and airfields in France and Belgium were also attacked.

On 27 May, more than 1,100 bombers were dispatched to attack the marshalling yards at Mannheim, Karlsruhe, Strasbourg, Saarbrücken, Neunkirchen, and Kons/Karthus, industrial targets in Ludwigshafen, and coastal gun batteries at Fécamp and St. Valery. The *Luftwaffe* countered the attackers and, together with the inevitable flak, managed to shoot down twenty-four bombers. Six of these belonged to the luckless 351st Bomb Group, based at Polebrook. The 457th Bomb Group from Glatton lost three B-17s. The following day, both bomb groups would again be in the thick of the battle and suffer heavily.

During the afternoon, the formations of Fortresses and Liberators returned to the sky over England and separated to land at their respective home bases. Here, wounded crewmembers were removed from the ships, crews were debriefed, and battle damage repaired as quickly as possible. No one at the operational airfields knew if another mission was due for the next day, 28 May—Whit Sunday, or Pentecost.

That afternoon, however, the meteorologists had promised visual bombing weather, and thus the second opportunity for a mission in the oil campaign presented itself. Close to midnight, the teleprinters began to rattle at all bases. At Eighth Air Force Headquarters at High Wycombe, the decision had been made: Eighth Air Force Mission 376 would be launched on 28 May, with the aircraft departing England late morning.

CHAPTER 2

The Plan for a Mission

To be able to properly understand the events of 28 May 1944, it is relevant first to outline the organization of the Eighth Air Force on that day. The way the planning officers at its Headquarters at High Wycombe orchestrated this attack is also covered in this chapter.

The basic bomber unit in the Eighth Air Force was a bombardment group (heavy).* It was composed of four bomb squadrons, each having an assigned strength of some twelve bombers. A bomb group was based at its own airfield, supported by its own logistic units and it was usually commanded by a colonel.

Three or four bomb groups were assigned to a combined bombardment wing, for both administrative and tactical purposes. The next higher echelon in the chain of command was the three air divisions: the First Air Division, with B-17-equipped units; the Second Air Division, with B-24-equipped units; and the Third Air Division, with a mixture of B-17- and B-24-equipped units. The three air divisions were under the direct command of the staff of the Eighth Air Force, which was commanded at the time by General James H. Doolittle. He was primarily known as a prewar flyer and as the leader of the daring bombing mission by carrier-based B-25 Mitchell bombers to Japan in April 1942.

On a combat mission, a combined bombardment wing put up a so-called combat wing, comprising bombers of each of its assigned bomb groups. To make matters more complicated, the organization of a B-17 combat wing differed from a B-24 combat wing.

In this stage of the war, three B-17 squadrons, with six bombers each and flying lead, low, and high in respect to each other, made up a bomb group formation. Sometimes one or more squadrons had one extra B-17, thus making a bomb group formation of up to twenty-one aircraft. Three bomb groups, again flying lead, low, and high, were then assembled into a combat wing formation, which in all was now at least fifty-four bombers strong. The positions of the groups within the wing rotated after each mission, so every

---

* Throughout the book, it will be referred to as bomb group.

Glatton, home for the 457th Bomb Group, was a typical Eighth Air Force bomber airfield. The three intersecting runways are circled by the perimeter track. The big T-2 hangar is plainly visible in the technical site. Just across the perimeter track is the control tower, with sheds for ambulances and fire trucks. More than thirty B-17s, both olive drab and natural metal finish, can be seen on the hard stands. Note Rose Cottage Farm closed in by the runways. Operations on the farm continued during the war.
JOHN WALKER

bomb group had its share of the responsibilities of leading a combat wing on a mission and all shared the particular risks of flying lead, high, or low group.

The B-24 units put up squadrons of around twelve ships each. Three squadrons were flying lead, low left, and high right in respect to each other. These thirty-six bombers were the A Group within a combat wing, which was complemented by an identical B Group. Thus, a B-24 combat wing comprised some seventy-two bombers.

In each bomb group formation, the very first ship carried the mission leader, or command pilot, flying with a so-called lead crew. The crewmembers of this lead crew were usually experienced and well on their way to finishing their tour of operations. Again, each wing had its own wing lead crew, thus flying in the first (lead) ship of the lead squadron of the lead group.

Who were the men who were to lead the entire Eighth Air Force into Germany on 28 May? The first wing to enter Germany was the 40th Combat Wing. The lead group in this wing was the 92nd Bomb Group, based at Podington. This group thus provided the command pilot. He was twenty-five-year-old Lieutenant Colonel André R. Brousseau. He was a 1940 graduate from West Point, and in March 1942, while still in the United States, he became the commanding officer of the 326th Bomb Squadron of the 92nd Bomb Group. With Brousseau in the lead ship, his squadron led the entire 92nd Bomb Group in the first nonstop flight over the Atlantic Ocean for a unit of this size in August 1942. Brousseau also took part in the first opera-

Typical Eighth Air Force control tower. The large panels with "PK" in the grass in front of the tower identify it from the air as Polebrook, home of the 351st Bomb Group. Next to the tower is the crash station, with an ambulance on standby.
ROBERT W. CONDON

tional mission of the group on 6 September. After that, he led the group on several combat missions. He was duly promoted and now served as the group's air executive.

Brousseau was to fly with the lead crew of Captain Clem B. McKennon. McKennon and his crew had arrived in England as replacements in early September 1943. They were then assigned to the 92nd Bomb Group and flew their first operational mission on 9 October, to Gdynia. The third mission of the crew, to Schweinfurt on 14 October, had nearly been its last. While six out of the eighteen aircraft of the group were shot down, McKennon's machine was damaged and one crewmember injured. He was just able to put it down in an English field, whereupon the crew returned to Podington by truck. McKennon's crew apparently stood out for its teamwork, and on 30 January, 1944, it was selected to fly its first mission as a lead crew for the group. Several missions as a lead or deputy lead crew followed, and on 18 March, it was transferred, on detached service, to the 305th Bomb Group at Chelveston. Here, a so-called Pathfinder section was formed, with each of the three groups in the wing detaching some of its lead crews to this section. The B-17s in this Pathfinder section were equipped with H2X radar to enable their navigators and bombardiers to navigate and bomb through cloud or smoke cover. The H2X radar was housed in a radome, protruding from the belly of the bomber and replacing the ball turret. If the 92nd

Bomb Group was to lead the wing and required an H2X lead aircraft, McKennon and most of his original crew took it from Chelveston to Podington, where the command pilot and some others then completed the crew for that particular mission. McKennon's co-pilot, 1st Lt. Jack D. Henderson, had to give up his seat in the cockpit for the command pilot and was assigned to become the formation observer. He, in turn, took the place of the tail gunner, and was to report to the command pilot on the status of the formation behind him.

Flying on 28 May with Brousseau and most of McKennon's combat crew were four other officers. They were 1st Lt. S. F. Renscok and 1st Lt. R. P. Flinn, both regular navigators; 1st Lt. H. G. Davis, operating the H2X radar; and Capt. Edward T. O'Grady, the lead bombardier. O'Grady was a veteran as well, as he was already the lead bombardier of a wing on the infamous Schweinfurt raid in October 1943. For his actions that day, he earned a Distinguished Flying Cross. The bombing of a formation was generally done at a signal from the lead bombardier. When he dropped his bombs, all other

This unusual picture shows four commanding officers in the chain of command of the Eighth Air Force listening to a speech by Marshal Lord Trenchard, "the father of the Royal Air Force." Second from left is James H. Doolittle, commander of the Eighth Air Force. On his right, with glasses, is Robert B. Williams, commander of the First Air Division; on Doolittle's left is Robert F. Travis, commander of the 41st Combat Wing. At far right is Kermit D. Stevens, commander of the 303rd Bomb Group. Both Travis and Stevens flew on the 28 May mission. KERMIT D. STEVENS

A standard bomb load for a B-17—ten 500-pound incendiary bombs—waiting to be loaded in a Fortress of the 508th Bomb Squadron, 351st Bomb Group. Note the little portable gasoline engine under the nose of the ship, which was used to provide power at the hardstand for the aircraft's electrical systems. The officers are Robert H. Gunster and Robert W. Condon, co-pilot and pilot in the squadron. ROBERT W. CONDON

bombardiers dropped theirs, thus hoping to obtain maximum concentrated coverage of the target. Others means of signalling the moment of release were smoke marker bombs, flare signals, or radio code words. These concepts applied to both types of combat wings.

Several bomb groups flying on 28 May were very experienced, having flown from England for more than a year and a half. Others had just started operations; some had suffered no combat losses at all. The longest-serving bomb group was the 92nd, now based at Podington, which flew its first mission on 6 September 1942. The "rookies" of the day were the crews of the 34th Bomb Group from Mendlesham. This group became operational on 23 May and this was its fifth scheduled mission. Since the early days of the Eighth Air Force, the bomb groups had steadily come in from the United States. No fewer than thirty-six bomb groups would take part in this day's attack, twenty equipped with B-17s and sixteen with the B-24s.

Most of the crews in the older bomb groups were replacements. They had trained in the States, and after having ferried a brand new aircraft to England, they were then assigned to a group in which where another crew had either finished its tour of operations or had been shot down. The fresher bomb groups were still flying with their original crews. These had assembled and trained as a group in the States, flew together to England in their own aircraft, and commenced operations from there. An example of this was the 457th Bomb Group, based at Glatton, which flew its first mission on 21 February 1944. Its original crews were now nearing the end of their tours—that is, those which had survived three months of combat.

The tremendous effort of training so many crews, nearly all of whom had come straight out of civilian life, must not be underestimated. Alvin G. Determan, a pilot in the 303rd Bomb Group, describes his training and arrival in England and his experiences serve as an example of so many others: "I enlisted in the air forces on 18 May 1942 at Minneapolis, and was put on inactive service, without pay, until 4 November, when I was called to Minneapolis and was to embark by train to Santa Anna, California, to become an aviation cadet. Here I underwent pre-flight instruction until 28 January 1943. From 1 February to 15 April, I had primary flight instruction at Sequoia Field in California, then basic flight instruction at Lemoore Air Base, also in California until 22 June that year. From 27 June to 30 August, the advanced flying training followed at Douglas Army Air Base in Arizona. At last, from 1 to 10 September, I was able to spent some days with my wife, back home, at Lake Benton in Minnesota. Afterwards transition flying training for B-17s at Roswell, New Mexico, until November 15. At Salt Lake City, Utah, I picked up my combat crew in the next two weeks and went with them to Dalhart Air Base in Texas for combat flying training. From 15–26 March 1944, we were in staging preparations for overseas movement and finally on 1 April, we left the States for England. We expected to be sent to some bomb group, but no; from 4 to 18 April, Pre Combat Ground School at Bovingdon. On 21 April we arrived at our combat station, Molesworth, and were assigned to the 303rd Bomb Group, 358th Bomb Squadron, the famous 'Hell's Angels.' We flew our first combat mission on 29 April, to Lyon in France. On 28 May in the early-morning hours, we were facing the twelfth combat mission of our tour in just this one month's time."[1]

The length of this tour of operations was cause for bitter discussion in this month of May 1944, mainly in the combat messes and barracks for flying personnel at the airfields. Until then, the normal tour of operations for a bomber crew had been twenty-five missions, something that very few of the early crews ever achieved. When more bomb groups and crews became available, and overall losses diminished, General Doolittle decided to raise the number of required missions to thirty. He reasoned: "The crews now had a much better chance of making a full tour. It took about ten missions before a team really became first class. Adding five missions to the crew's tour, in fact, resulted in not a fifth, 20 percent, but a full 33 percent improvement in the effectiveness of a crew. You were keeping them when they had gotten best."[2]

Not surprisingly, the bomber crews, were not too pleased with this decision. Some crews were given one or more mission credits to comfort their feelings. But the decision to keep them, because they had become such a good team and the overall combat losses were lowering, was to claim some of their lives on 28 May.

Eighth Air Force Fighter Command used the fighter group as its basic tactical unit. Just like the bomb group, it usually had its own airfield and was commanded by a colonel. But whereas the bomb group had four squadrons, the fighter group had only three, consisting of more aircraft, roughly about thirty per squadron. Administratively, the fighter groups were assigned to fighter wings, but all operational orders usually went directly from Fighter Command Headquarters to the fighter groups.

The normal fighter group strength on a mission was forty-eight fighters, all three squadrons providing four flights of four aircraft each. Every squadron had its own radio call sign, and the four flights within the squadron were referred to as white, red, blue, and green. Within a flight, number 1 was the leader; his tail was covered by number 2; and number 3 was covered by number 4. Thus, by using short radio call signs, everyone was directly able to identify the one who had sent the message. This was essential when, during air battles, fractions of a second could mean the difference between life and death for a fighter pilot.*

The most experienced fighter group of the Eighth Air Force to see action on 28 May was the 4th Fighter Group, equipped with the P-51 Mustang and based at Debden. It had flown its first mission on 2 October 1942. Many of its original pilots had transferred from the Royal Air Force. Here they had formed the voluntary Eagle Squadrons at a time when the United States still was not present on the European battlefront. At the other end of the scale of experience was the 479th Fighter Group, based at Wattisham. It flew its first operational mission with P-38 Lightnings on 26 May 1944. The Eighth Air Force Fighter Command had then reached the planned total of fifteen operational fighter groups. All these groups were employed on 28 May, four each operating the P-38 Lightning and the P-47 Thunderbolt and seven operating the P-51 Mustang.

However, it was not only the Eighth Air Force that provided fighter escort. There were two other sources that were used on almost all missions in this stage of the war. The first was the United States Ninth Air Force. This was a strong force, consisting of bomb groups equipped with medium bombers (mainly B-26 Marauders) and fighter groups. After the invasion of

---

* For example, "Cobweb Green 4" was the pilot in the number four position of the green flight in the 334th Fighter Squadron, which belonged to the 4th Fighter Group.

the continent, they were to be employed for tactical purposes, supporting the ground forces. But with the invasion still in the planning phase, these available fighter groups were used to support the Eighth Air Force when necessary. No fewer than eleven fighter groups of the Ninth Air Force would fly escort missions for the Eighth on 28 May. The other source for fighter support was the Royal Air Force, and its P-51 Mustang units were regularly requested to provide escort. On 28 May, fifty-six Mustangs from five different RAF squadrons were supporting the Americans.

As explained in the first chapter, seven high-priority targets were selected to be attacked on 28 May. In addition to these seven targets, large marshalling yards were selected for the first operational test of the GB-1 "glide-bomb."

The First Air Division was assigned to bomb the Braunkohle-Benzin A.G. oil refinery in Ruhland and the Junkers Flugzeug und Motorenwerke A.G. aircraft factory in Dessau. Division Headquarters decided that two combat wings, the 40th A and 40th B, would attack the refinery in Ruhland, and three combat wings, the 1st, 41st, and 94th, would deal with the factory in Dessau. Each combat wing comprised the standard three bomb group formations.

In addition to the normal bombing missions, the 41st Combat Wing was to drop the still secret GB-1. It was to be released against the huge marshalling yards in Cologne for its operational debut. This had nothing to do with the planning and execution of the main mission, and the aircraft destined for Cologne left their bases more than an hour earlier than those flying deep into Germany.

The Second Air Division, equipped with B-24s, was to deal with two major oil refineries, Braunkohle-Benzin A.G. in Zeitz and the I.G. Farbenindustrie A.G. plant in Merseburg/Leuna. Two of its combat wings, the 96th and the 14th, were scheduled to fly to Zeitz. Two others, the 2nd and the 20th, were to attack Merseburg.

The Third Air Division, comprising some bomb groups equipped with B-17s as well as some with B-24s, was assigned the Braunkohle-Benzin A.G. oil refinery in Magdeburg, the *Wehrmacht* tank ordnance depot in Königsborn and the huge Wintershall A.G. oil refinery in Lützkendorf. Here, two B-17 combat wings, the 13th A and 13th B, were sent to Magdeburg, and two other combat wings, the 45th and 4th, to Königsborn. Three B-24-equipped bomb groups were scheduled to make up two combat wings, the 92nd and the 93rd. They would attack Lützkendorf and were to fly at the rear end of the bomber stream.

The bomber forces were now made up as per the table on page 18, with the B-17-equipped units in forces I and II, the B-24 units in forces III and IV. Force V was the separate force for the glide-bomb mission.

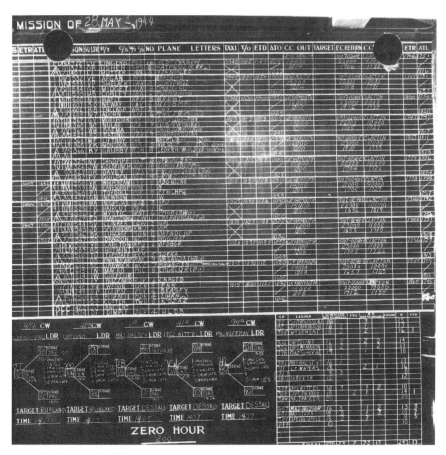

Status board for the First Air Division for the mission of 28 May. The columns show, from left to right, the bomb groups with their distinguishing triangle markings on the tails of their ships; the bomb squadrons with their fuselage codes; radio call signs and wireless call signs; number of aircraft for the mission; and their individual code letter. Then information on time for taxi, estimated time of departure, actual take-off time, altitude, time and place where the English coast was to be crossed, and the same information for the return journey. On the far left, in the columns of the 303rd, 379th, and 384th Bomb Groups, is information for the secret "Operation Grapefruit" to Cologne. NATIONAL ARCHIVES

The four main forces, excluding the one to Cologne, were to depart the English coast, near Great Yarmouth, at 1200, 1211, 1230, and 1242 hours, respectively, and follow a common direct-penetration course to a point northeast of Brunswick. From there the combat wings were to proceed to their respective targets, bombing on east-southeast downwind headings, taking them between the most heavily defended areas to minimize the effect of ground defenses.

All forces were to rejoin again approximately 150 miles south of their point of separation and return along a substantially direct route, deviating only to the extent necessary to remain south of the strong Ruhr defenses. The order of the forces during the withdrawal would be altered, due to the varying locations of the targets. The first force was to maintain an altitude of 22,000 feet over the entire route, with the Dessau combat wings climbing to 25,000 feet before bombing. The second force was to penetrate, and withdraw, at 20,000 feet and climb to 24,000 feet over the target area. The third force was to fly at 20,000 feet until approaching the Dümmer Lake area, climb to 22,000 feet to cross this well defended zone, and return to 20,000 feet for the remainder of the penetration and through the target area—except that the Merseburg combat wings were to remain at 22,000 feet until past their target. All combat wings of this force were to descend to 18,000 feet for the withdrawal. The fourth force was to fly at 22,000 feet during the penetration and over its target and descend to 20,000 feet for its withdrawal.

EIGHTH AIR FORCE ORDER OF BATTLE,
28 MAY 1944—BOMBER FORCES

	Target	Combat Wing	Lead Group	Low Group	High Group
Force I	Ruhland	40 A	92A	92B	305
	Ruhland	40 B	306A	306B	398
	Dessau	1	381A	91A	381B/91B
	Dessau	41	379	303	384
	Dessau	94	457	401	351
Force II	Magdeburg	13 A	390A	100A/95B/390B	100B
	Magdeburg	13 B	95A	388A	94A
	Königsborn	45	96	452A	388B/452B
	Königsborn	4	385A	94B/385B/447B	447A
Force III	Zeitz	96 A	466	466	467
		96 B	458	458	467
	Zeitz	14 A	492	492	392
		14 B	44	44	392

(continued)

	Target	Combat Wing	Lead Group	Low Group	High Group
	Merseburg	2 A	445	445	389
		2 B	453	453	389
	Merseburg	20 A	448	448	446
		20 B	93	446	93
Force IV	Lützkendorf	93	34	34	34
	Lützkendorf	92 A	487	487	487
		92 B	486	486	—
Force V	Cologne	41	303	379	384

The route and timing for the glide-bomb mission was independent of the principal operation. In order to reach the target area at the time of maximum predicted visibility [13.00 hours], this force was to depart Clacton at 11.36 hours and fly the mission at 20,000 feet, except when diving for additional speed in the target area.

The scheduled fighter support consisted of fifteen Eighth Air Force fighter groups, four of which were to fly double sorties; eleven Ninth Air Force fighter groups; and five Royal Air Force Mustang squadrons. With the exception of two groups detailed to provide close escort to the combat wing executing the glide-bomb attack against Cologne and one group that was to carry out a penetration sweep in advance of the main bomber forces, all other units were to operate in direct support of the four main bomber forces.

It was the 56th Fighter Group from Halesworth that would carry out the so-called "Zemke fan," invented by and named after its commanding officer, Col. Hubert A. Zemke. In this concept, a fighter group would fly in group formation to a designated point. There, the three squadrons would "fan" out in different directions to intercept any German fighters assembling over their fields and confuse and prevent their building up to a battle formation. An extra section would stay in the center so that if any squadron called in enemy fighters, this section could come up and assist. The first operational use of the "Zemke fan" was on 12 May, and it turned out to be a great success. On 28 May, the 56th Fighter Group would again try out the concept. The group was to fly to the Dümmer Lake area and then fan out in squadron strength towards Bremen, Nienburg, and Hannover.

EIGHTH AIR FORCE ORDER OF BATTLE,
28 MAY 1944—FIGHTER FORCES

	Target	Penetration Support	Target Support	Withdrawal Support
Fighter Sweep		56 FG (T)		
Force I	Ruhland	78 FG (T)	355 FG (M)	367 FG (L)
	& Dessau		352 FG (M)	358 FG (T)
			363 FG (M)	50 FG (T)
			4 FG (M)	
Force II	Magdeburg	356 FG (T)	357 FG (M)	474 FG (L)
	& Königsborn		359 FG (M)	362 FG (T)
			354 FG (M)	36 FG (T)
Force III	Merseburg	353 FG (T)	361 FG (M)	370 FG (L)
	& Zeitz		20 FG (L)	373 FG (T)
Force IV	Lützkendorf	479 FG (L)	339 FG (M)	19, 65, 129,
			55 FG (L)	306, & 315
				Sqdns RAF (M)
Force V	Cologne	364 FG (L)	406 FG (T)	406 FG (T)
General				356 FG (T)*
withdrawal				364 FG (L)*
escort				

(L) = unit equipped with P-38 Lightning   (T) = unit equipped with P-47 Thunderbolt
(M) = unit equipped with P-51 Mustang   * = second sortie for the group

The other fighter units were arranged to provide unbroken escort to each force from the west shore of the Zuider Zee* in Holland on the penetration, and to the Belgian coast on the withdrawal. Two groups rendering support during the penetration were to make second sorties, and sweep the final portion of the withdrawal route to aid any stragglers—bombers which were forced out of their protective group formations for some reason and were flying back to England alone.

German forces in the West were not only pounded by the Eighth Air Force. The Ninth Air Force dispatched over 600 B-26 Marauder and A-20 Havoc medium bombers to attack marshalling yards, naval yards, railway bridges, and V-weapon sites in France and Belgium. In addition, various P-47

* Its official name was the IJsselmeer, since it became a lake in 1933 after a dike was built at its northern end. However, the Americans always referred to it by its old name, either because their maps did not carry the new name or because it was so much more difficult to pronounce!

fighter groups executed dive-bombing attacks on targets in the same area. Also RAF Spitfire- and Typhoon-equipped squadrons were scheduled to attack fuel stores, bomb dumps, and switching stations. Unfortunately, their actions on 28 May are beyond the scope of this book.

The field orders were sent by teletype from the Headquarters of the Eighth Air Force to those of the First, Second, and Third Air Divisions, where additional orders and details were added. Again the teletypes chattered, this time sending the field orders down to wing headquarters, where further coordination took place and specific details were attended to. Shortly before midnight, operations officers on all bases were alerted for another raid: "Operation 376" was scheduled for 28 May. At these bases, a frantic activity developed. Many people went to work in the middle of the night. This ranged from the group operations officers who selected crews and aircraft for the mission and worked out the hundreds of details which would mean the difference between failure and success, to the ground crews who worked all night to bring the aircraft that were needed for the mission into tip-top condition. The armament sections loaded the Fortresses and Liberators with hundreds of bombs and thousands of rounds of machine-gun ammunition.

The combat crews were in their quarters, usually metal Nissen huts, dispersed all over the fields. If not playing a card game, reading, writing letters, or just lying awake and staring into the darkness, they were sound asleep.

Lt. Col. André R. Brousseau briefs crews of the 92nd Bomb Group for a combat mission. CATHERINE BROUSSEAU

Since the mission didn't have a very early start, the crews scheduled to fly were alerted only around 0600 hours. After washing and dressing, they had breakfast and proceeded to briefing. Here all details of the mission were revealed and all necessary information given.

We are fortunate that the personal speaking notes of the officer of the 401st Bomb Group conducting the briefing have survived in the archives. These brief notes clearly point out what he said to the combat crews in the briefing room at Deenethorpe.[3]

TARGET:

Your target for today is the number one priority target in Germany at this time. It is comprised of four individual targets as follows:

A The AERO-ENGINE FACTORY—Junkers engines [Ju 88] and jet engines [Me 262].

B The FACTORY AIRFIELD

C The BOMBER AIRCRAFT ASSEMBLY FACTORY

D The INJECTION PUMP WORKS—engine injection for better performance

This complex is the center of the Junkers aero-engine and aircraft organization. As such, the works are primarily engaged in design of new aircraft and aero-engines, production of prototypes, and development and experimental work on existing models, as well as setting up production series.

Your Mean Point of Impact is located in the AIRCRAFT ASSEMBLY FACTORY. This factory has been established since 1910 and has grown very large since that time, producing all known types of Junkers aircraft. You are familiar with their Ju 52, Stuka, Ju 88 [the fighter], Ju 188, Ju 290, etc. After the new models are successfully tested here, they are passed to other Junkers plants for mass production. All assembly details are first worked out at this parent factory, and thus eliminates all the bugs common to mass production.

You will see from the photographs, the hugeness of the target area—total area being about 3,000 × 1,800 yards, and roughly rectangular. SIX MPIs have been assigned to THREE WINGS attacking, and should provide ample coverage, and serve to cripple the whole efficiency of this great asset to the German Air Force. YOUR MPI is one of three final assembly shops.

SECONDARY TARGET:

AIRFIELD about 5 miles NE of Leipzig. This target is producing Junkers aircraft engines which are used in Ju 88s.

The map as used at Horham, base of the 95th Bomb Group, to brief the crews for the mission of 28 May. The circled areas are well known to be saturated with flak. The route to and from the target and details about the fighter escort are presented, and general information on targets for the other bomb divisions is shown. NATIONAL ARCHIVES

SECONDARY PFF:

CHEMNITZ Industrial Town, probably target large marshalling yard.

LAST RESORT:

Any military installation in Germany or any airfield in occupied territory not adjacent to a populated town.

FRIENDLY ACTIVITIES:

—40th 'A' and 'B' Wings' target.

—2nd and 3rd Divisions bombing in general area of Magdeburg.

—South of Leipzig [total five targets].

ROUTE AND FIGHTER ESCORT:

—1 Group P- 47s 1 Group P-38s; also extra sweep Dümmer Lake [47's]

—1 Group P- 51s 1 Group P-47s; also extra sweep Liege [38's—stragglers]

—1 Group P- 51s 1 Group P-47s; also extra sweep St Quentin [47's]

EPIDIASCOPE PROCEDURE:
  PRIMARY
  SECONDARY VISUAL
  —2,500,000 chart—Night target chart
  —Night target chart—Photographs
  —Photograph
  —Perspective

FLAK ROUTE:
  —Cover very carefully [Dümmer Lake, Nienburg, Celle, Oschersleben, Target area, Secondary and Secondary PFF];
  —route out okay, except for coast.

LAST MINUTE INTELLIGENCE:
  Possibly one South Bound convoy on the route back

SPECIAL INSTRUCTIONS:
  —P/W Poop
  —Tempest A/C operating over Europe
  —Escape Aids [shoes, dog tags, photos, purses and kits]

DON'T MENTION THE TARGET !!!!

Of course many other details were brought up during the briefing. The
formation plan of each bomb group was the subject of much attention, as it
could literally mean the difference between life and death to be in a well-

Uninjured crewmembers seen after the crash into Deenethorpe village, pictured on
11 December 1943, following their mission to Emden. Standing in the center is tail
gunner Robert V. Kerr; standing far right is pilot Walter B. Keith. ROBERT V. KERR

protected spot in a group—instead of in "Purple Heart corner," the squadron in the combat wing which was most exposed to possible German fighter attacks. Other details were the anticipated weather conditions, the times and places of assembly into group and wing formation, and the color of the flare signals used for identification purposes on that particular day. Also a "time hack" was given so that all crew members could synchronize their watches to the exact second.

One of the men attending the above briefing at Deenethorpe was Staff Sgt. Robert V. Kerr.* He was to be the tail gunner on the B-17G *Fitch's Bandwagon* (42-107043), leading the high squadron of the 401st Bomb Group. He recorded in his diary: "Felt pretty tired after flying the day before. Went down to the orderly room and waited until the rest of the crew got there. We piled into the trucks and went down to eat. After eating went to the briefing room and we sat toward the back. Looked at the blackboard and saw that we were leading the high squadron of the low group. Finally, the colonel came in and briefing started. Saw Keith sitting on the left and about six rows up. He looked kind of cute all dressed up in his flying clothes. He looked back at me and grinned. During the briefing someone said something funny and Keith looked back at me and laughed. After the briefing I talked with Keith a few minutes and having noticed that he was to lead the second element in our Squadron, I said 'I see you will be flying right behind me.' He said: 'You keep those God-damned guns going, cause if we get in any trouble, I'm coming right up underneath them, so keep them going.' I said: 'O.K., I'll protect you.'

"We went down to the armament shop and got the guns, cleaned them in a hurry and dropped them off at the ship. Sent the truck back after the officers. After putting the guns in, I went over and got a flak suit to put in the ship and then went and got another one and put them both near the tail wheel. I then proceeded to change clothes. In the meantime the officers had arrived and were coming out of the tent, saying that it was almost 'engine time.' Talked with the rest of the crew and ground crew for a few minutes while the pilot and co-pilot were up in the cockpit getting organized. Finally, the green flare went up and we scrambled in, as the first engine was started."[4]

One by one, the Fortresses and Liberators on the various bases came to life. With squealing brakes, the ships of a group followed the perimeter track around the airfield until the first ship, carrying the command pilot and lead crew, had reached the beginning of the runway. All eyes then turned to the control tower, waiting for the flare signal to commence take-off. Suddenly, there it was, and Operation 376 was on.

---

* Kerr was the tail gunner aboard the B-17G *Zenodia-el-Elephanta* (42-39825) of the 401st Bomb Group when it crashed during take-off on the mission of 5 December 1943. Miraculously, the entire crew of 2nd Lt. Walter B. Keith survived the incident. However, Keith's crew was split up due to injuries to several of the men.

CHAPTER 3

The German Defenses

Opposing the mighty armada from the Eighth Air Force was the German *Luftwaffe* and its ground-based flak units. The *Luftwaffe* was a hard-pressed service. With Germany fighting on three fronts since 1941 (the Russians in the East; America, England, and the other Western Allies in the South and West), the *Luftwaffe* was in big demand. Its units were stretched to their limits, both in number of aircraft and in pilots. To counter the daylight attacks on Germany by the Eighth Air Force, the *Luftwaffe* had some 600 day fighters available, of which just over half were serviceable. These were assigned to *Luftflotte Reich* and were stationed on various bases within Germany itself. In addition, *Luftflotte 3* was responsible for France, Belgium, and Holland, and this command had another 100 day fighters available in these occupied countries.

The *Luftflotten* were established on a territorial basis. The commander of the *Luftflotte* was responsible for all field formations under him, regardless of their operational role. For its operations a fighter unit would be controlled by a *Jagdfliegerführer* or *Jafü* (fighter commander). The *Jafü* was, in turn, subordinated to a *Fliegerkorps* or *Fliegerdivision*, under the final control of the *Luftflotte*.

The highest operational level for fighter units was the *Jagdgeschwader* (fighter wing), or JG for short. Its commanding officer, the *Geschwaderkommodore*, was usually a *Major* or above in rank and flew operations with his *Geschwaderstab*. The control of the entire *Geschwader* was normally exercised from the *Gefechtsstand* (battle headquarters) situated on the *Geschwaderstab's* airfield, but this was not always the case, and it was fairly common for the *Geschwader* to have its *Gruppen* scattered over several airfields in a wide area. A *Geschwader* normally consisted of three *Gruppen* (groups), with a fourth *Gruppe* used officially as an *Ergänzungsgruppe* (operational training unit) for the *Geschwader*, though in reality this unit was used operationally with most *Geschwadern* in the *Luftflotte Reich*.

The *Gruppe* was led by a *Gruppenkommandeur,* an executive post held by an aircrew member whose rank could vary considerably—normally a *Hauptmann* (captain) in fighter units. He had his own operational and administrative *Gruppenstab* and flew combat operations with his *Stabsschwarm* (staff

A Bf 109 G-6 and its pilot, Werner Möszner, of 9./JG 26 on Schiphol airfield. Clearly visible are the 30mm cannon in the propeller hub, the 20mm cannon in the gondolas under both wings, and one of the 13mm machine guns on top of the engine cowling in front of the cockpit. WERNER MÖSZNER

flight), usually of three to four aircraft. Under his command, there were three or sometimes four *Staffeln* (squadrons) led by a *Staffelkapitän*, an executive post that could be held by any aircrew officer from *Leutnant* (lieutenant) to *Hauptmann*. In the temporary absence of the *Staffelkapitän*, the unit was led by a *Staffelführer*. In combat the *Staffel* was split into *Schwärme* (sections of four aircraft) or *Rotten* (pairs of aircraft), just like their American counterparts. The *Staffel* normally comprised between twelve and sixteen aircraft, with the number of aircrew varying according to the strength; normally, there were to 25 pilots and 150 ground crew in the case of single-engined fighter units.

The *Gruppen* and the *Geschwader* were identified by Roman numerals before the abbreviation JG and Arabic numerals after it, respectively. So, for example, I./JG 11 was the First *Gruppe* of *Jagdgeschwader 11*. Within the *Gruppen*, the *Staffeln* were usually evenly distributed. The first three belonged to the first *Gruppe*, the fourth, fifth, and sixth belonged to the second *Gruppe*, and so on. The *Staffel* number also preceded the JG and, if used, replaced the *Gruppe* number. So 3./JG 11 was the Third *Staffel* of *Jagdgeschwader* 11; it was automatically assigned to the First *Gruppe*.

The backbone of both *Luftflotten* were the Messerschmitt 109 (Me 109) and Focke-Wulf 190 (Fw 190) day fighters. Both were combat-proven types, with many modifications since their fielding in the early days of the war. The main armament of the Me 109G-6 were a 30mm cannon, firing through the propeller hub, two 20mm cannon under the wing and two additional 13mm machine guns in the fuselage, forward of the cockpit. The Fw 190A-8 bristled with four 20mm cannon and two 13mm machine guns. Both were dangerous opponents for the American aircrews, especially when in the hands of skilled pilots. The new German jet fighters were only just entering service and would not play any role on 28 May.

Experience among *Luftwaffe* fighter pilots varied widely. Some, usually the *Staffelkapitäne* and *Gruppenkommandeure*, were very experienced combat pilots. Often they had been flying since the early days of the war. Since the *Luftwaffe* did not have a set tour of operations, like the USAAF and RAF, *Luftwaffe* pilots simply continued flying until death or wounds prevented their further service in combat units. A typical example of such an experienced pilot was *Oberleutnant* Walter Krupinski, the *Gruppenkommandeur* of II./JG 11. He had enlisted just before the outbreak of war on 1 September 1939 and came to 6./JG 52 in February 1941. During the 1941 campaign in Russia he claimed seven victories. In 1942, however, he quickly became one of the most successful pilots in his unit and ended the year with sixty-six victories. He had also been the recipient of the coveted *Ritterkreuz* (Knight's Cross). After a brief spell as an instructor pilot, he was assigned to the post

Fw 190s of 6./JG 1 on Störmede in April 1944. Clearly visible are the markings on the aircraft nearest the camera. This aircraft is *Gelbe 5* (*Yellow 5*), and the red band around the fuselage in front of the tail denotes JG 1. The bar in the red band denotes the *II Gruppe*. Also visible are the emblem for JG 1 (a winged "1") on the engine cowling and the white spiral on the propellor hub. HANS LÄCHLER

of *Staffelkapitän* of 7./JG 52 in March 1943 and continued to increase his score. On 5 July 1943, he shot down eleven Russian aircraft, but collided with another Me 109 during landing and was badly wounded. After his recovery in hospital he returned to business. His 100th victory was scored on 18 August and his 150th victory by 12 October. After 174 victories, all on the Eastern Front, he was awarded the *Eichenlaub* (Oak Leaves) in addition to his *Ritterkreuz*.[1] On 18 April 1944, he was recalled to the West, his transfer serving as a good example of the impact that the Allied offensive was having in the *Luftwaffe* ranks at that time. After a brief theater-familiarization period as *Staffelkapitän* of 1./JG 5 at Herzogenaurach in Germany, he was appointed in May 1944 as *Gruppenkommandeur* of II./JG 11 at Hustedt.

Another old hand, whom we will also meet in this book, was Austrian *Oberleutnant* Rüdiger Kirchmayr, *Staffelkapitän* of 5./JG 1. It is also interesting to note the vast difference in the numbers of victories scored, Krupinski and Kirchmayr both having about the same amount of combat time. Since the summer of 1941, Kirchmayr had been stationed at various bases on the North Sea coast and gained his first victory on 20 September 1941. His victories steadily mounted, and at the end of 1943, he had fifteen victories confirmed. In June 1943, he had become *Staffelkapitän* of 5./JG 1, a position he still held now nearly a year later. His victory list had risen to seventeen victories, all obtained in the West.[2]

Both Krupinski and Kirchmayr are typical of those who were the backbone in the *Luftwaffe* fighter force in May 1944. They were the ones who were leading the less experienced pilots into battle. *Unteroffizier* Rudolf Strosetzki of 8./JG 11 may serve as a typical example for them. His story also illustrates the enormous effort to train sufficient numbers of pilots for the *Luftwaffe*: "I started my flying days with gliding lessons, as a member of the *Hitler Jugend*. As I was afraid to miss something of the war (and who wasn't in those days) I signed up for pilot training in the *Luftwaffe*. On 1 May 1941, I was assigned to *Flieger-Ausbildungs-Regiment 32*, first at Pardubitz in Czechoslovakia, then in Rochfort, France. After these four months of basic training, I went to the *FliegerAnwärter-Battallion* in Langenlebarn, Austria, for a noncommissioned officers course. Then, from October 1941 to April 1943, I attended *Flugzeug-Führer-Schule A/B 113* in Brünn, again in Czechoslovakia. This was the training school where I finally obtained my pilot's license. From April 1943 to June 1943, I went to the *Zerstörerschule* in Paris/Orly, France. But before my group of students could really start learning to operate types like the Me 110, we were reassigned to the Jagdschule in Bad-Vöslau, Austria. This was apparently because of a shortage of pilots for the single-engined fighter types. From November 1943 to January 1944, I received the type training on the Me 109E at *Jagd Ergänzungsgruppe Ost* in St. Jean d'Angely, France. This was followed by two months at *Jagd Ergänzungsgruppe*

Süd in Marignane, near Marseille in France, for training on the Me 109G. Finally, in March 1944 I was assigned to a combat unit and was posted to 6./JG 11, then based at Wunstorf in central Germany."[3]

The first flak that would greet the Eighth Air Force was that of the German Navy. Its flak batteries were protecting many Dutch towns along the North Sea coast, and although the courses of the bombers were plotted to stay out of reach of the most well protected areas, some flak was always encountered. But all over Germany, flak units were stationed. Some were more or less static, protecting vital industries, major railway intersections or other high priority targets. Others were mobile and could be moved at short notice, to appear in places where Allied intelligence officers had not expected them to be. Based on the latest information, often coming from debriefing reports of previous missions, they prepared flak maps and during the morning briefing the latest status of the flak was given to the bomber crews. However, no prepared flak map or information could keep these crews free from fire, as the industrial targets in Germany itself were all well protected by batteries. Some targets were heavily defended by many batteries

This picture of the pilots of 6./JG 11 was taken in April 1944 at Wunstorf and is a grim illustration of the heavy losses that the *Luftwaffe* sustained. All seven pilots were either killed, severely wounded, or made prisoner of war in a period of just six weeks. Left to right: *Feldwebel* Martin Müller (KIA, 19 May), *Unteroffizier* Alfred Vüllings (WIA, 24 May), *Unteroffizier* Rudolf Strosetzki (POW, 7 June), *Leutnant* Andreas Trockels (KIA, 29 April), *Leutnant* Helmut Grill (KIA, 7 June), *Unteroffizier* Werner Althaus (KIA, 29 April), and *Unteroffizier* Heinz Kunz (KIA, 28 May).
RUDOLF STROSETZKI

and although this flak could not fully stop a bombing attack, it nearly always claimed victims within the bomber formation. Some aircraft literally disintegrated after a flak hit, others lost engines or suffered other structural damage that forced them out of formation. Quite often, this damage later led to a crash-landing or bail out of the crew. For many Eighth Air Force crews in May 1944, the German flak was a more feared opponent than the *Luftwaffe*'s fighters were. Flak was there on almost every mission they flew, while the fighters were not, and while one had the feeling that one could do something about fighters, (such as taking evasive action and returning fire), there was nothing to be done about flak, except to sit and take it and hope that no shell would find your aircraft or its immediate vicinity. But, nearly always and at total random, aircraft were hit and crewmembers wounded or killed by flak fire. The main German flak guns were of 88mm and 105mm. The bombers, with their bombing altitudes at about 21,000 feet, were easily within the range of these guns. The crews manning the flak guns were an odd collection. Some were regular *Luftwaffe* or *Wehrmacht* personnel. They were assisted, mostly in positions requiring less skill, by boys from the *Hitler Jugend*, sometimes not older than fifteen years, and slave laborers or Russian prisoners of war.

Eighteen-year-old Helmut Schade was a member of a flak gun battery and recalls: "It required a unit of about 120 to operate a typical six-gun flak battery. The aiming crew had various duties, including deflection, declination, azimuth and range, which showed as a triangle, rhombus, square, trapezoid and a circle on the range-finder, or *Entfernungsmesser*, which was a four-meter-wide optical device. When these symbols all came together on the viewfinder, which, when focused on the invading bombers, gave the final aim, the command to start firing was given by radio. Its normal magnification was 12 power. It could be raised to 24 power and 36 power to fill the viewfinder with the image of a single plane. The *Entfernungsmesser*, or E-1, rangefinder operator was the only man in the gun crew that had to go to school for his trade; all the others were trained on site. At the first telephone notice of approaching aircraft, usually seventy-five or more miles away, we dropped everything we were doing and raced through trenches to man the guns. Each of the six guns were on four legs, with pivots to turn it in any direction by hand cranks. All the ammunition was stored in racks alongside each gun. During an attack, the 'farm boys' pulled the large casings from the rack and handed them to a second man who plunged the grenade-end into a box which set the distance that the grenade would travel before exploding. The pointed end of the grenade had two small flat spots opposite each other, which served as a grasp for the range box to turn the fuse to set the distance the grenade would travel before exploding. This man then handed the shell to the third man, who slammed the shell into the breech of the gun and yanked the lanyard at command from the final aimer. All six guns fired in unison. If the grenade hit a plane, it would usually not explode on impact, but would explode only after travelling the distance set into the fuse.

"The final aimer with the rangefinder kept his sights pointed at the left wing root of the lead plane and the necessary nearly two mile lead was automatically calculated, so that the grenades would arrive at a spot in the sky that the target should occupy when it arrived there. All the guns operated in unison, as the information was fed to each gun through a large umbilical from the rangefinder's position. The guns were aimed in parallel to spread the pattern a little, the guns being some fifty feet apart. A slow turn in either direction by the target aircraft was enough to throw off the aim of the flak gunners. This is why the flak was heaviest during the final bomb run by the bombers, when they had to fly a straight and steady course, to give the bombardiers the best opportunity to hit the target. Our flak gunners would be tracking a straight line, and if the target aircraft disappeared behind a cloud, the line of aiming was continued as if the target could be seen. If the target aircraft re-appeared, adjustments would be made at that time. Even under the most ideal conditions, the target would only be in range for three minutes. When the bomb bay doors were opened on a clear day, it could easily be seen by the gunners at the flak battery."[4]

A gun crew posing at its battle stations. Note the ammunition storage in the dugout walls and the painted clock indications.
BUNDESARCHIV KOBLENZ

While the heavy flak was mainly protecting industry, the light flak protected the operational airfields of the *Luftwaffe*. These lighter pieces were also quite often put on wagons to provide flak cover for trains. This was a menace for strafing Allied fighter pilots, and many of them fell victim to the enormous firepower of the *Flak Vierling*—a lethal four-barrel 20mm cannon or 37mm guns, hidden in the edge of a wood, next to an airfield. The crews serving these weapons were regular *Wehrmacht* or *Luftwaffe* personnel. Both the heavy and the light flak will play their part in the story of Mission 376.

A typical German 88mm flak battery protecting an industrial area. The six guns in a battery were referred to as Anton, Bertha, Caesar, Dora, Emil, and Friedrich.
BUNDESARCHIV KOBLENZ

CHAPTER 4

Ruhland

At exactly 0100 hours on 28 May, Capt. Clem B. McKennon lifted B-17G 42-97592 off the runway at Chelveston. As mentioned, McKennon and his crew were part of the Pathfinder section for the 40th Combat Wing. They landed their B-17, equipped with H2X radar, just ten minutes later at nearby Podington, as they had been assigned to fly for the command pilot of the 92nd Bomb Group. Since the 92nd Bomb Group was also leading the first combat wing heading for Germany, McKennon's crew would spearhead the entire Eighth Air Force force. With this "Eighth Air Force lead," McKennon was coincidently celebrating his twenty-ninth birthday.

The first units in the Eighth Air Force armada were two combat wings, formed by six bomb group formations, assigned to bomb Ruhland. The 92nd Bomb Group from Podington, contributed two full group formations (lead and low) to the first wing, and the 305th Bomb Group from Chelveston filled in the high position.

At 1000 hours, the first B-17, that of McKennon and command pilot Andre R. Brousseau, took off from Podington. It was followed, within thirteen minutes, by another seventeen Fortresses to comprise the lead group. They assembled near the airfield at 8,000 feet into a textbook bomb group formation and left that point at 1108 hours to commence wing assembly.

The low group also took off from Podington, in the wake of the lead group, starting at 1013 hours. The low group assembled at 7,000 feet and rendezvoused with the lead group upon departing the Podington buncher—the radio beacon used during assembly.

Soon afterward, the high group, provided by the 305th Bomb Group, moved into its position, and the wing left the English coast at Great Yarmouth, at 1155 hours, five minutes ahead of schedule.

By then, two Fortresses had already aborted the mission. One from the lead group, because of a fuel pump failure on its number three engine. The other abort was in the low group, when a pilot suffered severe stomach cramps. Both places in the formations were taken over by spare aircraft, which according to standard operational procedures followed the Groups to mid-Channel for just this purpose. At 1205 hours, there was an unusual

35

The first of the many. The lead crew for the Eighth Air Force consisted mainly of crewmembers of Capt. Clem B. McKennon's combat crew of the 92nd Bomb Group. Aboard the lead bomber on 28 May were lead pilot Clem B. McKennon (kneeling, far left), tail gunner/formation observer Jack D. Henderson (kneeling, second from left), engineer Karl J. Bromley (standing, far left), radio operator Joseph W. Brown (standing, fourth from left), and left waist gunner Clyde W. Martin (standing second from left). JO NELL MCKENNON

incident that caused another B-17 to return to base. Another standard operational procedure in the Eighth Air Force, required the test-firing the .50-caliber machine guns just after leaving the English coast, to make sure they were working properly. And thus, as required, the lead group test-fired its guns. Unfortunately, the tail gunner in the lead ship in the low squadron was careless, and accidentally fired a .50 round into the nose of the B-17 flying just behind him. The armor-piercing round entered the glass nose, hit the navigator, then went through the instrument panel, hitting the co-pilot's leg and arm, and finally exited the ship on the right-hand side. The pilot immediately informed his group leader, Lieutenant Colonel Brousseau, and returned to Podington, where he landed at 1257 hours, no doubt furious about the carelessness of a gunner, which could easily have cost the life of one or more members of his crew. While flying at 15,000 feet, a cylinder head split on the number one engine of another B-17 in the lead group. The engine then failed, and this ship also returned to Podington.

Capt. Clem B. McKennon of the 92nd Bomb Group was the lead pilot for the 92nd Bomb Group. His aircraft spearheaded the nearly 1,300 bombers on 28 May.

JO NELL MCKENNON

Meanwhile, the third group in the combat wing, the 305th Bomb Group, experienced no problems at all. One spare returned to Chelveston, the other had tagged on to the 92nd Bomb Group and continued toward the target.

The second combat wing assigned to attack Ruhland was led by the 306th Bomb Group from Thurleigh, which also furnished the low group. The high group formation was provided by the 398th Bomb Group, based at Nuthampstead. Another H2X-equipped B-17G, *Mercy's Madhouse* (42-97557), flown by 1st Lt. P. J. Field, was the lead aircraft for this combat wing. No B-17s of this wing developed trouble, so four unused spares of the 306th Bomb Group turned back at 12.22 hours, and returned to Chelveston. Just five minutes after the spares left, Lieutenant Kata in the 306th low group formation, found his chin turret inoperative. Why this was not discovered or reported earlier, since the guns were test-fired shortly after leaving the English coast, is not known, but he left his place, which then stayed vacant during the mission.

Consequently, four bomb group formations of eighteen planes and two of seventeen aircraft entered the enemy coast near Bergen in Holland at 22,000 feet. Lieutenant Colonel Brousseau's B-17 was the very first at 1234 hours. Just twelve minutes later, the countdown of B-17s in the two combat wings continued. The number three propeller on the B-17 of Lieutenant Brye of the 305th Bomb Group ran away at 23,000 feet, and he turned back to England. At 1309 hours, Lieutenant McDaniel of the 306th Bomb Group returned, because the flaps of his B-17 refused to stay in position. This caused the use of excessive amounts of fuel, and he could not possibly endure the whole mission on the contents of his tanks. At 1320 hours, another number three propeller ran away, this time on the 306th Bomb Group's B-17 of Lieutenant Malsom. He dropped his bombs in the vicinity of the German city of Meppen, close to the Dutch border. One B-17 left the 398th Bomb Group formation, due to unknown causes. Lieutenant Chamberlain from the 305th Bomb Group then found his number two engine freezing up and, unable to keep up with the formation, he dropped his bombs in some rural area and returned home.

The fighter support for the so-called penetration phase of the mission was provided by the famous 78th Fighter Group from Duxford. Its fifty-four P-47s took off at 1137 hours, led by Maj. Harold E. Stump, commanding officer of the 84th Fighter Squadron. Nine Thunderbolts of the group aborted for various reasons.

For the bombers, the flight to the target area was uneventful, except for some meager, inaccurate flak near Dümmer Lake and Celle. As the formation arrived at the initial point at 14.13 hours, patchy clouds were found covering some of the target area. The combat wing "uncovered" at this time, meaning that it changed its formation, so that the three groups now flew in trail for the bomb run, so as not to interfere with or block each other. However, the low squadron of the low group lost its position and found itself under the open bomb bays of the B-17s in the high group. Consequently, the entire high group was unable to bomb the target.

Captain O'Grady, the lead bombardier, and responsible for bombing sequence of the first wing, took immediate action upon seeing the clouds. He made intricate bombsight corrections, while ordering his lead pilot, Capt. Clem B. McKennon, to fly a course parallel to the briefed one. Then, leading the combat wing into the target area, he found a break in the clouds. With a bomb run of less than a minute, the lead group formation was able to bomb the assigned primary at 14.24 hours. Lieutenant Colonel Brousseau was then faced with a serious problem. He knew that two of the Groups in his Wing still carried their bombs, but he could not spend too much additional time in the target area, since the next Wing was due to arrive within minutes. The low group made a second bomb-run, dropped its bombs, and rejoined the lead group, at 14.43 hours. The high group, forced off its bombing run by the stray squadron from the low group, was ordered to make a large circle to the right. Its lead bombardier, 1st Lt. T. D. Wynn, was unable to pick up his target and his pilot 1st Lt. W. P. Coburn intended to start another run. But Lieutenant Colonel Brousseau intervened, and ordered him to proceed to the secondary target, obviously with the purpose of giving the following Wing a good chance at the primary target.

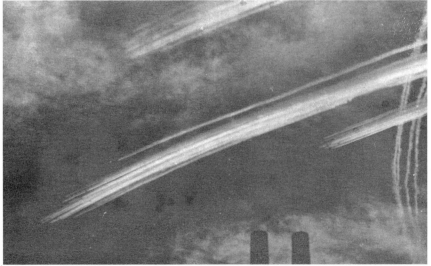

These pictures were taken in occupied Holland in 1944. They show a combat wing heading for Germany and clearly show the lead, low, and high groups and the fighters weaving above them in flights of four. Note the trailing bomber in the lead group-the aircraft is dropping from the formation, probably because of engine trouble. With no enemy fighters in evidence, it was wise to turn back for England at this stage. AUTHOR

"Bombs away." The lead bombardier in a PFF-radar-equipped B-17G has just released his bombs, signalling the release for all aircraft in his group. Note that the first bomb is a smoke marker, an extra means to mark the moment of bomb release. The two flak bursts are too close for comfort. Also note the extended radome housing the radar and replacing the ball turret. The white triangle on the tail, without a letter, denotes that the aircraft was serving as a wing or division asset, rather than with its parent bomb group, the 305th, which would have a letter G displayed inside the triangle. This aircraft did not fly on 28 May and was lost on 24 August 1944 while leading the 305th Bomb Group to Merseburg. CATHERINE BROUSSEAU

The bombing results of both 92nd Bomb Group formations were good, as a concentration was achieved in the central part of the plant, and many buildings and ovens were hit. It was estimated that damage to gas holders, and gas generators, would reduce the normal gas capacity by nearly 50 percent, and that damage to contact ovens would result in a five to ten per cent reduction in output. Captain O'Grady, the lead bombardier, was later presented with another Distinguished Flying Cross in recognition of his excellent work on the bomb run.

The high group, furnished by the 305th Bomb Group, located its secondary target, an aircraft repair factory at Zwickau, while still flying in a turn. Despite this, lead bombardier, 1st Lt. T. D. Wynn, decided to drop at

1508 hours, but missed the aiming point. However, he and the rest of the group succeeded in hitting a control tower, a marshalling yard, and several parked aircraft. On the B-17 piloted by 2nd Lieutenant LeBlanc, nineteen bombs stuck in the bomb racks and were brought back to Chelveston.

Ground defenses were almost non-existent during these attacks. Only one B-17 from the 92nd and two from the 305th were slightly damaged by flak fragments, but mechanical trouble played tricks on one crew. Flying in the number three position in the low squadron of the 305th Bomb Group formation, was B-17G 42-39878. The aircraft was nicknamed *War Eagle*, and its pilot was 2nd Lt. Julius F. Herrick. *War Eagle* was a relatively old machine having arrived at the 305th Bomb Group on 3 January 1944. It had flown several rough missions, during which it sustained considerable damage. After the necessary repairs it was given to Herrick's crew, when it arrived at Chelveston. The crew had a short, but intensive career, very typical for the intensive bombing campaign in this phase of the war. It flew missions on 23 May (Metz, France), 24 May (Berlin, Germany), 25 May (Thionville, France), 27 May (Mannheim, Germany), and 28 May to Ruhland. The regular engineer and tail gunner were grounded for medical reasons, and their places were filled by two old hands, Tech Sgt. Charlie Gillespie and Staff Sgt. John C. Napier, both of whom had almost completed their tour of operations.

Lt. Col. André R. Brousseau, the executive officer of the 92nd Bomb Group, is pictured between Lt. Col. Robert B. Keck (standing), the operations officer, and Lt. Col. William R. Reid, the group's commanding officer. On 28 May, Brousseau was wing leader for the 40th Combat Wing, bombing Ruhland. At the same time, he was leading the entire Eighth Air Force into Germany that day. For his leadership, he was awarded a Silver Star. CATHERINE BROUSSEAU

The navigator was nineteen-year-old Leon W. Lobdell, who gave the following account of the events on this day: "We went out to our ships in the bright sun to the accompaniment of church bells. Not long after, we formed up and started our climb for altitude over the North Sea. We hit several spots of moderate flak along the route, but felt reassured when an oil leak that we'd had all the way across the North Sea stopped. Finally, we hit the Initial Point and started on the run with the bomb bay doors open. The formation had been hurrying all morning and we had to strain our old crate just to keep up. She just had an engine replaced since one was knocked out over Berlin. On the run, the visibility, which had been unlimited all morning, changed, and the ground was obscured by 5/10th clouds. The lead crew was unable to find the target, a synthetic oil plant at Ruhland, and we made two 360 degree turns trying to find it. Soon after the second turn, one of our engines (number two, the new one) overstrained by the continual jockeying of the morning, had a runaway prop and we had to feather it.* With our load of eggs still stowed away and bomb bay doors open, we lost altitude rapidly and fell 4,000 feet before we managed to get levelled off. We found it impossible to climb with our load of bombs; consequently we were unable to rejoin the formation."[1]

---

* The photo below indicates that number three was feathered. Each propellor on a bomber had a feathering mechanism, which, if activated, stopped the rotation of the propellor and turned the blades into the wind, thereby reducing drag. If this feathering mechanism did not work, the propellor started to "windmill," which caused severe vibrations and heavy drag.

B-17G *War Eagle* (42-39878) of the 305th Bomb Group, 365th Bomb Squadron, is inspected by curious German personnel. The number three propellor was feathered before its belly landing near Zerf. The man in front of the number four engine may be a crewmember. MIKE HALEY

In the group formation, it was noticed that *War Eagle* lagged behind and gradually disappeared from view. Lead navigator, Gerald V. Vega, duly made an entry in his log and brought the information up at the debriefing, following his return that afternoon.

Leon Lobdell continued his account: "I managed, after a lot of jockeying, to get the ship set on a course for home. The bombs were salvoed near a small town in south-east Germany. Shortly after that, number three engine ran away and we found it impossible to feather and had to leave it windmilling. As we were still losing altitude, Jeff [pilot Julius F. Herrick] gave orders to salvo the ball turret and the enlisted men all went to work on it. Also everything that we could find loose went hurtling out: flak suits, helmets, ammo boxes etc. until the ship was stripped. By this time we were down in the vicinity of the Rhine River and really 'on the deck.' Before this we were passed by one B-24 wing and one B-17 wing. A B-24 passed by us just clipping the trees after dropping from its formation at high speed (it seemed as if a couple of his props had ran away). We had been flying over forest, but at last we came to the Rhine and I was absolutely sure of our position. However, at this time, our number four engine ran away and joined number three in windmilling out there.

"We knew that we'd had it now, for we were way down and still losing altitude. Our old crate shot over the Rhine, encountering light flak that didn't seem to last long; I guess they saw we were done for. We were so low over the Rhine that we had to follow a small river valley to the West; we couldn't make it over the hill. Our speed had dropped below 120, and Jeff called for ditching positions. We raced back to the radio room, threw everything out, and prepared for a crash-landing. Just then we had a call from the cockpit that we were about to hit. We slammed the door to the bomb bay and flopped on the floor. A couple of seconds later, we felt a heavy jolt as the tail hit and then a resounding crash, and terrific pressure forward as the plane hit. Jeff had to set her down in a small ploughed field on the side of a hill. It was pure luck that we came upon that spot for there wasn't another for miles. When we hit, red clay from the field boiled up, through the hole where the ball turret was removed, and choked everyone in the radio room. We finally came to a stop and piled out the hatch. About all the strength we had at first was to flop on the ground and get our flying gear off. The pilots failed in setting the ship on fire, so we quickly divided in pairs and took off."

After a textbook belly-landing by Julius Herrick and his co-pilot, Lloyd H. Saunders, *War Eagle* came to rest near the Moselle River, close to the German-French border at the little village of Zerf. Landing safely, with one feathered and two windmilling propellers was quite a performance in the eyes of the crew, who were now in a hostile country, and looking for a way back to England.

War Eagle's crew. Back row, left to right: Julius F. Herrick, pilot (POW); Lloyd H. Saunders, co-pilot (POW); Leon W. Lobdell, navigator (POW); Herbert Borax, bombardier (POW); Benjamin R. Norris, waist gunner (evaded); and Harold Tubbs, engineer (not on 28 May mission). Front row, left to right: Daniel E. Dunbar, waist gunner (evaded); William S. Schwartz, radio operator (POW); Orval R. Busby, ball turret gunner (POW); and Allan Greene, tail gunner (not on 28 May mission).
LEON W. LOBDELL

Six of the ten crew were caught by civilians or police within an hour, including Leon Lobdell: "A few civilians were running up; one on a bicycle was wildly shooting a pistol. We got 'the hell' out of there, and made for the woods. We soon found out that we'd had it, though we had landed right on the border, which was well guarded. We had to cross an open field and a brook to get to the woods, for, on one side there were the civilians and a town, and another town to boot on the other side. Shortly after we crossed the brook and got into the woods, 'hot lead' started singing around our ears and we decided that we didn't want to get shot. Our capture occupied the guards, so that the enlisted men all escaped [two were caught within an hour]. We were kept in a small courtyard near the village while the whole town looked on. Some civilian officials came and tried to look as important as possible. Finally they came with a small Ford truck and took us off. We stopped in a small town and I was slammed by a Gestapo agent and struck in the groin by a rifle butt."

After a night in solitary confinement in Saarburg, the captured crewmembers of *War Eagle* were transported to Dulag Luft, the interrogation center near Frankfurt, and after that sent to various prison camps. The story of some of the enlisted men, still at large that first night, will be related later.

War Eagle and its crew were the only losses for the entire combat wing, which returned to England in good order. Wing leader André Brousseau was awarded a Silver Star for his part in the successful attack. The citation for his decoration reads: "For gallantry in action, while serving as Air Commander of a Division of Flying Fortresses on a bombardment mission over Germany, 28 May 1944. On the first run over the target, cloud coverage prevented all but the lead group from releasing their bombs. Determined to destroy the objective, Colonel Brousseau coolly manoeuvred his lead combat wing over the target a second and a third time. When it became evident that one group could not bomb, he reformed the combat wing and though deep in enemy territory, led this small formation to a secondary target, where the one group released its bombs with excellent results. Far behind the briefed schedule and thus without fighter protection, Colonel Brousseau rallied his units into a tight defensive formation and led them back to bases in England without the loss of an aircraft. The gallantry and tenacity of purpose displayed by Colonel Brousseau in accomplishing his mission under adverse conditions attest to his able leadership."[2]

The second combat wing scheduled to bomb Ruhland was less successful. The 306th Bomb Group contributed both the Lead and low groups, and the 398th Bomb Group flew high. At the initial point, bombardier 1st Lt. D. R. Ross in *Mercy's Madhouse*, the H2X-equipped lead aircraft of the wing, with command pilot Capt. R. S. Lund of the 306th Bomb Group aboard, opened his bomb bay doors. Due to a bomb-rack malfunction, twenty-six bombs were automatically released. Not only did those 100-pound bombs tumble out of the bomb bay, but the two smoke markers, carried by the lead aircraft to indicate the moment of release for all planes in the group, were dropped accidentally.

Unfortunately, all the bombardiers in the lead group, their eyes glued to the bomb bay of *Mercy's Madhouse*, in anticipation of the moment of bomb release, hit their own bomb switch when they saw both smoke markers go. As a result 494 100-pound high-explosive bombs exploded harmlessly in open fields short of the target, leaving a very confused and disappointed lead group. Captain Lund continued his course to the target at Ruhland, hoping that the low and high groups would do better, but found that the same clouds that had hampered the bombing by the first combat wing, now completely covered the target. Rather than breaking up the wing formation in a search for his secondary target, the lead bombardier of the low group, 1st Lt. Ted Boswell, decided to drop on the first town of some size on the route after Ruhland. This was Elsterwerda, which had to endure the impacts of 644 100-pound general-purpose bombs. The wing flew a little to the south of the briefed course on the way out, which enabled the high group to drop 655 100-pound general-purpose bombs on Meissen. The results of bombing at Elsterwerda and Meissen were not important enough to be noted in the official reports. Moderate, but very accurate tracking flak hit the wing formation along the route in the target area, damaging thirteen B-17s in the low group, seriously wounding a crewmember in one of them, and damaging two B-17s each, in the lead and high groups. The bombing by the second combat wing had been a total failure, but fortunately it suffered no losses on its return leg of the mission.

Not only enemy action caused American losses. The airspace, crowded as it was with many huge formations of heavy bombers and numerous smaller formations of accompanying fighters, was extremely dangerous. Not only unseen enemy fighters or flak meant death and destruction, but also collisions between friendly aircraft, which were all too common. On this day, it would mean death for one American pilot and captivity for another.

Returning from its escort duty, the penetration escort for the Ruhland-bound bombers, a flight of four P-47s of the 78th Fighter Group, led by Capt. Alwin M. Juchheim, met head-on with a formation of four P-51s of the 363rd Fighter Group, who were taking over the escort at that time.

Capt. Alwin M. Juchheim posing in front of his P-47. THOMAS G. IVIE

The wingman of Captain Juchheim was 2nd Lt. Lawrence R. Casey, who still remembers the accident that followed: "We had been on a penetration escort to the bombers, deep into Germany. On our return we were flying a wide fighter finger type formation, naturally for the purpose of covering the others' tails from possible attack. The day was beautiful, not a cloud in the sky for miles. We were in the Hannover/Dümmer Lake area when we picked up four specks in the sky, at approximately our altitude, dead ahead. Juchheim, who had the eyes of a hawk (he was our leading ace of the 83rd Fighter Squadron at the time) had called them out originally and immediately identified them as P-51 Mustangs. Suddenly, I saw a ball of fire and I took immediate action to avoid one of the Mustangs in the other formation. I broke to the right and continued in a circle to see what was happening. Juchheim and one of the Mustangs had collided in mid-air. I saw that the P-51 had exploded, and there was nothing but fire, smoke and debris. The Thunderbolt was spiraling down, minus a major portion of its left wing. A parachute had blossomed out, so we assumed Juchheim had bailed out. We circled Juchheim, and it was my intention if possible to set my P-47 down, if a landing site was available, and to pick him up. It had been done before, even against all regulations, and I suppose common sense. During this time, we had seen contrails of a single plane, diagonally over us. Either number three, 1st Lt. William M. McDermott, or number four, 2nd Lt. Frederick

First Lt. John R. Brown was leading the flight of the 363rd Fighter Group, which was involved in the collision with the flight of the 78th Fighter Group. JOHN R. BROWN

White (I don't remember which) called out the sudden absence of the contrails. By this time we were down to five or six thousand feet, where no contrails are formed. Suddenly, we all spotted an Me 109. Later, we figured he had seen the ball of fire and decided to investigate. I had the first chance. I broke into him and hit him with a good burst of .50-caliber machine-gun fire. He eluded me, and the other two completed his destruction."[3]

How this took place was described by 1st Lieutenant McDermott: "I called my wingman and we started after the Me 109, chasing it down to 1,000 feet. My wingman, Lieutenant White, fired a short burst at the enemy aircraft and I saw many hits all over the ship. Lieutenant White then overshot, as the Me 109 had evidently chopped his throttle. The enemy aircraft then attempted to turn into an open field, but I closed in and fired two bursts. I missed the first one, but closed in further and at about 200 yards caught him in the side of the fuselage. Many pieces flew off, the enemy aircraft burst into flame and crashed."[4]

Leading the P-51 formation was 1st Lt. John R. Brown. He later submitted the following official report: "Lieutenant Ladas was flying number four position in my flight. At 1400 hours, just west of Gardelegen, a flight of four red-nosed Thunderbolts approached us from two o'clock level. I pulled the flight about 200 feet above this formation in a slight left turn. This cleared the entire flight, but I believe one of the Thunderbolts pulled up also, causing the crash. Lieutenant Ladas's ship hit one wing of the P-47 and shattered it to bits. The P-47 spiraled down out of my sight. In my opinion, Lieutenant Ladas's chances of surviving this collision are nil. I continued with the remainder of my section, on course."[5]

He later recalled the incident: "I felt at least partially responsible for his demise and have suffered pangs of conscience ever since. Ladas was flying as number four in my flight. When I saw the returning flight of P-47s dead ahead, I did a quick calculation that we were more maneuverable than they at that altitude and determined to climb to avoid ramming. For some unknown reason, Ladas was late in responding to my maneuver, and pulled up to join the flight just in time to hit the P-47 enroute. I might have called my maneuver on the radio, but it did not seem necessary until it was too late. The explosion was spectacular. Major McWherter, leading our group, called out, 'What happened back there?' I replied, 'Ladas had a head-on with one of the Jugs.'"[6]

The American eyewitnesses were right. The collision killed 2nd Lt. Anthony E. Ladas in P-51 42-106486 of the 363rd Fighter Group. His body was found near the remains of his Mustang, in Sichau, a community eleven kilometers west of Gardelegen, where he was buried the next day. A house in the village was severely damaged by wreckage. The collision also marked the end of the successful career of Capt. Alwin M. Juchheim, an "ace" with nine

Second Lt. Anthony E. Ladas of the 363rd Fighter Group was killed in the collision with Capt. Alwin Juchheim of the 78th Fighter Group. EDWARD T. PAWLAK

confirmed air victories to his credit. He had shot down an Me 109 near Freiburg the previous day. His P-47D 42-26016 fell one kilometer southwest of Jeggau, only two kilometers from the wreck of Ladas's Mustang. Juchheim was captured, slightly wounded, and spent the rest of the war in captivity.

Lawrence Casey again: "After the mix-up with the German fighter we went back to the general area where Juchheim would have landed, but not having the gas and time to really search the area, we had to climb back to altitude and head for England. You can imagine three heartsick fighter pilots on the way home. We were encouraged, though, that he had bailed out and was alive, at least during his descent to the ground.

"You can imagine how I felt. I had been his wingman ever since I arrived at this group. He patiently, and sometimes violently, taught me everything about fighter tactics that I know. Even though, at the time of this particular mission, I was usually leading my own flight, he asked me if I wanted to fly on his wing that day. Since I hadn't been scheduled on my own, and his present wingman was not available, I jumped at the chance. Now I was heading back to Duxford without him, unbelievable."[7]

The losses for the 78th Fighter Group would increase however; on their way back to England, with almost all guns unfired and no bombers to look after, its pilots sought targets on the ground. Strafing, low flying and shooting up of barges, trains, trucks or airfields with parked aircraft, was an extremely hazardous activity, because the aircraft were very vulnerable to light flak and fire from small arms at this altitude. As mentioned previously, strafing contributed greatly to the eventual demise of the *Luftwaffe*. Losses

First Lt. Karl R. Wagner of the 78th Fighter Group was the sole survivor of a three-ship strafing attack on Plantlünne. He was able to nurse his badly damaged P-47 back to England and made an emergency landing. KALE S. WARREN

while strafing were quite common, as a three-aircraft flight of the 78th Fighter Group, 82nd Fighter Squadron, would find out that day. The flight was led by 1st Lt. Philip H. Hazelett from Fairfield, Ohio, who had flown with the Group since early February and who was on his 57th combat mission. His number two, 1st Lt. Lynn A. Hosford, was one of the nine pilots who had to abort early in the mission. Number three in the flight was 1st Lt. Karl R. Wagner from Lowell, Ohio, and his wingman was 2nd Lt. William S. Orvis, from Farmington, California, on only his third combat mission.

Karl Wagner submitted the following: "We left our bombers at 1350 hours and started home, looking for targets of opportunity. We saw five or six twin-engined enemy aircraft on a grass field, which I believe to be Wunstorf in the Steinhuder Lake area. Lieutenant Hazelett decided to give it the works, so my wingman Lieutenant Orvis and I, followed him north of the field about six miles, where we let down to the tree tops and lined up on the field. We had just gotten to the edge of the field, when Lieutenant Hazelett called out that he was hit in the engine by a 37mm burst. While Lieutenant Hazelett was calling me, I was hit by three 37mm shells in the rear; two behind the turbo from underneath and one from the left. I broke right and got two or three 20mm shells through the horizontal stabilizers and elevators. While breaking I called my wingman, Lieutenant Orvis, and told him it was too hot and he shouldn't follow. I didn't see him, as he was slightly behind me, nor hear anything from him.

First Lt. Philip H. Hazelett was killed in action after his P-47 was hit by light flak and crashed in Gildehaus, near Bad Bentheim, Germany. GARRY L. FRY

"In the meantime, I was dodging and weaving amongst the trees in the woods. While dodging, I saw there were twelve to fifteen flak towers in the woods at the north of the field, all shooting at me. They were camouflaged by tree branches around the towers. They must have been fully alerted. I heard Lieutenant Hazelett say he was at approximately 5,000 feet and going to bail out. I wished him the best of luck and got the hell out of there. I then started climbing, and as I reached 3,000 feet, I saw Lieutenant Hazelett's plane spin past me and blow up. I looked for the parachute, but couldn't locate it. The plane could have flown quite a distance, as I was at least ten miles from where I heard him say he was going to bail out. I'm sure he got out OK. I believe Lieutenant Orvis must have been hit over the airfield."[8]

Unfortunately, Wagner was wrong: both Hazelett and Orvis were killed. Orvis crashed with his P-47D 42-76318 at Elbergen, near Lingen, at 1437 hours. Hazelett, who apparently did not succeed in leaving his stricken P-47D 42-26064, crashed a few miles further at Gildehaus, near Bad Bentheim, close to the Dutch-German border, at 1440 hours. Both were buried on 1 June at the cemetery at Lingen-Ems.

The airfield they had set upon to strafe was not Wunstorf, but Plantlünne, farther west. Records indicate that just nine days earlier, during the mission of 19 May, Hazelett and his flight had strafed "Plantlünne landing ground" and had met very light opposition. They had destroyed two Me 110s and damaged one He 111 and three flak positions around the field. Most probably, Hazelett wanted to repeat this action, but the Germans seemed to have learned from their mistake and had reinforced their anti-aircraft defenses, with deadly results. The following flak units were credited

Second Lt. William S. Orvis was killed in action after his P-47 was hit
by light flak and crashed near Elbergen, Germany. GARRY L. FRY

with shooting down Hazelett and Orvis: 4th Battery of *leichte Flak Abteilung
942*, 6th Battery of *leichte Heimat Flak Abteilung 876*, *Heimatflakzug Plantlünne*,
and machine-gun platoons of the *Flugplatz Plantlünne* and the II./NJG 3, a
German nightfighter unit, apparently stationed on the base at that time.
Karl Wagner was able to nurse his badly hit Thunderbolt across the North
Sea, made an emergency landing at Wattisham, and, at his debriefing,
recounted this disastrous strafing attempt.

Surtax Yellow Flight, also of the 82nd Fighter Squadron, had better luck.
Its flight leader, Benjamin M. Watkins, reported: "After leaving the bombers
and setting course for home, I noticed an airport near Gifhorn. Near the
drome in open fields were what appeared to be twin-engined planes. Upon
strafing them, I noticed that they were dummies. Hits were registered on several. My flight became separated as we dodged the accurate light flak which
was coming out of the woods. The other three, Lieutenants Beck, DeWitt,
and Gladstone, then attacked some oil wells east of Hannover. There were
forty of them and they had strikes on several. Then Lieutenants Beck and
DeWitt strafed an electric locomotive on a train, both getting hits on it. They
then continued to Celle airdrome, where Lieutenant DeWitt damaged a Ju
52 on the field, getting strikes on it. Lieutenant Beck shot up and damaged
three barges on a canal near the airdrome. He and Lieutenant DeWitt were
hit by intense light flak on the field. All returned safely."[9]

The grave of 1st Lt. Philip Hazelett at the Ardennes American Cemetery and Memorial in Neuville-en-Condroz in Belgium. AUTHOR

This picture testifies to the ruggedness of the P-47 and also to the flying skills of Karl Wagner. He landed it in this condition at Wattisham after being hit by flak over Plantlünne in Germany. GARRY L. FRY

A deadly 20mm flak gun in an improvised field position. The picture clearly shows how easily these guns could be moved and quickly turned into a death trap for strafing fighter pilots. The gun shield displays previous successes. BUNDESARCHIV KOBLENZ

Lt. Charles W. DeWitt of the 78th Fighter Group smokes a cigarette after his eventful mission on 28 May. The picture shows some of the damage that the flak inflicted on his Thunderbolt. CHARLES W. DEWITT

CHAPTER 5

The First Two Combat Wings Strike Dessau

The largest force of the day, three combat wings in all, was sent out to bomb the Junkers Flugzeug und Motorenwerke A.G., an aircraft and aero-engine plant in Dessau. However, the size of the force in itself was to be no guarantee of success. In the end, it would prove to be the least successful of all missions flown on 28 May and result in the highest loss to the attackers. It is, therefore, covered in great detail.

Leading the force to Dessau was the 1st Combat Wing. This wing was composed of a lead group, furnished by the 381st Bomb Group from Ridgewell, a low group with aircraft of the 91st Bomb Group from Bassingbourn, and a composite group with aircraft from both groups in the high group position.

The second combat wing, the 41st, was led by the 379th Bomb Group from Kimbolton, the 303rd Bomb Group from Molesworth flying low, and the 384th Bomb Group from Grafton Underwood flying high.

The third and last combat wing, the 94th, was formed by the 457th Bomb Group from Glatton flying lead, the 401st Bomb Group from Deenethorpe flying low, and the 351st Bomb Group from Polebrook flying high. During the assembly of this last wing over England, problems arose. Ultimately, they would lead to a clash with the fully assembled German fighter force near the target and result in very heavy losses to these three groups. The exploits of the 94th Combat Wing are covered separately in the next chapter. In this chapter, the experiences of the 1st Combat Wing and 41st Combat Wings will be described.

Leading the 1st Combat Wing—and thus the entire force bound for Dessau—was Maj. Charles L. Halsey aboard 1st Lt. James L. Tyson's PFF-equipped B-17G, *Evenin' Folks! How y'all?* (42-97562). They took off from Ridgewell exactly at 1000 hours, followed by another eighteen aircraft that formed the lead group. Group assembly was over the field, which they left at 1054 hours for wing assembly.

Navigator aboard the lead ship was 2nd Lt. John W. Howland, who wrote in his diary that evening: "After only three hours of sleep, we were

Most of the lead crew for the 1st Combat Wing in front of their B-17G *Sunkist Special*
(42-97625). This PFF-equipped B-17 was damaged in an accident a day earlier, and
on 28 May, the crew boarded B-17G *Evenin' Folks! How y'all?* (42-97562) for the
mission to Dessau. Back row, left to right: Richard C. Jensen, engineer; Arnold
Farmer, tail gunner (not on mission); Robert H. Miller, right waist gunner; Charles
Churchill Jr., left waist gunner; and Henry N. White, radio operator. Front row,
left to right: John W. Howland, navigator; James L. Tyson, lead pilot; and William J.
Doherty, co-pilot, flying as tail gunner/formation observer. *Sunkist Special* was
salvaged after crash-landing on 8 March 1945. JOHN W. HOWLAND

awakened and instructed to take off from Bassingbourn for Ridgewell. We
landed there at 2300 hours and got to bed about midnight. The wakeup call
came at 0500 and we were briefed for Dessau, a small town north of Leipzig.
Major Halsey was flying with us in the lead ship, and Ted Homdrom was my
co-navigator.

"Take-off time was 1000 and we assembled without problem. However,
just as we were leaving the first control point, we discovered channels A, B,
and C on the VHF radio were not working. Evidently the wrong crystals had
been installed. Major Halsey requested me to contact the deputy lead using
the Aldis lamp and ask them to contact us on the command radio frequency.
It was a great opportunity to practice my Morse code, so I blinked out a message in dots and dashes and waited for reaction. I could see the pilot of the
deputy lead clearly, and saw him shake his head and motion for someone to

join him. I then blinked away at the two heads I could see, and saw two heads shake no in unison. About that time Major Halsey called on the interphone, saying, 'Navigator, forget the Aldis lamp. Deputy lead just called in on the command radio frequency asking why you are blinking that light in the nose of your ship?' We all had a good laugh, and I decided then that blinking lights were fine for communications between ships at sea, but a sorry substitute for radio between airplanes. With communications established between the lead and deputy lead ships, we continued in our lead position. Deputy lead transmitted all necessary signals on channels A, B, and C for us. We found that channel D was functioning properly which gave us one working VHF channel. We crossed over the enemy coast following out the same old 'highway'—52-deg 37-min N—into Holland and on in to Germany. We had perfect pilotage weather all the way to the target."[1]

The low position in the wing was filled by the 91st Bomb Group, with eighteen ships taking off from Bassingbourn from 1004 to 1020 hours. This group was led by Capt. Paul D. Jessop in B-17G *Sleepy Time Gal* (42-102527), flown by 1st Lt. Edward Waters. All aircraft of the group reached the wing assembly point, where they met the high group. This was a composite group comprising twelve B-17s of the 381st Bomb Group and another eight of the 91st Bomb Group. Leading this group was Capt. George Reese of the 381st

PFF-equipped B-17G *Evenin 'Folks! How y'all?* (42-97562) led the 1st Combat Wing to Dessau. WILLIAM R. HADLEY

Bomb Group, in B-17G *Rotherhithes Revenge* (42-31761), piloted by Milton F. Tarr. Instead of returning to Ridgewell, the assigned spare for the 381st Bomb Group, B-17G *The Tomahawk Warrior* (42-97267), piloted by Lt. Robert G. Beackley, tagged on to the formation, making nineteen aircraft in that group. The composite group even had two more B-17s than usual, since the 91st Bomb Group furnished eight instead of six aircraft for the high squadron, all of which flew the mission.

Upon completing its formation, the 1st Combat Wing left the English coast at Great Yarmouth at 1205 hours at 14,300 feet and reached the Dutch coast thirty-four minutes later at 19,600 feet. The route to the target was flown as briefed. However, two ships in the lead group aborted and returned to Bassingbourn. B-17G *Shoo Shoo Shoo Baby* (42-32076), flown by 1st Lt. Walter R. Langford, suffered from a drop in oxygen pressure in the pilot's, navigator's, and engineer's systems. Lieutenant Hartman's B-17G *Dear Becky* (42-38128) was almost impossible to fly because when right rudder was applied, it suddenly moved violently to the full right position. Both crews were credited with a sortie upon return.*

The penetration escort for the flight to Dessau was provided by the 78th Fighter Group, the same group that escorted the preceding two combat wings to Ruhland. North of Dümmer Lake, the escort was taken over by the 352nd Fighter Group at 1319 hours and was then strengthened by the arrival of the 355th and the 363rd Fighter Groups near Celle at 1331 and 1336 hours, respectively, and the 4th Fighter Group near Gardelegen at 1350 hours.

Upon arriving at the initial point at 1405 hours, the flak intensified. It was later reported to be heavy and accurate over the target. In addition to this flak, the ground view gradually became hampered by scattered clouds, ground haze and smoke. Only 2nd Lt. James R. Van Pelt, the lead bombardier of the low group, the 91st, was able to drop his group's 160 500-pound high-explosive bombs on the first bomb run at 1417 hours. Unfortunately, neither the lead nor the high group were able to see the primary target on this run. The combat wing now had to continue to a target of opportunity, since making a 360-degree turn and coming over the primary target again would interfere with the other two combat wings following it. The time interval between the wings was no more than ten minutes.

Lead navigator John W. Howland continued his account in his diary: "We flew northeast a short distance and then turned south. While we were making this turn, a few German fighters hit the low group. A whole mass of

---

* *Shoo Shoo Shoo Baby* would also fly on the mission the next day and sought sanctuary in Sweden. After many years of postwar civilian use, it is now displayed in its original colors in the Air Force Museum at Dayton, Ohio.

The bombs of the 381st Bomb Group explode in the northwestern corner of Brandis-Polenz airfield. Note the twin-engine aircraft, both He 177s and Ju 88s, parked across the field. CROWN COPYRIGHT / PUBLIC RECORD OFFICE

German fighters hit a wing behind us and kicked the stuffings out of them. The German fighters only made one pass, as our escort came to the rescue and beat them off. A large airport just east of Leipzig was selected as a target of opportunity and we made our bomb run. Really blew hell out of the hangar area. But the high group failed to see our bomb doors opening, and they didn't drop on us."

The airfield that the 381st Bomb Group had selected for its 170 500-pound high-explosive bombs was Brandis-Polenz. It was home to several units, among those a *Gruppe* of *Kampfgeschwader 1* and the *Flugzeug-führerschule B 31*. At least one He 177 bomber of KG 1, a Ju 88 of the school, and probably six other aircraft were destroyed. One of the three large hangars on the airfield was completely destroyed and was never reconstructed. Two men, a pilot and a student pilot, lost their lives under the bombs and four student pilots were wounded.[2]

The high group, the composite group of both the 91st and 381st Bomb Groups, still had its bombs aboard. On the return flight to England, its lead bombardier picked out the Frankfurt marshalling yards at 1535 hours, and dropped 160 500-pound high-explosive bombs, creating havoc on the track. Maj. Charles L. Halsey, leading the combat wing, later recalled: "The primary was covered by patchy clouds and haze, so we went on to an airfield near Leipzig, where we saw a flock of six-engined bombers on the ground, so we let them have it. There was only a little flak over the primary when we went over it, but the formation that followed ours, really got it. It looked

When units of the U.S. 9th Armored Division entered the airfield at Brandis-Polenz on 16 April 1945, they found the wreckage of Ju 88 "20" of *Blindflugschule B31* still in the remnants of Hangar 2. This aircraft and probably six others were destroyed by bombs of the 381st Bomb Group on 28 May. Two members of the unit were killed and four wounded by the American bombs. U.S. ARMY

thick enough back there to make a good black cloud. We didn't get much over the target. Our high group didn't bomb with us. I picked up a place for them to hit on the way back, but they saw Frankfurt and went over there. In spite of the intense flak, they made a run on the marshalling yards and from where we were, it looked as if they did a beautiful job."[3]

No fewer than eight B-17s of the 91st and twenty-one B-17s of the 381st Bomb Group suffered slight to moderate damage from the flak over their respective targets. One of the B-17s of the 381st Bomb Group that was hit was piloted by Lt. Samuel H. Whitehead. He recalls: "Everything was pretty much routine until we started the bomb run. The flak became quite heavy and one of our waist gunners let us know there was oil streaming from the number three engine. The flak had hit a main oil line. I immediately hit the feather button, but it was too late, there was not enough oil left to feather the prop. We started falling behind, so I increased power on the other three engines. The windmilling prop caused the plane to vibrate so bad that we had to reduce power and drop out of the formation. At that moment we had a sinking feeling, we knew we had to return to Ridgewell alone. A damaged B-17 flying alone from the middle of Germany would be a sitting duck for enemy fighters. The formation, with all its gun power, was a real sense of security.

"We then salvoed our bombs, and I asked our navigator for the heading back to the base. We were very fortunate not to encounter any German fighters. We could only fly about 130 to 140 miles per hour due to the vibra-

From his combat position in the nose of B-17 *Patsy Ann* (42-97285), navigator Albert Saleeby can shake hands with his pilot Samuel H. Whitehead on the ground. The hole was made by the propeller after it separated from the number three engine.
SAMUEL H. WHITEHEAD

tion, so we really felt at risk. As we passed over Belgium we began to receive some flak, with shells bursting around us. So I banked the plane to take evasive action. Then the windmilling prop came off the engine and chewed a hole in the nose, barely hitting the navigator's heel. He was looking into the navigator's astrodome, which sits right in front of the cockpit. I could see sawdust whirling around. We thought maybe the bombardier or navigator were being chewed up. They let us know on the intercom they were OK. Once we got rid of the windmilling prop we were greatly relieved. I pushed the throttles forward, put the nose down and got the speed over 200 miles per hour and headed for home. We soon reached the English Channel— what a good feeling, we knew we had it made."[4]

Flak over Frankfurt had tragic consequences for another aircraft of the 381st Bomb Group. B-17G *Century Note* (42-107100) was piloted by 2nd Lt. Jack E. Sutherlin. He recalls: "I think we circled the target twice before going to another target. Our high group took a heading of approximately 230 degrees magnetic and flew on and dropped from 22,000 to 20,000 feet while skirting several other targets and with what they had in mind for a target. The weather was sunny and clear. Lt. Dave Schwartz, my navigator, plotted the course and called out nearby cities, rivers and what was ahead of us, the city of Frankfurt. Twelve airplanes* at 20,000 feet in clear weather flying

---

* Here Sutherlin refers only to the aircraft of his own bomb group in this high group. There were eight more from the 91st Bomb Group in this same composite group.

B-17G *Century Note* (42-107100) of the 381st Bomb Group, with bomb doors open, is flying through flak. On 28 May, its tail gunner, George Samuelian, was killed by a flak fragment. DAVID R. OSBORNE

the last twenty-five miles straight for a bomb run on Frankfurt was not normal practice, but this is how it happened. Bomb doors were opened and the 88 mm's started and they had our range and had many guns. It was the most intensely, accurate flak we experienced before or after. Black puffs, smell of exploding shells, occasional sound of exploding shells when close to the plane. Noise of fragments piercing the aircraft aluminium.

"Lt. Guy Feranti called bombs away and that we had dropped in the vicinity of the railroad yards in the city. Suddenly he became frantic, yelling that he was hit in the face and was bleeding badly. In what seemed seconds of time, George Samuelian, the tail gunner, said in a normal voice, 'I'm hit.' My intercom went out and I experienced something so close to my left forearm that I felt it pass. With my intercom out, I passed messages to Lt. Ray Sullivan on the pilots' briefing sheet for the day. Sergeant Valdez, waist gunner, went to check on Samuelian and passed out because of lack of oxygen. Tech Sergeant Du Pre, the radio operator, took a walk around bottle of oxygen to Valdez and revived him. They checked George Samuelian and said sadly that he was dead. During the time when Valdez passed out from lack of oxygen, I left the formation dropping to 18,000 feet. This wasn't the correct thing to do, but it was something I did in response with no reason. We were fortunate there were no enemy fighters in the vicinity. I also then discovered that the switch on the intercom had been turned to the 'off'

This picture of the crew of *Century Note* wearing different types of combat clothing was taken on the hardstand at Ridgewell only minutes before taking off on 28 May. Standing, left to right: William Hooper, ground crew chief; John Eckhoff, engineer; Jack Sutherlin, pilot; David Schwartz, navigator; Ray Sullivan, co-pilot; and Guy Feranti, bombardier. Kneeling, left to right: Tony Valdez, waist gunner; George Samuelian, tail gunner; John Du Pre, radio operator; and Joe Warner, ball turret gunner. JACK SUTHERLIN

position by flak. John Du Pre suggested a prayer, and there was an 'Our Father' for George Samuelian. We used the prayer on every following mission in memory of George."[5]

Another B-17G, *The Tomahawk Warrior* (42-97267), of the 381st Bomb Group would have a very close call. It also returned to Ridgewell alone on the deck, after flak damage forced it out of formation. Its pilot, 2nd Lt. Robert G. Beackley, stated that his troubles began in the target area, when his number two engine went out and it could not be feathered. The drag on the aircraft made it necessary to salvo the bombs at once, in order for it to keep up with the others in the formation. Ten minutes later, number three engine also went out, and although this engine could be feathered, the additional drag made formation flying impossible.

Beackley ordered his crew to jettison all equipment, and the gunners started heaving everything they could detach, out of the waist windows. With two engines out, he fell behind the group and tagged on to another formation, but was unable to stay with it. Beackley decided "to hit the deck" and started home, all alone. Flying at some fifty feet over hostile Germany had its

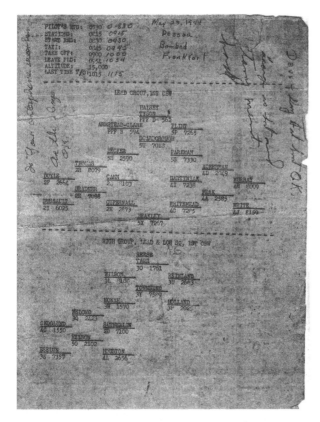

Jack Sutherlin and co-pilot Ray Sullivan used the formation diagram to exchange written information on the crew when flak over Frankfurt had shot out the intercom on *Century Note*. Sutherlin asked, "Is your inter-phone working?" and "Are the boys OK?" Sullivan replied, "Dave and Guy hit but OK" and "George is hit and Tony went back." Their handwriting can be seen on the paper. JACK SUTHERLIN

The *Tomahawk Warrior*, piloted by Lt. Robert G. Beackley, barely made it back to Ridgewell on 28 May and was photographed two days later. DAVID R. OSBORNE

own problems, as the crew soon found out. "We were too low for flak, but they went for us with small arms and machine guns. They didn't care what they hurt either. We saw bullets they were aiming at us, flying into German houses."[6]

The ball turret was then dropped, since it served no purpose flying at such a low-altitude, and ejecting its weight would help in getting home. Records clearly show, that only a touch of luck and some keen eyes kept Beackley and his crew from being shot down by German fighters. Returning from escort duty to the Ruhland force, a flight of P-51s of the 355th Fighter Group spotted Beackley's low-flying B-17.

One of the fighter pilots was 2nd Lt. Walter E. MacFarlane, who reported: "Coming out on withdrawal, I was flying Custard Red 3. I called in a bogie on the deck and led the flight down to investigate, as my flight leader didn't see it. We discovered it to be a Fortress with triangle 'L' markings, silver colour, with one engine out. The crew was jettisoning all of the equipment. We escorted it for about ten minutes when two Me 109s were observed coming in from the north on the deck to attack the Fortress. There was a third Me 109 which we did not see until later. I turned into the two and got on the tail of one and the third one got on my tail, but was shot down by my wingman, Lieutenant Eshelman. My enemy aircraft took evasive actions, but I was able to get several bursts in on him from 200 yards and at various angles, observing strikes all over the fuselage. He pulled up from 500 to about 800 feet and bailed out. I saw his chute open about 200 feet off the ground, and both he and his plane landed in a woods."[7]

Lt. Walter E. MacFarlane of the 355th Fighter Group spotted *Tomahawk Warrior* on the deck and shot down a German Bf 109 that tried to attack it. MacFarlane was shot down by a Bf 109 on 7 June and bailed out to be captured. WALTER E. MACFARLANE

Lieutenant Eshelman reported: "I was flying Custard Red 4. We were on the deck escorting a straggling Fort, when three Me 109s came in from the north to attack it. We turned into two of them and Lieutenant MacFarlane, Red 3, got on one's tail and at about that time I saw a third Me 109 coming in on Lieutenant MacFarlane's tail. I pulled back on this one's tail and opened fire at about 150 yards with 20-degree deflection. I hit him on the first burst in the cockpit. I fired a few more bursts, he straightened out and started diving and turning left and I followed him in this turn, firing in and getting more hits on the cockpit. He straightened out, faltered along, the engine began to run slow and the enemy aircraft crashed into small railroad tracks, exploding on impact."[8]

If the sharp eyes of Lieutenant MacFarlane had not spotted the lone Fortress, there is little doubt that *The Tomahawk Warrior* would have been no match for the German fighters, with its ball turret, machine guns, equipment, and ammunition gone. There is little doubt that the Mustangs' victims were pilots of 9./JG 1, who had taken off from Paderborn a little earlier.

One of these three pilots, *Leutnant* Hans Halbey, recalled: "It was Whit Sunday, sunny weather and a clear blue sky. On the edge of the airfield, we could see people going to church or going for a Sunday walk, appropriately dressed for the occasion. We were sitting fully dressed in the cockpits of our Messerschmitts, waiting for things to happen. 'We'—that is just three pilots remaining at Paderborn. Then, in comes a *Startbefehl* from some far away headquarters: 'Attack returning bomber formations.'

Lt. Francis L. Eshelman and his P-51 *Terry Fran.* Just visible under the canopy is the kill marking for Fritz Timm's Bf 109. Eshelman went down over France on 12 August but evaded capture and was back with the 355th Fighter Group in September.
KEN WELLS

"Three pilots are ordered to attack bomber formations! But one of us, *Hauptmann* Burkhardt (*Oberfeldwebel* Fritz Timm and myself are the other two), refuses the order and states that right at that moment some Mustangs were circling our field. His protests were honored. Then a new *Startbefehl*, this time with a specified course. Burkhardt orders us to fly as low as possible, to try to fly this route without enemy fighters noticing it. But it doesn't take long before eighteen Mustangs are upon us, at relatively low altitude. I notice two Mustangs behind me and I try, by climbing and turning steeply, to avoid them getting enough lead to shoot me down. Both Mustangs curve behind me, very close behind me. I try another tactic, dive my Messerschmitt down, pull up steeply, reduce power, and let it side-slip. This slows me down. As expected, the second Mustang behind me reacts too late (perhaps an inexperienced pilot) and passes me at high speed. With a little course correction, he is in my crosshairs and I fire: the Mustang shows a white trail and makes a turn downward. But at the same time, the pilot in the other Mustang has me in his crosshairs and fires. I notice that my bird has become uncontrollable, jettison the canopy, unbuckle, and get out. To my horror, I notice that we are really very low—will my chute open in time? I immediately pull my ripcord—the chute opens. I am just over some woods, see a Mustang flying toward me—it shoots at me. I have arrived in the tops of some trees and finally hang suspended between the branches. I turn the buckle on my harness, leave my chute in the trees, and climb down using some branches.

"Already the first people arrive at the scene. They have seen the dog-fight and have also seen that the Mustang fired at me in my chute. I am taken to the nearby village Mölln, and I learn what the people have also seen. *Hauptmann* Burkhardt was hit, his aircraft trailing smoke (I later learn that he had just managed to get to an airfield). The Mustang that I had hit made a belly landing; the pilot, who was uninjured, was lynched by the people, had not some *Wehrmacht* soldiers arrived who took the pilot in custody. Why lynch the pilot? Because before we came, just for the fun of it, they had shot at civilians walking in the sun.

"And *Oberfeldwebel* Timm? He lies burned next to the wreckage of his machine, only a small black package of human being. Unfortunately, I am not spared the look of him. The local doctor first puts an enormous syringe in my back to prevent tetanus, then removes a lot of glass fragments from my face.

"Two years later, I visit Mölln for the second time, and am brought by some inhabitants to the crash site. There I stand, at the edge of a reasonably-sized crater in thick woods, with thousands of fragments from my machine lying around, and still a smell of gasoline, metal, magnesium, and gunpowder in the air. And I had the rare feeling to be standing in front of what was almost my grave."[9]

Leutnant Hans Halbey of III./JG 1 had his portrait taken in October 1944. Under his left breast pocket, displaying his pilot's and glider pilot's badge, he wears the *Verwundetenabzeichen*, the German equivalent to a Purple Heart. It was awarded to him for wounds he sustained on 28 May when he was shot down by Lt. Walter MacFarlane near Ebsdorf.

HANS A. HALBEY

The Mustang that Halbey claimed to have shot down cannot be identified as no American loss matches the location where the dogfight occurred.

After the action, the P-51s, low on fuel, left the crippled *Tomahawk Warrior*, damaging one locomotive on the return to Steeple Morden. An unidentified P-38 Lightning took over the escort duty from that point. Over the coast, *The Tomahawk Warrior* was hit again by German ground fire, but kept on flying and eventually reached Ridgewell. There the ground crews could not count all the holes in her skin—there were just too many. Beackley was awarded a Distinguished Flying Cross for bringing back his B-17 on only two engines.

Jack Sutherlin, bringing in his damaged *Century Note* with three wounded and one dead crew member aboard, continues his account: "The Channel and England ahead, we let down and fired a red flare over the field, to notify wounded aboard, and landed first. We taxied to the ambulance at the end of the runway, and stopped. They checked George Samuelian and took Lieutenant Feranti, Lieutenant Schwartz, and Sergeant Valdez in the ambulance to the infirmary. George was taken to the hardstand to be unloaded. It was difficult to remove George, and medics did their job with difficulty. There was one good sized hole in the tail compartment and several others in the fuselage, wings and bombardiers compartment. The doctor said George had died seconds after he was hit. Even with the best of medical treatment it was impossible to prevent his death. May 29

was a day off for the crew to attend George's funeral at the Cambridge cemetery. He was not the only one buried that day. I keep thinking there were six
of them.

"Other crewmembers' wounds that day were superficial. Lieutenant
Schwartz was nicked by flak on the left hand. Lieutneant Feranti required
four stitches on the upper right hand side of his cheek below the eye.
Sergeant Valdez was hit at the very top of his left shoulder making a quarter-
inch-deep-by-quarter-inch-wide cut which required six stitches. I didn't know
of the latter two wounds until they got into the ambulance. On 30 May, my
crew, with a very reluctant Sergeant Valdez as tail gunner, flew to Dessau to
bomb what we didn't bomb on 28 May. Three ships from our Group were
shot down by fighters. Our last mission was on 11 August to Brest in
France—we never had any further casualties on our crew. George Samuelian
was not much of a conversationalist. He was pitcher on a softball team and
could also easily hit a home run. He was never late on a flight, always loved
to shoot and never said no to any command. George is a hero, wherever he
might be."[10]

The second combat wing assigned to bomb Dessau was the 41st, with the
379th, 303rd, and 384th Bomb Groups flying as lead, low, and high groups,

Hauptmann Lutz-Wilhelm
Burkhardt (on right) had
to use all his flying skills
to escape from a flight of
P-51s of the 355th Fighter
Group. Both other pilots in
his flight were shot down.

respectively. Leading the wing was Lt. Col. Robert S. Kittel in PFF-equipped B-17G 42-97699, piloted by Lt. D. S. Morrison. The 379th Bomb Group began its take-off from Kimbolton at 1040 hours and put up twenty-one aircraft in addition to two PFF ships.

One of the spare aircraft, piloted by Lt. Russell M. Olson, took over when B-17G 42-107213 of Lt. Milton S. Miller had to leave the formation while still over England because of personnel failure. The commanding officer of the group, Col. Maurice A. Preston, recorded: "The particular instance is being investigated and action is being taken by the medical department, rather than from a disciplinary standpoint."[11]

Two other spares returned unused. The lead group for this wing flew with an extra aircraft added to the low and high squadrons and thus had twenty aircraft in all. The high group for this wing, the 384th Bomb Group, also put up twenty aircraft in its formation. Group leader was Maj. Robert E. Thacker in B-17G 42-97072, piloted by 1st Lt. Phillip N. Bennett. No aircraft returned early to Grafton Underwood, and a normal group and wing assembly was made.

The low group, the 303rd Bomb Group, was led by Capt. Peter L.M. Packard in B-17G *Princess Pat* (42-102453), piloted by 1st Lt. Joseph A. Moreau. Two of the scheduled eighteen aircraft did not take off, one due to a flat tire and the other with a leaking wing tank. During group assembly, B-17G 42-107048, piloted by 1st Lt. Roy Eisele, aborted with a defunct oxygen system. Thus, only fifteen aircraft of the group made the subsequent wing assembly at 9,000 feet over their own field, Molesworth. Division assembly was made with some difficulty since the combat wings ran into a formation of Liberators. While the 41st Combat Wing was able to stay in formation and skirt around the obstructing Liberators, the 94th Combat Wing, which followed shortly behind and which was the last in the First Division's force, ran into great trouble. This will be described in the next chapter.

Lt. Col. Robert S. Kittel, leading the 41st Combat Wing, reported: "The division assembly was made amongst the B-24s. At the English coast, we were on course when a B-24 division came between us and the combat wing in front of us. We were first to cut in between the lead and second combat wing of the B-24s. It was a tight squeeze, but we made it."[12]

The English coast was departed at 1205 hours and 15,000 feet, and landfall in Holland was at 1241 hours and 22,000 feet. No unusual events occurred during the flight to the target area and the initial point was reached at 1406 hours.

An interesting account of the mission is given by Staff Sgt. John B. Pratt, the radio operator on Lt. Raymond R. Stevens's B-17 of the 384th Bomb Group. That evening, back at Grafton Underwood, he wrote in his diary: "Take-off 1023B—Left England at Cromer, south of the Wash. Went straight

Oberfeldwebel Fritz Timm of 9./ JG 1 scored his first victory, a Mosquito, on 9 October 1942 and claimed his fifth, a Mustang, on 24 May 1944. Despite all his combat experience, he was shot down by Lt. Francis Eshelman of the 355th Fighter Group on 28 May. He died when his Bf 109 crashed in flames near Ebsdorf.
ERIC MOMBEEK

east over North Sea to Holland. Passed over Zuider Zee and near Amsterdam. Kept going east over Germany towards Berlin. Near Hannover we went south-east and passed near Magdeburg to Dessau. We were supposed to bomb a JU engine factory at Dessau, but target was obscured by smoke from previous bombings. We turned south and went to Leipzig and bombed a synthetic rubber factory on the edge of Leipzig. Target was bombed from 26,000 feet, temp 29 degrees. We hit target hard. On route between Dessau and Leipzig, we saw several targets which had been hit by other groups. On run to Leipzig, a B-17 took a direct flak hit. It exploded and tail broke off at ball turret. Went down in flames and exploded again—no chutes. Medium flak (88mm black) at Dessau and medium inaccurate flak at Leipzig. Three Me 109s went over us on bomb run, but didn't attack. Two of our P-51s collided and went down in flames—I saw one chute. The high squadron in our group screwed up and their lead ship flew directly over us on bomb run. I looked up into his open bomb bay from radio hatch and just waited for him to drop them on us. I really was scared. He got back in place before bombs away—but we really sweat. We dropped ten 500-pound incendiaries on Leipzig and did a good job. Had a heavy escort of P-51s on way over and P-51s and P-38s on return—good deal! Returned northwest over Germany near Frankfurt and over Belgium near Brussels. Passed over French coast near Dunkirk and hit England near London. No flak or fighters on return. Group lost no B-17s. Our ship had no damage at all. Landed 1800B—7.5 hours, 6 hours over enemy territory. 6.5 hours on oxygen."[13]

The collision that Pratt witnessed was that between Captain Juchheim and Lieutenant Ladas, as described in the previous chapter. As Pratt wrote, the same smoke and haze around Dessau that fouled up the bombing of the 1st Combat Wing, now did the same to the bombing of the 41st. This wing also encountered moderate, but accurate flak over the target. The deputy lead aircraft of the wing, piloted by Lieutenant Lotz, was hit in two engines and had to leave the formation. It was last observed by the lead ship in the vicinity of Frankfurt, being escorted by three Thunderbolts. Lotz made it safely back to England and landed at Manston.

One bombardier in the 379th Bomb Group formation, thinking that he could identify the target sufficiently, dropped his bombs through the haze. The rest of the group held their bombs aboard and eventually dropped the remaining 186 500-pound high-explosive bombs on an airfield three miles west of Wustensachsen at 1515 hours, causing moderate damage.

The flak in the target area struck very hard at the crew of B-17G 42-107028 of the 303rd Bomb Group. This crew, commanded by 2nd Lt. Alvin G. Determan, was on its twelfth mission that month. Determan remembers that the day started badly: "As we taxied into position for take off, our plane canted a great deal to one side, as if one of the shock struts had collapsed. We radioed the tower and were given permission to pull off the runway. We deplaned and a flight engineer came tearing over in a jeep. He couldn't find anything wrong, but accused me of taxi-ing too fast. Then back to take-off and to find our group and squadron. We circled the area asking our squadron leader to fire a flare so we could join up, which we finally accomplished."[14]

Two of the crewmembers had swapped positions for this flight, a thing they were permitted to do, as they were both qualified engineers and aerial gunners. The regular engineer, Tech Sgt. Milton C. Hendrickson, left his top turret, and occupied the far more uncomfortable right waist gun position. The assistant engineer and right waist gunner, Sgt. Wayne E. Cope, moved up to the flight deck to man the twin .50s in the top turret. This seemingly hazardless exchange of combat positions would later mean the difference between life and death for the two men.

Alvin Determan: "Then to my horror, I found that I had forgotten to take pet my heavy flying jacket along. Sort of good luck jacket. I had the inclination to turn back to get the jacket but knew this was a ridiculous thought. The flight into Germany was routine, I believe, with no fighter attacks, and very little flak. At the time we were hit, I don't recall seeing any heavy flak at all."

The crew of B-17G 42-107028 of the 303rd Bomb Group was pictured at Molesworth only days before being shot down. Back row, left to right: Alvin G. Determan, pilot (POW); Ervin J. Pfahler, co-pilot (KIA); Jackson Palmer Jr., navigator (KIA); and Lamar E. Ledbetter, bombardier (not on 28 May mission). Front row, left to right: Milton C. Hendrickson, right waist gunner (KIA); Robert H. Asman, radio operator (POW); Manuel Vasquez, ball turret gunner (KIA); Acel E. Livingston, left waist gunner (KIA); Wayne E. Cope, engineer (POW); Albert R. Carroccia, tail gunner (KIA). ALVIN G. DETERMAN

But like Staff Sgt. John Pratt of the 384th Bomb Group, Tech Sgt. Francis H. Stender, the tail gunner in the lead aircraft of the 303rd Bomb Group, saw it happen all too well: "Lieutenant Determan was flying in the number three position just a little to the left and behind us. The aircraft received a direct hit, close to the number four engine from anti-aircraft gunfire at about 1435 hours in the vicinity of Leipzig. The right wing immediately caught fire and the aircraft then slid under our ship and on out of the formation past the number two position. The right wing came off and the aircraft then rolled over on its back and went down. As it did so, the tail came off at about the entrance door and I didn't observe any parachutes, although others report seeing one."[15]

All this took place in no more time than necessary to reading this statement. Lieutenant Determan again: "As we were hit, I reached under my seat to get my chest pack to attach it to my harness. I managed to get the pack on to one side, but was thrown violently into the passageway leading to the

nose. I didn't have time to even pull the bail out signal. I have often specu-
lated in later years whether it would have made a difference in saving the
lives of some of the other crewmembers. My only thought as I was being buf-
feted about was that I had 'had it.' My next recollection was being or falling
in the air with my chest pack above my head hooked only to one riser, the
tacking having pulled loose from my harness. I tried to get the pack down so
I could attach it to the other riser but to no avail. I finally managed to get a
hold of the rip cord, pulling it to open the chute. As it opened, being held
by only one riser I was subjected to a pendulum effect, swaying from side to
side, often being rotated at the peak of the swing. About this time I was hoping that someone would come by, pick me up and take me back to England.
I was feeling extremely lonely."

At the moment the aircraft broke up, not only Determan was thrown
clear, but also engineer Wayne Cope, from his combat position just behind
the pilots seats on the flight deck. The third and last man to escape was
radio operator Staff Sgt. Robert H. Asman. The seven other crewmembers
were all killed, either immediately by the flak burst or in the subsequent
crash of their B-17. According to a German report, the two larger parts of
the aircraft were found some 1,200 meters apart. One of the bodies was
found two-and-a-half months after the crash took place, on 11 August and
far away from both crash sites, giving graphic evidence of the suddenness
and force of the explosion.

The dazed Alvin Determan floated down beneath his parachute: "As I
approached the earth I could see human activity coming from four villages.
As I landed, ruining a few hundred feet of grass with my face, I was immediately surrounded by what I believe were *Volkssturm* civilians, with arm bands
and pistols and rifles. After divesting me of my outside flying coveralls, they
escorted me to one of the villages. Here everyone was friendly, serving me
with a bottle of terrible beer and ridiculing me as to my size (five foot, six)
and pointing to my lieutenant's insignia. After a short respite here, I was
escorted across a field where we met two regular German Army officers.
Evincing his hatred for the British, one of them jabbed me in the chest and
said, 'If you were Englander, I would shoot you right now.' I was then ush-
ered by the two officers to a detention building where there were a number
of prisoners that had been gathered in the past several days."

From there, Determan was taken to Dulag Luft for interrogation and
finally taken to Stalag Luft III. Both other survivors, Sergeant Cope and Staff
Sergeant Asman, were also captured. Six of the seven killed crewmembers
were buried on 29 May in the cemetery at Beucha, a village close to Leipzig.
The seventh man was buried on 12 August next to his comrades.

Staff Sgt. Harry Goland, the luckiest man in the 303rd Bomb Group on 28 May, looks out the exit hole of a flak shell that missed him by inches. After posing for this photograph, he willingly obliged the photographer's wish to show how happy he was to be back safely on Molesworth. Goland finished his tour of operations after one more mission, on 29 May. HARRY GOLAND

The German flak nearly claimed a second B-17 of the 303rd Bomb Group. Leading the high squadron of the group was 1st Lt. Paul R. Ellsworth in B-17G *Flak Hack* (42-97329). He reported later: "Everything was going along fine until 1435 hours when Leipzig flak came up and Lieutenant Determan, flying in the lead squadron, went down with two engines on fire, spinning and losing his tail. At that moment, the formation was just straightening out from a turn."[16]

This became a flak-assisted turn for Lieutenant Ellsworth, as a flak shell came up at an angle, through the bottom of the fuselage between the pilot and co-pilot, straightening the aircraft out with its impact. It was fortunate that Staff Sgt. Harry Goland in the top turret was standing erect. He had a very small margin of safety, and if he had been relaxed or even shifting his weight at that moment, his buttocks would have gone with the flak shell, which went out the port side of the fuselage, just above the wing root. As it was, the entire crew was thrown about. They found, to their surprise, that they were still flying and were reassured to hear Lieutenant Ellsworth tell them that everything was all right. They continued and dropped their bombs with the other remaining crews of the 303rd Bomb Group. In all, 140 500-pound high-explosive bombs were dropped at 1438 hours on the Molbis power station near Rotha, one of the largest of its kind, which supplied power to central Germany. Just two minutes later, the bombs were followed by the 198 500-pound incendiary bombs that the 384th Bomb Group added to the inferno. The three groups in the 41st Combat Wing had twenty-six Fortresses damaged by flak; three crewmembers were slightly wounded in aircraft of the 303rd Bomb Group. Target evaluation showed that the Molbis power station was well hit, with destruction of several offices, laboratories and barracks, very severe damage to the freight station, and indeterminate damage to the boiler house.

The heavy and accurate flak in the target area nearly accounted for another aircraft. Lt. William E. Satterwhite piloted one of the forty-eight P-38s of the 367th Fighter Group. The unit, one of those that the Ninth Air Force provided, was scheduled to provide withdrawal escort to the first force, the combat wings bombing Ruhland and Dessau and were to take over escort at 1500 hours.

Satterwhite recalls: "Upon intercepting the bomber stream we set-up our weaving pattern over the Groups we were assigned to protect. Our altitude was slightly more than 30,000 feet and we were throttled back to limit speed so as not to overrun the bombers. As the target was approached the flak became intense. A burst exploded especially close to my plane and that of my wing man. I felt an impact and concussion from the explosion. My wing man called saying I was hit and my left engine was smoking. It was actually coolant streaming out. I assessed the damage to the engine, feathered the prop to keep it from 'windmilling' and cut off fuel to the left engine and shut off the ignition. I had fallen from formation while checking the other engine, trying the flying characteristics to determine if controls were intact. Being stabilized, I dropped my exterior tanks, told the squadron leader I was damaged and I was authorized to turn back to England. My wing man, as was the custom, remained with me to provide cover if needed. Course was set to home with nearly 600 miles of enemy territory to cross. The weather was worsening. The next two-and-a-half to three hours proved to be uneventful which was helpful, as flying instruments, holding the torque against the powered engine, and navigating by chart when I could see a landmark was keeping me occupied. Somewhere nearing the Channel coast, my wing man and I became separated.

"Crossing the Channel, I made land-fall in mid-England, saw a grass strip and made my first single-engine landing in a P-38. It was a British/Australian fighter field. I was pleased to be back on friendly turf. To say I was tired would be an understatement. It felt like 'home', though I was not on my own base. It was close enough. I was not about to fly on and try to find my field near Stoney Cross. My base was advised I was down and safe. The next day I was picked up, taken to my base and made ready to go again. It was a memorable day. But, subsequent days supporting the landings at Normandy, 'beating-up' enemy airfields, strafing the retreating German Seventh Army, knocking out Tiger tanks for General Patton's Eleventh and Ninth Armored Divisions and softening the drop area at Nijmegen for paratroopers became even more exciting!"[17]

Satterwhite, very appreciative that a P-38 had two engines, had landed at Ford.

As mentioned, the third and last combat wing assigned to hit the Junkers plant at Dessau—comprising the 351st, 401st, and 457th Bomb Groups—had already got into trouble over England. Their story is told in the following chapter.

CHAPTER 6

The 94th Combat Wing over Dessau

THE FLIGHT TO THE TARGET

The 457th Bomb Group was assigned to lead the 94th Combat Wing on the mission to Dessau. Its lead aircraft was B-17G *Geraldine* (42-97630), equipped with H2X radar, and piloted by 2nd Lt. Charles D. Brannan. The command pilot for the wing, and flying in the co-pilot's seat of this aircraft, was Maj. George C. Hozier, the commanding officer of the 748th Bomb Squadron. There were three navigators aboard, 2nd Lt. James H. Kincaid and Capt. Patrick W. Henry were regular navigators and 2nd Lt. Gordon H. Lowe was operating the H2X radar. The lead bombardier was 2nd Lt. James E. Fast, and 2nd Lt. Walter F. Creigh, normally a co-pilot, was at the tail guns, acting as formation observer. The others aboard were engineer John T. Matovina, radio operator Joseph Colechia, and waist gunners Edward F. Hardin and Charles R. Vandeventer.

The lead bomber left the main runway of Glatton at 1029 hours, loaded with ten 500-pound bombs and one smoke marker, destined for Dessau. It was followed by twenty other Fortresses, including three spares, to form the lead Group of the 94th Combat Wing made group formation without any difficulty and was accomplished by 1122 hours and at 8,000 feet. Then the wing had to be assembled.

The low group for today was furnished by the 401st Bomb Group from Deenethorpe, which also took off with twenty aircraft starting at 1030 hours. Command pilot was Maj. Leon Stann, the operations officer of the 613th Bomb Squadron, in B-17G *Son of a Blitz* (42-31081), piloted by 1st Lt. Charles F. Hess. The assembly of the 401st Bomb Group went smoothly, and they too proceeded to the wing assembly point over the Deenethorpe buncher.

Not everyone aboard the bombers was fully aware of where he was going today, as the story of Staff Sgt. James E. Wells, engineer aboard Lt. Walter B. Keith's B-17 of the 401st Bomb Group, illustrates: "Our crew was awakened and alerted for a bombing mission on the morning of 28 May. Their routine was the normal getting dressed, toilet, breakfast, mission briefing, prayer, checking out of personal equipment, and going to the airplane. I say this was their routine, because I was not there. Our crew had flown a mission to Ludwigshafen on Saturday, 27 May. Upon returning from that mission, and completing our post-flight duties, we returned to the squadron area. One of our required duties was to read the squadron bulletin board. As I read the latest notices, I found my name on the guard duty roster for that night. I immediately went to our hut, and changed from my flying gear to my fatigue uniform. I proceeded at that time to the mess hall for chow prior to reporting for guard duty.

PFF-equipped B-17G *Geraldine* 42-97630 led the 94th Combat Wing to Dessau.
WILLIAM R. HADLEY

"I first found out that we were flying a mission when a squadron runner in a Jeep came to the hardstand where I was standing guard and informed me. The airplane crew chief relieved me, and I was taken by the runner to our hut to change into my flying gear. From there we proceeded to the mess hall for a very quick breakfast. From there the runner drove me to the personal equipment section, where I checked out my parachute bag with all the necessary equipment, then back to the hardstand where the crew were already going about their pre-flight duties. I went to the armament shack and gave my twin .50-caliber machine guns a thorough going over, prior to taking them to the airplane and installing them in the upper turret which was my combat station. After all my pre-flight duties were completed, I joined the rest of the crew as we awaited crew station time. I noted at this time that all the crewmembers were very quiet and subdued, which for our crew was not normal, as the waiting time was normally spent in horseplay. I asked where we were going, and some of the crew said it was going to be a rough one. So I asked again and Lieutenant Keith said he would brief me later. As events of the day unfolded, the briefing was forgotten, and as a result, I did not know where we were going, nor did I know what the target for the day was to be."[1]

The high group for the 94th Combat Wing was the 351st Bomb Group from nearby Polebrook, led by Capt. Harry B. Holsapple in B-17G *Linda Ball II* (42-97381), piloted by Capt. Bruce F. Winton. Nineteen B-17s left on schedule, only Lt. David M. Heller, who was to lead the high squadron of the group, experienced difficulties, and took off late. Subsequent group assembly was without difficulties, Heller's position staying vacant for the time being, as wing assembly was started.

The lead group left the wing assembly point, the Deenethorpe Buncher, on time. The 401st Bomb Group then assumed its position and the 351st Bomb Group joined shortly thereafter. Until then, everything had gone as planned, and nothing pointed to the mishap that would befall this Wing before the end of the day. Trouble started just before leaving the English

Part of the lead crew for the 94th Combat Wing. Kneeling, far left: James H. Kincaid, navigator. Third from left: Charles D. Brannan, lead pilot. Standing, far left: John T. Matovina, engineer; third from left: Charles R. Vandeventer, waist gunner; and fourth from left: Edward F. Hardin, waist gunner. MRS. JAMES H. KINCAID

coast at Great Yarmouth, when the wing ran into another wing, all B-24 units, and had to make a right turn at the division assembly line. The high group, the 351st Bomb Group, had the most trouble with the Liberators and was forced to execute a full 360-degree turn to prevent possible midair collisions. Shortly thereafter, Major Hozier ordered a sharp left turn that was then made by the lead and low groups. The 351st Bomb Group, having manoeuvred to avoid the B-24s, had now lost the wing formation completely.

Upon leaving the English coast, Lt. James V. Elduff of the 457th Bomb Group returned to Glatton, with his number one supercharger out and number two engine short on power. His place was taken by Lt. Winfred L. Pugh, one of the three spares. Both other spares, piloted by Lieutenant Stevens and Lieutenant Pashal, soon returned to base. None of the three 401st Bomb Group spares, piloted by Lieutenant Wells, Lieutenant Myrtetus, and Lieutenant Opie, was needed, and they returned to Deenethorpe. The 351st Bomb Group, now flying alone and trying to catch up with the formation, fared worse. Flying as deputy lead of this Group was 1st Lt. Clyde W. McClelland. His navigator, 1st Lt. John B. Duncan, recalled: "This mission was the thirtieth and last which I would have been required to fly in the European theater of operations. It was the only time during my tour of duty that there was some confusion during the formation of our wing over the assigned assembly point on the east coast of England. The result was that the other two groups had already departed across the North Sea, and our group found itself all alone over the English coast. Our group leader circled the assembly point several times, then headed east in an effort to overtake the other two groups."[2]

Second Lt. Walter F. Creigh, on his fifth mission, and acting as tail gunner/formation observer in *Geraldine*, the wing's lead aircraft, remembers: "We took off at 1030 hours. After assembly and at mid-Channel, the pilot cleared us to charge our weapons and fire a few rounds. I fired a short burst from each gun high over the right wing of the number 4 'slot' plane. As the pilot saw me start to fire, he slid up closer under the tail of our ship to avoid the clips and empty casings that fell away from my guns. Then I got my first call from Major Hozier. He asked the position of the High and low groups. Were they too close or too far back? This seemed to me the only justification for having a pilot in the tail gun position. My answer was that 'I thought they were more than two minutes behind us.' His next question was should we make a dog leg to the left or to the right? To shorten their radius turn I suggested a left dog leg and by now I felt I had earned my keep! The other Groups now caught up and we were on our way across northern Germany."[3]

Over the North Sea, Major Hozier, ordered a double drift to the left in an attempt to allow the 351st Bomb Group to join the formation. Unfortunately, it did not completely catch up and, probably due to increased air-

On his very first operational mission, 2nd Lt. Gerald F. Carter had to ditch *Reds Rogues* in the North Sea. VERA WEPNER

speed and having to climb fully loaded, aircraft in the 351st Bomb Group formation began to malfunction, and some had to abort.

After Lt. Alfred D. Neal returned to Polebrook with a sick bombardier, Lt. Martin Karagiannis followed, with the report that his number two supercharger lost power in climb and that it was impossible to maintain formation. Both Lt. Robert E. Taylor and Lt. Augustus J. Cesarini turned back when the number four engines on their respective B-17s malfunctioned. Both dropped their bomb load in the North Sea. The fifth and last to return to Polebrook was Lt. David M. Heller, the man who had a late take-off, and consequently never managed to find and overtake the Group formation. Both spares, piloted by Lt. William M. Power and Lt. Charles F. Anderson filled in, the first on Cesarini's position, number three in the lead squadron. Anderson decided to occupy the vulnerable number six position in the low squadron, originally intended for Lieutenant Taylor. It was to prove a fateful decision.

Upon reaching the enemy coast, the 351st Bomb Group was still behind, and Hozier had no other option but to make another double drift to the left, this time over Holland. Now, one B-17G in the low group had to abort. Excessive oil spilling from number four engine was pouring on its exhaust and burning. The propeller would not feather, the engine was shut down, and the propeller windmilled until the plane, piloted by Lt. Richard D. McCord, safely reached Deenethorpe.

The airspeed of the 457th and 401st Bomb Groups was reduced, again in order to enable the 351st Bomb Group to catch up. Engineer James E.

Sgt. John L. Wepner, tail gunner of
Reds Rogues.

Wells, in the 401st Bomb Group's formation, remembers the flight to the target area: "When the crew station alert flare was fired from the control tower, we then took our positions in the airplane and went about our duties. We started engines, took up our assigned position in the parade of Flying Fortresses taxiing to the active runway and engine run-up pad. Engine run-up was normal, so when the take off flare was fired, the group began taking off. When our turn came, we took the runway and began our lumbering take-off roll. We became airborne in a normal fashion and began our climb out. At this time we encountered very strong gas fumes throughout the airplane. At the direction of Lieutenant Keith, I made a visual check of the airplane, especially the bomb bay area where all of the fuel transfer lines were located. I found no evidence of fuel leaks, and reported my finding to the crew. We opened windows, and shortly the fumes dissipated, so we pressed on.

"The climbing and joining in formation went along normally, but somewhat raggedly. As we took up our easterly heading and began crossing the English Channel, our airspeed dropped so low on several occasions that Lieutenant Keith was required to extend wing flaps so as to keep the airplane from stalling and to maintain our station in the formation. As we reached our cruising altitude of somewhere around 25,000 feet, and coasted in over Fortress Europe, our formation did not improve appreciably, and I believe that our entire crew had a very bad feeling for this particular endeavor."[4]

Finally, near the Dutch-German border, the 351st Bomb Group caught up and occupied the high group position. However, the 94th Combat Wing had now lost eight minutes of precious time in the meticulously planned operation, and another combat wing, the 13th A heading for Magdeburg, had passed on time and on course. Major Hozier was now forced to take up position behind this wing, squeezing his own wing just in front of the 13th B Combat Wing, which was also heading for Magdeburg. In all, fifty of the intended fifty-four B-17s were left in the 94th Combat Wing—not too bad in view of things to come.

When the wing reached the vicinity of Dümmer Lake, trouble started for B-17G *Reds Rogues* (42-39837) from the 401st Bomb Group, piloted by 2nd Lt. Gerald F. Carter and 1st Lt. Clayton A. Johnston. Flying in the number five position in the lead squadron, Carter's crew was on its very first combat mission. Lieutenant Johnston, however, was an experienced pilot on his twenty-second mission and was breaking in the crew in the habits of operational flying. Johnston had already been involved in a crash-landing at Deenethorpe in early March.

The oil pressure on number one engine fell drastically, so that the propeller began to windmill and would not feather. Carter made an attempt to remain with the formation on the other three engines, but the aircraft began to drop back and it was decided to turn back. At that point, number four engine also went out, and oil began to spurt out from its top.

This propeller could be feathered. The bombs were jettisoned in an open field, and the same route flown going in was used in an attempt to return to England. The aircraft then began steadily to loose altitude, being pulled down by the windmilling propeller, with altitude loss of about 500 feet per minute. Maximum power was applied in an effort to get back on two engines, but the aircraft was indicating an airspeed of only 90 to 100 miles per hour, barely above the stalling point, and was down to 5,000 feet when it left the Dutch coast. Some flak was thrown up from the vicinity of Egmond, but it was very inaccurate. At this time Staff Sgt. John N. Heinlon, the radio operator, sent out coordinates and an SOS, announcing the crew's intention to ditch, and when the aircraft was at 2,000 feet, he clamped the key down.

The rescuers. Most of the twelve-man crew of High Speed Launch 2579, including its captain, Flight Off. J. Martinson, sitting with cap. JIM HAMMOND

Others in the aircraft meanwhile had thrown out all removable equipment, and as the aircraft neared the sea, power was boosted to maximum. For nearly fifteen minutes, the bomber mushed along at about fifteen or twenty feet above the water. Finally, when airspeed showed eighty-five miles per hour and the aircraft neared a stall, engines were cut, and *Reds Rogues* was eased into the sea. The tail hit first, without a violent impact, and finally the nose crashed into the water. The sea was calm at the time of ditching, 1438 hours, and the aircraft landed parallel to a mild swell.

Almost immediately, the ball turret floated to the surface, and the aircraft filled with water and began to sink. Because the radio operator, John Heinlon, was an expert swimmer, he was the first out. Water was already up to his waist before he left the machine. When the last man left the radio room, where the crewmembers were assembled in case of a ditching, water was chest-high. Neither dinghy was automatically released, and Heinlon manually released the left dinghy and was forced to hold the inflation bottle before it would inflate. Lieutenant Johnston left through the co-pilot's window and pulled out the right dinghy, which immediately inflated. Since the aircraft sank in less than forty-five seconds and the tail began to rise, the dinghies were forced backward.

And the rescued. The crew of *Reds Rogues* a few days after ditching in the North Sea. Left to right: John Hafko, waist gunner; 2nd Lt. Willard O. Locklear, bombardier; Sgt. Floyd A. Truax, engineer; 2nd Lt. Lloyd G. Deaton, navigator; 2nd Lt. Louis H. Ludeman, copilot (not on mission); Sgt. John L. Wepner, tail gunner; 2nd Lt. Gerald F. Carter, pilot; and Sgt. Stanford M. Hardister, ball turret gunner. VERA WEPNER

Three men were in each dinghy and two were hanging onto each, but those in the water soon climbed inside without difficulty. In the left dinghy were Lieutenant Carter, Lt. Willard O. Locklear (navigator), Staff Sgt. Heinlon, Sgt. Floyd A. Truax (engineer), and Sgt. John L. Wepner (tail gunner). In the right dinghy were Lieutenant Johnston, Lt. Lloyd G. Deaton (bombardier), Staff Sgt. Carl J. Miller (left waist gunner), Sgt. Stanford M. Hardister (ball turret gunner), and Sgt. John Hafko (right waist gunner). Both dinghies were then tied together. Two parachutes and the dinghy radio, as well as several kits which had been thrown out of the aircraft were picked up, and the dinghy radio with balloon antenna was set up.

Almost immediately, two P-47s arrived, and from that time, for three hours and twenty-five minutes—at which point the crew was rescued—P-47s circled overhead. At the end of that period, while one P-47 pilot was directing an air-sea rescue high-speed launch to the dinghies, another pilot was so enthusiastically buzzing the bomber crew, that he snapped off the balloon antenna with the propeller of his P-47. The crew was picked up by high-speed launch no. 2579 at 1800 hours and was then taken to the air-sea rescue hospital at Great Yarmouth. After a spell in the hospital, the men returned to Deenethorpe the following day.

Two pilots of the 508th Bomb Squadron, Lt. William J. Condon and Lt. Robert W. Condon, portrayed in front of barracks at Polebrook. On 28 May, the latter had to leave the 351st Bomb Group formation, drop his bombs in enemy territory, and fly back to Polebrook alone. The first was shot down by German fighters and killed along with five of his crew. On the left is Robert H. Gunster, co-pilot on Robert Condon's crew. ROBERT W. CONDON

Another B-17 would have to abort from the combat wing, again due to engine trouble. Flying in B-17G 42-38146 of the 351st Bomb Group was the crew of Lt. Robert W. Condon, who recalls: "Our aircraft was slow and we had to use a little more power than usual and both right wing engines were running a little hot. At about 120 miles inland and southeast of Hannover, Germany, at 26,000 feet, we lost the oil pressure on number three engine. As oil was coming over the wing, we feathered the engine and started to fall back. I decided to make a left descending 180-degree turn under control and we lost about 2,000 feet, as we still had our 5,000-pound bomb load. Alone, we were sitting ducks, if there were any German fighters in the area; however, we did not see any and we knew friendly fighters were due to arrive. So, heading west we were looking for a target of opportunity. The navigator, Joe Isoardi, spotted a military barracks area and bombardier Bill Witten took aim and dropped the bombs in trail. Tail gunner Sam Silver said a few of the bombs hit the target. We had lost a lot of altitude now and we were down to 18,000 feet. Now that the bombs were dropped, we lowered the power on the engines which resulted in a low indicated airspeed of 125 miles per hour. It was going to be a long slow trip to England.

"When trying to make it back from Germany alone, the standard operational procedure, was to hit the deck and fly at low-altitude, but with the stress on the remaining engines one of them might go at any minute, I decided to stay as high up as we could and hope the friendly fighters had cleared the corridor to the North Sea. All eyes of the nine-man crew were looking out for fighters. While still in Germany, we spotted one at three o'clock high, with his nose pointed at our aircraft. It looked like an Me 109. Just as he came into range of our guns, he turned and flipped his wings, and we could see it was a P-51 and were much relieved. A little later we saw another aircraft at a distance, which was easy to spot—it was a P-38.

"We were now getting close to the accurate antiaircraft batteries in northern Holland, and with our altitude and airspeed, they would surely have a good shot at us. We had seen them hit aircraft with a single initial shot and a burst of four 88mm shells. We sacrificed time for additional altitude when we reached the Zuider Zee. We then started our climb out of range, making 360-degree turns. Our plan was to make a zigzag dive to the Channel. At about 19,000 feet on a west heading, we made our dash, diving at over 170 indicated airspeed and changing our heading 10 to 15 degrees every twenty seconds. We made it across the Zuider Zee peninsula in a few minutes without incident; they didn't even fire a shot at us. When we reached the North Sea, we saw a P-51, which gave us cover, doing a few barrel rolls for us as we were both on our way to England. The navigator selected the nearest airfield and we landed safe and sound at an RAF base. I checked in at base operations and called Polebrook to report our status."[5]

Lt. Robert W. Condon and his crew safely returned from a mission in the summer of 1944 having just boarded a truck heading for interrogation. The thirteen .50-caliber machine-gun barrels to be cleaned and stored are clearly visible. Left to right: Robert W. Condon, pilot; Joseph Isoardi, navigator; Sergeant Fennell (not on 28 May mission); Sam Silver, gunner; Lawrence W. Jones, gunner; Robert H. Gunster, co-pilot; William Whitten, bombardier; unidentified (not on 28 May mission); and Frank E. Petrucci, engineer. ROBERT W. CONDON

Another B-17 from the high group had to leave the Wing before the target was reached. Only about forty-five minutes before the assigned primary was reached, Lt. Ivy L. Belote in B-17G 42-97318 turned back to England. One engine was feathered and, unlike Condon, he chose for a return on the deck. On the way out he was hit several times by antiaircraft fire but the damaged plane was landed safely at Polebrook.

Here the engineering officer reported on the damage to the aircraft: "Numerous flak holes in underside of right outboard wing panel and wing tip. Flak damage to underside of number one nacelle. Two .30-cal holes in underside of right-hand wing panel near leading edge. Two .30-cal holes in left side of fuselage under bombardier's window. One 20mm hole through rudder. Two flak holes in left side of fuselage. One 20mm hole in top of fuselage, left and rear of top turret. Flak damage to number one engine and number three propeller. One flak hole in top of left wing tip."[6]

Two crewmembers, navigator Lt. James R. Lechner and top turret gunner Sgt. Earl H. Meyers, were wounded and admitted to Polebrook base hospital.

In all, only forty-seven of the scheduled fifty-four B-17s remained in the 94th Combat Wing when the initial point was reached. The main problem that had arisen with the fact that Major Hozier had taken a position behind the 13th A Combat Wing was that this wing and the ones following it were units of the Third Air Division, which was scheduled to attack Magdeburg. Hozier's combat wing had been the last of the units sent out by the First Air Division and detailed to attack Dessau. At Fighter Command headquarters, the available escorting fighter groups had been assigned to the various air divisions. The sudden change of place of the 94th Combat Wing into another division's force did not cause any problems as long as all bombers flew the same route in the main bomber stream. But trouble started when a point north of Brunswick had been passed, and Major Hozier, the 94th Combat Wing's leader, had to turn for Dessau and leave the stream of bombers heading for Magdeburg. This left him temporarily unescorted, since the assigned fighter escort to his own air division flew miles away.

The Germans soon recognized this opportunity on their radar, and at 1401 hours, a radio transmission was intercepted in England. The *Jagdführer*, the German fighter controller, was heard to call his pilots and advise them to attack in the Magdeburg area, preferably against the second wave and not the first. This links with the fierce attacks, both the Magdeburg-bound 13th A Combat Wing and the last Dessau-bound 94th Combat Wing (that of Hozier) were about to endure.

The 56th Fighter Group had executed the "Zemke fan" as briefed, its fighter squadrons fanning out in different directions, well in advance of the bomber formations. However, they did not have any success in locating German fighters in the early stage of their assembling and returned to Halesworth without contact. Now, somewhat later, the assembling German fighters were spotted by the 355th, 352nd, and 363rd Fighter Groups, protecting the force bound for Ruhland and Dessau.

DOGFIGHTS OVER DESSAU

The 355th Fighter Group was led by Capt. Carl C. Colson after Lt. Col. Claiborne H. Kinnard had aborted early in the mission. Its 354th Squadron sighted more than fifty enemy aircraft assembling in the vicinity of Wittenberg and Jüterbog at 20,000 feet, with a top cover of some fifteen aircraft at 32,000 feet, south of the bomber track and making a wide orbit in front of the route. Although every pilot in the group was alert, some *Luftwaffe* pilots managed to elude them and suddenly bounced Blue Flight of the 354th Fighter Squadron.

The German fighters were those of 6./JG 11. One Me 109 was piloted by *Unteroffizier* Rudolf Strosetzki, who recalled: "I flew as number three in the flight of *Fahnenjunker-Feldwebel* Willi Schorr, a very experienced pilot. We flew as *Holzaugenrotte*, the aim of which was to protect the flight leader and his wingman (*Unteroffizier* Fischer) in the opening phase of the attack, when

Unteroffizier Rudolf Strosetzki of 6./JG 11 (center) in a typical *Luftwaffe* pilot outfit. He shot down a P-51 in the Magdeburg area on 28 May.
RUDOLF STROSETZKI

the flight hadn't been dispersed by combat. In other words, the *Holzaugen-rotte* remained at altitude and kept track of the attacking pair of the flight, to warn them in time over the radio of any threat from behind or to protect them by attacking the hostile aircraft. During this mission, we approached the intruding enemy formations.

"Beneath us, a P-51 unit turned, as they apparently had seen our contrails above them. Schorr used our advantage in altitude and attacked the lower flying P-51s, with his wingman, coming out of the sun. I remained at altitude. The P-51 pilots recognized our intentions and went into a defensive circle, in which the one can watch the other's back. The attacker has, when he enters this circle, an enemy aircraft in front of him, but also at the same time, one in his back. This now happened in this encounter. A P-51, known to be able to make steep turns, was trying to maneuver into a firing position.

"I couldn't get a warning over the radio to Schorr or Fischer, as our frequency was heavily used in this phase of the combat. I decided to attack from above on this Mustang, came into firing position and fired short bursts with my MK 108 30mm cannon on the target, which was now flying just in front of me. The hits were visible in the tail, fuselage, and cockpit. Parts of the aircraft started to fall off. The Mustang I had hit, fell away over his right wing and spun down uncontrollable. I couldn't observe it hitting the ground, as I was engaged by other Mustangs immediately thereafter."[7]

His flight leader, Willi Schorr, gave this account of the action: "After I recognized them as enemy aircraft, I bounced the twelve Mustangs, from behind and out of the sun. They were flying at an altitude of 8,500 meters. During the engagement, I ended up behind the last Mustang and fired on it at a distance of 50 to 100 meters, while executing a right-hand turn. I then observed hits on its right stabilizer, cockpit and fuselage. It then trailed thick white smoke and spun down over its right hand side. I last observed it, on fire, at about 6,000 to 7,000 meters. I couldn't see it crash, as I was engaged immediately thereafter."[8]

The day's events were vividly and honestly recorded in the 354th Fighter Squadron's war diary: "Frankly, the lack of experience throughout the group, now consisting of many fresh pilots who yet have to become battle-wise, cost us an opportunity to take some sort of sizeable toll of the enemy formations which were sighted. Lack of combat experience, plus a weakening loss of aircraft through mechanical failure, hurt our chances to a very great extent. There were sixteen early returns in the group due to mechanical difficulties. Wing tanks would not release, or coolant shutter doors stuck, or coolant regulators failed to function properly, or radio failed.

Fahnenjunker Feldwebel Willi Schorr of 6./JG 11, here pictured in the center of this *Staffel* line-up in November 1944, shot down a P-51 in the Magdeburg area on 28 May. RUDOLF STROSETZKI

"Lieutenant Colonel Kinnard [leading the 354th Squadron, but at the same time the group], his face reflecting his disappointment, returned shortly after take off with a faulty ignition. Jim Austin took over command of the 354th Squadron. By the time the squadron had penetrated enemy territory, the abortives had begun to weaken us. We finally ended up with an eight-plane section. We picked up the bombers, all right, and Jim Austin, as directed, took our eight planes over to the right side of the formation. The group somehow became spread out: the very point which Lieutenant Colonel Kinnard had warned against. So when three gaggles of enemy fighters were observed in the Wittenberg-Juterbog area, there wasn't a helluva lot anyone could do about knocking them down. We chased them away, which protected the bombers, but the Jerries made us look rather silly. Jim Austin spotted some fifty enemy aircraft to the right of the bombers, making a wide port orbit across the bomber track, in front of them. He reported them to Captain Colson [the new group leader], and then took up the chase. Meanwhile, Jimmy could see that the fifty Jerries had a top cover of about fifteen or more 109's, circling up at 32,000 feet. We were at about 26,000 feet, and the fifty Jerries, Jim's section was chasing were at about the same level.

"Trying to keep an eye on the top cover, trying to catch the fifty, and trying to watch in other directions, all with the knowledge that he was

First Lt. Clarence R. Barger had a close call before. A bullet entered his canopy and exploded. The armor plating behind his head saved his life that day. On 28 May, he was shot down by a German fighter near Magdeburg. His remains were never recovered or positively identified, and his name is recorded on the walls of the missing on the Henri-Chapelle American Cemetery and Memorial in Belgium. JULIUS J. MOSELEY

unsupported, proved to be a trying experience for each pilot in that section. The top cover Germans were cagy, this time. They were smart. They sent a flight of eight down toward us, but broke into two units of four each. One squad would bounce us, and then the other, and with their advantage of altitude they were faster than we were. The first time the Jerries bounced us, everybody was warned. 'Fid' Barger acknowledged that he had heard the warning by saying, 'Okay, watch 'em.' A moment later the section had broken to right and left in order to meet the Germans' attack, and from that time on, no one saw 'Fid' or Walt Christensen, who had been flying his wing."[9]

Leading Blue Flight of the 354th Fighter Squadron was 1st Lt. Clarence R. Barger. He was already credited with six ground and a one-third air victory. He was flying in P-51B 43-6631, and his wingman was 2nd Lt. Walter M. Christensen. Blue Three and Four were Lt. Robert L. Harness and Lt. Gilbert S. Wright respectively. Both Harness and Wright managed to break away in time from the incoming *Luftwaffe* fighters, calling over the radio to Barger and Christensen to do the same. Although Barger apparently acknowledged the warning, both he and Christensen were shot down in the bounce. Christensen crashed to his death in his P-51B 43-6983 at 1415 hours at Buhlendorf, one kilometer north of Zerbst. Christensen was buried on 29 May in the Moritz cemetery.

According to German reports, another Mustang crashed "500 meters north of the shooting range of the airfield Zerbst." Some mortal remains of its pilot were found and buried in the Russian cemetery in Zerbst. There is a strong possibility that these were the remains of Clarence Barger. How-

With proud pilot Lt. Clarence Barger looking on, ground crew member Webster McMurray paints the sixth swastika on Barger's P-51. All six were ground victories, obtained while strafing enemy airfields.
JULIUS J. MOSELEY

ever, after the war, Clarence Barger's remains were never recovered or positively identified, and his name is recorded on the Wall of Missing at the Henri-Chapelle American Cemetery and Memorial in Belgium.* The other pilots of the 355th Fighter Group were unable to intercept any German fighters in this encounter, so they returned to Steeple Morden, with no claims to their credit. On its way back home, however, a flight of the group's 357th Fighter Squadron escorted a straggling B-17G of the 381st Bomb Group and managed to shoot down two Bf 109s, as related in the previous chapter.

The 352nd Fighter Group, led by its operations officer, Maj. Stephen W. Andrew, was more successful. After taking off at 1200 hours from Bodney, escort was started north of Dümmer Lake at 1319 hours at 25,000 feet. Andrew reported: "The bombers had a good formation within the wings, but the five wings of the task force were strung out beyond the limit of visibility, so that only three of the five wings were visible at one time. The other two squadrons of our group became engaged at around 1400 hours. At about 1410, I took my squadron [the 486th] up to 30,000 feet to investigate some thirty or forty contrails. My Red Leader turned off to port and found some Me 109s among the contrails, but my contrails turned out to be P-47s, so I went down a bit and resumed close escort on the bombers, during the time they were in the target area.

---

* After extensive research, it is the author's firm believe that Barger was the pilot who crashed near Zerbst, close to his wingman, Walter Christensen.

Second Lt. Walter M. Christensen served with the 355th Fighter Group for less than a month. On his eleventh combat mission, he was shot down and killed in action near Zerbst. RAY SHEWFELT, 355TH FIGHTER GROUP ASSOCIATION

"Soon after the bombing, my number three, Lieutenant Colby, sighted Me 109s attacking a box near us. There were about seven or eight Me 109s in front of this box and above. I chose them for attack. They approached us head-on and from about 200 feet above. I was careful to avoid a head-on pass, but one of them did fire head-on at Lieutenant Colby, who said that the Me 109 had three chevrons and he thinks it is the one I shot down a few seconds later. I made a sharp 180-degree turn to starboard and fell into a curve of pursuit on a 109 that was crossing my path at 90 degrees, and which was somewhat above me. I opened fire at about 300 yards after having fallen almost directly astern. My first burst went wild as I over-deflected. I ceased fire and started over again, this time obtaining better results. There were many strikes on the port wing, tail and fuselage and pieces flew off. I broke off when the 109 fell into a violent right-hand spin. My number two, Lieutenant Karl, said he saw the pilot bail out, but he did not open his parachute. The 109 trailed a lot of smoke when it fell. The above combat began at about 28,000 feet and terminated at 21,000 feet. We climbed back up to rejoin a box of bombers, but we set course for home shortly thereafter, when my number two reported engine trouble. The entire group had to withdraw at about this time, as we were forced to drop tanks early."[10]

Maj. Stephen W. Andrew relives his latest combat with 1st Lt. Henry W. White. Both scored a victory on 28 May. Lt. Garland Rayborn is looking on. Andrew went down on 2 July, Royborn on 11 September, and both were captured. MARC HAMEL / SAM SOX, 352ND FIGHTER GROUP ASSOCIATION

The Bf 109 was Andrew's eighth, and penultimate, air victory. The chevrons he is referring to in his report may identify a *Gruppenkommandeur*. As we will later see, the German units involved in this dogfight did indeed loose some experienced veterans in the fight.

The Blue Flight of the 486th Fighter Squadron consisted of only three Mustangs, since one had aborted earlier. Leading the flight was Capt. Woodrow W. Anderson, an experienced pilot with 3.5 air and 9 ground victories to his credit. He was flying in his regular P-51B, *Texas Bluebonnet* (42-106635). Blue Two was Lt. Lester L. Howell in *Hot Stuff*, and Blue Three was Lt. Edwin L. Heller in *Hell-er-bust*. Heller reported: "Captain Anderson was leading our flight and we saw many contrails above the bombers. We climbed to meet them. At 30,000 feet, they came down at us from nine o'clock. There were three of us and about twenty-five of them. It was impossible to stay together and Captain Anderson tagged on to one and headed down on his tail while I took another one on. By that time we were both in a fight and on our own. Lieutenant Howell saw Captain Anderson get many good hits on his ship, before his attention was taken away by his own fight. I got on the tail of an Me 109 and we split-S'd toward the deck. I finally got him right over Dessau at 20,000 feet, where he bailed out. I never saw him

P-51B *Texas Bluebonnet* (42-106635). The picture shows the distinctive blue nose that identified the Mustangs of the 352nd Fighter Group and also the map of Texas on the left side of the nose. MARC HAMEL / SAM SOX, 352ND FIGHTER GROUP ASSOCIATION

open his chute. I was by myself and finally joined up with three red-nosed P-51s with QP-markings. One of these and myself saw another Me 109 at the same time, but he got there first, so I stayed back to cover him. He got a few hits and overshot, so I came up and finished him off. I had to break away to avoid a collision with the P-51, but I saw the 109 going down smoking at 3,000 feet. From his actions I know he could not pull out in time."[11]

The red-nosed P-51 was piloted by 1st Lt. Joseph L. Lang of the 4th Fighter Group, who had provided support to the beleaguered first Fortress formation heading for Magdeburg, and who had lost his own wingman during the engagements, as will be described in the Magdeburg chapter.

Blue Two, Lester Howell, now on his own in his *Hot Stuff,* managed to shoot down an Me 109. Its pilot bailed out and was seen to open his parachute. Howell also joined some 4th Fighter Group aircraft and eventually returned to Bodney with the 328th Fighter Squadron of the 352nd Fighter Group.

First Lt. John F. Thornell was leading this 328th Fighter Squadron in *Patty Ann II* and reported: "At approximately 1400 hours, about fifty-plus Me 109s came at us head-on, intent on attacking the bombers at 25,000 feet. I called the squadron to drop their tanks and proceed to attack the enemy aircraft. Our squadron, with the help of a few friendly fighters dispersed the enemy. I picked out one that was turning to get behind us. I followed him to 5,000 feet and closed to 75 yards range before I opened fire. He burst into flames and the pilot bailed out. My flight was with me all during this air battle. We went back to 23,000 feet and resumed escort for a few minutes and then attacked two more Me 109s, which broke for the deck. I followed to 15,000 feet and then came home with my flight."[12]

The fighter pilot combat reports clearly indicate the size of the enemy fighter formation and the confusion of the dogfight that ensued. It is small wonder that, when these dogfights took place, other German fighters were given an unobstructed approach to the bombers, as will be recounted later.

Leading Yellow Flight of the 328th Fighter Squadron was 1st Lt. Henry W. White in *Dallas Darling.* He reported: "I was leading Yellow Flight when we saw fifty-plus bandits coming up the bomber track, in the area of Magdeburg. A few would peel off and hit each box of bombers. They were on the far side and above the bombers at about 30,000 feet and we couldn't get to them, so we made a 180-degree climbing turn to catch them. They outdistanced us, so I went back up the bomber track. In the vicinity of Magdeburg I saw many contrails high-crossing the track of the bombers going west. I climbed up to their level chasing them and identified them as Me 109s. When they saw us, some broke for the deck and about half of them went into Lufberrys at different altitudes. I attacked tailend charlie of the top Lufberry. He was turning to the left until I bounced him. Then he turned right, letting me get right up his tail. I pulled the trigger. Just as I did, a P-51 came up between me and the Me 109, so

Woodrow Anderson, Thomas W. Colby, and Stephen W. Andrew, pictured next to the 486th Fighter Squadron operations building at Bodney. All three would fly the mission of 28 May, which was to be Anderson's final flight. MARC HAMEL / SAM SOX, 352ND FIGHTER GROUP ASSOCIATION

I broke off left to miss him. I ended up on the tail of an Fw 190. I gave him a deflection burst from about 200 to 300 yards, then closed to about 100 yards in trail. I gave him another burst, then broke to avoid an attack from an Me 109. I evaded the Me 109 and tried to get on the tail of the Fw 190 again. I closed on him from about 90 degrees in a left turn. His prop was windmilling an he was practically standing still. I was going so fast that I couldn't reef it hard enough to keep from over-shooting him. I chopped everything, pulled it in and up to slow down, so I could go back to work on him. I saw him slowly spiraling down as I pulled up. I also saw an Me 109 on the tail of a P-51, so I made a pass from about 90 degrees at the Me 109. He broke off his attack on the P-51. I looked for the Fw 190, but didn't see any enemy aircraft any more; however I did see a chute drifting 10,000 feet below me. All this time there were so many enemy planes about and events were happening so fast I'm not sure this sequence of events is in order. It was about a fifteen-minute real old dog fight. After it was over, I circled the area to get my flight together. My number three and four men were with me, number two being lost from the flight. I had used so much gas that I had to start home. On the way out, flak at Munster dispersed the flight. I came home alone, not being able to find and reform the flight."[13]

Lt. Edwin L. Heller was flying
P-51B *Hell-er-Bust* (43-6704) in
Anderson's Blue flight. He
managed to shoot down one
Bf 109 during the dogfights
on 28 May and shared the
destruction of another with 1st
Lt. Joseph L. Lang of the 4th
Fighter Group. EDWIN L. HELLER

The Fw 190 was credited as destroyed, for White's first air victory.

The last pilot of the 352nd Fighter Group to get a confirmed kill was 1st Lt. Harry H. Barnes, who reported: "I was flying White 2, and as the 487th Squadron leader and I pulled up from a bounce, we saw three enemy aircraft attack and destroy a P-51 from dead astern. We followed these three down in a long dive from 25,000 feet and I closed on the enemy aircraft on the left. Observing no hits while firing at 600 yards, I fired again at 300 yards, observing strikes on the wing and canopy. The aircraft started smoking and broke slightly to the right and I closed up to 150 yards and fired a burst causing the fuselage and tail to explode and the ship to fall apart. This was at 15,000 feet. I then followed the other two Me 109s down to the deck into a smoke screen west of Leipzig and fired at one from 300 yards, 30-degree deflection, getting hits on the wing root and observing smoke coming out of the left wing radiator. I broke off and lost sight of him, as his wingman started to break into me and I turned into him. I was alone at this time, so after turning into this enemy aircraft, I headed out and rejoined White Leader above the smoke."[14]

Elated, the group's pilots landed at around 16.50 hours, claiming to have shot down seven-and-a-half German fighters in air combat. But, when most of the aircraft had returned, both Howell and Heller became concerned about their flight leader, Woodrow W. Anderson, whom they had last seen in combat over Dessau. Harry Barnes, after claiming his Me 109 destroyed, then also reported about a P-51 he had seen shot down by the Bf

First Lt. John F. Thornell of the 328th Fighter Squadron had a successful week. After shooting down two German fighters on 27 May, he shot down one on 28 May and another two on 29 May. Thornell ended the war as one of the Eighth Air Force's top-scoring aces. MARC HAMEL / SAM SOX, 352ND FIGHTER GROUP ASSOCIATION

109s: "We saw a P-51 flying straight and level at 20,000 feet. This was just west of Leipzig at approximately 1410 hours. Suddenly three Me 109s pulled up behind the P-51 in a line astern. The leader of this formation fired a short burst at the P-51 and hit him on the fuselage and canopy. The Mustang started to smoke and fell into a steep dive to the right. Pieces were flying from the plane and we feel sure that we saw the pilot in a free fall. We are also quite certain that this P-51 was from the 352nd Fighter Group, because it appeared to have a blue nose similar to the design used on the ships of this group."[15]

The only pilot of the 352nd Fighter Group who did not return to Bodney was Woodrow Anderson, and it was feared Barnes had witnessed his being shot down. When dusk fell, Anderson was officially reported missing in action. Edwin Heller and Lester Howell, the two other pilots in his flight, submitted a claim for a German fighter destroyed for him, which was eventually awarded by the victory credit board. This brought Anderson's total of air victories at the time of his death to four and a half, in addition to nine ground victories.

Second Lt. Lester L. Howell flew as wingman to Capt. Woodrow Anderson. He shot down a Bf 109 during the engagements for his first air victory. Howell was shot down and killed on 2 July. MARC HAMEL / SAM SOX, 352ND FIGHTER GROUP ASSOCIATION

It is highly probable that Anderson was shot down by *Leutnant* Hans Fritz, piloting a Bf 109G of 3./JG 3. Fritz reported: "I took off at 1315 hours from the airfield Burg near Magdeburg. At 1400 hours and flying at about 28,000 feet, we saw the enemy with about 300 Fortresses and Mustang and Lightning fighter cover. We immediately started a dog fight with the Mustangs, above the Fortresses. To the right of our unit, which became split up in individual combats, flew six Mustangs. Another eight Mustangs attacked us from behind and above. I then fired from about 100 yards at a Mustang which crossed in front of me at a 90-degree angle. Immediately, parts of the right wing flew off and the canopy was jettisoned. The Mustang flew faltering on and a short time later the pilot jumped out of it, using his parachute. This happened at 1417 hours southeast of Aschersleben. I had another fight, with Lightnings this time, however couldn't score and had to land at 1455 hours due to lack of fuel at the airfield in Halle. To shoot down the Mustang, I used twenty 20mm cannon shells and sixty 13mm rounds."[16]

German records show that the wreck of a Mustang was found near Aschersleben, seventeen kilometers east of Quedlinburg. However, despite the statements by Barnes, who saw the pilot in a free fall, and Fritz, who saw him jump out using his parachute, some mortal remains of the pilot were recovered from this burned out wreckage. These could not be identified and were interred as "unknown." The name of Woodrow Anderson is recorded on the Wall of Missing at the Henri-Chapelle American Cemetery and Memorial.*

First Lt. Henry W. White shot down his first enemy aircraft on 28 May, while leading Yellow Flight of the 328th Fighter Squadron. MARC HAMEL / SAM SOX, 352ND FIGHTER GROUP ASSOCIATION

The other fighter group scheduled for target escort was the 363rd Fighter Group, a Ninth Air Force Mustang-equipped unit. It departed Staplehurst at 1149 hours, led by 382nd Fighter Squadron commanding officer, Maj. Robert C. McWherter. They made rendezvous near Celle at 1336 hours. Three of its fifty Mustangs had aborted, and the group had already lost Anthony E. Ladas in the collision with the Thunderbolt of Capt. Alwin M. Juchheim of the 78th Fighter Group, as covered in the Ruhland chapter.

The 363rd Fighter Group was to have its biggest single-day score during its entire war service. Leading White Flight in the 380th Fighter Squadron was 1st Lt. Morton A. Kammerlohr, who reported: "Just after rendezvous with Forts, I saw a gaggle of hundred-plus Me 109s, Fw 190s, and Me 410s in a tight box formation, firing from six o'clock and at our level of 26,000 feet, approximately 350 yards away. I called for Hassock White Flight to break left

---

* It is the author's firm belief that Anderson was the pilot who crashed near Aschersleben.

and down; at this time, I heard Lieutenant Clemovitz say, 'Kammy, I'm hit, I'm going to bail out.' I saw Lieutenant Clemovitz at 24,000 feet going down, trailing white smoke in a 45-degree dive at five o'clock to a gaggle of enemy aircraft. This occurred at approximately 1415 hours."[17]

Second Lt. Feodor Clemovitz, flying in his P-51C *Little Joe* (42-103004), recalled events: "Almost immediately, we encountered a box formation of German aircraft flying 180 degrees to our flight path in what you might call a parade formation, slightly above and to the left of our flight path. We immediately dropped our wing tanks, broke left and gave chase. After we levelled off on our chase run, we could see another box formation approaching us at a lower altitude. This formation, as was the previous one, was made up of Me 109s, Fw 190s, and Me 410s, about a hundred in all. As we approached, I made ready to start firing. Suddenly, my aircraft was hit in front, apparently by an exploding 20mm shell in the coolant tank. The coolant enveloped the plane in a white cloud. As I could not bail out until I cleared the enemy formation, I commenced firing until I was past the formation. I could not see if I hit any of the enemy aircraft because of the spraying coolant. I called Lieutenant Kammerlohr, told him my plane was hit and that I was bailing out. I jettisoned my canopy and attempted to roll over and push out of the cockpit. I was unsuccessful and on my third attempt I finally got out. I made a delayed fall until I saw the horizon going above me, then pulled the rip cord, since I was falling through a major dog fight. I landed in a cleared field with no chance to get to any cover. Before I was captured, I saw an Me 109 crash and another one go overhead, badly smoking. I was escorted by two Home Guardsmen, taken behind a wall in a small town, and searched."[18]

First Lt. Harry H. Barnes posing with P-51D *Williams-Villian* (44-13619). Barnes was shot down on 13 August, but escaped to friendly territory. The aircraft seen here was lost a day earlier. MARC HAMEL / SAM SOX, 352ND FIGHTER GROUP ASSOCIATION

Capt. Woodrow W. Anderson was leading Blue Flight of the 486th Fighter Squadron in *Texas Bluebonnet.* He obtained his final air victory, bringing his total to four and a half air and nine ground victories before he was shot down. He is still listed as missing in action, and his name is recorded on the walls of the missing at the Henri-Chapelle American Cemetery and Memorial in Belgium.

THOMAS W. COLBY

Clemovitz had landed in Eichenbarleben, about twelve kilometers west of Magdeburg, and *Little Joe* came down in Schackensleben, three kilometers farther to the north. He was shot down by *Feldwebel* Horst Petzschler of 4./JG 3, who recalls: "I came from Russia, with 126 fighter bomber missions flown on Fw 190s—so some experience was there when building up new *Staffeln* for the defense of the Reich. We were the *4. Staffel; Oberleutnant* Bohatsch was our *Staffelkapitän.* Our *Staffel* with the Me 109s was the high-altitude protection (*Hohenschütz*) for the *Gruppe.* They attacked the bomber boxes first, and we were supposed to go in after them, but got mostly engaged before that.

"Higher-flying P-51s did get on our tails; they flew 150-octane and reached about 32,000 feet, while our engines were finished in 30,000 feet, no more power. When my wingman, *Unteroffizier* Hans Herdy, twenty years old and just out of flying school, screamed, 'Mustangs from above and behind,' we were attacked. I did not attack anybody, and Herdy went straight down. A blue-nosed P-51* apparently overshot me at high speed, and I gave him a good burst of 30mm MK 108, plus everything from my two 13mm machine guns. He showed a glycol streak, very heavy, and went down. I could only report a 'probable,' northwest of Magdeburg. At the same time, another P-51 gave me a good hit in my left wing. I lost one third of it and did go into a flat spin, soon recovered, but spun the other way. Recovering several thousand feet lower, I realized that my Me 109 was no longer controllable.

---

* Clemovitz's unit, the 380th Fighter Squadron of the 363rd Fighter Group, carried a blue propeller spinner and a blue band around the nose of its P-51s.

Prepared to bail out; I did so when reaching the height of our balloon barrages over the Elbe ship locks near Rothensee-Magdeburg at 1,600 meters. I got out of my crippled *Schwarze 14* and hit the silk! Shortly later, I landed safe and unhurt near the wreckage of a downed B-17. Met some of the crew of the shattered plane, who came later with me to our base at Burg. They were treated well in our mess hall and, next day, went to Frankfurt for interrogation. I got a new *Schwarze 14* the same night, to be ready for the next day. Lucky enough, after fourteen action-packed missions over Germany, my unit in the East requested me back because of the heavy losses they had in JG 51."[19]

Another Mustang of the 363rd Fighter Group was shot down by enemy fighters. This was P-51B 42-106481, piloted by 2nd Lt. Curry P. Wilson. Upon his return to Staplehurst, 2nd Lt. Jack A. Warner reported: "I was number three man of White Flight in Sunshade squadron [382nd Fighter Squadron]. Lieutenant Wilson was White number four, flying my wing. At about 1410 hours, I looked around and saw an Me 109 on Lieutenant Wilson's tail. I called him on the r/t to break, and at the same time, I broke into the Me 109 and chased him off Lieutenant Wilson's tail. He never broke but went into a slight dive, and the last I saw of him, at 1415 hours south of Magdeburg, he was still in the dive with what appeared to be coolant coming out of his air scoop. I dove down from 26,000 to 15,000 feet to try and pick up Lieutenant Wilson, but was unable to find him."[20]

Maj. Robert C. McWherter led the 363rd Fighter Group in action and shot down a Bf 109. He is posing with his P-51D *Hoo Flung Dung* (44-13380). STEVE BLAKE / EDWARD T. PAWLAK

Four pilots of the 363rd Fighter Group during training in the United States. Left to right: Charles R. Reddig, Feodor Clemovitz, Morton A. Kammerlohr, and James E. Hill. On 28 May, both Hill and Kammerlohr scored a victory, while Clemovitz was shot down and made prisoner of war. JAMES E. HILL

Curry Wilson's Mustang crashed around 1430 hours on the eastern side of Bennstedt, a village eight kilometers west of Halle, and Wilson himself was captured, slightly wounded, around the same time. But for the loss of Clemovitz and Wilson, the 363rd Fighter Group claimed no fewer than sixteen enemy aircraft destroyed, one probably destroyed, and five damaged.

It is quite unfortunate that most pilot encounter reports for the 363rd Fighter Group have not survived in an archive or private collection. Only a few accounts of their engagements have survived. Lt. Gordon McEachron of the 380th Fighter Squadron was awarded a Distinguished Flying Cross for this day's actions. His citation reads in part: "Lieutenant McEachron was leading a flight on a bomber escort mission when he spotted a large number of enemy aircraft overhead. He immediately ordered the flight to drop their wing tanks and made a sharp turn to the left. By the time the flight had completed the turn, the enemy aircraft could no longer be seen. Suddenly a break was called, and as Lieutenant McEachron turned, he saw more than 100 enemy planes approaching from the rear. Intercepting a group of Me 109s just as they were pressing their attack on the bombers, Lieutenant McEachron picked a target, closed to about 300 yards, and fired a long burst. Strikes were noted along the fuselage and wing, and the enemy aircraft rolled over and split-S'd with dense black smoke pouring from the engine. Suddenly an Me 410 appeared just in front of him. As the enemy turned, Lieutenant McEachron turned with him and fired a long burst. Strikes were observed along the fuselage of the enemy plane.

"Together with his wingman, Lieutenant McEachron went after the main group of enemy aircraft which were ahead. Another target, an Me 109, came into view. Lieutenant McEachron chased in on the enemy fighter and began firing from 500 yards. Pieces of the plane began to fly off as round after round went home. Suddenly, black smoke began pouring from the plane and it caught on fire. The enemy pilot bailed out."[21]

It is possible that the Me 410 that McEachron hit belonged to *4. Staffel* of *Zerstörergeschwader 26*. This unit had taken off from Königsberg, and when it returned there after the battle, two of its aircraft had to belly-land due to battle damage. The radio operator on one of these aircraft, *Unteroffizier* Johann Kubetzki, was found to be dead upon return at Königsberg.

Lieutenant Schmidt was flying as wingman for Maj. Robert McWherter, and he remembers witnessing McWherter's first kill in the European theater: "McWherter spotted an Me 109 slightly below us and in we went. I was sticking to his wing like glue as he manoeuvred for position. Closing rapidly and now dead astern of the Me 109, Mac let him have it. The plane began coming apart and as we flew through the pieces, the Jerry bailed out and I believe he was hit by Mac's prop."[22]

After return to England and careful study of the available gun-camera film, the pilots of the 363rd Fighter Group were awarded twelve enemy fighters destroyed in air combat. In addition to that, the flight led by 1st Lt. John

Feodor Clemovitz of the 363rd Fighter Group, 380th Fighter Squadron, posing in front of P-51 *Little Joe* (42-103004), in which he was shot down on 28 May. FEODOR CLEMOVITZ

Feldwebel Horst Petzschler of 4./JG 3 flew top cover for his *Gruppe*. During combat in the Dessau area, he shot down Feodor Clemovitz of the 363rd Fighter Group.

R. Brown had strafed a German airfield near Frankfurt on its way back to England. This flight had lost Anthony Ladas in a collision early in the mission. The three remaining pilots—Brown, Lt. James H. Clark, and Lt. Robert E. Proctor—gave the airfield a good beat-up. Brown destroyed an He 111 and damaged a Ju 52 and two unidentified twin-engined aircraft, Clark destroyed an He 111 and three Ju 88s and damaged another He 111. Proctor damaged an Fw 190 and a training aircraft.

The German units involved in the air action were probably JG 3, JG 5, and JG 27. *Jagdgeschwader 27* was hit especially hard, with no fewer than six pilots killed in action. Most painful for the *Luftwaffe* was the loss of its experienced unit leaders. JG 27 lost two *Staffelkapitäne* on 28 May. *Oberleutnant* Josef Jansen, commanding 1./JG 27, was badly wounded in action and succumbed to his wounds on the thirty-first. *Oberleutnant* Eberhard Bock, *Staffelkapitän* of 5./JG 27, was killed when his Bf 109 crashed after a dogfight near Helmstedt. Losing experienced pilots like these quickly eroded the combat effectiveness of the *Luftwaffe*.

FROM THE INITIAL POINT TO THE TARGET

It was not enough. Despite the efforts of the available fighter escort, it did not prevent large groups of German fighters of all types from reaching the bomber formation, and especially the exposed 94th Combat Wing. Because of the fierceness of the battle and the mass of the attacks, it is simply impossible to establish an exact sequence of events. Too much was happening at once in limited air space. Based on extensive research, this author has made the best possible reconstruction.

Second Lt. Walter F. Creigh, at the tail guns of *Geraldine*, the wing's lead aircraft, recalls: "As our formation approached its initial point near Magdeburg, the intercom came alive with 'Bandits . . . bandits.' We were being attacked by large formations of German single- and twin-engine fighters. They hit us in three waves. The intercom was filled with frantic and excited chatter. Each crew station calling out directions of incoming fighters and about hits on ships in our own group; also desperate calls to those in ships going down to bail out. Of course they could not hear!"[23]

One of the first hit in the 351st Bomb Group formation was the number five aircraft in its low squadron. B-17G 42-31757 was piloted by 2nd Lt. William J. Condon and 2nd Lt. Joseph P. Kolceski. Radio operator William H. Morris recalls events: "After flying several missions, we became aware that it was pretty rough staying alive, as the air war was at its peak at this time. On 28 May, we took off with our group to bomb the Junkers plant in Dessau, Germany. We flew with several other groups for a while and then separated

Another German pilot also took part in the action of 28 May: Oscar Boesch, seen here with his Fw 190, *Schwarze 14*, in August 1944. Horst Petzcheler kept Boesch's tail clear as he attacked the bombers. HORST PETZSCHLER

from them, for their mission was to bomb Berlin [Magdeburg]. As we approached the initial point, we encountered severe flak, and then the fighter planes came at us in their usual attack position, head-on from the south. On the first pass they shot out our number four engine. We lost power and had to fall out of formation, unable to keep up with the rest of the Wing. In order to lighten the load, we had to drop our bombs. Flying on our own, they singled us out and fired on us from every position. We were all busy firing back from every position when I was hit in the right forearm by a machine gun slug from an enemy fighter, and it shattered both bones in my arm."[24]

Wounded around the same time was the waist gunner, Sgt. Harry M. Norris, who received head wounds. Norris, on his very first combat mission, became frantic. He took off his own oxygen mask and ran toward the radio room, possibly for the purpose of just letting somebody check his wounds. Unfortunately, the crew flew with only one waist gunner, so Norris did not have anyone near him to help him. Now he stumbled toward the nearest crewmember, William Morris in the radio room. However, the lack of oxygen—and possibly the head wound—caused Norris to fall into the electrically operated gear train of the ball turret, which was in full operation at this time. He subsequently was caught in the rotating gear and died instantly.

Second Lt. Curry P. Wilson of the 363rd Fighter Group, 382nd Fighter Squadron.
EDWARD T. PAWLAK

Still in his radio room, Morris looked for help and opened the doors to the bomb bay: "I looked to the front of the aircraft and saw the wind-shield was shattered and that both pilots and the engineer, Staff Sgt. Junny O. Jackson, were dead. I assisted the ball turret gunner, Sgt. Charles G. Jenkins, out of the ball turret and snapped his parachute on him. He seemed as though in a daze and sat on the radio table, possibly from lack of oxygen. The tail gunner, Sgt. John J. Jackson, and I jettisoned the waist escape door. That's all I remember since I passed out from lack of oxygen. When I regained consciousness, I was very confused and in shock, but very relieved to find my parachute had opened by itself. The rip cord had been shot away while it was lying on the floor prior to snapping it on, and the parachute itself had eight holes in it. There were fighter planes all around me, dogfighting. I saw one P-51 fighter strafe a flak position in a straight, vertical dive from which he never pulled out. I saw his crash and flames shoot all around the area. I think the town I landed in was Bernburg."

Morris indeed came down in Bernburg, close to Dessau, where he was captured and admitted to a hospital for treatment of his wounded arm. It was here that he saw the crews' bombardier, Lt. Edward S. Onken, bleeding badly. Since Morris believed Onken was bleeding to death, he offered a blood transfusion, which was declined by the German medics, saying they didn't care whether American pigs and Chicago gangsters died or not. After his wounds were dressed, Morris followed the normal procedure of

First Lt. Gordon T. McEachron and his P-51 *Beachcomber II*. He flew this aircraft on 28 May when he shot down a Bf 109 and earned a Distinguished Flying Cross for his actions that day. He later transferred to the 354th Fighter Group and was shot down and made prisoner of war on 1 December. GORDON T. MCEACHRON

being sent to Dulag Luft and then to Stalag Luft IV at Kiefheide near the Baltic Sea.

He continues his story: "I found out sometime in October 1944 that Sgt. John J. Jackson was in the same camp as I. I did not know the fate of the rest of the crew until I was liberated and was at Camp Lucky Strike in France. It was here that I found our bombardier again. He told me that the navigator, Lt. Laddie J. Zindar, had taken a direct hit from a 20mm cannon shell and was blocking Lieutenant Onken's escape route. He said all he could do was sit and pray to God for help. Suddenly, an Fw 190 fighter plane fired at the nose of the plane and shattered the plexiglas nose to bits, and the air stream sucked him out. He was tangled in his chute strings and came down head first, landing in a flak gun position. The German soldiers took him to a hospital, where he was found to have sixty-eight shrapnel and bullet wounds in his body. That was the place where I saw him and believed he was bleeding to death. Needless to say, I was thrilled to see that he did survive."

But only three of the nine crewmembers survived. All but one of the six others killed were on their fourth operational bombing mission; Norris was only on his first. Their bomber crashed at 1419 hours at Waldau on the outskirts of Bernburg.

Flying on the left wing of Lieutenant Condon's crew, in the number six position of the low squadron, was the crew of Lt. Charles F. Anderson. They had taken off as a spare but had taken over the position of Lieutenant Taylor when his B-17 malfunctioned. The crew belonged to the 510th Bomb Squadron; their mount for the mission, B-17G 42-97472, was from the 511th

McEachron receives the Distinguished Flying Cross.
GORDON T. MCEACHRON

Bomb Squadron's stable of aircraft. The radio operator on this crew was Sicilian-born Staff Sgt. Casper Vecchione, who recalled: "Fighters were attacking, and occasionally, we were hit by the explosive 20mm shells the fighters were firing at us, because when one hit or hit close by, I remember little holes suddenly appearing in the walls of the plane. Just before the pilot said something about three engines out (numbers two, three, and four, leaving number one on the extreme left the only one running), a shell hit the plane, and a fragment of this shell hit the waist gunner in the chest (we were flying with a nine men crew, I had taken place on the other waist gun), knocked him down, stunned him, but it did not penetrate his flak suit (his is the only face I remember—I can picture this in my mind as if yesterday).

"We helped each other with our parachutes and, at the pilot's order, bailed out. I had always been, and still am, terrified of great heights, and when I looked down, there was such a bluish haze that I really didn't have a sense of height, as when ground objects are easily discernible. And fearing the feeling of falling and with the absolutely crazy thought that if the chute didn't open I might reach up and grab the plane again, I jumped out and immediately pulled the ripcord. It took a long, long time to hit the ground. On the way down I felt a very sharp pain in my right ear and when I hit the ground the wind had me swinging forwards and backwards, and I landed going backwards on a high mounded row of dirt. I felt a sharp pain in my back and I remember I had dry heaves—that is like vomitting, but with nothing coming out. I was quite groggy, so after kicking me, spitting on me, and yelling at me, the Germans who had been waiting for me pulled me up to my feet and one of the three soldiers reached behind him, pulled what looked like a small handgun, pressed it to my forehead and yelled at me at the top of his voice. I noticed about 100 feet from me there was a cabin with a flat roof, on this roof there was a big tripod with a huge pair of field glasses about twenty-four inches long."[25]

Vecchione had landed in the immediate vicinity of a German flak unit, the 1st Battery of *Flak Abteilung 567* near Jütrichau. Just like Vecchione, the rest of the crew was captured sooner or later and spent the rest of war in prison camps. Their bomber came down near Westdorf, three kilometers south of Aschersleben. It is possible that they were attacked by *Unteroffizier* Fritz Rudert in a Bf 109G-6 of 1./JG 27, who reported: "After take-off at 1255 hours, I was flying number two to *Feldwebel* Rohr. During the engagement with a Fortress II formation near Magdeburg, I attacked a Boeing from behind. It flew to the left of the formation, and I shot both his right engines on fire. Then the enemy aircraft dove away to the left, from the formation. I could not watch any further, because I pulled up for another attack. From my new position, I couldn't see the Boeing any more and attacked another."[26]

First Lt. John Robertson of the 363rd Fighter Group shot down a Bf 109. EDWARD T. PAWLAK

Another pilot in the German formation backed up the claim from Rudert. This was *Unteroffizier* Hilbman, who stated: "After the first attack from behind on a Fortress formation, I saw a Boeing, flying to the left in front, dive away to the left from the formation. The right engines were afire."[27] Rudert was awarded a *Herausschuss*, a successful attack resulting in a bomber having to leave its protective formation.

Another 351st Bomb Group B-17 was hit. It was B-17G 42-97191, nicknamed *Silver Ball*, which was flying in the number six position in the high squadron. The plane had flown sixteen previous missions, but the crew of 2nd Lt. Carl F. Miller was already on around its twentieth. The exception was substitute navigator 1st Lt. Russell A. Brown. He had flown thirty-five combat missions from Foggia, Italy, and now was on his fifteenth mission with the group from Polebrook. He had been transferred to England at his own request, together with his original copilot, Frank J. Hoder. Brown recalls: "On approach to the target, we were attacked by three waves of Me 109s, Fw 190s, and Me 210s, with twenty to twenty-five aircraft in each wave. The Fw 190s in four to six aircraft in three waves. I remember that, although the day had bright sunshine at 22,000 feet, the air turned to a smoky grey, I supposed because of the amount of gunsmoke each air force was dispelling in the defense of their cause."[28]

When *Silver Ball* was raked with gunfire, the oxygen lines were destroyed and the ball turret gunner was mortally wounded. Staff Sgt. Isidor P. Kaplowitz had left his ball turret to replace his used oxygen bottle for a new one of the low pressure type, and at the moment he was reentering his turret, a 20mm shell exploded the full oxygen bottle which killed him instantly. His body lay half in and half out of his turret. Several other crewmembers were slightly wounded.

When a fire broke out that could not be extinguished, Miller rang the bail-out bell. All the crew, except Kaplowitz, safely cleared the aircraft. When co-pilot 2nd Lt. Maurice G. Fikes left, Miller was alone in the cockpit, where things seemed to be under control at that moment. However, he did not survive. The other crewmembers believe that he took the full responsibility of

First Lt. Burl L. Williams of the 363rd Fighter Group shot down an Fw 190.
STEVE BLAKE

being a pilot and aircrew commander, and that he went back through the aircraft to make sure everyone else was out. Germans later told captured crewmembers that one body was found in the crashed bomber and another several hundred feet from it, with an only partially opened parachute.

Apparently, Lieutenant Miller took too much time in the aircraft and bailed out too low to safely open his chute. Russell Brown picks up the story: "After diving out of the burning aircraft wishing to separate myself as far as possible from the fighting and the burning aircraft, I fell many seconds without opening my chute. As I approached in descent, a layer of clouds that I knew to be at about 5,000 feet, I pulled the rip cord and watched my chute open, then to my dismay, and terrible fear, watched my shroud line wind together up toward the silk that blossomed above me. Immediately I flung my arms and legs out to resist my spinning which was nearly causing the collapse of my life-saving parachute. This peril being averted, I entered the low cloud bank, only to discover that a more terrible threat to my life was approaching in the form of the aircraft from which I had escaped a few seconds ago. It was bearing down on me through the clouds, and which I could not see, and could not escape even if I could see, as I hung helpless in my chute. As the plane went screaming by on it's own mission of death, I broke through the clouds to see the welcome earth below. I fell into a ploughed field in a corner created by dense cultivated pine thickets. I gathered my chute together and ran into the thicket. After burying my chute I walked deeper into it and sat down with my back resting against the trunk of a tree in such a manner that I could watch down the rows of pine to the end of the row."

Second Lt. James E. Hill shot down an Fw 190 for the first of two air victories. He was made prisoner of war on 14 June.
JAMES E. HILL

Russell Brown managed to stay at large until June 1, when he was captured while trying to cross the railway bridge over the River Elbe at Barby. He joined the seven other survivors of the crew in various Stalag Lufts. Their Fortress crashed at 1430 hours along the railway line between Deetz and Nedlitz, fifteen kilometers northeast of Zerbst. Miller and Kaplowitz were buried on 30 May in the Nedlitz cemetery.

Flying on the right wing of Lieutenant Miller, in the number five position of the high squadron, was B-17G *Pin Ball* (42-39987), piloted by F/O Robert E. L. Probasco and 2nd Lt. Stephen B. Lewellyn. Their regular navigator, Donald Rude, did not fly with them since he reported to sick call that morning. He was replaced by 2nd Lt. William P. Bragg, who recalled: "We were attacked by a superior number of various types of German fighters near Magdeburg at an altitude of 27,500 feet. Our ship was knocked out of formation on about the third pass. Due in part to the fact that our ship was old and already had difficulties keeping up, we tried to salvo our bombs. Our pilot, in attempting to get our ship from above another ship, so salvo could be accomplished, hit the propwash from another B-17 and we were thrown from formation.

"The attacks continued, various types of fighters making passes. Crew members, including myself, were wounded from time to time. Our oxygen and number three engine were shot out. Number two engine was running away periodically. Had lost altitude to about 19,000 feet. Decided with pilot to hit deck and take up a course generally in the direction of Switzerland. Was working on course when bombardier returned from vicinity of cockpit

Second Lt. Donald W. Ray of the
363rd Fighter Group scored his one
and only air victory on 28 May. He
accounted for an Fw 190 in the
Dessau-Magdeburg area. RICHARD RAY

and prepared to bail out, stating pilot could not pull ship out and had
ordered abandonment. Bombardier bailed out. Co-pilot bailed. Noted altitude as approximately 11,000 feet and bailed out myself. Noted engineer
coming behind me as I left ship.

"On way down noted enemy fighters in area; however, no attack made
on parachutists in vicinity. Noted chute (later identified as co-pilot) coming
down over little village to my right. This village I believe I can positively identify as Falkenburg, about fifty miles south south east of Dessau. I would not
have believed we were that far from Dessau; however, only cursory navigation was possible during the fight and, as I remember, our course was laid
out for a long east leg after target. The co-pilot was shot at by civilians while
he was descending over the village; when he came down in the village he was
manhandled to some extent but was extricated from this difficulty by the
police, who turned him over to *Luftwaffe* authorities at the nearby airfield. I
believe I was about two or three miles south of the village. I landed in a grain
field near a railroad track and a canal and was picked up by two enlisted
members of *Luftwaffe* and assisted into airfield which was nearby.

"Believe plane crashed not too far away, as observed plane flying on
automatic pilot in large circle, while I was descending. Also, the *Luftwaffe*
had various items from plane next morning. Observed crew member, I
believe to be Singleton, the tail gunner, brought into Nazi medical office,
while I was leaving. He was shot through the stomach and in very bad shape.
Was presumed dead by us while in prison. Germans made vague statement

28 May was the highlight in the career of 1st Lt. Edwin E. Vance of the 363rd Fighter Group. He was able to obtain two victories before his death during a dive-bombing mission on 11 June. Both were scored on 28 May, when he destroyed two Bf 109s and damaged a third. STEVE BLAKE

to one of the survivors something about chute or chutes not opening. Singleton, by engineers account, was OK when he left; therefore, presume may have been shot on ground. A good bit of shooting at airmen by civilians was going on that day, from the accounts of other crews, and from co-pilots experience."[29]

The crew's bombardier, 2nd Lt. Bruno Branch, recalled his story: "I was not injured in the plane, but sustained a spine fracture on landing with my parachute. On 28 May, the crews' ninth mission, the 351st Bomb Group was in trouble before we left England. Our group was supposed to be the last one in the 1st Division of bombers leaving England at checkpoint Yarmouth. When our group, arrived the 2nd Division composed of all B-24s were already crossing the Channel on the way. Our group leader circled until all the B-24s had passed by and took our group in behind the B-24s and in front of the 3rd Division which was all B-17s.* We were twenty minutes late when we crossed the Channel. The group made up ten minutes en route and were approximately ten minutes late at the target area, with no fighter escort in sight. Bombs away scheduled for 1410 hours, arrived 1420 hours.

"The *Luftwaffe* sent up Me 109, Fw 190, and Ju 88 planes to attack. I was sitting in my position preparing for the bomb run when at three o'clock high, I noticed this group of planes. Our 511th Squadron was positioned high in the group, which was 27,500 feet. The crew was alerted to German fighters in the area and all guns were manned. My bomb bay doors were

---

* Here Branch's memory is incorrect. As we have seen, it was indeed a B-24 formation that they ran into, but they followed the first B-17 wing of the Third Air Division into Germany.

Oberfeldwebel Erich Klein of 3./JG 5 was shot down by a P-51 south of Salzwedel. A .50-caliber machine-gun round hit his right knee, and Klein bailed out. Later, his right leg had to be amputated. ERIC MOMBEEK

open. I noticed the German fighters had disappeared into the sun out of my view. In less than a minute we were attacked from one o'clock high. I was supposed to release our bombs when the group bombardier did so, as he had the bomb sight aboard.

"On this first pass, an Me 109 with its firepower struck our number three engine, hit our ball turret and injured Ringstmeyer. He was able to get out of the turret with help. Bragg was firing from the right nose gun during the first attack, was knocked to the other side of the plane with fragments of the shell exploding in his right side from head to foot. The lead bombardier made a dry run on our primary target Dessau which was an aircraft engine plant used on Ju 88 planes. The secondary target was Magdeburg, the oil depot located there. The group, still under attack, headed there. We lost our communication system aboard shortly after. The number three engine was leaking oil, the pilot wanted to keep it going as we needed the power. Soon it started to windmill and lost so much oil it could not be feathered. Soon the numbers two and four engine started to run away due to the additional strain, and our plane started to lose altitude and formation.

"I salvoed the five tons of bombs to help the plane. The plane was at 14,000 feet and losing altitude fast. I went to the pilot and told him it looks like we have to bail out. He told me yes and to go ahead. I went back into

Oberleutnant Josef Jansen, the experienced *Staffelkapitän* of 1./JG 27.
He was badly wounded in action on 28 May and succumbed to his
wounds on 31 May. AB A. JANSEN

the nose section and told Bragg we were going to bail out. I said to him 'you
want to go first' and his reply was for me. I told him, 'This is no time to
argue,' and said, 'So long,' and I went out the nose escape door head first. I
left the plane at about 1430 hours, altitude 12,000 to 13,000 feet. Bragg,
Lewellyn, and Probasco followed immediately from the nose escape door. I
was in a free fall to about 5,000 to 6,000 feet when I pulled my ripcord. I
counted five parachutes in the air plus my own and saw the plane make a
turn to the right as it was descending struck the ground with an ensuing
puff of black smoke.

"All survivors of the plane were taken to a nearby *Luftwaffe* air base and
transferred by rail the next day to Dulag near Wetzlar, a *Luftwaffe* interrogation center for captured airmen. I was in solitary confinement twenty-four
hours and asked the interrogating officer who spoke English fluently what
happened to the other four crewmembers. He said their chutes did not
open. In my conversations with Ulreich and Frankowski who bailed out
from the rear of the plane, there was no apparent reason for them not to
jump. What happened to lost crew members is conjecture. Ulreich and
Frankowski were sent to an enlisted airmen *Luftwaffe* camp. Probasco,
Lewellyn, Bragg, and I were sent to Stalag Luft III near Sagan, which we left
on 27 January 1945."[30]

The flight of the 363rd Fighter Group with 1st Lt. John R. Brown in *Big Mac Junior* and 1st Lt. James H. Clark (left) in *The Mighty Midget* strafed an airfield in the Frankfurt area. Brown destroyed an He 111 and damaged a Ju 52 and three unidentified planes. Clark destroyed three Ju 88s and an He 111, damaging another He 111.
STEVE BLAKE

As has already been related, all the officers escaped from the front of the aircraft, but the enlisted men in the back were not as lucky. Ball turret gunner Sgt. Norman W. Ringstmeyer was hit by fire from the German fighters and called in to report his wounds. Co-pilot Lewellyn directed the radio operator, Staff Sgt. Arlie W. Moore, to help him out of the turret. Then they were hit again by fighters. Apparently, Moore was hit by this burst, as just seconds later the bail-out signal was given, and both Moore and Ringstmeyer were seen lying on the floor of the aircraft, covered with blood, observed by right waist gunner Sgt. Edward J. Frankowski. Since Frankowski was wounded and dazed, he was unable to help them, and so he bailed out. Why the other waist gunner, Sgt. Raymond G. Seaman, did not jump is not known, and he crashed with the bomber. The tail gunner, Sgt. James D. Singleton, jumped from his own escape hatch, and his parachute opened properly.

As William Bragg has already reported, shots were fired from the ground at the descending airmen, and several bullets hit the unfortunate Singleton. He died the same evening, at 1935 hours, at the hospital at Torgau-Elbe, from wounds caused by shots through the right pelvis, right shoulder, left hip, and left foot. The author has been unable to find out if the person or persons responsible for this cowardly killing were ever brought to trial, but it seems unlikely. Singleton was buried on 1 June at the Torgau municipal cemetery. The other three gunners were buried on 31 May at Schmerkendorfer Wald near Falkenberg-Elster, close to the location where their *Pin Ball* crashed. The airfield where the prisoners were brought was Alt-Lönnewitz, some five kilometers north of the crash location. So within just two or three minutes, the Germans had shot down four B-17s from the 351st Bomb Group, flying as numbers five and six, in both the low and high squadrons. This graphically illustrates the relative vulnerability of these combat positions within a bomb group formation. The 401st Bomb Group formation, flying low in the wing, bore the brunt of the German attacks. Its high squadron was hit especially hard.

The tail gunner aboard the squadron's lead aircraft *Fitch's Bandwagon* was Staff Sgt. Robert V. Kerr, who recorded in his diary: "We reached the initial point and the bomb doors were opened. Looked over my shoulder at eleven o'clock and saw a formation a way ahead of us and saw a fighter going down trailing smoke. Flak started coming up ahead of us. Looked out to our left and saw several green flashes at nine o'clock as shells exploded right near us and the navigator had said, 'There's flak right near us.' I

P-51B *Big Mac Junior* (42-106647) of the 363rd Fighter Group, 382nd Fighter Squadron, Ninth Air Force, forms a handy backdrop for pilot 1st Lt. John R. Brown and his ground crew at Staplehurst, England.

pressed the button and said, 'Those are 20mm's.' Just then someone yelled, 'Fighters at ten o'clock,' and it sounded like all guns on the ship let go at once. Looked over my right shoulder and saw a whole formation of enemy planes diving at us right through their own flak. I grabbed the guns and got ready for action, but none of them came within range of where my guns were pointing. Had my parachute [chest type] attached to one hook through the side of my flak suit, in case of emergency. Pulled helmet down tighter, turned face away and ducked my head behind metal frame as air was filled with exploding 20mms. There was a terrific racket.

"I looked out and saw a ship from another group (Polebrook/351st?) roll over on its back and go down in a vertical dive. Watched until it went out of sight. Another went into a steep glide and I saw one chute come out just before the ship went out of sight beneath us. The *Luftwaffe* went off to four o'clock and got back into formation again. I looked high up at six o'clock and saw vapour trails from the escort and thought they were coming to our rescue. But I got a rather sickening feeling as I saw them make a left turn and head north.

"All of a sudden somebody yelled, 'Fighters coming in at two o'clock,' and it seemed like every gun on the ship opened up at once again and the whole ship shuddered and seemed to jump sideways. The noise made by the

The officers of the crew of B-17G 42-31757 of the 351st Bomb Group. Left to right: Joseph P. Kolceski, co-pilot (KIA); William J. Condon, pilot (KIA); Laddie J. Zindar, navigator (KIA); and Edwin S. Onken, bombardier (POW). WILLIAM H. MORRIS

guns firing and the exploding shells was terrific and as I turned and looked over my left shoulder through the green flashes of the 20mm I saw what appeared to be the whole German Luftwaffe pouring in on us with their guns blazing."[31]

The number five position of this squadron was occupied by the experienced 1st Lt. Walter B. Keith and his crew in B-17G 42-31557. Staff Sgt. James E. Wells, the engineer, recalls: "As we approached the target area, the *Luftwaffe* made its first appearance. They were first called by Peter Beckowitz from the ball turret. The attacks were made from the front and level with our formation, making it difficult to get very long shots at them. The attacks were made by the German fighters in a wing abreast formation and they came in wave after wave. I do not recall how many enemy fighters we encountered that day, but there were many of them.

"At some time during the battle, our number two engine was shot out and I noticed a large hole in the top of the cowling that could have been the exit hole of an 88mm flak shell. Lucky for us that it did not explode. As I slewed my turret around, I was amazed at the number of holes and the damage that had been inflicted on our plane. At one time Arthur Mahler, the radio-operator, reported that there was a fire in the bomb bay. I made a

The enlisted men of the crew of B17G 42-31757 of the 351st Bomb Group. Back row, left to right: Harry M. Norris, waist gunner (KIA); Lawrence Kofoed, waist gunner (not on 28 May mission); Charles G. Jenkins, ball turret gunner (KIA). Front row, left to right: William H. Morris, radio operator (POW); John J. Jackson, tail gunner (POW); Junny O. Jackson, engineer (KIA). WILLIAM H. MORRIS

visual check at this time. I could see no evidence of any fire, but the bombs had been salvoed, and I assumed that either the bombardier or the pilot had salvoed them. I later talked with the bombardier, and he said he did not remember doing it, so it must have been Lieutenant Keith. After all that had transpired, we were still functioning all right. At some time during the battle, we found ourselves flying all alone. There was a vacancy in the lead squadron formation, so Lieutenant Keith slid our airplane into that spot, so we would not be so alone.

"The formation began a turn to the left, which put us on the outside, so as a result, we began falling behind. I heard Lieutenant Keith call for #10 on the turbos. This was an emergency setting, so that we could obtain all available power from the engines to attempt to maintain station. There was no response to his request, so he repeated it. There was still no response, so I heard Lieutenant Keith say, 'The hell with it, I will do it myself.' At this time, I heard the turbos wind up, but it was too little too late. We continued to fall farther and farther behind the group formation.

"It was not long before two Fw 190s queued up on our tail and began the final assault on our B-17. One attacked from the five o'clock high position, the other from the seven o'clock high position. At this time I had no interphone communications with other crew members. I noted that the radio-operator was firing at the fighter coming from the seven o'clock position, so I selected the one coming from the five o'clock position. The final blow was a 20mm shell which entered the airplane in the dorsal fin area, came between the waist gunners, snipped the radio operator's boot, contin-

Waist gunner Harry M. Norris and ball turret gunner Charles G. Jenkins. Neither of them survived their fight with the *Luftwaffe*.
LAWRENCE KOFOED

ued through the aft bomb bay bulkhead door and impacted and exploded in the forward bomb bay bulkhead among the fuel transfer lines. Flames immediately erupted and enveloped my turret, so I decided that it was time to make a hasty retreat from the turret. I slid down out of the turret, and opened my eyes long enough to locate my parachute pack which I kept stowed on the floor to the right of my turret.

"As I retrieved my parachute pack, someone started beating on me. I can only assume that it was Lieutenant Keith and he thought I was on fire. I wiggled trying to get free, so I could get out of the airplane. When the beating stopped, I made my way to the crawl way to the emergency exit. Later I wished I had taken the time to check the cockpit area, but I did not. I believe that 2nd Lt. John J. Maloney, the co-pilot, must have been dead in his seat, because he did not respond to Lieutenant Keith's request for the turbo setting earlier. As I entered the crawl way, I stopped and attempted to hook my parachute pack to my harness. I was so doubled up, that I could not get the pack between my upper legs and my chest. I momentarily put the pack under my arm, and figured I would make my exit from the airplane, and then connect the pack on my way down. I immediately vetoed that decision, and made one more attempt to hook it. This time I succeeded in hooking the right side only, so I felt that would have to do.

"As I approached the exit, I found it had already been opened, and bombardier Lieutenant Weiss was there. Since he was there first, I felt he had priority so I motioned for him to go. He shook his head and motioned for me to go, so away I went. Against all of our verbal training, I opened my parachute immediately, as did most of the other crewmen that I know. As I made my descent, I counted seven parachutes in a stair step fashion, so I assumed at this time that at least seven of us got out. Since I had only one side of my parachute fastened, I made a sliding fall and drifted away from the rest of the parachutes that were descending. As I was descending, a German fighter approached me, and my first thought was that he was going to strafe me. As it turned out, he wanted to have some fun at my expense. As he went by me, he kicked his rudder so that I was directly behind him and he then gunned his engine an got me swinging in my parachute like a giant pendulum.

"My contact with the earth was a crashing fall through some very tall trees. I came to a halt short of the ground hanging from the trees. I freed myself from my parachute harness, and began looking for some place to hide. It seemed that the Germans planted their trees in straight rows, and kept all underbrush cleared from beneath them. It was not very long before I was captured. I guess I was fortunate because my captors were military. The civilian population did not care much for the American aviators. I was transported some distance, where I was put in a shed of some type, and there I saw some of my crew members.

The crew of B-17G 42-97472 of the 351st Bomb Group. Back row, left to right: William H. Baird, bombardier; Charles F. Anderson, pilot; Robert L. McFetridge, co-pilot; and Robert E. Ryan, navigator. Front row, left to right: George P. Nitzberg, ball turret gunner; Guseino P. Lostocco, radio operator (not on 28 May mission, KIA on 19 July); Walter R. Subora, right waist gunner (not on 28 May mission, POW on 14 June); Edward E. VanHorn, tail gunner; and Neal W. Williams; engineer. All on board on 28 May were made prisoners of war. WALTER R. SUBORA

"Lieutenant Weiss landed in trees like I did, but he was held by the branches until his parachute canopy collapsed, and he free fell to the ground, getting broken up quite a bit. Tail gunner Victor d'Agostino was blown from the airplane when it exploded. He was battered up pretty badly. One of his boots was completely blown from his foot, and the ankle appeared to be three times its normal size and he appeared to have some broken ribs. He was covered with scrapes, abrasions and cuts. Arthur Mahler landed in a ploughed field and badly sprained an ankle. Merle Barnes, the left waist gunner, appeared to be in the best shape of all of us. We never did see Lieutenant Keith.

"Of the crewmembers that did not make it, I offer this. As I previously mentioned, Lieutenant Maloney was apparently killed sometime during the aerial battle. Lieutenant Weiss told me later on the ground that he assisted 1st Lt. Jack B. Priest, the navigator, from the airplane. What happened to him, we never found out. Arthur Mahler and Merle Barnes felt that Peter Beckowitz was killed on about the first pass the fighters made on us. Barnes also said that Leo Cass, the other waist gunner, was still firing his gun when he tried to get him to leave the airplane, but he refused. We never knew the

Staff Sgt. Casper Vecchione, the radio operator on B-17G, 42-97472 of the 351st Bomb Group, in the open radio hatch of a B-17 of the 510th Bomb Squadron, showing the retractable machine gun that was operated by the radio operator.
CASPER VECCHIONE

reason. We were taken by a farm cart pulled behind a vehicle to an airbase at Magdeburg. The next day, we started on our way to Frankfurt and finally ended up in Stalag Luft IV."[32]

The four men who did not survive were buried on 29 May in the community cemetery of Setzsteig. Lieutenant Keith's bomber crashed at 1410 hours, eight kilometers southeast of Belzig and fifteen kilometers southwest of Niemegk. Additionally, the neighboring B-17 was lost in the early stages of the attacks. And again, as in the 351st Bomb Group, it was the bombers in the most vulnerable positions that were hit first by the German fighters.

The number six position in the high squadron was occupied by 1st Lt. William F. Protz, and his crew in their B-17G 42-102580. This crew was on its eighth mission and its demise was quick and deadly. The suddenness of its loss caused speculation among returning crews that it may have been a direct flak hit which resulted in the crash. This hit, or perhaps a concentrated burst of cannon fire by a German fighter, caused a fierce fire in the radio room of the aircraft, immediately followed, before any of the crew had a chance to parachute, by an explosion, which literally tore the machine apart. Five crewmembers, including the pilot, were able to pull the rip cords on their chutes in time after the explosion and were captured. Five others, the co-pilot, navigator, bombardier, engineer, and radio operator were killed and later buried in the Susigke cemetery. Pieces of the aircraft and the five bodies were strewn across the countryside six kilometers east of Aken and only five kilometers west of Dessau, their intended target.

The German pilot who claimed to have shot down Protz's B-17 was *Leutnant* Alexander Ottnad, flying in an Me 109G of 8./JG 27. At 1244 hours, he had taken off from Götzendorf-Leitha airfield. He reported: "I flew as *Staffelführer* on a mission against a reported enemy formation. At 1410 hours, we encountered two waves of Fortress IIs with fighter escort, between Dessau and Magdeburg. Our group attacked from the front, I fired on the enemy aircraft, flying third from the right. I observed hits in the front part of the aircraft and right wing. When I broke off the attack I was hit in my engine and fuselage. I then observed how the Fortress II I had hit went straight down, with its right wing burning. I then parachuted from my own aircraft, because it was heavily smoking. I could not observe the actual crash of the bomber I had hit. The impact should have been at 1428 hours, south

The crew of B-17G *Silver Ball* (42-97191) of the 351st Bomb Group. Back row, left to right: James D. McCann, radio operator (POW); J. Adams (not on 28 May mission); Frank Avry, engineer (POW); Isidor P. Kaplowitz, ball turret gunner (KIA); Carl F. Miller, pilot (KIA). Front row, left to right: Maurice G. Fikes, co-pilot (POW); Anthony J. Bushlow, right waist gunner (POW); Albert L. Lien, left waist gunner (POW); and George A. Stafford, tail gunner (POW). MRS. GEORGE A. STAFFORD

or southwest of Zerbst. Other remarks: I also observed another Fortress going down after our same attack."[33]

Feldwebel Franz Büsen, flying in Ottnad's formation, backed up the claim, and since the time and location in Ottnad's report exactly matched the crash of Protz's bomber in *Planquadrat JE 4*, German authorities awarded him the destruction of this bomber. As we have seen, it was not always a one-sided affair. Apparently, the gunners in the B-17 formation had hit Ottnad's Bf 109, forcing him to bail out. Ottnad was not the only pilot who was hit. Both *Gefreiter* Herbert Curth, who also claimed an *Herausschuss* over a B-17, and *Unteroffizier* Otto Mühlbauer of 8./JG 27 had to belly-land their damaged Bf 109s. *Unteroffizier* Günther Weth of 7./JG 27 was mortally wounded during these engagements and crashed with his Bf 109 near Dessau.

First Lt. Vincent J. Kaminski, a veteran pilot with twenty-eight missions to his credit, was flying with his crew in the number three position of the low squadron, in B-17G 42-97073. This crew was not his regular one, but that of Lt. Joseph E. Ferdyn, who was on leave that day. Co-pilot was 2nd Lt. Robert J. Enstad, on his twenty-fourth mission. The rest of the crew had about the

Staff Sgt. George A. Stafford, tail gunner of *Silver Ball* standing next to the tools of his trade. He was shot down in this aircraft on 28 May and made a Prisoner of War.
MRS. GEORGE A. STAFFORD

same number of missions finished. Enstad recalled: "Some minutes prior to the initial point, the crew observed and discussed what we thought was another bomb wing off to our right, at about three o'clock level. However, this wing was moving faster than our 94th Combat Wing. At this point, it was well ahead of us and made a 90-degree left turn and flew to a point where it was directly in front of our wing. It then made another 90-degree left turn and came at us at twelve o'clock level. The Germans put every type of aircraft that would fly into this attack—even fixed landing gear aircraft were present.

"Our plane was badly damaged on the first pass. 20mm shells entered our left wing, damaging manual controls and knocking out superchargers on number one and two engines. Our airspeed dropped to 135 to 140 miles per hour and our maneuverability was very poor. We jettisoned our bombs as we dropped from the formation. Three-aircraft elements of fighters started attacking our lone aircraft. We actually survived three or four attacks and shot down some enemy fighters. The final attack came from six o'clock

The crew of B-17G *Pin Ball* (42-39987) of the 351st Bomb Group. Back row, left to right: Robert E. L. Probasco, pilot (POW); Stephen B. Lewellyn, co-pilot (POW); Bruno Branch, bombardier (POW); Donald B. Rude, navigator (not on 28 May mission). Front row, left to right: Herman T. Ulreich, engineer (POW); Edward J. Frankowski, right waist gunner (POW); Arlie W. Moore, radio operator (KIA); Norman W. Ringstmeyer, ball turret gunner (KIA); Raymond G. Seaman, left waist gunner (KIA); and James D. Singleton, tail gunner (KIA). BRUNO BRANCH

with 20mm shells spraying the entire aircraft. One shell exploded in my back-pack type parachute. Other shells or fragments hit the hydraulic system and oxygen supply, engulfing the cockpit in flames."[34]

Bombardier James V. Walsh of the crew of Lt. Edwin A. Post, who was flying next to Kaminski, saw the last moments and reported about it back at Deenethorpe that evening: "Number one engine on fire, peeled over on back and went down."[35]

Enstad: "The aircraft did a wing over and exploded. That Charlie and I got out is truly a miracle. My backpack chute had been badly damaged by shell fragments so I came down fast—fortunately landing in a freshly ploughed or cultivated field. Another miracle! I did have a number of shell fragments in me, but no broken bones. Lt. Charles Manning, our navigator, didn't have a scratch. I came to, surrounded by Charlie and German civilians. We were taken to the village town hall at Mühro. Three members of other bomber crews joined us there. After a period of time we were taken to a nearby cemetery. There were the remains of the eight other members of our crew. With difficulty, Charlie and I managed to identify them. Charlie, the three other uninjured airmen, and some slave labourers were ordered to strip the clothing from the remains and, with the aid of shovels and some boards, buried them in a common grave. Under heavy guard we were then transported by truck to a large airport. Our group grew to about fifty. Here we were strip-searched and all personal belongings were taken from us. Treatment at this location was harsh, there was little or no first aid for the injured. We were held there overnight."

One of other three airmen who was ordered to help bury the eight men, has been identified as Charles H. Bedell, the radio operator of the crew of Lt. Paul Scharff. Kaminski's aircraft had crashed in a wooded area near Steinberg, 800 meters northeast of the village of Mühro, in the Zerbst district. The eight crewmembers were buried in the village cemetery.

Flying in the number four position of the Lead Squadron, just behind the Lead aircraft, was B-17G *Bonnie Donnie* (42-31034). Both the aircraft and her crew, piloted by 1st Lt. George E. West, had been at Deenethorpe for some time already.

Bonnie Donnie was one of the original aircraft that the group had received while still in the United States. It had survived a crash-landing at the base, on return from a mission in March, but was repaired to fly many more. The crew of 1st Lt. George E. West was the first replacement crew for the 612th Bomb Squadron. They sailed to England on the *Queen Elizabeth* in the early part of November 1943. All crewmembers were nearing the end of their now thirty-mission combat tour on 28 May. But instead of their regular B-17, *Hangover Haven*, they had been assigned *Bonnie Donnie* that morning.

Second Lt. Bruno
Branch, bombardier of
Pin Ball during training
at Dalharst Army Air
Force Base in Texas,
January 1944. He was
shot down on 28 May
and became a prisoner
of war. BRUNO BRANCH

Navigator on the crew was 1st Lt. Lloyd A. Nutter, who recalled: "Magdeburg was heavily defended and there was lots of flak. Near the initial point
we were attacked by fighters of all kinds, Me 109s, Fw 190s, Ju 88s, and some
we did not identify. In all the missions I had flown, we had not encountered
as many aircraft—they came at us from every direction. After we turned on
to our bomb run and had opened the bomb doors, they simply disappeared,
having been shot off. We struggled over our primary target and dropped
our bombs, but we were in a very bad shape, and had dropped from the formation. We were losing altitude and airspeed and because of the severe
damage to the aircraft, we discussed the options we had open to us. We considered abandoning the aircraft at this time, and had made this decision.

"I had destroyed all classified information along with the various charts,
and was in the process of almost jumping out of the ship, when the bombardier tapped me on the shoulder and told me the pilot had decided to
hold out a little longer. We then held a conference and decided to hold all
the altitude we could and try to stay as close as we could to our group for
fighter support. We knew that if we did get back to England, we would have
to abandon the aircraft there as there was no way we could land it and there

was so much damage we could only turn the thing to the right. We were flying over a complete cloud deck and about twenty minutes later we saw a clearing in the clouds, right over the city of Leipzig. We were able to steer around this city—if it had not been for the break in the cloud deck, I would not have been writing this. A lone B-17 would have had no chance against the anti-aircraft guns surrounding that city. At this time we were down to about 18,000 feet, starting from 24,000 feet.

"The rear part of the plane had been severely damaged and there was no oxygen, so the crew of gunners had moved up to the radio room where oxygen was available. At this time I heard that one of the waist gunners, Staff Sgt. Hugh D. Russell, had been wounded in the head by a 20mm shell.

"We continued on our heading, trying to hold altitude, but now we were down to 17,000 feet. Suddenly someone called over the intercom 'right wing on fire.' I believe I heard the word 'fire' as I bailed out the forward escape hatch. The bombardier was right behind me. I bailed out head first, he bailed out feet first and we both got out OK. We had always argued as to the best way to go. To the best of my knowledge we were the only ones to bail out, the rest blew up with the ship and simply opened their chutes. The tail

Staff Sgt. Robert V. Kerr, tail gunner of B-17G *Fitch's Bandwagon* (42-107043) of the 401st Bomb Group.
ROBERT V. KERR

gunner, Staff Sgt. Michael Lefkin, was killed when his chute had a 'streamer' and failed to blossom. The waist gunner with the bad head wound might not have been able to open his chute at all. I actually saw both bodies later. The co-pilot, 1st Lt. Douglas H. McKinnon, was standing in the bomb bay preparing to jump, when the ship exploded. Most of his clothing was blown off, but he got out OK. The pilot was last seen standing between the pilot and co-pilot seats, holding the wheel, trying to keep the ship steady for the rest of the crew to bail out. The rest of the crew, in the radio room, simply opened their chutes after the explosion. I might add there was no communication with the radio room, all these facilities had been destroyed.

"As we had been instructed, I delayed my chute opening as long as possible. I made a free fall from about 17,000 to about 2,000 feet, and my first attempt to open the chute failed. For some reason, the pilot chute, supposed to pull out the main chute, failed to pop out. My chute, being a chest type, was easy to get at, so I reached in and pulled out a handful of silk. That was all it took, it opened and when it did, I thought every bone in my body was broken.

Standing amidst his original combat crew is 1st Lt. Walter B. Keith, who piloted B-17G 42-31557 of the 401st Bomb Group on 28 May. He was shot down and made prisoner of war, just like his former navigator, 2nd Lt. Carl T. Floto, who is kneeling on this picture. The latter flew as navigator on the crew of 2nd Lt. Frederick H. Windham on 28 May. WARDLAW M. HAMMOND

Standing at left is Sgt. Merle E. Barnes, left waist gunner
(POW). At right is Sgt. Peter Beckowitz, ball turret gunner
(KIA). Kneeling at left is 2nd Lt. Irving Wolliver, navigator (not
on mission). At right is Cpl. Arthur P. Mahler, radio operator
(POW). JAMES E. WELLS

"We had bailed out somewhere southwest of Leipzig and I came down in
the middle of a grain field. We had been instructed to hide the chute immediately, but I was so scared I couldn't even get it off. I could see civilians
coming at me in the distance, and not wanting to be captured by them, I
began running the other way. After some bullets started coming very close
to my head, I stopped and became a 'Comrad' [he means *Kamerad*, German
for "buddy"]. I was being beaten up rather badly by these civilians when a
German guard, on a bicycle, appeared from a fighter base, which was
nearby. He took charge and I walked alongside him over to this base.

"During this walk, we were both pelted by various objects that were
thrown by the civilians. I am positive that this guard saved my life. As we
walked to the base, I observed the wreckage of our aircraft. The remains
were so close to where I landed that I am sure it exploded within seconds of

the time I bailed out. The rest of the crew all landed in or near the base and were captured by the military. Sometime later, I volunteered to go and identify the bodies of the two gunners. This was a kind of grey area in those days, but I felt a responsibility to the families of these men to identify them. The rest of the war was spent in various German prison camps."[36]

Bonnie Donnie had crashed between Otterwisch and Pomssen, and all surviving crewmembers were made prisoner of war in the small village of Pomssen, close to Grimma.

OVER THE TARGET

The aggressive German fighter attacks had now battered the wing, and gradually the protective combat wing formation fell apart. Forty-seven B-17s had reached the initial point, but at least eight were shot down between the initial point and the target and several others were damaged.

Dense smoke and haze covered the target area and the wing leader, Major Hozier, decided to make a turn and make a second run to the target. During this turn, the fighter attacks continued, and upon their second arrival over Dessau, the lead bombardiers in the 457th and 351st Bomb Groups were again unable to identify their mean point of impact and decided to keep their bombs aboard and head for the secondary target.

Staff Sgt. James E. Wells, engineer of B-17G 42-31557 of the 401st Bomb Group. JAMES E. WELLS

Many crewmembers now just wanted to get rid of their bomb loads and were not appreciative of the efforts of their bombardiers to get the bombs on target on a second run. A waist gunner in one of the ships, due to be shot down in the next few minutes, recalled: "Of course, the bombardier missed seeing the target, so we had to go around again. The German fighters only had to make one turn to hit us again. This happened again on the next bomb run, which they also missed. Maybe the lead and deputy lead got knocked out. On the third bomb run we got it. If the bombardier had done his job the first time, maybe we would have been home free. As far as defense against the fighters, all we could do was spray bursts of fifties hoping to hit a few as they went by.

"I have never forgiven bombardiers, for this was not the first time they missed and had to around again. When we would look at the pictures, we saw they still missed."[37]

The 401st Bomb Group, which had already lost four of its B-17s, was able to find its designated mean point of impact on the second run, and the Group's lead bombardier, Lt. Robert W. Rowe, decided to drop, and the twelve remaining B-17s in the formation dropped their bombs, with good results.

However, the bombing had put them somewhat behind the other two groups of the wing, and again the German fighters hit. One of the pilots still in the formation, 1st Lt. Dan C. Knight, flying B-17G *Mary Alice* (42-31983), recalled it this way: "I must say that of my thirty missions, Dessau was the one that gives me nightmares. When we turned on our initial point toward Dessau we noticed way off in the distance many specks in the sky that none of us gave too much thought to as there were many instances when other bombers would be headed for other targets. Little did we realize that what we had seen would turn out to be between 200 and 300 German fighters. As we passed over the target the first time, our group lead bombardier had a malfunction in the bomb sight and our bombs did not get away. Anyway, our group commander called our wing commander to advise that our bombs had not gone away. He informed our group commander to do a 360, go back over the target, get our bombs away and that the other two Groups would stooge around and wait for us, so that we all could go back to England together.

"This is when everything started to happen. As we came off the target after getting our bombs away, all hell broke loose. As I mentioned, those specks we had seen in the distance turned out to be fighters of all types, Me 109s, Fw 190s, and even an assortment of twin-engines. They were all over us like a swarm of bees. They would come at us from all directions—above, below, both sides. They were everywhere. We saw some collide with each other, as they couldn't get out of each other's way. There simply wasn't enough sky to avoid each other. I don't know when we realized it, but at some point, we became aware that the 457th and 351st Bomb Groups had not only not waited for us, but were nowhere in sight. We were eighteen bombers against the whole *Luftwaffe* it looked like. There was no way that I could imagine that any of us could survive with the odds stacked against us like that. I'll never forget my thoughts about dying. I was sure it was inevitable, but you keep on holding that tight formation that you know you have to do, but I kept wondering how it was going to feel to be killed. It had to happen. It was just a question of 'when.' This is the part I'll never forget—I kept thinking to myself that 'I'm still thinking, I'm still thinking, I'm still thinking. If I can still think, it hasn't happened yet.' It was a strange feeling. After a while you begin to think that maybe, just maybe it isn't going to happen to you, even though planes are going down all around you. I think that they estimated later that this went on for about forty minutes. It seemed like an eternity.

"At one point, our group commander called the high squadron leader to 'tuck it in,' don't be hanging way out there away from the group. He radioed back as to how could he, with his formation behind him. Then he was informed that there were no more planes behind him, all five had gone down. That was the 613th Squadron. My ship was, among others, hit by a

Victor d'Agostino, tail gunner of B-17G 42-31557 of the 401st Bomb Group. JAMES E. WELLS

20mm shell, which had gone through the right horizontal stabilizer, through the fuselage, up against one of the ammunition boxes in the tail and had fallen on the floor behind Charlie Paceley, my tail gunner, without exploding. We radioed in, when we arrived back over Deenethorpe late that afternoon, and the armament people came and defused it and Charlie kept it as a souvenir.

"The loss of seven ships out of one group in one day is a tremendous amount, but it is a miracle that any of us got back. We, the 615th Squadron, were really lucky, since we only lost one ship, the one piloted by Vincent Kaminski. Probably what helped us the most in my squadron was the tight formation that we always maintained. Bill Seawell, our squadron commanding officer had always trained us to fly with wings overlapping. He used to say that if you don't, you don't belong in the 615th Squadron."[38]

Flying in the element just in front of Dan Knight was 2nd Lt. Edwin A. Post in B-17G 42-102674. During the furious fighter attacks, the ball turret received a direct hit from a 20mm cannon shell fired by one of the German fighters. The unfortunate occupant of the turret, Staff Sgt. Frank R. Lutzi, until that moment defending his aircraft and crew, was mortally wounded. With great difficulty and care other crewmembers removed him from his battered battle station and made him as comfortable as possible in the radio

Leo C. Cass was last seen firing his right waist gun of B-17G 42-31557.
FRANKLIN D. CASS

room of the bomber, where he soon died. Unhesitatingly, the radio operator, Tech Sgt. Charles F. Casner, climbed into the damaged, blood-spattered ball turret, and stayed there during the fighter attacks, and until the formation had left the enemy coast, with the sub-zero gale rushing through the holes in the Plexiglas. For this gallant action, he was awarded a Distinguished Flying Cross upon return in England.

The next aircraft to go down were two B-17s flying in the already hard hit high squadron of the 401st Bomb Group. The first of the two to fall was *Lonesome Polecat* (42-102581). It was flying in the number four position and was piloted by 1st Lt. Paul F. Scharff, another experienced pilot in the Group. The crew had already lost both its wingmen, piloted by Lieutenant Keith and Lieutenant Protz, before the target.

Scharff's tail gunner was Staff Sgt. James M. Smallin, who recalled: "Our crew was grouped in the twenty-four to twenty-eight mission range, except for Lt. Robert E. Hoover, our bombardier, who was wounded in a fighter attack over France and missed about ten missions. I am not sure about Staff Sgt. Roscoe D. Tomlinson, the left waist gunner, who came to our crew as a replacement for Sgt Leking, who was shot down and killed with Lieutenant Sheahan's crew on 2 March over Frankfurt. As we approached the initial point, the co-pilot, Lt. Charles A. Eckert, was monitoring the fighter channel and over the intercom reported heavy fighter activity over and around the target area. By this time, we could see heavy and apparently accurate flak over the target, as many planes finishing the bomb run were trailing black smoke, indicative of an oil fire in at least one or more engines. For whatever reason, we were crowded off the initial point and I heard Lieutenant Sharff tell the co-pilot over the intercom we would have to go around again.

"About this time the fighter attacks began. We were never sure how many German planes were in the area, but we estimated fifty to sixty fighters at a time made two firing passes at us by the time we came around to the initial point again and the attacks were continuous to the heavy flak area. All were head-on firing passes and at close range. Obviously veteran fighter pilots, at least those heading the attacks. I was the tail gunner and could feel the 20mm cannon shells hitting the plane, but to my knowledge we apparently suffered no severe damage from the fighter attacks before or during the bomb run. The flak was every bit as accurate as we had thought it was. As we came close to the bomb release, I could hear the anti-aircraft shells explode and feel the flak hitting the bomber, but again there was no apparent damage. Immediately after bombs away, the radio operator, Sgt Robert C. Strong, checked the bomb bay and reported three bombs still in the bomb racks. Whether damage from fighter attacks or antiaircraft fire prevented their release, no one will ever know.

The crew of B-17G 42-102580 of the 401st Bomb Group. Back row, left to right: William F. Protz, pilot (POW); John J. Maloney, co-pilot (KIA on Keith's crew); Alvin J. Stiegel, navigator (KIA); and Sam B. Bennett, bombardier (KIA). Front row, left to right: Jim K. Morrow, engineer (KIA); Albert P. Reinhardt, left waist gunner (POW); Wayne W. Wicks, radio operator (KIA); James C. Appleby, tail gunner (POW); Glenn I. Cliff, right waist gunner (POW); and Frank S. Bartak, ball turret gunner (POW). On 28 May, Maloney was replaced by Richard S. Barnett, who was killed. Maloney flew as co-pilot in the crew of Lt. Walter Keith and was also killed. WILLIAM F. PROTZ

"Sergeant Strong had just released the talk button when Lieutenant Hoover reported another massed fighter attack was coming and this time they were on target. With all seven forward-firing .50-caliber machine guns going and the 20mm shells hitting the plane, I wondered if it was going to come apart. Number two and three engines caught fire and shut down immediately. The aircraft made a slight climbing turn to the left and threatened to stall out; although the stall alarm never went off. Lieutenant Scharff immediately requested assistance, saying his arm had been shot off and he was bleeding to death. The next voice on the intercom was that of Lt. Bernard Schwartz, the navigator, giving the order to bail out. What had transpired forward of the bomb bay, I was able to piece together in the prisoner of war camp. Lieutenant Eckert, the co-pilot, had been killed instantly, the top of his head had been blown off and he suffered wounds in the chest area. Lieutenant Scharff had his arm blown off, apparently so close to the shoulder that a tourniquet could not be applied. Tech Sgt. Robert X. Karl, the engineer, was temporarily blinded by shattered glass from the top turret gun sight and unable to see what was going on. He left the ship through the bomb bay. Lieutenants Schwartz and Hoover bailed Lieutenant Scharff out through the nose escape hatch, but due to the loss of blood Lieutenant Schwartz didn't think he would live long enough to reach the ground. That left the two up front and somehow Lieutenant Hoover didn't get out.

"When I heard the bail out order, I snapped on my chest chute and opened the door by the tail wheel and saw all four gunners lined up at the rear door, all with chest chutes on and all four were apparently all right. Sgt. Frederick G. Pynigar was the first in line. He pulled the emergency T-handle on the door, kicked the door and jumped. I did the same with the escape hatch in the tail section and followed him out. I never saw Sergeant Tomlinson again. It's almost certain some of the fighters came around again to finish the job. It's possible. Lieutenant Hoover and Sergeant Tomlinson apparently were both killed while still in the plane, before they could get out. However it is my personal belief that both were killed by hostile German civilians after they bailed out."[39]

This last statement of James Smallin is supported by the experience of some other crewmembers: "When I landed, a crowd of armed civilians gave me quite a beating and may have gone further if a couple of soldiers had not stopped them and took me in. The left waist gunner may not have been so lucky as myself."

"I saw all enlisted men, except Sergeant Tomlinson, at the prison of the Magdeburg airfield after my own capture by the Germans. Sergeant Karl had severe abrasions about the head and eyes, and Sergeant Bedell had been beaten by German civilians about the face. The others were in exhausted condition from lack of food and water."[40]

Right waist gunner Sgt. Frederick Pynigar recounted: "The pilot, when we were getting hit from the front, would pull the nose up. This time it didn't work. The co-pilot was killed and the pilot badly wounded. The right outboard engine was on fire. The pilot must have put the plane on automatic pilot because it was going around in circles. I got orders from the navigator to bail out. I made sure the ball turret gunner was out. I'm afraid of heights, hate elevators, can't look out windows more than two stories, and can't watch TV with guys fighting on girders. I did not have second thoughts about this. I'd seen too many ships blown up. I snapped on my parachute, went to the side door and pulled the emergency cord, nothing happened, jumped on the door, again nothing happened, then I thought to open the door handle and it flew off. I bowed to the tail gunner at his door to go first, he waved me out. I dove out and was hit with hot oil from the engine. I delayed my jump, I looked up and all I could see was bomb bay doors open and all I could hope was that they wouldn't let them go until I was out of there. When houses began to take shape, I thought it was time to pull the rip cord, it didn't pull, then I gave it a big yank and the chute opened up. We had been warned to have the parachute straps tight. I still got a real jolt when it opened. We had been instructed to pull on the shroud lines to steer, I saw a wooded area and that's where I went. I hung up in the trees about three feet off the ground. I had a knife in my jump suit pocket and cut the lines and took off on the run. I was able to hide and remain free for a day-and-a-half."[41]

Lonesome Polecat crashed at 1424 hours at Glienicke, thirty-six kilometers east of Burg, near Magdeburg. But events in the nose of the aircraft went somewhat differently to how Smallin reconstructed in the prisoner of war camp. The same burst of fire that killed co-pilot Eckert, had indeed severely wounded pilot Scharff. He lost one of his arms, just below the elbow and had several other wounds in his body.

The sights of air battle. This photo and the five that follow come from the private album of Friedrich Keller, the *Gruppenkommandeur* of II./JG 27. They were taken on 12 May, the day of the first "oil strike," and give a graphic example of a scene oft repeated on 28 May, the day of the next oil strike. In this photo, a B-17 without its tail section in its death throes. It is B-17G 42-97382 of the 96th Bomb Group, which collided with B-17G 42-102452 during a fighter attack. Only three crewmembers—the radio operator and both waist gunners—got out. In the other B-17, the navigator and bombardier were killed; the others bailed out.

With a tremendous explosion, the bombs and fuel explode when the aircraft hits the ground.

German soldiers run toward the American airman, who has just touched the ground, his canopy still catching the wind.

Mixed emotions show on the American's face as he picks up his chute. He is a prisoner of war now, but probably realizes that others of his crew have perished.
FRIEDRICH KELLER VIA JEAN LOUIS ROBA

Through the smoke, a parachute appears with a lucky crewmember.

Wreckage fell close to the airbase at Merzhausen, where
II./JG 27 was stationed in May
1944. A ground crewmember
takes cover behind a Bf 109, but
is curious enough to keep
watching the events.

A tourniquet was quickly applied by engineer Karl, himself also
wounded, and then Scharff was assisted from the cockpit area into the nose
of the aircraft. After fastening his chute, the escape hatch was opened to bail
out. But now there were three men in the cramped nose area of the aircraft.
Since Scharff was between bombardier Hoover and navigator Schwartz and
Schwartz in turn was between Scharff and the escape hatch, Schwartz had to
bail out first. This he did safely, assuming that the other two would follow
him out. That is also the story that was picked up by James Smallin. But
when the Germans found the wreckage of *Lonesome Polecat*, they found the
remains of three crewmembers aboard. These were later identified as the
bodies of Eckert, Scharff, and Hoover, who had apparently not made it out
of the hatch after Schwartz. The aircraft may have entered a spin, prevent-
ing Scharff and Hoover from getting to the exit or Scharff may have passed
out, blocking Hoover's escape route. Whatever the reason, together with the
death of Tomlinson, possibly at the hands of someone on the ground, four
of the crew perished, and six were made prisoners of war.

Next, the aircraft in the number three position of the same squadron
went down, which reduced the strength of this squadron to only two
bombers. Tail gunner Robert V. Kerr, aboard *Fitch's Bandwagon* leading this
beleaguered high squadron, recounted this stage of the attacks in his diary:

"My attention was attracted by a couple of Fw 190s that circled around to come up from behind to pick off the stragglers. Now, in the lull and in spite of it all, I noticed only two B-17s still with us—Hammond in one and Keith in the other.* Hammond was about 100 yards behind us and a little to our right and Keith was about 150 yards away at about eight o'clock when two Fw 190s came up on Hammond's tail and let go with their 20mm and then turned over toward Keith. I drew a bead on the second one and cut loose with both barrels and I began to wish I had my steel helmet on, after I had seen the 20mm exploding around Hammond's ship. (While all the fighters were coming through, my steel helmet kept coming down over my eyes, since there was no liner in it to keep it in place; I got mad in the excitement and had yanked it off and threw it down on the catwalk behind me).

"As the Fw 190 moved over near Keith's ship, I turned around to see where my helmet was. I reached back to drag it toward me with my foot, but it rolled further down the catwalk toward the escape hatch and out of my reach. Keith now moved closer to Hammond but was lagging 100 feet or so behind him as the Fw 190 circled and came in for another attack. Both Keith and Hammond were flying a little lower than we were, with Keith slightly below Hammond, as the 20mm started bursting around them again from the Fw 190 on their tail. Some of the shells went past them and started exploding around us. After one exploded practically in my face, I decided to put that helmet back on my head, where it belonged. I stopped shooting and jerked all the cords loose, as well as the oxygen hose and crawled up and got the helmet, threw it back by the ammunition box, then crawled into position and put on the liner and the helmet over it. I connected the ear phones and oxygen hose and resumed shooting.

"I noticed that both Keith and Hammond seemed to be getting several hits and there were still a couple of Fw 190s on their tail. I noticed one turn over on its back and dive down toward five o'clock after making its pass. We were right in the line of fire of the Fw 190 firing at Keith and Hammond and 20 mm's seemed to be exploding all around us. I noticed one string of flashes coming right toward us but they stopped just before they reached us. Keith was now dropping behind and over toward seven o'clock, and I saw the Fw 190 coming up on his tail again. I drew a bead and was just waiting to get a little closer, when I heard 'tail gunner from navigator' over the interphone. I didn't answer and when it was repeated a few seconds later I said, 'Just a minute—I'm going to be shooting.' He said apologetically, 'OK, OK.'

---

* In this account in his diary, Kerr mentions Keith as being the last to fall from the squadron. However, official group reports show that most probably Windham's crew was the last to go down. This view is supported by the author. However, Kerr's account is presented unchanged.

III./Jagdgeschwader 27
8. Staffel
(Truppenteil)

O. U. , den 31. . 1944
(Ort, Datum)

V.N.E. **A.C.M.**

3/475/44

Abschußmeldung, Zerstörungsmeldung

1. Zeit (Tag, Stunde, Minute) und Gegend des Absturzes: **28. 5. 1944, 14.25 Uhr, etwa S- SW Zerbst**

Höhe: **7500 m**

2. Durch wen ist der Abschuß / Zerstörung erfolgt? **Leutnant Ottnad**

3. Flugzeugtyp des abgeschossenen Flugzeuges: **Fortess II**

4. Staatsangehörigkeit des Gegners: **amerikanisch**

Werknummern bzw. Kennzeichen: **./.**

5. Art der Vernichtung: **durch Beschuss**

   a) Flammen mit dunkler Fahne, Flammen mit heller Fahne

   b) Einzelteile weggeflogen, abmontiert (Art der Teile erläutern) auseinandergeplatzt

   c) zur Landung gezwungen (diesseits der Front, glatt bzw. mit Bruch)

   d) jenseits der Front am Boden in Brand geschossen.

6. Art des Aufschlages (nur wenn dieser beobachtet werden konnte) **nicht beobachtet**

   a) diesseits oder jenseits der Front

   b) senkrecht, in flachem Winkel, Aufschlagbrand, Staubwolke

   c) nicht beobachtet, warum nicht? **wegen Fallschirmabsprung**

7. Schicksal der Insassen (tot, mit Fallschirm abgesprungen, nicht beobachtet) **./.**

8. Gefechtsbericht des Schützen ist in der Anlage beigefügt

9. Zeugen:

   a) Luft **Feldw. Büsen (7.Staffel)**

   b) Erde

10. Anzahl der Angriffe, die auf das feindliche Flugzeug gemacht wurden: **1 Angriff**

11. Richtung, aus der die einzelnen Angriffe erfolgten: **von vorne**

12. Entfernung, aus der der Abschuß erfolgte: **4oo - 2oo m**

13. Takt. Position, aus der der Abschuß angesetzt wurde: **Staffelführer**

14. Ist einer der feindlichen Bordschützen kampfunfähig gemacht worden? **./.**

15. Verwandte Munitionsart: **M.-Mun.,Pz.Spr.Gr.,Br.Spr.Gr.Patr.**

16. Munitionsverbrauch: **unbekannt**

17. Art und Anzahl der Waffen, die bei dem Abschuß gebraucht wurden: **MK 1o8, 2 MG 151, 2 MG 131**

18. Typ der eigenen Maschine (z. B. Me 109 E mit 2 Kanonen und 2 M.G.): **Bf 1o9 G-6/U4**

19. Weiteres taktisch oder technisch Bemerkenswertes:

20. Treffer in der eigenen Maschine: **Motortreffer (Fallschirmabsprung)**

21. Beteiligung weiterer Einheiten (auch Flak):

eing 6/4

Leutnant u. stellv. Staffelfüh
(Unterschrift)

Zu Ziffer 5-7 Zutreffendes zu unterstreichen.

The first page of the combat report that *Leutnant* Alexander Ottnad submitted following his mission on 28 May. He was awarded the destruction of the B-17 flown by Lt. William Protz of the 401st Bomb Group. In the same action, he had to bail out of his Bf 109. NATIONAL ARCHIVES

I then cut loose on the Fw 190, but he was a little too far away for me. It didn't look like Keith's tail gunner was firing at all.*

"When the Fw began getting pretty close to Keith I quit firing. A couple more fighters were going after Hammond, so I fired on them whenever I could get an opening and they weren't too close to Hammond's ship. I do not remember seeing Keith's ship again, the last I saw of it, it was still flying straight and level, although losing altitude. A few minutes later someone said that there were men bailing out of a B-17 at about ten o'clock and about a minute later I looked down below us on our left and saw four chutes floating down, which I thought to be of Keith's ship. Someone told me later that Keith's ship had a big hole through the radio room and one through the vertical stabilizer big enough to drive a jeep through.** Someone else said that the last they saw of Keith's ship it was doing things that even a fighter shouldn't do. But apparently this was after they had bailed out."[42]

The bomber Kerr saw being shot down by Fw 190s was the B-17G *BTO in the ETO* (42-102647). It was piloted by 2nd Lt. Frederick H. Windham and 2nd Lt. Donald P. Ferguson. The navigator was 2nd Lt. Carl T. Floto, who, like Robert Kerr, served on Walter Keith's original crew, which crashed into the village of Deenethorpe in December 1943.

Floto, who was badly wounded during this crash, returned to combat duty, and since the Keith crew was split up, he now served as navigator on Windham's crew. He reported after the war: "Flak was encountered near the initial point, at which time a burst outside the plane knocked out number three engine and killed co-pilot Ferguson instantly. Ship was subsequently hit by Me 109s and other German fighters. Part of the oxygen system had been knocked out by the flak burst and I was talking with the tail gunner, Sgt. Floyd O. Miller, and a waist gunner about the auxiliary supply. When the ship was hit by fighter fire, the tail gunner ceased talking and efforts to contact him over the interphone were fruitless. I asked one of the enlisted men to see about him, but in the confusion and excitement, I received no definite report regarding Miller. Immediately afterwards it became necessary to bail out. We bailed out a little north-east of the target area. That same evening I was accompanied in my jail by Windham, bombardier Angelo J. Melito, engineer Robert W. Rittmaier, and right waist gunner Clyde E. Irelan. All of these men were liberated in April 1945 and returned to the United States."[43]

---

* This supports the view that this was not Lieutenant Keith's B-17, but that of Lieutenant Windham. The latter's tail gunner was killed, whereas Keith's tail gunner was taken prisoner.

** Windham's radio operator was killed in action, whereas Keith's radio operator was made prisoner of war.

Second Lt. Robert J. Enstad, co-pilot of B-17G 42-97073. Miraculously, he survived the demise of his bomber and was made prisoner of war.
ROBERT J. ENSTAD

The following seven photos show crewmembers of B-17G 42-97073 of the 401st Bomb Group. All were killed in action on 28 May. ROBERT J. ENSTAD

Tech Sgt. Jack D. Agee, engineer.

1st Lt. J. Dee Black, navigator.

Staff Sgt. Larry R. Cooper, radio-operator.

Staff Sgt. William M. May, left waist gunner.

Staff Sgt. Everett M. Bushendorf, right waist gunner.

Staff Sgt. Harold Hertzan, tail gunner.   Sgt Joe R. Johnson, ball turret gunner.

BTO in the ETO crashed near the village of Niemegk, where the five killed crewmembers were interred on 29 May. Most probably, their assailants were fighter pilots of JG 27. Flying in an Me 109G-6 of 8./JG 27 was *Obergefreiter* Reuter. He reported: "After take off from Goetzendorf-Leitha at 1247 hours, we discovered a formation of Fortress II in the Magdeburg area around 1420 hours, flying at 7,200 meters. I was flying as wingman to *Unteroffizier* Burkel. During our second attack, the first one from behind, I was shooting at the fourth Fortress from right and observed after my first burst, bright flames on the far left engine and after some more bursts, black smoke coming from the inner left engine. The enemy aircraft then dove away from the formation at an angle of about 15 degrees. All this happened about forty kilometers northeast of Magdeburg. I couldn't watch the events any further, since I had to follow my element leader, *Unteroffizier* Burkel. Landing followed on Zerbst airfield."[44]

Only two aircraft were now left in the high squadron of the 401st Bomb Group. Leading this pitiful remnant was B-17G *Fitch's Bandwagon* (42-107043), flown by Lawrence E. Fitchett. The other bomber was B-17G *Lady Jane* (42-107009), piloted by 2nd Lt. Wardlaw M. Hammond. Fitchett's tail gunner Robert V. Kerr, with his grandstand view of all the events in the Squadron, recorded the following about this episode of the battle in his diary: "Intermittently, between fighter attacks, I took time to notice flak coming up and there was probably a lot that came up that I didn't notice, being preoccupied with fighters. At one time, we got several close bursts and especially one real large burst near the tail which really jarred the ship, the black smoke curling upward as it went past my window. At one time during the lull in the fighter attacks I called on the interphone and asked if anyone knew what we were doing up here, going around in circles. Either the navigator or pilot answered that he didn't know, and he'd like to know himself.

"Hammond began to drop behind a little. I noticed the cowling knocked off number one engine and a piece of it was hanging, being held there by the wind. His number one prop was feathered. I began to wonder why Fitchett didn't move us into another formation—we now had only one ship straggling behind us and it looked like we were all alone. Finally, Hank Kelsen asked the pilot why he didn't get up into the formation ahead, and Fitchett said, 'Let them catch up with us—we're supposed to be leading.' Hank replied, 'There's nobody behind us.' The pilot called me and asked how many ships we had behind us, and I said, 'One—there is just one ship behind us, and it has number one engine feathered—I think it is Hammond.' Fitchett replied, 'Roger,' and I could feel the ship pick up speed as we moved up into the formation ahead of us. Watched Hammond as he again caught up, but then he dropped out. I told the navigator that he was dropping further and further behind and he said to keep my eye on him. I thought I could see fighters around the ship, then it disappeared from view."[45]

B-17G *Bonnie Donnie* 42-31034 of the 401st Bomb Group after a belly-landing at Deenethorpe on 4 March 1944. She was repaired and flew again, but was finally lost on 28 May. VIC MASLEN

Wardlaw Hammond had started as co-pilot on Walter Keith's crew and was, just like Carl Floto and Robert Kerr, on the crew during the crash in Deenethorpe village. He was upgraded to first pilot and now had a crew of his own. He recalls: "The German fighters started firing cannon before meeting our formation. The 20mm cannon shell, which explodes at its maximum range of about 1,000 yards, created a firefly-like cloud that flashed through our formation just before their planes passed over, through, and under us with cannon continuously firing. I felt a shudder in the aircraft and looked out at the left outboard engine. The top half of the cowling was missing and there was a large hole in the top of the wing behind that engine. The aircraft lurched over to the left, and I instructed Lt. Dene C. Gober, the bombardier, over the intercom to dump the bomb load. He replied: 'I already have.' The ball turret gunner told me that the upper half of the cowling was dangling below the engine. It was scooping up the air creating a very large drag which made it impossible for us to maintain the necessary speed to stay in formation. Visually inspecting the damaged engine, I noticed large quantities of oil leaking out where one of the cylinders used to be. The co-pilot started to feather the damaged engine, but I stayed his hand, saying: 'We still have oil pressure, and we can get ten to twenty minutes out of that engine before it runs out of oil and starts to seize up.' We were losing altitude at about 150 feet per minute, but I stayed under our Group, turning inside of them at each turn to keep from lagging too far behind so that we would be protected by their ball turret guns. We soon lost the formation completely."[46]

The rest of the adventurous journey of *Lady Jane* and her crew will be covered later in this chapter.

The lead group, the 457th Bomb Group, was not able to escape the fierce fighter attacks. Flying as deputy lead navigator in H2X-equipped B-17G 42-97686 was 1st Lt. William H. Dupont, who recorded the events the next day in his diary: "Yesterday, I prayed for all the milk runs that I have had to date. It was a PFF mission so I flew with a strange crew. We were attacking a target near Leipzig at Dessau and about 100 miles from the target our fighter escort just suddenly disappeared. We were about fifteen minutes late so it was our own fault because the fighters have a schedule to make, too. The Germans are using a new technique now that seems to work pretty well. They fly in formation of about fifty or one hundred planes and never attack singly any more. The formation will fly parallel to you, just out of range of our guns and suddenly the whole formation will turn into you and all attack at once.

"We were flying along wondering where our escort was when a formation of about thirty planes appeared on our left and started to creep up to attack. We weren't very worried because we had fifty planes in our own formation and thirteen guns per plane give us 650 machine guns for our own protection. It was then I noticed another formation of about seventy-five fighters on our right doing exactly the same thing. It was then that I gave up hope completely. First, the formation on our left would come thru under or over our formation and start forming on the other side. Then the seventy-five planes on the right would attack doing the same thing.

"I was in the deputy wing lead position, and Pat Henry was alongside me in the lead [see reference to Henry later in this chapter]. A 20mm shell hit their number three engine and set it on fire and the first gruesome thought that occurred to me was that I was the new squadron navigator after Pat went down. Then it dawned on me that I wasn't going to get home either. Those fighters would knock down at least two Forts every time they came thru. We were getting our share of Jerries too but rapid calculation showed that they could outlast us. This went on for about twenty minutes and I knew the entire fifty airplanes would be annihilated before long when suddenly the fighters left us. We didn't know why at the time but before long we saw the beautiful double vapor trails above us made by our little friends, the P-38s. There weren't very many of them, but not very many are necessary."[47]

The crew of *Bonnie Donnie* of the 401st Bomb Group. Back row, left to right: Hugh D. Russell, waist gunner (KIA); Alfred J. Morini, ball turret gunner (POW); Michael Lefkin, tail gunner (KIA); and Thomas B. Montgomery, bombardier (POW). Middle row, left to right: Douglas H. McKinnon, co-pilot (POW); George E. West, pilot (KIA); and Lloyd A. Nutter, navigator (POW). Front row, left to right: Sergeant Stewart, waist gunner (not on 28 May mission); Robert L. Andrus, radio operator (POW); and Francis L. Russell, engineer (POW). LLOYD A. NUTTER

First hit in the lead group was B-17G 42-31520, piloted by 1st Lt. Clyde B. Knipfer, flying as number five in the low squadron. Again, this was a very experienced pilot and crew, well on their way to finishing their tours of operations. Later in 1944, bombardier 2nd Lt. Stanley V. Gray wrote in his diary: "At briefing, they said all indications were that there would be intense fighter attacks, as one of the last mass opposition attacks of the enemy. But as S-2 [Intelligence] was or at least has been wrong on several other occasions, we didn't pay much attention to it. So we started out over the Channel toward the coast. George's [navigator George R. Derdzinski] right gun was jammed and I spent most of the trip to the coast stripping it and trying to fix it. We finally got it to fire a few bursts. But then it jammed again and would only fire single shots. George only got to fire a couple of times in all the previous missions so we forgot it.

"We hit a little flak on the coast as usual and a little later on along the course. We heard nothing of fighter attacks over VHF so we felt safe as we could be. We were just about ten minutes off the initial point when a group of fighters appeared at three o'clock level. They proved to be enemy fighters and had evidently driven off our fighters beforehand. They flew along with us for about ten minutes. They seemed to be forming or just plain getting up nerve. Usually a fighter attack will come in or go on. But these fellows just flew along. We later figured they were probably flying slow to let the larger ships catch up into battle formation. I counted fifty-two and one of the crew counted sixty in that one group. They were made up of all types, Me 109s, Fw 190s, Ju 88s, Me 110s, and Me 210s.

Second Lt. Dan C. Knight, pilot of B-17G *Mary Alice* (42-31983) of the 401st Bomb Group, who flew in the number four position of the low squadron. DAN C. KNIGHT

"We came onto the initial point and opened our bomb bay doors. By this time the group of fighters was about at 1 o'clock flying parallel to our course. As we turned onto our run, which made us turn at an approximate 45-degree angle into the fighters, they turned into us and came in on us. The Me 109s came first, then the Fw 190s with the 110s and 210s sitting back and letting go with rockets and 20mm. We opened fire with everything we had, that is all except George. He was firing his single shot machine gun with all he had. We were in the number five position so we caught the main attack. The 20mm were bursting all around us, but mainly in front of us. Thank God we weren't fifty feet ahead of our flight position. Knipfer turned slightly into the fighters and lowered one wing.

"Just then we caught one or more 20mm incendiaries in our left wing, just aft of number two engine. A fire developed immediately in the main gas tank. Knipfer rang the bail out bell and set the ship on automatic pilot in a slow turn to the right. In the nose George and I had not heard the bell and were still shooting. I saw the fire and Richard A. Bruha, the co-pilot, told me to lighten the load. I dropped the bombs and tried to contact Knipfer. In the meantime Bruha had left his seat and opened the escape hatch in the bombardiers compartment. He saw George and I still in the nose, so came up to tell us to get out. Knipfer followed him, but bailed out the hatch. Bruha then did not want to bail out and since we hadn't exploded by then, went back to the cockpit and took it off AFCE [automatic flight control equipment] and headed west.

"George tried to find a map, but they were too scattered to do any good. So we gave Bruha a general heading and started praying. The fire was then blazing in a beautiful orange. I went to the cockpit to help Bruha if I could. He was off interphone and the rest of the crew was screaming for information. I tried my best to give it to them. Bruha was then trying to put the fire out by diving the ship. Number two engine was feathered by then. We leveled out at about 10,000 feet and headed home in an effort to get to France before we crashed, so that we might get help in an escape. We ran into some flak but nothing serious.

"As near as I can figure out now, it was about forty-five minutes after we were hit that the fire began eating into the main spar and heating up the rest of the gas and we decided that we could never make it much more. We had lived long enough on borrowed time. I informed the remaining crewmembers to bail out when they wished and to try and hit a forested area. Goldstein and Waltho left then. Bendino left later. Furrie was going out of the ball. The left wing showed definite signs of strain and began to fold up from the pressure. Voit then left the nose, then the remainder of us left in turn. The ship flew for a while in a circle, then the wing came off and it exploded, putting an end to a damned good B-17 and my last touch of American homeland for some time to come."[48]

The crew of Lt. Claude M. Kolb of the 401st Bomb Group. This crew was shot down, and all were made prisoners of war on a 6 March 1944 mission to Berlin, excluding the man kneeling at far right, 2nd Lt. Milton F. Maloney, co-pilot, and the third man standing from the left, Staff Sgt. Frank R. Lutzi, ball turret gunner. Maloney continued and flew fifty-five missions in the European theater. Lutzi was killed in action on 28 May, when the ball turret of B-17G 42-102674, piloted by Lt. Edwin A. Post, received a direct hit from a 20mm shell. He is buried at the Cambridge American Cemetery and Memorial in England. CLAUDE M. KOLB

The distance between the landing places of the crewmembers, left the Germans with a great intelligence puzzle regarding the aircraft to which they had belonged. While the first crewmembers had left the bomber and were captured a little south of Quedlinburg, others came down in the vicinity of Fulda, nearly 200 kilometers farther. Their bomber finally crashed at 1550 hours near Doellbach, eighteen kilometers southwest of Fulda and all its occupants were made prisoner of war.

In the same low squadron, 2nd Lt. William L. Brackley and his crew occupied the number three position in B-17G *Miss Cue* (42-31505). Brackley recalled: "The flak was intense, and contrary to their usual attacks enemy fighters pressed attacks in the thick of it. While we were on the bomb run, a half-dozen Fw 190s lined up abreast at our altitude, making a frontal assault. Glancing forward from my formation flying, I saw them coming, with cannons blinking in a grim code 'To whom it may concern!' A split second later we were hit, very hard! In that instant, number one engine was lost, afire and burning furiously. Fortunately, feathering it eventually put out the fire.

The turbo-supercharger and related induction system on number three engine were shot away. At high altitude, it delivered little power, barely enough to overcome its own drag.

"A 20mm cannon shell penetrated the cockpit from the front, passing between my co-pilot and me. It struck Sam Bernstein my top turret gunner, in the groin and exploded. He brushed my arm when he fell down the crawl way to the deck below the cockpit floor, landing in a heap on the nose hatch. Providence prevented the shell from exploding as it entered the cockpit. Our battle damage was critical. The group had not yet released its bombs, and I was unable to maintain altitude on two engines. I directed my bombardier to jettison our bombs immediately, and in the same breath asked my navigator to look after Sam. He soon reported that he was certain Sam was dead. I presumed as much, the interior of the cockpit was heavily spattered with blood and bits of flesh."[49]

Leading the high squadron of the 457th Bomb Group was 2nd Lt. Benny M. Flowers in B-17G *Delayed Lady II* (42-32079). His bombardier, 2nd Lt. John J. Gides, was hit in the head by a small-caliber bullet on the bomb

The crew of B-17G *Lonesome Polecat* (42-102581) of the 401st Bomb Group. Back row, left to right: Paul F. Scharff, pilot (KIA); Charles A. Eckert, co-pilot (KIA); Robert E. Hoover, bombardier (KIA); Bernard Schwartz, navigator (POW); and Sergeant Brown, radio operator (not on 28 May mission). Front row, left to right: Charles H. Bedell, ball turret gunner (POW); Frederick G. Pynigar, right waist gunner (POW); Robert X. Karl, engineer (POW); James M. Smallin, tail gunner (POW); and Sgt. Roger T. Leking (KIA, 2 March 1944]. JAMES M. SMALLIN

run. As a result of the concussion sustained from the bullet, he accidentally hit the toggle switch for his bomb load. Upon seeing the lead aircraft of the high squadron releasing its bombs, the entire low squadron released theirs as well, all bombs exploding harmlessly in the open fields below. The left waist gunner of the *Delayed Lady II*, Victor U. Meador, went up front and bandaged the head of the badly wounded Lieutenant Gides and held an oxygen mask to Gides's face for the duration of the return flight to Glatton.

Hit during the first fighter pass was B-17G *Oh Kay* (42-97470), flying number six position in the lead squadron. It was piloted by Lt. Bernard V. Connor and Lt. John W. Norton. The latter recalled: "We just turned on the bomb run when I saw, off our right wing what seemed to be a cloud of German fighters. I pointed them out to the pilot, who then informed me there were many on our left side too. We were hit on their first pass and it seemed as if, with us, half the Eighth Air Force left the formation with battle damage. We held our bombs, since there was a target of opportunity dead ahead. As we didn't carry a bomb sight, our bombardier, Morris F. Swerdlove, dropped them when he thought it was about right.

"We levelled the plane off at 10,000 feet with everything under control. Navigator Glen Thornton gave us a heading home and I was calling for fighter escort. Then we were picked up by three P-38s who were covering another B-17 which was flying below us with three engines going. We were down to two engines then, so I called the fighters and said: 'Hey, what about us? We only have two engines.' Then they left the other B-17 and came up and stayed with us until they ran low on fuel. On the way out we ran into some accurate flak that burst at just our altitude and off to our left, so we turned right until we flew at about 90 degrees from our original course and until we were out of their range. Then we resumed our heading for home and started to throw flak suits, ammunition, guns and oxygen bottles out. We were down to 2,000 feet and just hoping the engines would last. What we didn't understand was why the German fighters never came back. They had plenty of time to land, refuel and rearm and take off again to catch us and the others limping home. Luckily they didn't and we made it back to Glatton."[50]

The P-38s that came to the rescue belonged to the 364th Fighter Group from Honington. The group was up for its second mission of the day and scheduled to provide escort to stragglers.

One of the pilots was Lt. Max Woolley, who recalled: "We crossed the coastline at the southwestern tip of Schouwen Island, taking a southerly course of 165 degrees. The German gunners below fired their usual barrage of flak, keeping us alert to our ten seconds left, ten seconds right, ten seconds down, and ten seconds up flight, to minimize the possibility of being hit. We commenced to lose altitude and look for stragglers after leaving the coastal batteries. German fighter pilots were constantly on the lookout for stragglers knowing that they were damaged and easy prey. It was imperative that we locate any stragglers as soon as possible.

"Off to our right was the haze from Gent, with Brussels about twenty miles southeast of our position. However, there were no stragglers in the area. With Mons up ahead we made a 90-degree turn to the left, in hopes of intersecting a straggler if he were heading south, before he could get near the German fighter bases in northern France. Now flying at 11,000 feet altitude with no stragglers in the area, we could see the Sambre river as it wound its way through the green Belgian countryside. In the bend of the river before reaching Namur was Charleroi.

"Little did I realize at this time that in thirty days from this date on 27 June, my plane would be the target for a well-aimed projectile from German flak gunners, after leaving our target in the Sedan-Nancy area. I would be forced to bail out and while descending in my chute, be shot by German soldiers. Heading in an easterly direction and seeing no stragglers, we made a 140 degree left turn about twenty miles west of Liege. Now flying in a northwesterly direction, we were in hopes that a straggler would be somewhere within the day's bomber tracks. About fifteen minutes later, north of Brussels near Mechelen, a reflection in the sky caught our attention. It was a lone Fort, travelling south at our altitude, apparently lost because of a damaged compass. Flying within several hundred yards of the slow moving plane, we made a steep bank to the left so that the crew could recognize our silhouette as little friends, and not German fighters. We then turned right, and climbing several hundred feet, flew up and over the Fort, while waggling our

Staff Sgt. James M. Smallin, tail gunner of *Lonesome Polecat.* He was shot down and became a prisoner of war on 28 May. JAMES M. SMALLIN

wings, indicating for the lost crew to follow us. We immediately made a 360 degree turn to the right, with the Fort turning to the 290-degree course that we had previously set, flying over the crippled bomber.

"'White Leader to Red Leader, over,' Captain Ford called on the radio. 'This is Red Leader, go ahead, over,' was Lieutenant Sam Phillips's reply. 'Red Flight take the left side; White Flight take the right, over,' was Ford's order. 'Roger, out,' Phillips replied. With the instruction from the brief radio communication, Ford positioned his flight to the right and several hundred feet above the Fort, while Phillips placed our flight at the same altitude on the left side of the straggler. Using a snake like weaving pattern to maintain flying speed, to remain with the straggler for protection, we crossed the Dutch coast near Flushing about twenty-five minutes later. At mid-Channel, having seen no enemy fighters with not too much flak, we waggled our wings and headed for home base, arriving there at 1900 hours. The crew aboard the straggler appeared to be aware of their position, in control of the damaged plane, and on course for their home base."[51]

Also hit by the German fighters near Dessau was B-17G *Black Puff Polly* (42-97067), flying in the number six position of the high squadron. Its crew was also one of the originals, which formed the 457th Bomb Group in the United States, and were now fairly close to finishing their tours. Pilot was 1st Lt. Rudolph M. Stohl and Sgt. William F. Bemus, was the right waist gunner, who recalls: "This day I was flying top turret gunner, since I had traded positions with the engineer Robert C. Kriete. Over the Channel when test firing the twin guns I found that the left solenoid, which pumps the ammunition into the gun was out and I only had my right gun working properly. When we were coming in on the bomb run, we usually had fighter escort and had P-38s that day for the first part. Some P-47s and P-51s were supposed to take over. Evidently when our fighter escort left, the others were late. We had some cloud cover on the right and after a few minutes there came all these German fighters.

"They came out in swarms and in every kind and type. I had never seen that many concentrated at a time. We were flying on the right side of the formation. There was quite a bit of action up front and then there was this Focke-Wulf that barrelled in from up above. I only had the one gun working, and I fired and the ship next to us fired. That Focke-Wulf went straight down, and up to today I don't know who hit him. I think it was the other gunner, because keeping my sight on the fighter wasn't easy with one gun pulling the turret to the right. There was an Me 210 which barrelled in at two o'clock high; he came straight at us and fired at us. He hit both engines on the right, blew a large hole underneath my turret and knocked the tail wheel down. I don't know about the rest of the damage, but I know we couldn't feather the engines that were hit. The bombs were salvoed, but

Lt. Walter B. Keith's original crew in September 1943 at Cutbank, Montana. The crew was split up after a take-off crash on 5 December 1943. Kneeling, third from left, is tail gunner Robert V. Kerr. Standing, far right, is pilot Walter B. Keith. Next to him is co-pilot Wardlaw M. Hammond. Standing far left is navigator Carl T. Floto.
VIC MASLEN

when we tried to close the bomb bay doors, they stayed open. We then jettisoned everything we could, we even dropped the ball turret, flak suits, excess ammunition and some guns, since we were in no shape to fight. The engines on the left were on full steam, but we were losing altitude slowly. We were trying to make the coast and encountered a little flak, which didn't bother us too much.

"Then, near Bremen, we just ran into a mountain of flak and the whole thing just came apart. The flak hit the ship and she just raised up. I was still up in the turret and it seemed that flak directly hit our number three engine, which fell out. The windshield shattered and Stohl rang the bell to get out. Only later I learned that this was the moment that our radio-operator Tech Sgt. Walter W. Wagoner was killed; he received an almost direct hit from an 88mm shell and was pretty badly shot up. He crashed with the ship, but since I did not go backwards, because of the still open bomb bay and only a narrow catwalk available, this was told to me by the others who were in the back of the ship.

"My option was to go out through the bomb bay or the bombardiers hatch, I chose the latter. On my way to the hatch, I noted that I had buckled my chest chute up side down and stopped to correct it and turn it around.

Still the flak was hitting the ship, and suddenly there was a loud explosion and just as I left the escape hatch I was hit by a fragment of flak. The wind blew me straight back, and since we were always told never to pull the chute in the slip stream I pulled my rip cord a little later. When I did, nothing happened, so I gripped the chute with both hands and then it opened. Being so excited my wound didn't hurt much, it just burned a little. I was shot through the groin, the fragment entered one inch on the right side of my spine, it had come out through the left side of my leg and had penetrated my colon. I didn't know at the time, but I was shot pretty bad. I was all wet with blood, and the next thing I knew was that we were shot at from below. I slumped in my chute and the firing seemed to stop. Then I noticed that our ship was coming toward me in a circle, but it missed me by half a block, it levelled out and I thought for a moment it was going back to England without me.

"28 May was a Sunday, and I landed right in front of a church. The cemetery and church were together and I pulled my chute to prevent me from going straight into some tombstones and I hit the ground right in front of the church. Well, then the congregation came out, and I mean really came out. They got around me in a circle; they were scared because they thought I was wearing a .45 pistol. Anyhow, they never touched me, but just shouted and spat at me. Then an officer came up and looked for my pistol, which I didn't have. They brought up a horse-drawn wagon, when a German soldier hit me and broke my nose. God knows I was bleeding bad enough already. They threw me in the wagon over the side and there was my navigator John Millham, who had broken his leg while landing. When we were transported, I told Millham, 'I'm gut shot, and I'm going to die.' He then put his arm around me and said, 'I can smell it,' but told me I would be all right and gave me a real pep talk. We then were brought to a *Luftwaffe* camp, where everyone was kind and I was bandaged there. Millham and I were put in an ambulance and brought to the Saint Josef hospital in Bremen. A surgeon then did a great deal of work on my colon, and he did a perfect job."[52]

Eventually, Bemus recovered and, due to the severity of his wounds, was repatriated during an exchange of prisoners of war. He arrived in the United States on the SS *Gripsholm* in January 1945. The rest of the crew, excluding the dead radio operator, Walter Wagoner, were made prisoners of war and returned home after the war. Wagoner was buried in the cemetery at Bremen-Osterholz.

The now-deserted *Black Puff Polly* crashed at 1604 hours at Mahndorf, close to Bremen. It was to be the most northern geographical location where a bomber crashed during the day's operations. The "mountain of flak" Bemus spoke of was put up by *leichte Flak Abteilung 844* and *leichte Flak*

Abteilung 954 and *schwere Flak Abteilung 606,* all of whom had their batteries in the vicinity of Bremen.

Also in the high squadron was 2nd Lt. Jonathan M. Herbold in B-17G *Rampant Pansy* (42-107034). His right waist gunner, Charles D. Shebell, recalls: "The radio operator Richard R. Hazelhurst was between me and the other waist gunner, David V. Scharff, putting out chaff through a hole in the floor in front of the ball turret. I was watching for fighters in my view when I heard an explosion and a bump against me. At first, I thought it was the radio operator but no, the fighters got us. It took only seconds to check damage—the waist of the ship was a mess. The right waist window was shot out and the machine gun was hanging in its mount with a belt of ammo in it. Scharff and Hazelhurst were on their feet, so I felt better.

"The escape hatch was swinging open and side of the ship was torn into strips of aluminum, but we could walk around with care. One parachute opened up with the explosion. I looked at my feet where my chute and

The crew of Lt. Frederick H. Windham was pictured in early January 1944 at Rapid City, South Dakota. Unfortunately, all but two of the men on the picture (Sgt. Jose G. Garcia, kneeling at far right, and Lt. Angelo J. Melito, standing at far right) are unidentified. Windham's crew arrived at the 401st Bomb Group with three officers, all of whom were on the ship on 28 May. As the original navigator was apparently left behind, the crew was strengthened by Lt. Carl Floto. Five out of six original enlisted men were on the fateful 28 May mission. Only Sgt. C. S. Stephens was replaced by Staff Sgt. Floyd O. Miller. So eight out of ten men in this picture were flying in *BTO* in the ETO when the B-17 went down over Germany. GIL VILLALPANDO

shoes were and there was a hole about four inches wide and my fatigue hat lying next to it was ripped to shreds. The ball turret gunner, Johnny Miller, wanted to get out of his turret, but a spent cartridge blocked the gear ring. I got that out and he got out to be with us. I reported the damage to the flight deck and it was then I learned the inboard engine next to the pilot was hit. Couldn't feather the engine and the propeller just wind milled. I had the feeling something wasn't right with me. My left leg was bleeding, though I felt no pain. I reported this to the bombardier and Scharff, and Hazelhurst came to help.

"I thought for sure the radio operator was going through the floor and thanked God that we were still on good oxygen supplies. I wanted to, and thought I was able to stay at my station, but my heated suit was shorted out and then they got me into the radio room and wrapped me in an electric blanket with a tourniquet on my leg. I was still on my own oxygen and radio. I can't tell much about the return to base as I was only on oxygen and think I must have dozed off for awhile. After landing I was taken to the dispensary and then to general hospital, where I finally got sewed up around ten o'clock that night. I returned to combat status, but never flew any more missions."[53]

In addition to Shebell, the two others in the waist, Hazelhurst and Scharff, suffered only minor injuries—a miracle if one studies the pictures showing the damage that had been done to the waist of the aircraft.

B-17G *Fitch's Bandwagon* (42-107043). On 2 June, only five days after making it back from Dessau, it was involved in a collision while taxiing for takeoff and was subsequently scrapped. ROBERT V. KERR

B-17G *Lady Jane* (42-107009) of the 401st Bomb Group. On 28
May, it flew in the number two position of the high squadron.
After being hit by enemy fighters, it left the formation, and its
pilot, Lt. Wardlaw M. Hammond, landed at the emergency
field at Woodbridge, England. Four other B-17s in the high
squadron were shot down, and only the lead ship, *Fitch's
Bandwagon*, returned to Deenethorpe. *Lady Jane* was lost on
6 November 1944. MICHAEL L. GIBSON

Second Lt. Lawrence
E. Fitchett and 2nd Lt.
Bruce M. Campbell,
pilot and co-pilot of
Fitch's Bandwagon, looking at the number
three engine of their
aircraft. On 28 May,
they piloted the lead
aircraft in the high
squadron, the only air-
craft in the squadron
to return to
Deenethorpe safely.
ROBERT V. KERR

The lead crew for the 457th Bomb Group on 11 May 1944 mission to Luxemburg. Several of these men were also on the wing lead crew on 28 May. Standing, left to right: Walter F. Creigh, tailgunner/formation observer; Patrick W. Henry, lead navigator; Mark R. Belcher (not on 28 May mission); William H. Dupont, deputy lead navigator; George C. Hozier, command pilot; and Dino H. Tonelli (not on 28 May mission). WALTER F. CREIGH

Officers of *Lady Jane*'s crew pose with B-17G *Command Performance II* (42-32005). Left to right: Wardlaw M. Hammond, pilot; Alexander R. Livingstone, co-pilot; Dene C. Gober, bombardier; and Myrick J. Whiting, navigator. *Command Performance II* was lost on 24 July 1944. WARDLAW M. HAMMOND

This unique picture was taken during the German fighter attacks on the 94th Combat Wing near Dessau. It was taken from the cockpit of B-17G *Mission Maid* (42-38021) of the 457th Bomb Group. This aircraft, piloted by Lt. Green B. Poore, was leading the low squadron of the group. Clearly visible are a large number of German fighters coming in for an attack from one to two o'clock positions, two men hanging in their parachutes, and a piece of wreckage crashing to earth. It also shows the haze and smoke that the lead bombardier had to cope with on the bomb run and which eventually led to an attack on the secondary target, Leipzig-Taucha. GREEN B. POORE

B-17G 42-31520 of the 457th Bomb Group, 751st Bomb Squadron. Lt. Clyde B. Knipfer and his crew were shot down by German fighters near Dessau in this aircraft. JOHN B. WILSON

The crew of B-17G 42-31520 of the 457th Bomb Group. Back row, left to right: Nicholas D. Furrie, ball turret gunner; Percy Waltho, waist gunner; Harvey M. Conover, radio operator (not on 28 May mission); Harvey C. Cottrel, waist gunner (not on 28 May mission); Stephen T. Voit, engineer; and Joshua Goldstein, tail gunner. Front row, left to right: Richard A. Bruha, co-pilot; Clyde B. Knipfer, pilot; Stanley V. Gray, navigator; and George R. Derdzinski, bombardier. All were made prisoner of war. NICHOLAS D. FURRIE VIA TOM KRACKER

B-17G *Miss Cue* (42-31505) of the 457th Bomb Group was flown by 2nd Lt. William R. Brackley's crew. Staff Sgt. Harry Bernstein, the engineer, was killed by a 20mm cannon shell on the mission. WILLIAM R. HADLEY

The crew of *Miss Cue* during training in Pyote, Texas, in March 1944. Most of them were on board on the 28 May mission. Back row, left to right: Harry Bernstein, engineer; Glenn A. Jackson, radio operator; Miles McQueen, waist gunner (not on mission); Daniel D. Elieff, ball turret gunner; Bernard J. Geraghty, waist gunner; and Thomas W. Gougarty, tail gunner. Front row, left to right: William L. Brackley, pilot; John Hossack, co-pilot (not on mission); Winifred E. Stortz, navigator; and Anthony J. Kulczycki, bombardier (not on mission). THOMAS W. GOUGARTY

Second Lt. John J. Gides, the bombardier of B-17G *Delayed Lady II* (42-32079) of the 457th Bomb Group. During the fighter attacks, he was hit in the head by a .30-caliber bullet and severely wounded. JOHN J. GIDES

B-17G *Oh Kay* (42-97470) of the 457th Bomb Group returned to Glatton two hours after the rest of the group had landed. WILLIAM R. HADLEY

Oh Kay was lost exactly four months later, on the 28 September mission to Magdeburg. Her nine-man crew was taken prisoner of war. WILLIAM R. HADLEY

Lt. Max J. Woolley and his P-38J *The Homesick Angel* (42-67979) of the 364th Fighter Group. He was one of the pilots that escorted straggling *Oh Kay* safely to England. Woolley was shot down on 27 June in this aircraft and evaded capture. MAX J. WOOLLEY

B-17G *Black Puff Polly* (42-97067) flying as the only natural metal finish aircraft in an otherwise olive-drab formation in the spring of 1944. On 28 May, it was crippled by German fighters and eventually shot down by flak near Bremen, Germany. The aircraft with code letter A in the top righthand corner is B-17G 42-31520, which was also lost on the same mission. BERNARD E. BAINS

The crew of *Black Puff Polly*. Back row, left to right: William F. Bemus, right waist gunner; John R. Billington, radio operator (not on 28 May mission); Francis J. Lape, tail gunner (not on 28 May mission); Sheldon E. Moore, ball turret gunner; Robert C. Kriete, engineer; and Irwin A. Welling, left waist gunner. Front row, left to right: John O. Millham, navigator; Rudolph M. Stohl, pilot; David W. Schellenger, co-pilot; and James E. Thomas, bombardier. All aboard were made prisoners of war. JOHN B. WILSON

Sgt. William F. Bemus, right waist gunner of *Black Puff Polly*. He was badly injured on 28 May and was eventually returned to the United States in a POW exchange in January 1945. WILLIAM F. BEMUS

Second Lt. John O. Millham, navigator of *Black Puff Polly* in a picture taken shortly after his crew received its new Fortress. JOHN B. WILSON

B-17G *Rampant Pansy* (42-107034), flown by Lt. Jonathan M. Herbold in the number two position of the high squadron, returned to Glatton badly damaged. The aircraft was salvaged after a crash-landing in December 1944. WILLIAM R. HADLEY

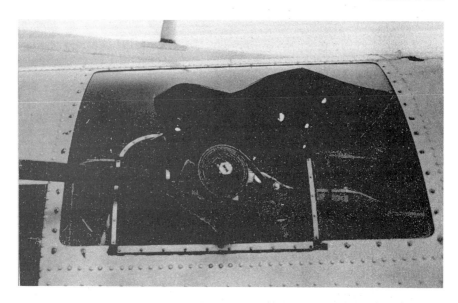

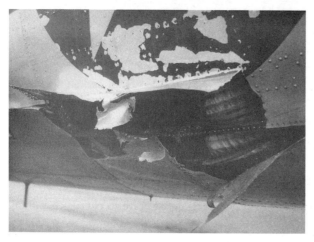

Part of the battle damage to *Rampant Pansy* of the 457th Bomb Group. Three crewmembers were wounded, all having their positions near this gaping hole—radio operator Richard R. Hazelhurst, left waist gunner Charles V. Shebell, and right waist gunner David V. Scharff. BERNARD E. BAINS

OVER THE TARGET AND BACK TO ENGLAND

Now, with two aircraft shot down from his own lead group, several others having that had to drop their bomb load to keep up, a battered low group with four aircraft already missing, and a trailing high group still under attack by German fighters and rapidly losing more and more Fortresses, Maj. George Hozier was faced with an agonizing decision. He knew that a large number of aircraft had already dropped their bombs somewhere along the route, including his own low squadron, when Lieutenant Gides was hit in the head by a small-caliber bullet. The question was whether he should turn for the secondary target at Leipzig and thus expose his formation to more German fighter attacks and fierce flak in that area or, whether he should lead the formation in the direction of England and thus possibly gain some fighter escort and find a target of opportunity along the route. Despite the odds facing him and his formation, Major Hozier decided to go to Leipzig, a very courageous thing to do.

Lead navigator Patrick W. Henry, whose name appeared in the diary fragment of colleague William Dupont earlier in this chapter, clearly remembers the situation aboard: "Lieutenant Brannan, the lead pilot, asked me for a heading and estimated time of arrival for the initial point for the secondary target. I gave him the info and the bombardier and I began getting ourselves ready for the secondary bomb run.

"As I studied the maps and considered our situation, I was seriously concerned about several factors. First, we had taken considerable damage from fighters and had lost at least one aircraft. Our radar was useless. The rest of the Eighth Air Force had gone their separate ways, so apparently we were to be the only ones hitting Leipzig. We were supposed to fly to an initial point northeast of the target, coming in to it on a southwesterly course. After the bomb drop, our most expeditious move to rejoin the rest of the troops would have been to turn immediately on a northwesterly heading. But our flight plan called for something different to avoid the flak areas surrounding the city of Leipzig. In face of the German fighters still attacking, crew fatigue, fuel remaining, the difficulties of maintaining tight formations in large-magnitude turns and finally the fact that the boundaries of the flak zones not always proved to be accurate, it was my belief that a deviation from the original flight plan was the best, using the shortest possible route.

"I called the pilot on the intercom and outlined the problem as succinctly as I could, explaining the pros and cons of each alternative, without recommending either one. After all, it was not my decision to make; the pilot was in command of the aircraft and empowered to make decisions regarding the safe completion of the flight, and Major Hozier had been designated by the wing commander as his representative to carry out the mission. In the discussion that followed, as I recall, Lieutenant Brannan did most of the talking to me over the intercom. I am sure he was discussing it with the major. He asked a lot of questions and finally it was decided to take the shortcut."[54]

Leipzig was reached, and the remaining six aircraft that still had bombs in the 457th Bomb Group, dropped on the Leipzig-Taucha aircraft factory. Hits were observed in the northeast corner of the target area. While the fighter attacks had subsided, the flak now increased, and was reported to be intense and accurate in the official report.

Patrick Henry, in the lead aircraft, recorded this frightening experience: "There was one thing on the bomb run in such abundance that it blocked out almost everything else and it is all I can remember: FLAK! Flak, flak, and more flak. Flak such as I had never seen before (and never saw again, thank God). Leipzig made Berlin look like a lightly defended city. I had heard some guys talk about missions where the flak was so thick you could get out of the plane and walk on it, and I had known that they were exaggerating, but now I began to believe it was possible. And the closer we got to the target the worse it got. Even Brannan, whom I knew from previous missions to be a very cool customer under fire, made some impassioned remarks about the severity of the flak, although such extraneous comments were strictly taboo on the bomb run. As soon as the bombs were gone, we turned on to

Maj. George C. Hozier on left and Capt. Patrick W. Henry on right have a laugh after completing yet another mission. They shared anxious hours in the lead ship of the 94th Combat Wing on 28 May. Hozier and Henry were shot down and made prisoner of war on 17 September on a mission in support of Operation Market Garden. BERNARD E. BAINS VIA WILLARD REESE

our new heading and I began to sweat out the withdrawal from beautiful downtown Leipzig. I think Brannan asked me for an estimate of how much longer we would be in the flak, which had not abated one iota; if anything, it was getting worse. I made some sort of estimate, based on the distance to the edge of the flak zone as shown on my chart, but at this time I had very little confidence in it; I might have said something like 'about three minutes.'

"Ordinarily at this point in a mission, I would be busy checking our position and progress by identifying landmarks on the ground and it would take my mind off such annoyances as flak or fighter attacks, but now the flak was so thick I could hardly see the ground. There was no chatter on the intercom, the only sound was the droning of the engines and the explosions of the flak bursts, which were rapid-fire but of varying intensity. There was nothing to do but hunker down and wait and hope and pray. Occasionally, when a burst came very close and the aircraft bounced a little bit, I thought I heard a noise like a grunt over the intercom, but it may have been my imagination or it might have been my own involuntary response to the stimulus. We droned on for what seemed like hours, but was probably two or three minutes. I had plenty of time to wonder about whether we had indeed taken the wisest course, but when I thought about where we would have been had we taken the other route, I reassured myself that we were better off here. But still, this was really BAD.

"Suddenly, a voice over the intercom brought me back to reality. 'Jesus Christ, Henry, when are we gonna get out of this stuff? You said three minutes' (or words to that effect). It was Brannan, and this also was very uncharacteristic of him. It strengthened, if possible, my conviction that no one had ever seen flak any worse than this. I gave him some sort of reply to the effect that the boundaries of the flak zones were not exactly as we had been told they were and that this stuff couldn't keep up much longer. It didn't, the intensity decreased and then the barrage stopped all together. Brannan expressed his relief in salty language and began a check on each crew member to determine if anyone had been wounded and if there was any serious damage to the plane. Everyone was okay, there were plenty of new holes in the plane and some time later the number three engine had to be feathered, but this would not keep us from getting back. I breathed a sigh of relief and said a quick thank-you to the good Lord. Then I got back to my navigating."

William H. Dupont, the deputy lead navigator, recorded in his diary: "Those who were left went on to the target and the flak nearly finished what the fighters started. A spare oxygen bottle saved my life when the flak was heaviest. It got in the way and took the beating instead of me. Anyway, when we got back we naturally kissed the beautiful ground, we were so thankful to get down in one piece. Pat Henry came home on three engines, but quite a few of the boys didn't. Our particular wing was the only one that had heavy fighter

The bombs of the remaining aircraft of the 457th Bomb Group explode in the vicinity of Leipzig. Results were classified as "poor." WILLIAM R. HADLEY

attacks and we lost fourteen ships. If I can get thru a day like yesterday I can get thru any of them, so I am no longer worried about the outcome."*[55]

One of the victims of the flak along the route was the deputy lead aircraft of the high group, the 351st Bomb Group. The B-17G *Black Magic* (42-31721) was flown by the experienced 1st Lt. Clyde W. McClelland, who had survived the fierce fighter attacks and now fell to the flak. Capt. Harry B. Holsapple, the command pilot, later reported: "I first noticed 1st Lieutenant McClelland, who was flying in number two position of my element just before bombs away. At that time, I noticed nothing wrong with him. Shortly afterward, I saw him and he had fallen out of his position and was directly below me with numbers one and two engines feathered. I think that he must have been hit by flak, which we encountered in moderate amounts just before bombs away. I did not see any fighters then and I feel certain that if there had been any that I would have seen them. Lieutenant McClelland was under control and was keeping an airspeed of 150 miles per hour. He was descending and peeled off to the left apparently heading toward France. He then went out of sight. I heard nothing over VHF and saw no parachutes."[56]

---

* Sadly, William Dupont was killed by a flak fragment over Osnabrück on 26 September 1944. He is buried in the Cambridge American Cemetery and Memorial in England.

After returning from Dessau, the officers of the 351st Bomb Group lead crew pose next to their ship, B-17G *Linda Ball II* (42-97381). Standing, left to right: Capt. Harry B. Holsapple, command pilot; 1st Lt. John H. Wrisberg Jr., tail gunner/formation observer; and Capt. Bruce F. Winton, lead pilot. Kneeling on the left is 1st Lt. John R. Duchesneau, bombardier; on the right, 1st Lt. Miles E. Manthey, navigator. HARRY B. HOLSAPPLE VIA JOHN R. DUCHESNEAU

B-17G *Black Magic* (42-31721) was assigned to the 351st Bomb Group on 20 January 1944 and shot down on its thirty-fifth combat mission on 28 May, piloted by Lt. Clyde W. McClelland. KEN HARBOUR

McClelland's original crew during training in the United States in October 1943.
Four of the men were aboard *Black Magic* on 28 May, flying as deputy lead crew for
the high group of the 94th Combat Wing. Back row, far right is Clyde W. McClelland,
pilot. Front row, third from left, is Junior H. Edwards, waist gunner; fourth from left
is Louis E. Poole, engineer; and fifth from left is Nathan L. Williams, ball turret
gunner. All four were made prisoners of war. CLYDE W. MCCLELLAND

Lieutenant McClelland, already an old hand in the air war over Europe,
was flying with a mixed crew, since groundings, illness, and leaves had
changed his original crew considerably. The replacement for his regular navigator, 1st Lt. Richard G. Miller who was lost aboard one of the six aircraft
that the Group lost on the mission to Ludwigshafen the previous day, was 1st
Lt. John B. Duncan. He was on the last of his required thirty combat missions and recalled: "I heard reports of our gunners on the intercom system,
that some of our planes had been hit and were going down. Then we lost
one engine, followed by a second engine, and we were forced to fall back
out of formation since we were unable to keep up. We certainly felt that we
had a chance of making it back to England, when we lost a third engine, following which we endeavored to lighten the plane's load by throwing over-
board heavy items such as ammunition cases and other heavy objects. When
we dropped to 3,000 to 4,000 feet, McClelland had no other choice than to
give the order to abandon ship.

"The bombardier, Lt. George F. Kiely, and I decided to go back to the
bomb bay and drop out there, since they still were open, because they malfunctioned when we wanted to close them. I assigned myself the task of
watching all of our gunners jump out of the waist door. Then I called
McClelland on the intercom, advising him that the gunners were out and

that Kiely and I were then leaving the ship. As I recalled afterwards, I felt quite certain that also tail gunner, Staff Sgt. LeRoy D. Cruse, did jump from the ship, but I have no idea what happened to him after his jump. I came down on the outskirts of Bad Soden. Since my parachute was turning during the last several hundred feet, I experienced a very bad landing and suffered a compound fracture of the left leg, both the tibia and fibula bones. As I hit the ground with my left heel, I felt a sharp pain for just a moment, then, when I tried to get up, I found that I was unable to move from the waist down.

"In the meantime, German civilians and Hitler Youth came running out of the village, greatly excited, as you can well imagine. I was kicked and struck on the forehead, with something like an axe handle while I was lying on the ground. Eventually, a German soldier or policeman arrived and appeared to assume control of the situation. Much to my surprise, they tried to get me up on my feet, but this only caused the ends of the broken and fragmented bones to go through the skin, causing me great pain. When they finally realized that I had a very badly broken leg, they brought in a crude wooden stretcher, placed me upon it and carried me into the village, where a German doctor put me to sleep and placed a cast upon my leg, but made no effort to set the bones in the leg. Their purpose was to prepare me for transportation elsewhere. From the doctor's office I was carried to a car on a stretcher, of sorts, and somehow placed inside. I was then driven some distance to a hospital for French workers in Germany, where I was interrogated by a very sinister German intelligence officer, who threatened to have me shot."[57]

Two of the men in this picture, taken in Cutbank, Montana, in October 1943 were aboard *Black Magic* on 28 May. Standing in the middle is George F. Kiely, bombardier, and standing on the right is John B. Duncan, navigator. Both were made prisoners of war. JOHN B. DUNCAN

However, after his recovery Duncan was transported to the regular inter-rogation center, from where he was sent to a hospital in Meiningen and then finally to Moosburg, where he was liberated in April 1945. One crewmem-ber, tail gunner LeRoy D. Cruse, was not so lucky. After parachuting, Cruse was killed on the ground by a civilian. A detailed account of his tragic death is given in the final chapter of this book. The rest of the crew was captured, copilot Richard E. Francis on 29 May and ball turret gunner Nathan L. Williams on 1 June. They spent the rest of the war in a prisoner of war camp. Their abandoned *Black Magic* crashed near the small village of Mernes, eight kilometers east of Bad Orb.

Also hit, probably by flak, on the last bomb run was B-17G 42-97452 of the 457th Bomb Group. The very experienced crew of 1st Lt. Emanuel Hauf was also nearing the end of its tour, having flown over with the Group from the United States to England in January 1944.

When leaving the target area, other crews in the vicinity observed that a fire had started in the aircraft's number four engine. What happened next can be told best by a very good friend of Emanuel "Skip" Hauf. He was 1st Lt. Green B. Poore, piloting B-17G *Mission Maid* (42-38021), and flying close to Hauf in the group formation: "Someone called over the radio that there were 'Bandits' from the north. My bombardier, Frank Rowe, was very alert

Tech Sgt. Leonard J. Kriesky (far right) and Staff Sgt. LeRoy D. Cruse (second from left), radio operator and tail gunner, respectively, of *Black Magic*. LEONARD J. KRIESKY JR.

and was able to get some pictures of them, coming in for an attack on us. I have been able to count about twenty-five of them and there were other aircraft that our right wing prevented from being included in the picture. I later learned from Intelligence sources that there were thirty-eight German fighters in this attack. There was no indication that they were in any type of formation, in fact the picture shows them to look and resemble a swarm of bees on the attack. They came from the north at the same altitude we were flying which meant they hit us from our right side. It is very difficult to find the proper words to describe the events that followed other than 'unadulterated living hell.' All fighters came in with all guns firing and they passed by so close that we expected some mid-air collisions. They only made one pass at the bombers and then they headed for the ground and the safety of their aerodromes. We were lead ship in the lower element of the formation and suffered some battle damage, but fortunately no one was injured. We also encountered moderate flak and Lieutenant Hauf was seen to receive a near burst of flak which set his right wing on fire between the number four engine and the wing tip. The fire soon went out and was seen to smolder at times.

"After the fighter attack, I do recall Lieutenant Hauf taking up a position in the lead element of the formation, which afforded him a much better protection should another attack be forthcoming. I, or should I say, our crew maintained a position slightly below and to the left of Lieutenant Hauf. From this position we could see no damage other than the engine which was on fire. The Hauf crew and our crew were always very close and the comradeship that developed was almost like brothers. The officers of the Hauf crew and our crew shared the same metal Nissen hut. Lieutenant Hauf did not shut down the burning engine and maintained a very good position which leads me to believe that one of the two pilots was at the controls. The engine fire was contained during our withdrawal from the target area. I attribute this to the fact that we were flying at 30,000 feet where the air is quite thin and there is not too much oxygen for the fire to spread.

"As we were approaching the English Channel from the east, I noted that Lieutenant Hauf left the formation and started a very rapid descent. I thought that he was planning to attempt to ditch his aircraft on the west side of the Channel, just off the English coast. We did have P-47 fighter escort at this time. I did not discuss my actions with our crew, but attempted to stay with Lieutenant Hauf, so that we could have some encouraging information to report of his attempted ditching. Lieutenant Hauf's initial rate of descent kept increasing until it was necessary for our aircraft to slow down. We were flying well above the recommended airspeed for the design limitations of the B-17 aircraft. Lieutenant Hauf's rate continued to increase until it was almost a vertical dive and his rate of speed was well beyond the airframe limitations. We noticed that the lower in altitude the more the fire increased.

The crew of B-17G 42-97452 of the 457th Bomb Group. This picture was taken on 22 May after the crew had led the group to Kiel in B-17G *Nancy K* (42-97451). On 28 May, the entire crew, then nine men, was killed when their B-17 crashed just off the Belgian coast in the North Sea. Back row, left to right: William R. Hawley, navigator; Emanuel Hauf, pilot; Donald V. Swain, co-pilot; and Richard E. Jaqua, bombardier. The six enlisted men in the front row are in alphabetical order: Louis F. Beske, ball turret gunner; Oscar A. Gascon, tail gunner; Willis H. Johnson, engineer; James J. Kilroy, radio operator; Paul R. Moore, right waist gunner; and Joseph S. Reid, left waist gunner. Of these six, Gascon, Johnson, Kilroy, and Moore died on 28 May; the other two were not on the crew that day. GREEN B. POORE

This, of course, was due to more oxygen being available which permitted the fire to increase. I would estimate that between 10,000 and 12,000 feet, the right wing of the Hauf plane came off and the aircraft went into a violent spin. After a spin of one turn or possibly another half, the aircraft exploded. I would estimate that we were about 7,000 feet above the explosion, and we had a very clear view of this disaster, no parachutes were observed and it was our contention that there were no survivors.

"As I previously stated, there were P-47 aircraft in the vicinity and two of them followed the wreckage to the water and the last I saw was that they were flying low over the water where the B-17 went into the Channel. I thought Lieutenant Hauf's intention was to attempt a ditching just off the English coast, but for some unknown reason, he gradually turned from a westerly course to a southerly course and as a result the wreckage entered the water about three to five miles off the Belgian coast. We were flying alone after leaving the formation and we beat a hasty retreat to Glatton. In fact, we landed before the remainder of the formation arrived. As a result of my impulsive actions in leaving the safety of the formation, I received a verbal reprimand and at the same time with a curious glint in his eye, the group commander said he was glad to know someone had firsthand knowledge of what had occurred."[58]

On 22 February 1944, the second combat mission for the 457th Bomb Group, B-17G 42-97452 sustained damage to its port wing. After the wing was repaired, the aircraft's operational life resumed, only to end on 28 May in a crash in the North Sea. BERNARD E. BAINS VIA WILLARD REESE

No details will ever be known about what happened aboard the B-17 of Emanuel Hauf. All nine crewmembers, having almost finished their tours, perished in the crash, and no trace of their remains was ever found. The names of six of them are recorded on the Wall of the Missing at the Ardennes Cemetery, and three at the Cambridge Cemetery. The P-47s to which Green Poore referred belonged to the 50th Fighter Group, a Ninth Air Force unit on withdrawal escort duty, which reported seeing a B-17 crash in the North Sea north of Ostend at 1708 hours, with no trace of chutes in the vicinity.

The 457th Bomb Group formation arrived back over Glatton at 1750 hours with some aircraft firing red flares, indicating wounded aboard. These were given priority in landing and wounded were removed from three battered Fortresses. Lieutenant Gides was gently evacuated from the *Delayed Lady II* with his terrible head wound. In *Snafusk Shamrock,* crewmember Walter F. Pittman had received a flak fragment in his left eye, and the hits in

Rampant Pansy had left three wounded. All five were quickly admitted to the base hospital and eventually recovered, including Lt. John Gides, who remembered: "I woke up four days later in the Seventh General Hospital, somewhere in England. I had been hit in the head by a shell from a Focke-Wulf 190 causing the removal of some brain tissue and the insertion of a silver plate in my cranium. Also, I had the tip of the middle finger of my left hand shot off. I suffered aphasia and was sent by hospital ship to Walter Reed Hospital in Washington, D.C., for rehabilitation. It was necessary to relearn speaking, reading and writing. Since that time, I've had to take medicine on a daily basis to prevent epileptic seizures caused by the head trauma. I also lost my sense of smell and hence, cannot taste food or drink. So, as you can see, the injury has left me with no memory of the events of that day and kept me from further service. I was awarded the Purple Heart and the Air Medal."[59]

This picture was taken on 30 May 1944 after a mission to Ochersleben. The crew of Green B. Poore of the 457th Bomb Group is celebrating the end of the tour of tail gunner Ralph R. Stowe, the man in the white underwear. He was one mission ahead of the rest of the crew. This crew flew lead in the low squadron of the 457th Bomb Group on 28 May and was flying near Lieutenant Hauf's B-17 when it exploded over the North Sea. Poore's crew claimed four German fighters destroyed during combat in the Dessau area. Standing, left to right: Green B. Poore, pilot; unidentified (substitute co-pilot); George W. Brice, navigator; Ralph Stowe; John F. Nechak, radio operator; Frank J. Rowe, bombardier; and Orin E. Hobbs, waist gunner. Kneeling, left to right: Frederick J. Smith, engineer; Lynn W. Rice, waist gunner; and George W. Murphy, ball turret gunner. GREEN B. POORE

The luckless engineer of *Miss Cue*, Staff Sgt. Harry Bernstein, was beyond medical attention. His body was interred at the Cambridge cemetery.

Lt. Roy W. Allen had to make a one-wheel landing in *Rene III*, the personal B-17 of the group commanding officer, Col. James R. Luper. He performed a great task, causing minimal extra damage and with no hurt to his crew. Two hours later, Lieutenant Connor, who at first had been given up as lost, came limping in with only one engine functioning properly on *Oh Kay*. Two engines had burned out in the target area and three cylinders on the third had been punctured by enemy fire. Connor had dropped out of formation and had everything movable thrown out of his aircraft on German towns. He flew all the way back to Glatton alone at 12,000 feet with an airspeed of 115 to 135 miles per hour.

George W. Brice, navigator on Lieutenant Poore's crew, clearly remembers that evening at Glatton: "Since they were our closest friends on the base

B-17G *Snafusk Shamrock* (42-31615) of the 457th Bomb Group. On 28 May, it was flown by the crew of Lt. Robert H. Magill in the number five position of the lead squadron. Its crew claimed two German fighters destroyed, but tail gunner Walter F. Pittman was wounded by flak in his left eye. The group's engineering department noted this battle damage after the mission: "20mm cannon shells hit right elevator and right horizontal stabilizer, both have to be replaced. Two flak holes in left wing tip. Flak hole in trailing edge of left outboard wing panel. Five 20mm cannon holes in dorsal fin and vertical stabilizer. Flak burst along left side of fuselage, from tail end to lower ball turret, resulting in extensive skin damage. Pilot's windshield shattered by flak. Flak struck number two engine cowling." The aircraft was shot down on 20 June 1944 on a mission to Hamburg. JOHN B. WILSON

we were sickened and devastated by the loss of Hauf and his crew—they too, were close to having completed their missions. One of Hauf's crew members had saved two bottles of bourbon to celebrate their completion of the final mission when their time arrived. That night we used those two quarts, and our own supplies, and for the first time during the tour we drank heavily in honor of, and to lessen the stunning loss of our room mates and friends."[60]

At Polebrook, it was another bleak day. After losing six aircraft on the twenty-seventh, the 351st Bomb Group had now lost five B-17s and their crews. Walter Bergstrom, ball turret gunner in one of the group's B-17s that made it back, recalled: "Of the twenty-four missions I flew, the Dessau raid was by far the worst and the most terrifying. I will never forget the scene as we flew through the bomb run with angry fires and black smoke rising from the target area. Worse still was the heavy flak and the German fighters attacking from positions in front of the formation. I emptied all 1,100 rounds of shells from my ball turret guns and am quite sure that I missed everything but the sky.

"Young men, especially in the military, are supposed to be he-men and not show emotions or express their fear. So, all during debriefing after we landed I put on the usual front of bravado. As soon as the debriefing was over I walked hurriedly to a large wooded area between the airfield and the ground crew quarters. There I sat beneath an oak tree and sobbed for what seemed like hours—stopping long enough at one point to vomit. All of the terror and fear I experienced that day were spilled out in my tears. After it became dark, I went to my barracks and crept into my bunk, where I finally drifted off to sleep."[61]

At Deenethorpe, a shocked 401st Bomb Group counted their losses; seven aircraft were lost, although one crew was picked up by Air Sea Rescue. One crewmember lay dead in a returning bomber, three others were wounded, and all nine aircraft that returned were damaged by fighters and flak. Especially, the 613th Bomb Squadron had been hit very hard. Six of its aircraft had formed the high squadron, and only *Fitch's Bandwagon* returned to base. Its tail gunner Robert V. Kerr recalled: "It sure looked good to see the coast of England again. After we got a ways over England I went up into the radio room, now that we no longer had to wear the oxygen mask and were free to move around. I ate a candy bar and opened some gum and we talked over the big battle. We figured that Hammond had gone down and that we were the only crew from the squadron to get back. I changed clothes in the waist and went back and took the guns out before we reached the field. We circled the field, then landed. As we taxied from the south-east end of the short runway, around by the hangars and operations office, guys were standing along the taxi strip and in front of operations watching us. I guess they wondered where the rest of the group was. Bright and Hicks and a few other guys were waiting in the dispersal area as we taxied in, and the pilot swung the ship around and cut the engines. I then jumped out and took the equipment bag out and set it down; then got my guns and set them on it.

Spectacular series of pictures of the landing at Glatton of B-17G *Rene III* (42-38113) of the 457th Bomb Group on 28 May. Lt. Roy W. Allen and crew had flown in the number three position of the high squadron. The ship was damaged by flak and fighters, whereupon Allen skillfully made a one-wheel landing. *Rene III* was repaired to fly many more missions before it was finally lost in action on 21 March 1945. Allen and his crew were shot down on 14 June 1944. All but one of the crew survived and evaded capture. BERNARD E. BAINS / JOHN WALKER

"Everybody started crowding around the ship looking for holes. A couple of guys were standing there, and as I set them down, I said, 'I don't think these guns are much good anymore,' and they said, 'Man, look at that,' as they looked them over. The left one especially was burned pretty bad and pretty well-worn in the grooves. Everybody started asking us all about it and all the rest of the crew were raving about it, but I didn't say much. All the other dispersal areas in the squadron were empty and the guys all started coming over to our ship to find out what had happened to their ships. One crew chief, Sullivan, came down in the armament truck and kept saying, 'What the hell happened? What the hell happened?' He wanted to know if any of us had seen what happened to his ship. It was a silver-colored ship and was on about its second mission. We loaded the guns into Sullivan's truck and he took them to the armament shop. He said that we didn't have to clean them, he would do that for us. We took our stuff to the equipment room and then went to interrogation. We didn't have to wait for a table, there were plenty of 'empty tables.'

"We were interrogated by Lieutenant Meredith. The Catholic chaplain, Burke, was there. Had coffee and cake while being interrogated. Lieutenant Meredith asked the navigator and bombardier the usual information and the time and strength of fighter attacks, etc. He asked how many fighter claims there were and the whole crew claimed eleven. When he asked about complaints, I told him about the escort flying so high that they couldn't see what was going on below them. I told him that just between the first and second attacks, I could see the vapour trails from the escort above us and they hadn't the slightest idea of what was going on below them. Remembering the vow I had made a few hours earlier, if I was lucky enough to get back, I wasn't going to claim any fighters, but the rest of the crew talked me in to it. We went over to the table where they were putting in claims. The other guys put in their claims, and I waited until there was an opening, and I was interviewed by the lieutenant. I told him about the one that I thought it was most likely that I got, and then Sassi and Kelsen told me to put in for another one, so I told him about another that it appeared that I had nailed. After interrogation, we went to the mess hall and ate, then went up to the barracks. We talked for quite a while about the mission and went to bed at 10 P.M., I guess, hoping that we wouldn't have to fly again the next day for the third day in a row."[62]

But contrary to the somber opinion of the crew of *Fitch's Bandwagon*, *Lady Jane* had not gone down over Germany. She had carried her crew safely to the emergency strip at Woodbridge and was thus the tenth, and final, surviving B-17 of the 401st Bomb Group. Its pilot, Wardlaw M. Hammond, who was awarded a Distinguished Flying Cross for bringing it back to England, recalled events after he lost the formation over Germany: "I feathered the

Home, sweet home—a most welcome sight to returning crews. B-17G *Mollie Mule* (42-107124) of the 351st Bomb Group returns to Polebrook. On 28 May, this aircraft flew to Dessau in the lead squadron of the group, piloted by Lt. William Crockett. Battle damage sustained that day necesitated replacement of number three propellor and number four engine. KEN HARBOUR

left outboard engine as the oil pressure finally dropped off and instructed my co-pilot to call for fighter support on the VHF radio since we still were deep in German territory. We finally saw a squadron of P-38s approaching, but were going too slow for them to stick with us, even though they made lazy S-turns above us. We were alone for a while and were attacked with one pass by an individual Me 109; he must have been low on gas since he did not return. We apparently did not sustain serious battle damage from this attack. After a while a squadron of P-47s accompanied us until we approached the Belgian cities of Antwerp and Ostend. The P-47 pilots knew about the intense flak we could expect if we flew over either one of those cities. The navigator, Lt. Myrick J. Whiting, tried to keep us between the cities, but the flak guns had a long range and we were low, at about 15,000 feet. I heard a tremendous bang and the left wing flipped up. I helped it with a hard turn to the right, trying to avoid the next round of four shells, which would follow the first one.

"One of the shells from the single battery that was firing at us, had exploded directly below the left inboard engine and blew off the propeller dome. The next four shells exploded exactly at our altitude, but harmlessly to our left. The oil pressure began dropping, and I shut down this engine without being able to feather the propeller. The drag of the windmilling propeller and the hanging cowling on the other left engine made it necessary for both me and the co-pilot, Lt. Alexander R. Livingstone, to apply aileron and rudder to keep the aircraft out of a spiral dive. We were now losing about 500 feet per minute and we still had to cross the English Channel. Lieutenant Whiting said, 'I think we might be able to make the English coast if we're lucky.' I instructed the radio operator to call the Air Sea Rescue Service just in case we had to ditch the aircraft in the Channel. We threw out everything removable, including the gun barrels, the long distance radio, the flak suits and the ammunition. We contemplated releasing the ball turret, but reconsidered because this action would make ditching more hazardous. We totally burned up the good engines trying to get the aircraft back without ditching.

"Lieutenant Whiting directed us to Woodbridge Air Base, which had a long emergency airstrip on the coast. We crossed the water at no more than 350 feet and flew over the field. To come into the runway upwind, I had to make a left turn into the dead engines. I did not have enough altitude to fly further downwind and turn to the right. To make the left turn, I had to simultaneously roll out all the right aileron trim and rudder trim which I had used to offset the unbalanced thrust of the two good engines which had been running for over three hours at full throttle.

"When the engineering officer of our group came to the base to pick up the plane, he was upset because he had to change all four engines. He

Sgt. R. H. Hampton, a ground crewman, takes a good look at the battle damage to the left wing of B-17G *Son of a Blitz* (42-31081). It was the lead ship of the 401st Bomb Group and was piloted by Lt. Charles F. Hess.
VIC MASLEN

wanted to know why we did not operate the engines at normal rated power. I did not bother to give this stupid question a reply, knowing that if I had done so the plane would be in the Channel on the bottom or possibly in a pile of junk somewhere in Belgium."[63]

Of course the interrogation reports of this group reflect the horrors its crews had gone through that day. Capt. Fred D. Grinham, who had led the low squadron, was of the opinion that the leadership of the 94th Combat Wing was exceptionally poor on this day. Two other pilots in the same squadron, Edwin A. Post and Elmer C. Gillespie, were very critical of the fact that a second run was made over the target.

Also the crews of the 351st Bomb Group were quite outspoken during their debriefing. Lieutenant Hales remarked that "the leader was going so fast, it beat the whole formation to death." Lieutenant Bland remarked that "the lead stalled us out in the turns and these turns were too steep." And Lt. John Wellbeloved simply stated, "Do not see any reason for going over target so many times."

But life went on at the respective airfields after the crews returned home. There is no better way to illustrate this than the fact that: "William H. Ballenger, co-pilot of the Ochsenhirt crew, was infuriated and extremely critical of the fact that Staff Sgt. William McIntyre, who flew as his bombardier, was scheduled to do a tour of guard duty that night and even did not have time to eat or shower after this very rough mission."[64]

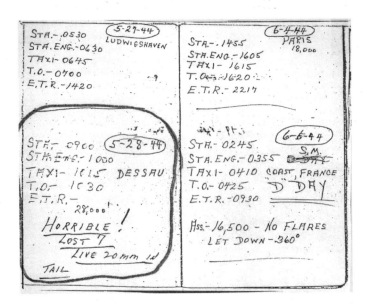

First Lt. Dan C. Knight, pilot of B-17G *Mary Alice* (42-31983) of the 401st Bomb Group, kept a small log of his missions. He noted the target and the most important times of the mission after the morning briefing. The notes that he added in the evening of 28 May are self-explanatory.
DAN C. KNIGHT

CHAPTER 7

Magdeburg

Force II consisted of no fewer than four combat wings. Two of these, the 13th A and 13th B, were assigned to bomb the oil refineries near Magdeburg. Both others, the 4th and the 45th, were to attack the military depot at Königsborn. All were B-17 units of the Third Air Division. The 13th A Combat Wing was led by the 390th Bomb Group from Framlingham, with the 100th Bomb Group from Thorpe Abbotts flying as the high group, and a composite group of the 95th, 100th, and 390th Bomb Groups flying as low group.

The 13th B Combat Wing consisted of the 95th Bomb Group from Horham leading the 388th Bomb Group from Knettishall, flying high, and the 94th Bomb Group from Bury St. Edmunds, flying low.

The 356th Fighter Group provided the penetration support for these Wings. Its forty-four P-47s took off from Martlesham Heath at 1204 hours, commanded by Lieutenant Colonel Baccus. This take-off was marred by an accident. One of the pilots, Lt. William G. Craig, lost power just as he lifted off the runway. Though he managed to set the aircraft back down, it flipped over after hitting a ditch at the end of the runway. Although the Thunderbolt immediately caught fire, Craig was pulled out safely, with minor injuries and he returned to duty three days later.

The 13th A Combat Wing formed up without any noticeable difficulty near Felixstowe and left the English coast at 1211 hours. Wing leader was Col. Frederick W. Ott, commanding officer of the 390th Bomb Group, in B-17G *Mary Jane* (42-102634), piloted by Lt. Orice D. Settles.

In the formation of the 390th Bomb Group, the B-17 piloted by Lieutenant Dayton had to abort, due to mechanical trouble. One of the assigned spares, piloted by Lieutenant Ingram, took his place in the lead squadron of the group. When it appeared there were no more vacancies to fill, the two other spares returned to Framlingham. Shortly thereafter, however, Lieutenant Parke had to abort when the supercharger on his number four engine failed.

Lieutenant Wolf and Lieutenant Simmons, piloting *Fever Beaver* and *The All American Girl*, respectively, left their positions in the high squadron of the 100th Bomb Group formation. Two spares, piloted by Lieutenant Bethea and Lieutenant Williams, immediately took their places.

Second Lt. William G. Craig of the 356th Fighter Group crashed with his P-47 on take-off from Martlesham Heath. KENT D. MILLER

In the composite group, two aircraft from the 390th Bomb Group, aborted; one with number one engine out, and the other due to the failure of the ball turret hearing system. The 390th Bomb Group's only spare for this composite group, piloted by Lieutenant Chadwick, took over one of the positions. The other was filled by the spare from the 95th Bomb Group, piloted by Lt. Jonathan H. Bullard, since there were no vacancies to fill in the low squadron, that was provided by his own Group. All 100th Bomb Group aircraft in the composite group proved satisfactory, their one spare returning to Thorpe Abbots. In all, an almost complete combat wing, minus only one B-17 in the lead group, entered enemy territory at 1246 hours.

We have seen in the previous chapter that the last combat wing of Force I, scheduled to attack Dessau, experienced difficulties in forming up. This Wing and the first Magdeburg-bound wing, the 13th A, then traded places in the bomber stream, with the unfortunate effects as described in the previous chapter. However, more formation mishap was at hand. The assigned second combat wing in Force II, the 13th B, now had to fly as the third combat wing and its assembly was not going smoothly, despite the excellent visibility. The assembly of this wing will now be studied in greater detail, to illustrate the complex process of forming a combat force of this magnitude, even under most favorable weather circumstances.

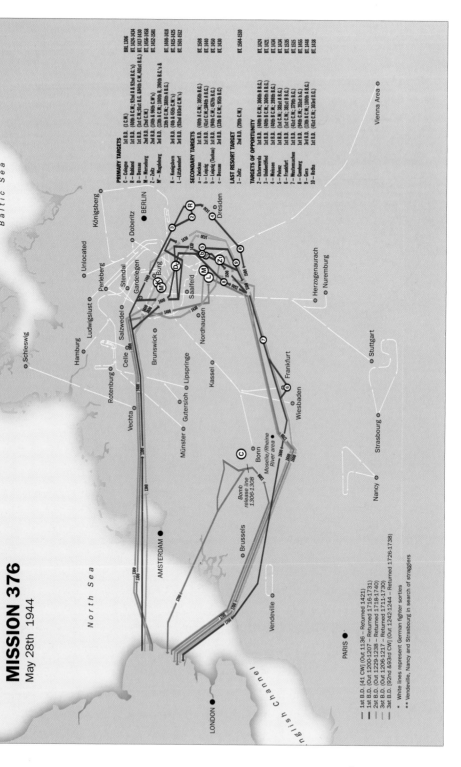

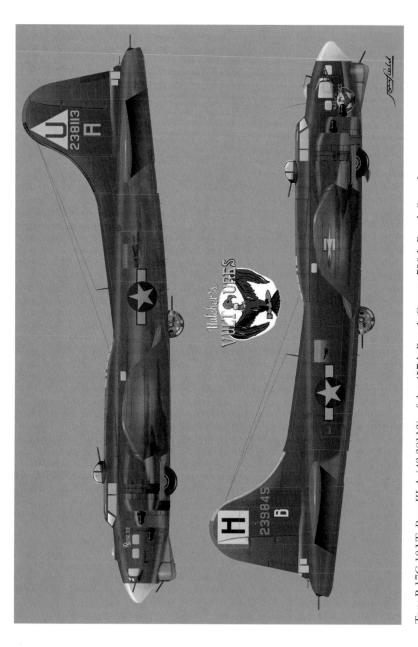

Top: B-17G-10-VE *Rene III*, A (42-38113) of the 457th Bomb Group, 750th Bomb Squadron.
Bottom: B-17G-1-VE *Hulcher's Vultures*, B (42-39845) of the 388th Bomb Group, 563rd Bomb Squadron.

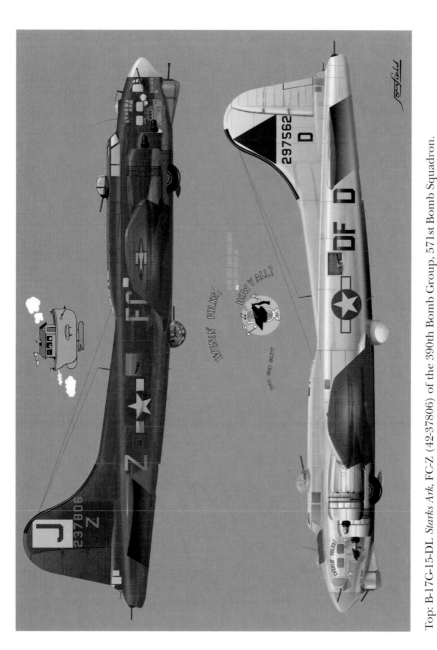

Top: B-17G-15-DL *Starks Ark*, FC-Z (42-37806) of the 390th Bomb Group, 571st Bomb Squadron.
Bottom: B-17G-20-VE *Evenin' Folks, How Y'All?*, DF-D (42-97562) of the 91st Bomb Group, 324th Bomb Squadron.
Note H2X fitted, no ball turret.

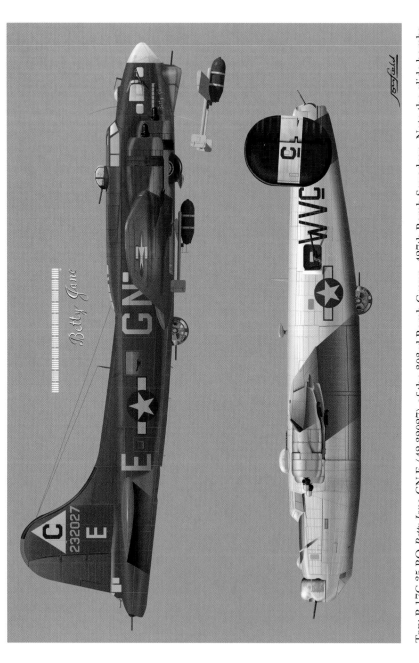

Top: B-17G-35-BO *Betty Jane*, GN-E (42-32027) of the 303rd Bomb Group, 427th Bomb Squadron. Note the glide bombs.
Bottom: B-24H-30-FO WV-C (42-95308) of the 445th Bomb Group, 702nd Bomb Squadron.

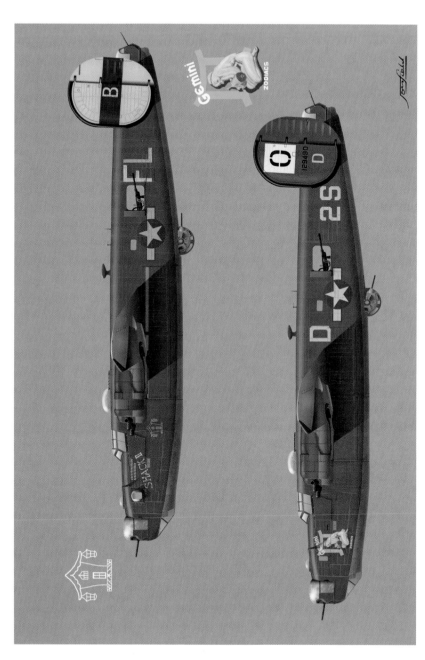

Top: B-24H-1-CF *The Shack II*, FL-B (41-29143) of the 446th Bomb Group, 704th Bomb Squadron.
Bottom: B-24H-15-CF *Gemini*, 2S-D (41-29490) of the 486th Bomb Group, 834th Bomb Squadron.

Top: P-51B-10-NA *Big Mac Junior*, C3-D (42-106647) of the 363rd Fighter Group, 382nd Fighter Squadron, flown by 1st Lt. John R. Brown. The aircraft was later fitted with a "Malcolm"-type frameless hood. Bottom: P-51B-5-NA *Hurry Home Honey*, C5-T (43-6935) of the 357th Fighter Group, 364th Fighter Squadron, flown by Capt. Richard A. Peterson.

Top: P-51D-5-NA *Swedes Steed III*, FT-T (44-13383) of the 354th Fighter Group, 353rd Fighter Squadron, flown by 1st Lt. William Y. Anderson.

Bottom: P-51D-5-NA 44-13619 of the 352nd Fighter Group, 487th Fighter Squadron, Williams Villian, HO-B, flown by 1st Lt. Harry H. Barnes.

Top: P-47D-22-RE *Lady Jane*, HL-J (42-26020) of the 78th Fighter Group, 82nd Fighter Squadron. This was the regular aircraft flown by Capt. Alwin M. Juchheim, but not on 28 May, when he was involved in a midair collision over Germany.

Bottom: P-47D-11-RE 42-75457 of the 353rd Fighter Group, 351st Fighter Squadron, YJ-A, flown by 2nd Lt. Joseph Farley.

Supermarine Walrus HD917, BA·U, is known to have been on strength with No. 277 Squadron of the RAF in May 1944. On 28 May, Squadron Leader Raoul Wallens piloted a Walrus of this squadron and rescued two crewmembers of B-24J 42-110074 of the 389th Bomb Group from the English Channel.

A belated tribute to the men of the RAF Marine Branch. This is BPBC 68-foot High Speed Launch 2579, operating out of Gorleston and shown as it appeared on 28 May 1944, manned by Flight Off. J. Martinson and his crew, when it rescued the entire crew of B-17G *Reds Rogues* (42-39837) of the 401st Bomb Group after they were obliged to ditch in the North Sea.

Top: Messerschmitt Bf 109G-6 *Black* < (412163) of 6./JG 11, flown by *Unteroffizier* Heinz Kunz. The illustration is a reconstruction based on similar machines and shows typical fighter camouflage of RLM 74/75/76. Bottom: Messerschmitt Bf 109G-6/U4 *Black 6* (441324) of 5./JG 27, flown by *Hauptmann* Eberhard Bock. This illustration is a reconstruction based on typical practice in the unit at the time.

Top: Focke-Wulf Fw 190A-8 *Red 24* (730386) of II./JG 1, flown by *Oberleutnant* Rudiger Kirchmayr. Bottom: Focke-Wulf Fw 190A-7 *Yellow 13* (642540) of 3./JG 11. A reconstruction based on similar aircraft in the unit in May 1944.

At Duxford, Capt. Alwin M. Juchheim talks to his crew chief, Staff Sgt. Robert McCord, prior to yet another combat mission of the 78th Fighter Group from Duxford. On 28 May, Juchheim survived a midair collision with a P-51 of the 363rd Fighter Group over Germany and was made a prisoner of war. Note the auxiliary fuel tank under the fuselage of Juchheim's P-47. It contained 108 gallons of fuel, giving the fighter precious extra time over Germany. The individual aircraft letter J is also displayed on the cowling for identification purposes on the ground. USAAF

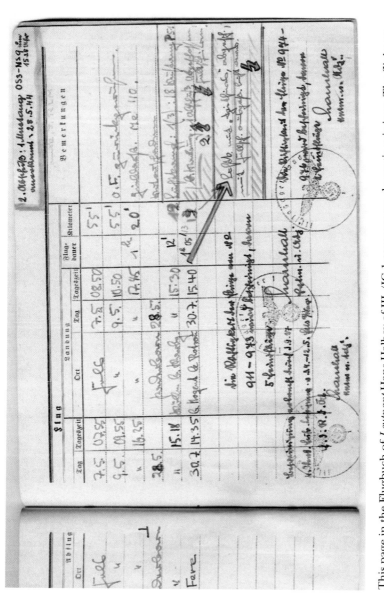

This page in the Flugbuch of *Leutnant* Hans Halbey of III./JG 1 covers some dramatic missions. The flight on 28 May lasted a mere twelve minutes since Halbey was shot down near Mölln by Lt. Walter MacFarlane of the 355th Fighter Group. Having recovered from his wounds, he went back on operations on 30 July over France. He was shot down again and so badly injured that his next flight was not until Christmas that year. HANS HALBEY

Robert Bailey A.S.A.A. © 1997

This painting by Robert Bailey depicts *Feldwebel* Horst Petzschler of 2./JG 3, flying in his Bf 109 G-6 *Schwarze 14*, turning to meet P-51s diving onto the German fighters. With Petzschler and other pilots of the *Hohenstaffel* covering them, pilots such as *Feldwebel* Oscar Boesch in his Fw 190 *Schwarze 14* head for the B-17s in the bomber stream. During this fight, Petzschler shot down Lt. Feodor Clemovitz of the 363rd Fighter Group before he was shot down himself and bailed out of his fighter near Magdeburg. ROBERT BAILEY

This painting by Troy White depicts 2nd Lt. Ralph "Kid" Hofer of the 4th Fighter Group rolling out behind a Bf 109G-6 flown by *Unteroffizier* Heinz Kunz of 6./JG 11. Moments later, the Bf 109 dove into the ground, killing Kunz. Thus, the Kid claimed his fifteenth and last air-to-air victory in his P-51B *Salem Representative* (42-106924). During the engagements in the Magdeburg-Dessau area, Hofer's aircraft was hit in the rudder, but he managed to return to Debden. His luck ran out on 2 July, when he was killed in action.

TROY WHITE / WWW.STARDUSTSTUDIOS.COM

Some members of the lead crew of the 13th A Combat Wing, which led the Magdeburg-bound force, pose in front of B-17G *The Sweetheart of ?* (42-31728). Front row, left to right: Orice D. Settles, lead pilot; Fred W. Murray, bombardier; William E. Orr, navigator; Turner W. Hibbits, co-pilot. Bottom row, left to right: John H. Hill, engineer; Bernard J. Storms, waist gunner; Jeff Garland, ball turret gunner (not on mission); Daniel A. Wright, waist gunner; Joseph Vitaz, radio operator; Robert P. Schrouder, tail gunner (flew with Gilmore crew on 28 May). FRED W. MILLER

The 13th B Combat Wing should have assembled as follows: at 1146 hours, the 95th Bomb Group, leading the wing, was to approach Clacton from the east at 16,000 feet. The 388th Bomb Group was to come in from the south at 17,000 feet and the 94th Bomb Group from the southeast at 15,000 feet. Wing leader was Lt. Col. David C. McKnight, flying in B-17G *Silver Slipper* (42-32066), piloted by Lt. J. W. Hagenbauch. The 388th Bomb Group formation was led by Capt. Leo G. Burkett in B-17G *Gydina* (42-31802) and the 94th Bomb Group by Capt. William C. Healy in B-17G *Belle of the Brawl II* (42-32020).

The events are best described by the report that the operations officer of the 94th Bomb Group submitted: "We took off from base at 1010 hours and made a normal group assembly. We circled out over the Channel and arrived at Clacton at 11.46 hours, from the southeast at an altitude of 15,000 feet, as briefed. We called the combat wing leader before we reached Clacton, and he said he would be on time and on course."[1]

At this point, Lieutenant Vogel left the 94th Bomb Group formation, his radio operator having become unconscious. Although he soon regained consciousness, he was so ill that Vogel took him back to Bury St. Edmunds as soon as possible. The report continues: "Upon arrival at Clacton, we looked for the combat wing but did not see another aircraft within a radius of five miles. On the horizon we could see a number of groups and partially formed wings but they were too distant to have Clacton as their point of assembly. As we left Clacton, we called the wing leader and asked where he was. He said he would be about a minute late, but then called again to say he was four minutes late. We did not see any aircraft in his direction, east.

"Assembly point number 2 was Buncher number 22, where our wing leader reported he would be one minute late. On the way there we had everybody available looking for the other two groups that comprised our wing. Repeated requests to fire flares were complied with by the combat wing leader, according to his VHF, but no formation near us was seen to fire flares. At this time we asked him whether he would be on time at Buncher number 12, the third assembly point. He replied he would be there on time and in as much as we were making the correct time we stayed on course and made every point as briefed, going through Buncher number 22 on time, 1154 hours, and proceeding to Buncher number 12, arriving there on time. This was assembly point number 3 and the beginning of the division assembly line. There were partially formed wings near us when we arrived there at 1158 hours, as briefed, but nowhere could we find a two-group wing. No wing in that area fired a green flare which was assigned to our combat wing. Under these circumstances, there was nothing else to do but proceed along the Division assembly line on course and continue to look for the combat wing leader, using the VHF to establish our relative positions."

Between the lines in this detailed report, which was submitted on 30 May, it is easy to imagine the tension mount aboard the *Belle of the Brawl II*, the calls over the VHF, anxious eyes looking in every direction, lead navigator and pilot constantly checking their briefing notes and actual location.

The report continues: "We arrived at Splasher number 9 at 1203 hours and turned on course to Great Yarmouth, continuously calling the wing leader to find out where he was, whether he had seen our flares and requesting flares from him. A short time later, we observed a three-group wing firing green-green flares but upon closing, we were requested by the leader to stay out of the formation. Our leader's flares were never visible to us or to any aircraft in our formation. This being the case, we decided to proceed to Great Yarmouth, figuring that by the time they reached the coast, the Wings would all be formed in their proper position and that a well formed two-group wing would be readily apparent. We crossed the coast thirty seconds before briefed time, 1213 hours, and upon crossing we called the wing leader again, asking where he was. The reply we got was that he thought he saw us to the right and that we should 'S' to the left, which we did, even though there was no formation apparent. When we contacted him again, he said he was directly behind us, requesting that we 'S' out to the right, which we did and then back on course, but still no formation apparent. We were never at any point given a geographical position from which to work. His explanation of position in terms relative to our own group could by no means have been sufficient, unless the wing leader was actually where he said he was in respect to us. We therefore continued 'S'ing, calling and asking for flares and firing flares in an effort to determine where he was and to form our combat wing. The wing leader used up all the flares in his aircraft in an attempt to aid us in locating him. His high squadron leader then continued to fire flares, according to VHF conversation.

"At a point about twenty miles out, on course from control point number 1, our officer/tail gunner called to say that approximately ten miles behind us there was a two-Group formation. At that time we called the wing leader and asked what his position was in relation to the coast. He replied that he was just crossing the coast at the time of my call; thereupon I notified him that we were some distance out in the Channel and would 'S' to the right in an attempt to pick him up. (Previous to this, he had called me to say that he spotted us several miles behind him and would slow down so that we could effect assembly with him; however, there were no two-group wings within sight in front of us at that time.) We did 'S' to the right and then proceeded back to the left. After this procedure we came quite close to the two-group wing which our tail gunner had spotted and, thinking it was our wing, we called the wing leader and asked him to fire some flares again. No flares were fired from the formation near us and, further, we noticed that the formation behind them had four groups.

"Behind the four-group wing there were no aircraft whatsoever. Therefore, it was only logical to assume that the wings which were near us were the 4th and 45th Combat Wings, which were the last two in the division formation and that one wing had acquired a group from the other, making two and four-group wings. At that time it was in my mind to join the two-group wing and go on the mission with them. However, upon calling the bombardier, I found that he did not have any target maps for the target which was to be bombed by that wing, nor did I or my navigator have the plan of bombing, which would be important in effecting the peel-off at the initial point before bombing and also in re-assembling after the target had been hit. At that time, and even now, after some reflection, it does not seem to me that it would have been a wise choice to risk aircraft and men in a mission on which we could neither defend ourselves properly nor put the bombs in the place where they would do the most good."

At this point, the 94th Bomb Group formation turned back to England. All twenty aircraft and their crews landed at Bury St. Edmunds, each returning its load of thirty-eight 100-pound general-purpose bombs. Chagrined, the operations officer concluded: "The time of reaching assembly points and control points were corroborated by the other lead navigators in our group. Since visibility was very good, it is incredible that we would not have seen our combat wing if they were at the proper place at the proper time. At no time did the wing leader give us a geographical position from which we could work at effecting an assembly or an interception at a point further along the briefed courses. No member of any crew in the group, although they were all alerted, spotted the formation we were trying to join and which was continuously shooting flares."

Obviously, the operations officer of the 95th Bomb Group also had to submit a report. He made a much briefer one: "The 95th Bomb Group, flying as lead group in the 13th B Combat Wing, took off from base at 0950 to 1004 hours and assembled over the field at 2,000 feet by 1025 hours. Leader began climb to rendezvous altitude and made the first rendezvous point, at 1148 hours, two minutes late at 16,000 feet and three miles south of Clacton. The other two groups in the wing, the 388th and the 94th, were ahead of us at the wing rendezvous—so the 95th leader cut short his course and picked up the 388th Group before leaving the English coast. The 94th Group was still unsighted. Shortly before leaving the English coast, a group of B-24s crossed the wing's path and in order to avoid a collision; the wing leader made a sharp left turn and back on course—which caused a further loss of time. Therefore, the wing left the coast seven miles north of course, Great Yarmouth, and three minutes late at 1215 hours at an altitude of 16,000 feet. Climb to 20,000 feet was begun. While crossing the Channel, the 94th Group, which was still up ahead, decided to make a 180-degree turn in order to contact the 13th B Wing, if possible. While making this turn, the group lost sight of the division and was forced to abandon the mission. Therefore, only two groups composed the 13th Wing."[2]

Again, an interfering B-24 formation was used as an excuse for troubles during assembly. The matter was never pursued, as the pace of operations was so high in this period of the war.

During formation of the 95th Bomb Group, Lt. E. L. Rossetti aborted and returned to Horham because the number two engine on his B-17G *Pride of Vhelhalis* (42-37889) failed. His place as a spare was taken by Lt. Norman A. Ulrich in B-17G *Ol' Boy* (42-31924). The two other spares returned unused. The third and last group in this wing, the 388th from Knettishall, fared worse. This group took off from 0940 to 1000 hours with twenty-one aircraft, eighteen for the formation and three spares. No fewer than six of these returned before reaching the enemy coast. Lieutenant Maple's number one engined failed over the base, Lieutenant Elliot found his own oxygen system out and Lieutenant McArthur returned as a scheduled spare. But after this last spare had left, Lieutenant Phillips's number three supercharger went out at altitude, Lieutenant Newell's number two propeller ran away, and Lieutenant Salles returned when he suffered badly from sinusitus. So a depleted 13th B Combat Wing, with only thirty-three aircraft instead of the briefed fifty-four, crossed the coast of Holland at 1254 hours, seven minutes late, but on course and at an altitude of 20,000 feet.

For both combat wings, landfall and flight to the target were routine, but troubles began near the initial point, when the "misplaced" 94th Combat Wing had to go to Dessau. The two wings it was flying in between—the 13th A and B—had to turn for Magdeburg. As we have seen before, Maj. George Hozier, leading the Dessau-bound Fortresses, had to cut short near the initial point to make up time, and consequently the available fighter escort was strung out in the target area.

As the bombers droned over the North Sea and Holland toward Magdeburg, several fighter groups had taken off in England to relieve the 356th Fighter Group from their escort duty. Among these were the 354th and 357th Fighter Groups, assigned to the Magdeburg wings and both destined to engage in fierce encounters with the *Luftwaffe*. After departure at 1139 hours from their base at Lashenden, near Maidstone, the forty-nine Mustangs from the 354th Fighter Group climbed out over the North Sea at an economical speed to reduce gas consumption. No fewer than ten of the pilots had to abort the mission. A flight of four was unable to find the formation at all, a pilot became ill and five had other reasons for aborting.

Just back from a mission, with the strains of his oxygen mask still visible on his face, his hair uncombed and his pistol still in a shoulder holster, 1st Lt. Don McDowell is treated with coffee and a doughnut. On 28 May, he disappeared over the North Sea, and his body washed ashore in England nearly two months later.
STEVE BLAKE

One of these five was 1st Lt. Don McDowell, an experienced and popular pilot in the group, flying in P-51B 42-106712. He was already credited with the destruction of nine German aircraft in air combat, including three on the same day (21 February 1944). At about 1247 hours, McDowell gave a brief radio call to his flight leader, 1st Lt. Carl Frantz, and stated that he had to return to base. The Mustangs were at an altitude of 22,000 feet and only five minutes before landfall at Brielle, Holland. Frantz acknowledged receipt of the message with a simple "Roger."

McDowell then dropped from formation and turned back on course toward England. The reason for McDowell's abort only became clear, when 1st Lt. Philip D. Cohen wrote: "I was flying as number four on Don McDowell's wing on this escort mission and I had to abort due to a toothache. On the ground, the tooth felt fine, but at 22,000 feet it really hurt. I immediately turned around, being just over the coast of Holland, and turning with me, to accompany me home was Don McDowell. We immediately dropped to 14,000 feet for two reasons. The first was the oxygen mask, which you could take off at this altitude, the second was to smoke a cigarette. We were fifty feet in distance, to cover each others tail. I turned to my right and Don was there, I turned to my left and it was blue sky, turned to my right again and Don was gone. I circled around about three times and barked in the radio—in code—and finally called: 'Don, where are you?' There was no reply. This was in the middle of the North Sea. In about thirty or forty minutes, I landed at Lashenden, got out of the P-51 and, after reporting Don's disappearance, took a jeep to the dentists tent and sat in his chair. This was a loose tooth and after the dentist had pulled it, he then showed it to me."[3]

No explanation was ever found for Don McDowell's sudden disappearance. Whatever the cause, he did not survive the North Sea. His body was washed ashore in England in the second half of July and was buried at the American Military Cemetery in Brookwood. The 354th Fighter Group formation continued and would revenge the death of their comrade later that day.

At the same time that Major Hozier's Dessau-bound 94th Combat Wing was hit by the large formations of German fighters, the same thing happened to the 13th A Combat Wing, heading for Magdeburg. The 390th Bomb Group, leading this wing, bore the brunt of the attack. Although the escorting fighters of the 354th and 357th Fighter Groups tried as hard as they could, *Luftwaffe* fighters were able to close in on the bombers, and a fierce battle developed.

Col. Frederick W. Ott, the recently appointed 390th Bomb Group commanding officer, flying as wing leader in *Mary Jane*, piloted by Lt. Orice D. Settles, saw five or six formations of enemy fighters, assemble in front of him. At 1407 hours, they came in, firing on the lead group from head-on.

One of these formations, with some twenty Fw 190s, fifteen Bf 109s, and five Me 410s, made a saturation attack on the group from between twelve and two o'clock. The enemy aircraft were stacked up in a line abreast, from low to level, in three or four rows.

The Me 410s broke off their attack about 3,000 yards out of the formation, firing rockets to break up the formation. The other enemy fighters hit the group en masse, with some going through to make individual attacks on the low group of the wing, although most of them broke off down and away. No fewer than five B-17s of the 390th Bomb Group were hit fatally during this attack.

It is a tribute to the experience and leadership of the commander of the major German formation, *Oberleutnant* Rüdiger Kirchmayr of JG 1, that despite American fighters all around, he had been able to maneuver his unit so as to be able to execute such a head-on attack on a B-17 formation.

One of the assailants was *Feldwebel* Rudolf Lehmann of 4./JG 1, in Fw 190A-8 *Weisse 13* (170416): "On 28 May, after having been on readiness for some time, I took off at 13.05 hours as a *Rottenführer* (element leader) in II./JG 1. We were ordered to assemble with I./JG 1 and III./JG 1 at a height of 1,000 meters over Paderborn and were ordered to fly a course of 100

The crew of B-17G *Mountaineer* (42-32089) of the 390th Bomb Group. Front row, left to right: Adolph J. Matthias, pilot; Henry J. Gerards, co-pilot; Lieutenant Little, navigator (not on 28 May mission); and Quentin R. Bass, bombardier. Back row, left to right: Jerry Wolf, engineer; Charles M. Oliver, ball turret gunner; Leon C. Walker, tail gunner; and Charles N. Abbot, radio operator. All were made prisoner of war.
QUENTIN R. BASS

degrees. After a few course alterations, we met a formation of Me 109s and Me 410s at 1400 hours in the vicinity of Magdeburg. At the same time we sighted five enemy bomber formations on an easterly heading at 7,500 meters, with a heavy fighter escort.

"We attacked the Boeings head-on at 1407 hours. During this concentrated attack on the first group, I fired on the left, outward-flying Boeing. Parts of its right inboard engine flew off, and in addition I could see strikes in the cockpit area and fuselage. The Boeing started to burn, emitting dark smoke, and fell away from the formation. Because I was immediately engaged by the enemy fighter escort, I could not observe further developments."[4]

This B-17 was probably B-17G 42-32089 of the 570th Bomb Squadron, flown by 1st Lt. Adolph J. Matthias and 2nd Lt. Henry J. Gerards in the number three position in the lead squadron. Some years later, Gerards wrote down the events of the day: "It so happened I was flying the ship as we reached the initial point, where we turned for the bomb-run. From the initial point to bombs-away, a two-minute run, we had to fly straight and level to give Bass [2nd Lt. Quentin R. Bass, bombardier] a chance to aim. This was when flak became deadly. Flak began to come up thick for a short time, then suddenly stopped and all hell broke loose. Head on we saw about 25 enemy planes attacking. I called over the intercom 'enemy fighters, twelve o'clock low.' Then we saw they were hitting our low group. They were Me 410s. But up ahead about the same number of Fw 190s were coming in. This time I could feel the recoil of our guns spitting and five or six seconds later they had gone through us. Some above and some below. A few of our planes dropped out of formation, and we knew these boys would not be in their bunks that night, talking and laughing about the mission just completed. Then another group, another twenty-five Me 109s, were coming in head-on. Wow! I could see one with a bead right between my eyes.

"Our guns started spurting. Then I could see fire from his wings and nose. A row of small caliber bullets hit our windshield at eye level all the way across and along my side window. Wham! A 20mm shell exploded below us in the cockpit. As the Me 109 slipped about ten feet under our wing, the cockpit filled with smoke. I opened the window slightly and the smoke cleared out immediately. We had been badly hit. Numbers one, two and three engines were all hit. Matt tried to feather the props, but they failed. I tried again but no good. The engines were too badly shot up. Even the cowling and some of the cylinders had been blown off by the 20mm shells. The ship was hard to hold level now with just number four engine running and the vibration was terrific. Matt ordered bombs away and coincidentally Bass dropped ours with the groups' bombs. Wanting to use our altitude to carry us as far as possible to safety, I called the navigator for a heading to Sweden. Bass answered back, 'Joe's hurt.'"[5]

Second Lt. Quentin R. Bass, the bombardier of *Mountaineer*. He was shot down and became a prisoner of war on 28 May. QUENTIN R. BASS

Miraculously, the cannon fire had injured only one crewmember. Navigator 2nd Lt. Joseph P. Freyland was hit by a 20mm shell in his right leg, which almost severed it just below the knee. Bombardier Quentin R. Bass, busy firing at the oncoming German fighters, immediately administered first aid and, upon command of the pilot, helped Freyland out of the nose escape hatch, with his parachute fixed and the rip cord in his hand. To the great relief of the crew, they saw his parachute open and descend slowly to the ground.

Lieutenant Freyland was picked up by Germans and admitted to a hospital in Wolmirstedt, where he underwent surgery. Unfortunately, his right leg had to be amputated, and eventually, he was returned to the United States during an exchange of prisoners of war. In January 1945, he came home on the SS *Gripsholm*, a Swedish ship chartered by the International Red Cross. Gerards continues his account: "I sat there with a sort of helpless feeling, trying to fly a straight heading. But with full right rudder and stick, we were still circling to the left. Then Matt poked me and motioned to bail out, and I asked why. He pointed to number two engine. I stretched my neck and looked. The engine was on fire back of the fire wall. In another few seconds it would blow up. I flipped on the automatic pilot, pulled the cords and wires on my chest releasing my flak suit, oxygen mask and all that junk. Then I hooked on my chest pack-chute and crawled through the catwalk to the nose hatch. Bass and the engineer were waiting, so out I went.

Second Lt. Joseph P. Freyland, the
navigator of *Mountaineer*. He was
badly wounded in his right leg
during the fighter attacks on 28
May and was bailed out by bombardier Quentin R. Bass. His leg
had to be amputated, and he
returned to the United States
in January 1945 during an
exchange of prisoners of war.
MRS. DORIS FREYLAND

"For a few seconds, I fell lying flat on my back. There was no sensation
of falling and it was like lying on the softest bed ever. The wind made a loud
roar as I fell through space. I began to think it was time to pull the ripcord,
but I couldn't see how far it was to the ground. Then a new experience. I
stuck my arm out slightly to turn over. I had heard stories of men soaring
like birds, but I never thought I would try it. The result was a series of outside loops, snap rolls, Immelmanns, chandelle's, spins, spirals and slow-rolls.
I did them all and some new ones too. It was on a slow roll, I guess, that I saw
the ground clearly and could make out the trees plainly. I had passed
through a broken layer of clouds at about 10,000 or 12,000 feet and it was
time to pull. With a quick, hard jerk, the ripcord pulled clear out and I
dropped it. Although it was only a second, it seemed like an hour till that
chute opened. But open it did—and with a bad jolt. It looked wonderful up
there all blossomed out and floating me down to earth safely. There were
about eight or ten small holes along the bottom edge of one panel, and I
wondered if a bullet had passed through the chute or perhaps a mouse had
been hungry back at the base. It was really fun floating down like that but
the chute straps bit into my legs pretty bad and there was no way to relieve it.

"The ground was getting closer and I could see that I would land in one
of two forests. One had large trees thinned out and the other was a field of
young pines planted in neat rows and very dense. My hope was to come

down between the large trees. But no, it had to be the other way. I crossed my legs and put my arms over my face. Then I waited and prayed for a good landing. The tree limbs brushed me as I settled easily between the rows. I was down with my feet on good solid earth again—and all in one piece. Thank God! My back hurt a bit and I had a cut on my hand. Otherwise, I was in tip-top shape, it was now 14.15 hours."

German records indicate that Gerards was captured at 2035 hours near the village of Colbitz, at the road from Magdeburg to Stendal. His experiences during that afternoon and early evening are described in chapter 13. He then was transported to the airfield Magdeburg-Ost, where he met half of his crew. Four crewmembers still at large were all captured within a few days. Their bomber crashed at Holzhausen, twenty-six kilometers north of Magdeburg.

Unteroffizier Fritz Wurl of 6./JG 1 was flying in Fw 190A-8 *Gelbe 14* (W.Nr. 170437) and reported: "After making contact with the enemy in the vicinity of Magdeburg at around 7,500 meters, we attacked a group of twenty-five to thirty B-17s with fighter escort, heading east, at 1407 hours.

"We made a concentrated attack on the front of the bombers. During this attack I fired three bursts on the B-17, flying second from right in the formation. At 300 meters, I fired the first burst. The B-17 immediately caught fire in both righthand engines and emitted black smoke. During the second and third bursts I was able to hit the front of the fuselage. During my attack, I saw how a part of the glass canopy of the B-17 flew off. When I broke down right, I saw how the B-17 I had attacked went down burning, falling away over its left wing. Emitting white smoke, it then went straight down. At around 6,000 meters the Boeing exploded. One crewmember parachuted. I couldn't observe the impact of the burning parts of the plane, because I was having a dog fight with six enemy fighters. During this fight, I received a hit in my cockpit."[6]

The bomber which met such a fiery end was probably B-17G *Devil's Aces* (42-31985). It was flown by the crew of 2nd Lt. John H. Ingram, who had been scheduled as a spare, but had to fill in, since another aircraft had aborted the mission in an early stage. *Devil's Aces* flew in the number five position in the lead squadron. Results of the fighter attack were disastrous. Left waist gunner Edward Czyz recalled: "It was an easy flight to the target area. Then, all of a sudden, we were attacked by a large number of German fighters, coming in from twelve o'clock. Already during their first pass, we were heavily hit. I am sure that we lost the navigator and one or both of the pilots in this attack. At the same time also the entire tail section, with gunner Arnold McKee in it, was shot off. I recall somebody yelling to bail out, before the intercom went out. The plane was then going into a sort of flat spin and at the same time spiralling down. I was pinned to the side of the fuselage by

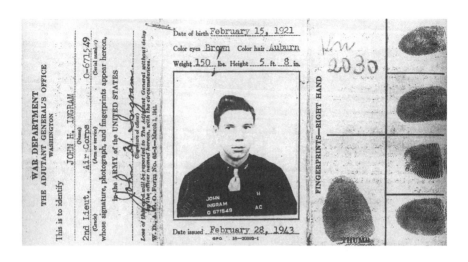

The Germans recovered several personal documents from the wreck of *Devil's Aces*, among them John Ingram's identification card as well as some slips of paper that should not have been taken on an operational mission since they gave the Germans much information about the unit to which the crew belonged. Such information could be of benefit in future interrogations of other crews from the 390th Bomb Group. NATIONAL ARCHIVES

the centrifugal forces. I managed to grab my parachute, but caught it by the handle of its ripcord. It then sort of popped open inside the aircraft. I snapped it on my harness, holding the chute together. Somehow I then managed to reach the waist door and pulled myself out, or was pulled out by the partially opened chute. I wasn't in the air very long before reaching the ground. I have no idea how the other two survivors, bombardier Daniel Cosgrove and engineer William Buntin managed to get out."[7]

Devil's Aces crashed near Lostau, ten kilometers northeast of Magdeburg. Four crewmembers were buried in the Hohenwarte cemetery. One crewmember was not found until 25 June and buried in Körbelitz. The bodies of two other crewmembers, McKee and Lewis, were never found, and both men remain missing in action.

One of the other aircraft in the lead squadron of the 390th Bomb Group was B-17G *Bomboogie* (42-31974), piloted by Lt. Robert C. Gilmore

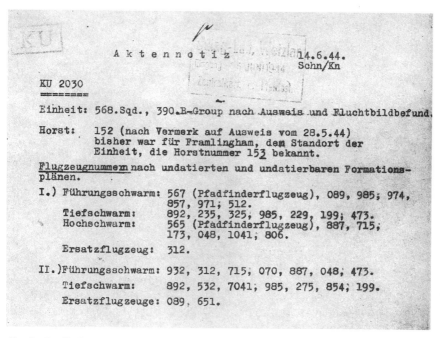

```
                        A k t e n n o t i z                    14.6.44.
                                                               Schn/Kn
     KU 2030
     ========
     Einheit: 568.Sqd., 390.B-Group nach Ausweis und Fluchtbildbefund.

     Horst:   152 (nach Vermerk auf Ausweis vom 28.5.44)
              bisher war für Framlingham, dem Standort der
              Einheit, die Horstnummer 153 bekannt.
     Flugzeugnummern nach undatierten und undatierbaren Formations-
     plänen.
     I.) Führungsschwarm: 567 (Pfadfinderflugzeug), 089, 985; 974,
                              857, 971; 512.
         Tiefschwarm:     892, 235, 325; 985, 229, 199; 473.
         Hochschwarm:     565 (Pfadfinderflugzeug), 887, 715;
                          173, 048, 1041; 806.

         Ersatzflugzeug:  312.

     II.)Führungsschwarm: 932, 312, 715; 070, 887, 048; 473.
         Tiefschwarm:     892, 532, 7041; 985, 275, 854; 199.
         Ersatzflugzeuge: 089, 651.
```

Also in *Devil's Aces*, one or more old formation diagrams were found. These provided the Germans with much information. At one glance, they had the last three digits of the serial numbers of many 390th Bomb Group aircraft and were able to piece together the lead squadron (*Führungsschwarm*) with its Pathfinder aircraft (*Pfadfinderflugzeug*), low squadron (*Tiefschwarm*), high squadron (*Hochschwarm*), and the spare aircraft (*Ersatzflugzeug*). With this information in hand and provided with some data on a crashed B-17, a German interrogator at Dulag Luft could catch out a 390th Bomb Group crewmember who was trying to stick to the rule of just mentioning name, rank, and number. NATIONAL ARCHIVES

and Lt. Charles N. Baker. The latter recorded the events in his diary, after his safe return to Framlingham that evening: "When we arose early this morning, little did we realize we would come home to an almost empty barracks. Both Matthias and Ingram went down, no chutes reported. Our target for today was Magdeburg. Got usual flak in for our route was straight for Berlin, which was a feint. However, we turned south and to the target some eighty miles before Berlin.

"With our bomb bay doors open and just three minutes before bombs away, we noticed high at one o'clock, five P-51s drop their belly tanks, and head for six o'clock; evidently fighters had been sighted there. About one minute later Gillie nudged me and pointed out front at another formation. I picked up the binoculars and what I saw could chill a persons blood for instead of B-17s all I saw were twoengined and single-engined ships.

"Here they came, some forty or fifty of them heading straight for us and every one firing. 20mm cannon shells were exploding all around us. With this one pass they knocked Ingram, who was flying on our right wing down, and also Matthias who was right above us.

"As these fellows came by, I got a picture of one. At this time, Ordel [Arthur W. Ordel, bombardier] was shooting at one at a hundred yards, which then exploded. Hope I got it in the picture. I hadn't noticed, but later Gillie told me an Fw 190 had to turn up in a ninety degree bank in order to come between us over our left wing. Don't know how many Jerries went down on this pass, but rest assured there were a good many.

"As they went by, they began to queue up at once to come through again. Made a pass from eleven and from one. Got usual flak on route out as we 'sweated,' even shot at us as we were going out over the Channel."[8]

One B-17 in the high squadron was badly hit in the fighter attack. It was B-17G *Silver Slipper* (42-102440), flying in the number four position. It was last observed by others in the formation, on fire and in a steep, descending spiral. Co-pilot F/O Charles A. Richardson was wounded in one arm, but the rest of the crew escaped injury. With two engines out on the same side, one of which was on fire, pilot 2nd Lt. Walter P. Weigle had no choice but to ring the bail-out bell. Right waist gunner, Sgt. Gale W. Minor, made sure that ball turret gunner, Sgt. Irvin T. Mniszewski, got out of his turret and put on his chute properly and then followed the other crewmembers out. All crewmembers landed safely and were quickly captured, since they landed near the *Luftwaffe* base at Burg, near Magdeburg. Their abandoned B-17 crashed at Gut Lüben, four kilometers northeast of Burg.

Two other B-17s, numbers one and two in the high squadron, were hit by the sudden attack, but, although damaged, managed to keep their positions and returned to Framlingham. Both the loss of Weigle's B-17 and the damaging of two others can be attributed to a number of pilots of JG 1. One of

The crew of B-17G *Silver Slipper* (42-102440) of the 390th Bomb Group. Back row, left to right: Walter P. Weigle, pilot; Charles A. Richardson, co-pilot; Herman H. Preusser, navigator; and Elmer D. Severson, bombardier. Front row, left to right: Thomas J. Curiston, engineer; Gale W. Minor, right waist gunner; Donald F. Rudolph, radio operator; Joseph M. Becker, left waist gunner; Alexander Spotanski, tail gunner; and Irvin T. Mniszewski, ball turret gunner. All were made prisoners of war. GALE W. MINOR

them was *Unteroffizier* Erwin Steeb of 6./JG 1, in Fw 190A-8 *Gelbe 2* (W.Nr. 730403), who reported: "During the first head-on attack, I fired at a range from 600 to 100 meters on a Boeing, flying to the right in the formation. I obtained hits in its fuselage, cockpit and left wing. While large parts from the fuselage and cockpit flew away, the left inboard engine started to burn, with dark smoke emitting. When I turned right, I noticed that the Boeing that I had attacked lost height and started to fall behind the formation. I could not observe it any further, because I became engaged in a dog fight with enemy fighters."[9]

He was awarded a *Herausschuss*, not an *Abschuss*. This meant the board which evaluated fighter claims judged that Steeb succeeded only in forcing a bomber to leave its formation instead of actually shooting it down. However, the bombers which left the protection of the combat wing formation were later often jumped upon by other fighters and then shot down. Two other German pilots, this time of 4./JG 1, also claimed an *Herausschuss* over an American B-17.

Feldwebel Adolf Schulz was flying in Fw 190A-8 *Weisse 8* (W.Nr. 37331): "I fired at a distance from 400 to 100 meters on the Boeing flying second from left in the first formation. I observed hits in the forward half of the aircraft and small parts flew off. After I had cleared the formation, I noticed that the Boeing I had fired upon was lagging behind and gradually lost altitude. I was attacked by the enemy fighter escort and could not observe any further."[10]

Gefreiter Walter Gehr in Fw 190A-8 *Weisse 9* (W.Nr. 680143) reported: "At 1400 hours, flying in the vicinity of Magdeburg at 7,500 meters, we sighted five formations of enemy Boeing F IIs, with strong fighter escort. During our first concentrated attack at 1407 hours I attacked a Boeing F II in the first, high-flying formation of about twenty-five to thirty Boeing F IIs. I scored hits in the cockpit. In addition some parts of the aircraft flew off. The Boeing lost altitude and dropped away from the rear of the formation. Due to attacks by their fighter escort, I could not observe the Boeing any further."[11]

Both Schulz and Gehr were among the many pilots the *Luftwaffe* would lose in the battles ahead. Schulz had to make a belly-landing the next day, returned to combat and was killed in action on 31 May. Gehr was killed in action on 20 July in France.

Unteroffizier Erwin Steeb in the cockpit of his Fw 190A-7 W.Nr. 40282 of 6./JG 1. He was awarded a *Herausschuss* in the Magdeburg area during his attack on B-17s of the 390th Bomb Group on 28 May. The next day, he had to bail out of this aircraft and was wounded. HANS LÄCHLER

One of the German pilots who actually saw some of the crewmembers leave a stricken bomber after he had hit it was *Feldwebel* Alfred Bindseil of 6./JG 1, flying in Fw 190A-8 *Gelbe 11* (W.Nr.110303), who reported: "On 28 May, I took off at 1305 hours and flew as *Rottenführer* (element leader) in II./JG 1. After sighting the enemy, our group attacked a formation of about twenty-five to thirty Boeing B-17s in the vicinity of Magdeburg at 1407 hours. We attacked head-on. After turning away after the pass I momentarily lost sight of the formation. I immediately pulled up again and saw a formation of twenty to twenty-five Boeing B-17s about 1,000 meters above me, heading east. I pulled up from behind and positioned myself in a good firing position. I then fired multiple bursts at the last Boeing at a range from 800 to 200 meters. I hit him in the fuselage and right wing and at the wing root white smoke appeared. Already during my attack, I observed two crewmembers jumping out with their parachutes and that the bomber lagged back considerably. I then was attacked by enemy fighters and could not observe further events."[12]

His victim was probably the B-17 flying in the vulnerable number six position of the low squadron of the 390th Bomb Group. This was B-17G *Decatur Deb* (42-31651), flown by 2nd Lt. Herbert V. Strate and his crew, all on their third or forth mission. It peeled out of formation with the cockpit afire, and part of the vertical stabilizer shot away. It was seen to attempt to regain its position, then started going down in a spin. From the doomed bomber, only three men were able to save themselves and parachute into captivity. These were the engineer, Staff Sgt. Edward C. Stoy, the left waist gunner, Sgt. Harold B. Bolton and the tail gunner, Sgt. Edward D. Molenock.

Staff Sgt. Stoy recalled: "We were flying in our B-17 *Decatur Deb*, loaded with thirty-eight 100-pound high-explosive bombs. On the front of each bomb was an eight-inch rough-cut propeller, which was unscrewed by the wind while falling and armed the bomb. After we crossed the Channel, Lieutenant Strate informed me that one of the generators was not working. I tried but was unable to repair it in flight. He asked me if we should turn back or continue. I wanted to turn back because I did not think the engine would last for eight hours without a generator, but he made the decision to continue. After some two hours, and fairly heavy flak, we approached the bomb-run and the bomb bay doors were opened.

"It was exactly 1400 hours when we started the bomb-run. At that time someone on our intercom called out bandits at twelve o'clock. In the distance there were hundreds of fighter planes coming towards us. Within seconds they were all over us and all hell broke loose. The plane was shuddering from all of our guns, when suddenly we were hit by something big. I found out later this was when part of the tail was shot off. The plane

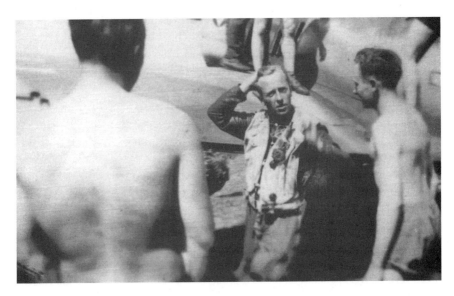

Feldwebel Alfred Bindseil of 6./JG 1 has just landed in his Fw 190A-8 170393 *Gelbe 11* at Störmede, and ground crews, dressed for the weather, are anxious to learn about his combat experiences. Bindseil probably shot down *Decatur Deb* of the 390th Bomb Group while flying this Fw 190. Note the insignia for JG 1, a winged "1" in a white diamond on the cowling. ERIC MOMBEEK started into a dive and started to roll to the left. I dropped down from the top turret to remove my oxygen mask and put on my chute. The pilot and co-pilot were down in the forward escape hatch, which had smoke coming out of it. The hatch is only big enough for one person at a time and time was running out for me. I pushed my way through the door into the bomb bay. The arming props of the bombs were about one and a half feet from the forward bulkhead and I dove headfirst between the props and the bulkhead. I didn't make it. The arming props caught on my pants and jacket which caused me to be hung upside down on the end of the bombs, with no way to get loose.

"After a short period of time trying to get loose and wondering what my mother and wife would think when I didn't return, something amazing happened. All of a sudden, something or someone salvoed all of the bombs, with me stuck to the bottom bomb. With the plane in a dive and rolling over, the bombs drove me head-first into the left forward corner and side of the bomb bay. The bombs hit me as they tore out part of the side of the plane.

The crew of B-17G *Decatur Deb* (42-31651) of the 390th Bomb Group. Back row, left to right: George Vincent, navigator (not on 28 May mission); Robert L. Woolfolk, bombardier (KIA); Samuel R. Elliot, co-pilot (KIA); and Herbert V. Strate, pilot (KIA). Front row, left to right: Nick Mamula, radio operator (KIA); Arthur E. Reed, ball turret gunner (KIA); Robert B. Smart, right waist gunner (KIA); Edward C. Stoy, engineer (POW); Edward D. Molenock, tail gunner (POW); and Harold B. Bolton, left waist gunner (POW). MRS. ANN ZURAVIC VIA EDWARD C. STOY

The top of my head was cut by the dive into the corner, and my face, back, and arms were cut by the arming props. My chute was OK, so I backed up to the jagged edges of the plane and fell out backwards. As I fell, I looked up and saw what was left of the plane. It was a ball of flames and had no tail or wings. I was the only one in the front of the plane to survive. Three survived, seven died, I was lucky."[13]

Staff Sgt. Nick Mamula was radio operator of *Decatur Deb*. On 28 May, he was flying on his third combat mission. His aircraft was hit by enemy fighters and went down in a spin. Only three of the crew survived. Mamula was killed and is buried at the Lorraine American Cemetery and Memorial in France. MRS. ANN ZURAVIC

Oberleutnant Rüdiger Kirchmayr prepares for take off in an Fw 190A-6. Note the red band around the fuselage, known as the *Reichsverteidigungsband* (Defense of the Reich Band). The bar in it denotes that the aircraft belongs to *II Gruppe*.
ERIC MOMBEEK

Decatur Deb crashed at 14.08 hours near Ebendorf, four kilometers northeast of Magdeburg, close to the location where a B-17 of the 100th Bomb Group would crash within a few minutes. The remains of the crewmembers who were killed were buried on 6 June in the Westerhüsener cemetery in Magdeburg.

The fifth and last B-17 the 390th Bomb Group lost in this fierce attack flew in the number three position in the low squadron. It was B-17G *Starks Ark* (42-37806). This aircraft, flown by 1st Lt. Henry C. Holmes, was last observed at about 7,000 feet with number two engine and the left wing afire, going straight down. It probably fell victim to experienced *Oberleutnant* Rüdiger Kirchmayr, the *Staffelkapitän* of 5./JG 1, who flew Fw 190A-8 *Rote 24* (W.Nr. 730386). His combat report states: "I took off and led the formation of *Jagdgeschwader 1.* At around 1400 hours, we sighted the enemy, about 400 B-17s and B-24s with a strong fighter escort, on an easterly heading. During the first concentrated attack on a group of about twenty-five to thirty B-17s, I attacked the B-17 flying furthest left. The group formation was stacked fairly flat, not high, but broad. The Boeing I fired upon lost parts of the cockpit area and fuselage, white smoke poured out and it went down in a tight left spin. While we were pulling up and forming up for a second attack, I could only see eleven B-17s, some of them pouring smoke, still in the group that we first attacked. The other Boeings were lagging far behind. I could see that one of the Boeings that was still flying in the formation, and was emitting smoke, suddenly exploded, without being attacked any further."[14]

Pictured just after a successful mission in early 1944 are pilots of JG 1. In the center, below the cockpit, is *Oberleutnant* Rüdiger Kirchmayr. He led JG 1 in battle on 28 May and claimed a B-17 and a P-47 for his forty-seventh and forty-eighth victories.
ERIC MOMBEEK

Oberleutnant Rüdiger Kirchmayr's log book with the entries for his actions on 28 May. The first was credited to him; the latter was not. RÜDIGER KIRCHMAYR

Miraculously, all of this doomed B-17's crewmembers survived and parachuted. However, one of them, radio operator Tech Sgt. Forest L. Knight, was killed by German civilians on the ground. Engineer Tech Sgt. Victor L. Baccaro, recalled the events: "It was our twenty-fifth mission this day. Just before we began our bomb run, a group of about forty-five enemy fighters were spotted just off our right wing and were flying parallel to us. At this point, we were still waiting for our fighter escort to come in and 'break-up' the enemy's formation. Our escort never did show. The enemy aircraft included Fw 190s, Me 109s, Me 110s, and various others. The enemy flew ahead of us, made a left turn, lined-up in a couple of layers and then attacked in a frontal assault. They flew through our formation, attacking with all they had and all our ships guns were facing forward to meet this attack. At this point, both our starboard engines [official report says port engines] were hit, and on fire. We were flying at 28,000 feet at the time of the attack and were able to drop our bomb load on the target prior to being hit. We exhausted our mounted fire extinguishers and found they had no effect on the engine fires. We began a rapid descent and again were hit by the enemy aircraft. At this time the pilot gave the bail-out order. Five of the crew, including myself, bailed out through the hatch under the cockpit and another four went out through a rear door. The tail gunner had his own escape hatch located in the tail and went out there. All crewmembers had to clip on our parachutes after the bail out order was given.

The crew of B-17G *Starks Ark* (42-37806) of the 390th Bomb Group. Back row, left to right: Victor L. Baccaro, engineer (POW); Harold R. Roock, left waist gunner (POW); Sgt. John Tomasko, right waist gunner (not on 28 May mission); Paul A. Kast, tail gunner (POW); Forest L. Knight, radio operator (KIA); and Frank R. Watson, ball turret gunner (POW). Front row, left to right: Henry C. Holmes, pilot (POW); Charles B. Kruger, co-pilot (POW); Walter Steck, navigator (POW); and Oral C. Thompson, bombardier (POW). VICTOR L. BACCARO

"I fell head first through the hatch and stayed that way for about two miles. I pulled my rip cord and the chute 'righted' me. An enemy fighter circled me a couple of times and I hoped and prayed that he wouldn't machine-gun me or turn his tail to collapse my chute. This aircraft left me alone. I landed in a plowed farmers field and many civilians came running toward me. These civilians included women and children. One man in the group pointed a very long rifle at me and kept repeating, 'Pistole, pistole.' I raised my hands and said, 'No pistole, no pistole.' A German patrol arrived and dispersed the crowd and captured me."[15]

No evidence was found as to the actual cause of death of Tech Sgt. Forest L. Knight, whose parachute was seen to open. Since he was described by other crewmembers as headstrong, it is possible that he ran into trouble

Starks Ark was named after 1st Lt. Robert F. Starks. He, his crew, and his aircraft were pictured at Framlingham on 20 January 1944. They were flying another B-17 on the first major Berlin raid on 6 March when they were shot down on their twenty-fifth and final mission of their combat tour. *Starks Ark* was then inherited by the crew of Lt. Henry C. Holmes. They, too, were on their twenty-fifth mission, their thirteenth in *Starks Ark*, when they were shot down near Magdeburg on 28 May. USAAF

when civilians were trying to capture him. He was buried at the community cemetery in Walternienburg and, after the war, was brought to the Lorraine American Cemetery and Memorial in France, where he still rests. *Starks Ark* crashed near Walternienburg, twenty-eight kilometers southeast of Magdeburg. Some of the German fighters continued their attacks into the high group of the wing. It was composed of B-17s of the 100th Bomb Group and was led by 418th Bomb Squadron commanding officer Maj. Magee C. Fuller.

Staff Sgt. William E. Hill was the left waist gunner on B-17G 42-31895 in its lead squadron. He noted in his diary that evening: "We were awakened this morning to go bomb a synthetic oil factory at Magdeburg, Germany. We had beautiful weather today and we made the trip to the initial point just nice. Then, all of a sudden, we were attacked by about thirty-five enemy fighters coming in from the nose and we were No. 2 ship today in the lead

Starks Ark and other 390th Bomb Group B-17s are bracketed by accurate flak on their way to Bremen on 16 December 1943. USAAF

squadron. The group ahead of us was hit by the same ships and they lost six at one time. Our bombardier and navigator got one of them and we scattered the rest. Then, another group of about the same number hit us and a Fortress went down from the high squadron just over our ship and I think they got one in the low squadron too. I was too busy to pay too much attention to our ships as there were enemy fighters all over the sky. We were attacked again twice more by about the same number of fighters but, we scattered them before they reached us. Thank God. Our bomb load for today was 10 x 500-lb GPs [general-purpose bombs]."[16]

Among the *Luftwaffe* pilots sweeping through the 100th Bomb Group formation was *Unteroffizier* Bernhard Golinger of 6./JG 1, flying in Fw 190A-8 *Gelbe 12* (W.Nr.730358). He reported: "I took off at 1305 hours as number four man in the first *Schwarm* [flight] of the *6. Staffel* of II./JG 1. After sighting the enemy, we attacked a formation of twenty-five to thirty B-17s flying east at 7,500 meters head-on, at 1407 hours in the vicinity of Magdeburg. During this attack, I fired at a range from 600 to 100 meters on the Boeing, flying fourth from right. Its righthand engines immediately started to burn and emitted dark smoke. Already during my attack I noticed how parts of the nose section flew off. I could not observe the fall of the Boeing, while I flew through this enemy formation and attacked the first Boeing in the next formation. During this I was attacked from behind by an enemy fighter. I was hit in the engine and left wing. My engine started to burn and flames entered the cockpit. I pulled my plane up and jumped out with my parachute."[17]

Golinger's claim was backed up by *Unteroffizier* Wurl, who saw that the B-17 which Golinger had hit went down "over its left wing with burning engines on its righthand side."

This Boeing, whose demise was also mentioned in Staff Sgt. Hill's account, was B-17G 42-31389, flying in the number four position in the high squadron. The aircraft was aptly named *Lucious Lucy* after its pilot, 1st Lt. Lucius G. Lacy. He was flying with a mixed-up crew, as the co-pilot of his original crew was killed on the 6 March mission to Berlin, and his engineer was killed on the 11 April mission to Poznan. His co-pilot for this mission, 1st Lt. Claude E. Schindler, was held in high regard by the other men, one of them stating: "He flew the roughest missions and was the coolest, calmest co-pilot that ever flew in combat."[18] And bombardier Herbert Greenberg wrote: "If I recall correctly, Schindler was still carrying stitches from a previous wound."[19] The cannon shells mainly struck the right side of the cockpit and started a fire in number four engine.

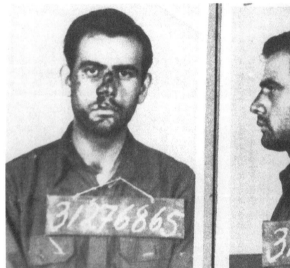

Tech Sgt. Victor L. Baccaro, the engineer of *Starks Ark*, was pictured after his capture on 28 May. He was lucky to escape with his life, as there is strong suspicion that radio operator Forest L. Knight was killed by angry civilians he bailed out from the stricken aircraft. VICTOR L. BACCARO

Lacy recalls the events: "It all happened so very fast. We were hit all over the aircraft. I was temporarily stunned and blinded. When I got my vision back I reached over and saw that my co-pilot, Claude Schindler, was dead. The number one and four engines were on fire. Looking backwards I noticed that the engineer had left, he had probably gone to the waist of the ship. I couldn't see too well and dropped through the hatch into the nose of the aircraft. Here I found that the navigator and bombardier were also gone, as their escape hatch was open. I then bailed out through that hatch, with my chute in my hands. I managed to get it hooked on, but had turned it upside down. This caused a good deal of spinning until I reached the ground. I was picked up almost immediately by German troops."[20]

Three of Lacy's crew were killed by Golinger's fire. Schindler was last seen slumped in his seat with his left arm hanging still and not moving. Also

B-17G *Lucious Lucy* (42-31389) of the 100th Bomb Group above a complete under-cast. On 28 May, it fell victim to fighter attacks near Magdeburg. Three of its crew were killed in action. 100TH BOMB GROUP PHOTO ARCHIVES / MICHAEL FALEY

Lt. Lucius G. Lacy, front row on right, during pilot training. RAY CARY

right waist gunner, Staff Sgt. Joe S. Folsom, was killed by a shell. Ball turret gunner Staff Sgt. Chester L. Powell either was killed by the fighter attack or never had a chance to get out of his turret. Probably, with the electrical systems shot out, he went down with the doomed bomber, which crashed at Barleben, five kilometers north of Magdeburg, very close to *Decatur Deb* of the 390th Bomb Group, that was shot down just moments before. Tail gunner Staff Sgt. Michael Rotz, with several panels blown from his chute, had a rough landing and was taken to a hospital in Magdeburg. All survivors of the crew were captured.

It was, however, not entirely a one-way battle. The gunners in the bombers fought back savagely and spent thousands of rounds of .50-caliber ammunition and claimed several German fighters destroyed. For example, Lt. Vernon O. Breazeale, the bombardier on the B-17 flying in the number five position of the high squadron, reported: "An Me 109 was attacking our

Posing in early 1944 in front of B-17G *Mason and Dixon* (42-31412) is the crew of Arch Drummond. Two of these men were aboard *Lucious Lucy* on 28 May. They are Claude E. Schindler (standing, second from right) and Sidney A. Cary (kneeling, third from right). Co-pilot Schindler was killed in action. Engineer Cary was made a prisoner of war. TALBERT E. SPENHOFF

The six enlisted men of Lieutenant Lacy's original combat crew. Three of them were on the fateful 28 May flight in *Lucious Lucy*. Back row, left to right: Joseph A. Howell (not on 28 May mission); Joe S. Folsom, right waist gunner (KIA); and Herman H. Hilburn (not on 28 May mission). Front row, left to right: Raymond J. Mitchell, left waist gunner (POW); Chester J. Carknard, engineer (KIA on 11 April 1944); and Clarence H. Wood Jr., radio operator (POW). RAY CARY

element leader [Lieutenant Lacy]. I started firing at him at 800 yards, and I gave him four to five short bursts before he got out of range. Pilot bailed out under our left wing tip and the enemy aircraft went down with flames coming from the engine."[21]

His pilot, Lt. Burdette Williams confirmed the claim and stated that this was the enemy fighter which had shot down Lieutenant Lacy. On the same aircraft, 42-107011, the navigator Walter M. Pickett aimed his two machine guns in the nose turret on an Fw 190: "I started firing at the enemy aircraft at 500 yards, I gave him two bursts and he started smoking from engine."[22]

Then tail gunner, Lyle E. Nord, reported over the intercom that he saw the pilot bail out as his aircraft passed the tail, but that he did not see the chute open. Pickett, and Breazeale, were awarded a fighter destroyed.* It is likely that this Fw 190 was that of Bernhard Golinger. The crew on the other

---

* The fortunes of war saw Breazeale killed the very next day, going down with Lieutenant Williams's crew on the mission to Leipzig. Tail gunner Nord was also killed; Pickett and Williams were taken prisoner of war.

aircraft that filled in as a spare, flying as number six in the high squadron and just to the left of Lieutenant Lacy and Lieutenant Williams, was also busy. Ball turret gunner Staff Sgt. Symington was credited with a Bf 109 destroyed, and tail gunner Staff Sgt. Harris got two Fw 190s damaged.

The group lead bombardier, 2nd Lt. John E. Dimel, although occupied with getting everything ready for the bomb run, reported: "Nine Fw 190s started attacks at eleven o'clock level. I started firing at 1,200 yards at the leader and at 800 yards he started to break up. The rest of his formation peeled off to the right and as he went under us, the ball turret gunner saw the enemy aircraft begin to break up completely and the pilot bailed out."[23]

Lieutenant Dimel was given credit for destruction of the Fw 190, but ball turret gunner Sgt. Carl K. Platkin would also claim an Fw 190: "Three Fw 190s came in at one o'clock low and I swung my turret around in time to open up at the first one at about 800 yards. Pieces started to fly off his wings, then he passed by, and I continued firing at the other two and later the tail and right waist gunners told me over the interphone that my first ship blew up, at about 700 yards behind our plane after going into a spin."[24]

In all, gunners aboard the Magdeburg-bound bombers claimed sixteen German fighters destroyed, eight probably destroyed and six damaged. The American fighter escort also extricated a heavy toll of the attacking Germans. The forty-four Mustangs of the 357th Fighter Group from Leiston, led by Lt. Col. Thomas L. Hayes, were strung out along the bomber stream heading for Magdeburg and Königsborn, and those flights which could, did everything possible to turn back the German fighters.

The confusion and stress of aerial combat is very evident in Hayes's own combat report: "I was Dryden Leader at the time of engagement and was leading Greenhouse Red Flight.* About fifty to sixtenemy aircraft of mixed Me 109s and Fw 190s came into the bombers at 25,000 feet from twelve o'clock. Because of our position at the time [rear of the bombers] we could not stop the attack, but caught them on the way out. My White flight in support became separated from me when I turned onto the tails of the enemy formation, as other P-51s cut that flight out. When about to fire, I had to leave my target and turn into some aircraft approaching me from twelve o'clock. They turned out to be P-51s. Taking up pursuit again I was able to get on one of the Me 109s which now began to dive. I fired three short bursts. After the first strikes, he skidded, I suppose to look back. I fired again, seeing debris and canopy come off. Just as the third burst was fired it looked like the pilot started out. However, at that instant, strikes were noticed on and around what looked like the pilot. Then the ship actu-

---

* Dryden denotes the 357th Fighter Group and Greenhouse its 364th Fighter Squadron.

Part of the lead crew of the 100th Bomb Group. Kneeling, left to right: Manly W. Hall, co-pilot; Lloyd W. Coartney, navigator; Charles E. Harris, pilot; G. Peterson (not on 28 May mission); John E. Dimel, bombardier. Standing, left to right: two ground crewmen; Joe H. Blume, right waist gunner; Bob Pion (not on 28 May mission); Jack B. Gaard, radio operator; Norm Howden, engineer; and two ground crewmen. CHARLES E. HARRIS

ally disintegrated. I went out of control myself, indicating 500 miles per hour at 20,000 feet and so did my wingman. I picked up my element leader, Lt Howell, quickly and covered him as he nailed an Me 109 with the pilot parachuting. We climbed back to the bombers from 12,000 feet and continued the escort."[25]

It was Hayes's sixth air victory, but although he thought at the time that 1st Lt. John C. Howell had "nailed" a Bf 109, it later appeared to have been a very easy victory, as Howell reported: "Fifty-plus Me 109s and Fw 190s made an unsuccessful [*sic*] run on the bombers and my leader [Lieutenant Colonel Hayes] turned into position on the group's tail and we dove after them. He got one, and then I went after two Me 109s with him covering my element. I gave chase to 8,000 feet from 15,000 feet, where the two split. After a few seconds, I closed and for no reason the pilot bailed out of the 109."[26]

Elated over his first and so easily achieved air victory, Howell returned to Leiston, where his own wingman, 1st Lt. Robert M. Shaw, confirmed the story.

In the meantime, the leader of Greenhouse Blue Flight, Capt. Richard A. Peterson, went into action: "We had made rendezvous with our bombers

Lt. Col. Thomas L. Hayes on the wing of his P-51 with his ground crew. On 28 May, Hayes led the 357th Fighter Group in action over Magdeburg and shot down a Bf 109. JOSEPH M. DESHAY / THOMAS L. HAYES

First Lt. John C. Howell after returning to Leiston with a badly damaged P-51. On 28 May, he was able to strike back and accounted for a Bf 109, the first of his three air victories.
JOHN C. HOWELL

just before the initial point. After they made their turn on the initial point, the front box was bounced by approximately fifty to seventy-five enemy aircraft. My flight immediately engaged the enemy, tagging on the rear of the enemy formation. I fired on a straggler, observing numerous strikes on the canopy, engine and tail. The enemy aircraft swerved to one side, rolled on its back, tumbled once or twice out of control, and then broke into a violent spin at approximately 8,000 feet. I observed a large section of the plane rip off, but I do not know if it was the pilot or just the canopy. I observed no chute and I claim this Me 109 destroyed, with 150 rounds fired from my own guns."[27]

This victory, confirmed by his wingman 2nd Lt. Nicholas J. Frederick, was his eleventh in the air so far. Peterson would end his tour among the high-scoring fighter pilots in the European theater of operations with fifteen air victories to his credit. Number three in Peterson's Greenhouse Blue Flight was 1st Lt. LeRoy A. Ruder: "My flight leader made an attack on a large formation of Me 109s. We approached the enemy formation from the rear and gradually got within firing range. I picked out one of the enemy aircraft and he broke off the large formation, with me following him. I fired a burst at about twenty degrees deflection and observed strikes on the fuselage. The enemy aircraft immediately turned sharply and after closing to about 275 yards I again fired on him. I did not observe strikes at this time

The sleek nose of P-51B 43-6935, the first of three P-51's that Richard A. Peterson named *Hurry Home Honey*. While flying this aircraft, Peterson shot down a Bf 109 during combat in the Magdeburg area. MERLE OLMSTED

but the Me 109 straightened out and dove for a cloud. As he neared the cloud I observed the canopy coming off, but continued to fire and observed numerous strikes in the cockpit and fuselage. A large object that was either the pilot or part of the tail section fell from the aircraft a few seconds later. The aircraft emerged from the cloud in a vertical dive and crashed in flames. I fired 511 rounds and claim this Me 109 as destroyed."[28]

Again a wingman, this time 1st Lt. Hollis R. Nowlin, confirmed events, and Ruder was awarded this victory. It brought his total to 5.5 in the air and gave him the coveted status of an "ace." He would have little pleasure from it, however, since he scored no more victories until his death in combat during the 6 June invasion of Normandy, just nine days later.

First Lt. Charles K. Peters was leading Cement White Flight and saw the enemy fighters attack the bombers: "I dropped my wing tanks and started for them. I saw one black Me 109 trying to get on the tail of a blue-nosed Mustang. I got on his tail and fired. I saw numerous strikes in the cockpit. Smoke poured out and the canopy came off, but the pilot did not get out. I believe he was killed, as the plane started into a slow spiral, trailing smoke and prop windmilling. I did not see it crash, because I started after another enemy aircraft."[29]

The strikes on the tail and fuselage were no doubt noted in the combat report of the American pilot who engaged *Feldwebel* Alfred Heger of 4./JG 11 in the Magdeburg area. Heger managed to get away from his attacker and belly-landed his Bf 109 *Weisse 10* at Schönebeck near Magdeburg. It is possible that Heger fell to Richard Peterson's fire. HANS LÄCHLER

First Lt. LeRoy A. Ruder shot down a Bf 109, which brought his total to five and a half and brought him ace status. He was killed over Normandy on D-Day, 6 June 1944.
KENT D. MILLER

However, the confirmation by 2nd Lt. William S. Davis, his number two, brought Peters's total to three and a third air victories. Another pilot in Cement Squadron, Capt. Edwin W. Hiro, damaged a Bf 109 in the same combat. Despite his positive report regarding the destruction of the Me 109 and a later resubmission of this claim, it was regarded only as "probably destroyed."

In the 362nd Fighter Squadron formation, two pilots managed to down a German attacker. Maj. Joseph E. Broadhead spent 170 rounds on an Fw 190: "We had just made rendezvous when a large number of enemy aircraft (approximately hundred) started making head-on passes at the bombers, coming at them in large formations in a line abreast. After the first wave passed through, I peeled off and started following. One Fw 190 peeled off, leaving the formation and I started after him. He was unaware that I was following him, so I held my fire until I had pulled up within 200 yards maximum. I was directly in back of him at 8,000 feet, doing 450 knots indicated air speed. I took careful aim and gave him one long burst, hitting him in the tail, fuselage and wings. Smoke immediately started coming from him and he did a roll to start a split-S and I overshot him. As I crossed him, I saw fire starting from his belly. The bombers were in trouble, so I rejoined them, since considering the fire which I had seen, it was enough to destroy the Fw 190."[30]

First Lt. Charles K. Peters and his P-51 *Daddy Rabbit*. Peters scored his last victory on 28 May, shooting down a Bf 109 in the Magdeburg area. MERLE OLMSTED

He was awarded his victory, one of the eight he managed to achieve during his tour of operations. Then 1st Lt. Leonard K. Carson, who was to become one of the great aces of the Eighth Air Force, went after his victim. His fight took him to the deck: "The enemy aircraft had made three passes at the bombers, which we were escorting. About 300 yards to the left of my flight, an Fw 190 was making an attack on a P-51. I broke from my flight to attack the Fw 190 and he broke off his attack and dove for the deck. I fired several times during the dive, but we were going so fast that I couldn't get an accurate shot. I got a few hits on his wings during the dive, however. He levelled off at about 300 feet above the ground, chopped his throttle, dropped flaps and made a steep turn to the right. I overshot him, but came back and he got into a lufberry. I fired several times from 250 to 300 yards at 140 miles per hour. I saw several strikes on his fuselage and wings. He levelled off and started to glide towards the ground, his engine burning. About twenty feet off the ground he jettisoned his canopy. His ship went into a slight bank to the left, hit the ground, cartwheeled and burst into flame. The pilot was killed in the crash."[31]

Carson's victim was *Oberleutnant* Heinz-Helmut Brandes of 8./JG 11. Brandes, a former Me 110 pilot with *Zerstörergeschwader 1* on the Russian front, had been transferred to the *Reichsverteidigung*, received additional training on the Fw 190, and had served with JG 11 for less than a month.

Maj. Joseph E. Broadhead and his P-51B *Baby Mike* (43-12227). Broadhead shot down an Fw 190 northwest of Magdeburg as his sixth air victory. MERLE OLMSTED

Having been briefed for a mission, pilots of the 357th Fighter Group, 362nd Fighter Squadron, have picked up their equipment and are leaving the operations building for their aircraft. Standing with one leg up in the weapon carrier is Leonard K. Carson. On 28 May, Carson scored the third of his overall total of eighteen and a half air victories. On his left arm is a note pad on which he no doubt wrote important information during the mission, such as navigation control points and radio call signs. MERLE OLMSTED

During that month, however, he had obtained two victories, a B-24 on 13 May and a B-17 on 19 May. He now crashed to his death near Gross Börnecke.

Finally, Capt. Kenneth E. Hagan managed to damage an Me 410, bringing the total for the 357th Fighter Group to seven single-engine enemy fighters destroyed, one damaged, and one twin-engine fighter damaged, with no losses on their own side.

In mid-June 1944, the father of Heinz-Helmut Brandes visited the field near Gross Börnecke where his son crashed to his death two weeks earlier. Clearly visible is the track in the field where the belly of the Fw 190 first hit the ground. Here the canopy and Brandes's field cap and gloves were found, probably sucked out by the airstream when he jettisoned the canopy. The aircraft then slid toward a dyke camouflaged by the wheat. At the last moment, Brandes pulled up to prevent crashing head-on into the dyke, but crashed on the far side of it. The aircraft then exploded and burned. In the rubble, his father found the charred and melted Iron Cross that his son had worn. WILFRIED BRANDES

Help for the beleaguered Fortresses attacking Magdeburg came from an unexpected direction. The 4th Fighter Group from Debden, led by the 336th Fighter Squadron's commanding officer, Maj. James A. Goodson, had joined the bomber stream at 1350 hours near Gardelegen at 22,000 or 23,000 feet. The group's escort duty was primarily to be with the Ruhland/Dessau-bound force, and the three squadrons positioned themselves around the combat wings. Just after joining up, the pilots saw more than twenty Bf 109s and Fw 190s approaching at 26,000 feet to attack the wing that had just left the main bomber stream and that was headed for Magdeburg. The 335th and 336th Fighter Squadrons were positioned on the outside of the bomber stream, flying at 26,000 to 27,000 feet and unable to help.

The 334th Fighter Squadron, however, led by Capt. Winslow M. Sobanski in P-51B *The Deacon* (43-6898) and flying behind and above the bomber stream at more than 30,000 feet, bounced the enemy aircraft, and a raging battle developed. Sobanski managed to destroy a Bf 109, firing only eighty-nine rounds. He reported: "Our squadron used it's superior height (32,000 feet) and followed them in the turn in a shallow dive. As soon as they made their turn we dropped our tanks and went down fast. I spotted a few P-51s trying to climb from below and sort of following the tail end of the 109 formation—without closing though. This rather upset my plan of attack as I

Oberleutnant Heinz-Helmut Brandes was assigned to 8./JG 11 on 2 May 1944 after serving as an Me 110 pilot on the Eastern Front since April 1942. He was severely wounded in action in September that year and was out of action for nearly a year. He fell to the guns of Leonard Carson on 28 May and died trying to crash-land his Fw 190. WILFRIED BRANDES

couldn't very well tell where the P-51s and the Me 109s began in the gaggle below. I missed out on a couple of chances when P-51s either cut me off or made passes at me. We managed though to split up the enemy formation and I found a single bluish-grey Me 109 flying a perfect line abreast formation with a P-51 at some 150 yards distance. They both didn't seem to realize their mistake, and only caught on when I attacked the 109. He dove straight down and momentarily I lost him in the haze, finding him again when he started pulling back up. I fired a few short half-second bursts closing in and was just going to position myself better on him, as I saw no strikes. Much to my surprise, he jettisoned his canopy and bailed out. I watched his a/c half-roll and crash, and then took a picture of him in the parachute. I claim one Me 109 destroyed, and a scared Hun."[32]

In Red Flight, led by 2nd Lt. Ralph "Kid" Hofer, only three P-51s were still operational, as Lieutenant Sharp had aborted earlier. All three pilots managed to destroy a German fighter each, and one damaged another Bf 109 in the action. Hofer reported: "I was leading Cobweb Red Section, near Wittenberg, when fifteen-plus enemy aircraft came in high head-on to the middle bunch of bombers. Shortly after that, I saw four Fw 190s go through the Forts, bringing one bomber down in flames. I dropped my tanks and gave chase. Four P-47s cut me out and destroyed one enemy aircraft. I had pulled up to rejoin our Big Friends, when an Fw 190 dove past. Lieutenant

Capt. Winslow M. Sobanski led the 334th Fighter Squadron on 28 May and shot down a Bf 109. On D-Day, 6 June, he was killed in action.
TIMOTHY KIRKUP VIA BRUCE ZIGLER

Siems shot him down at 6,000 feet, after I had broken into some more 109s. I jumped one enemy aircraft out of this bunch and closed to seventy-five yards, getting strikes. The enemy aircraft poured glycol, rolled over and dived into the deck."[33]

During this combat, Hofer was hit by a 20mm shell in the rudder of his *Salem Representative*, but he made it safely back to Debden and awed everybody on the ground, doing a victory roll over the base despite the damage to his tail. This was his fifteenth and last air victory. "Kid" Hofer was killed on 2 July during a shuttle mission to Russia.

Second Lt. Grover C. Siems submitted the following report: "Flying Red 4 and then Red 2 to Lieutenant Hofer, at 28,500 feet, we saw some Fw 190s attacking a box of B-17s in the Magdeburg area. We dropped tanks and went over to see what we could do. One B-17 was going down and one chute opened from it. Being circled by P-47s, I took a quick picture of it, as two Fw 190s went by going for the deck. However there were too many enemy aircraft above to bother with the two, so we started a climbing starboard orbit and saw more Fw 190s. One was coming head-on to us, a little to starboard, which Lieutenant Hofer said to leave alone because it was bait. There were more ahead and above. As we passed the Fw 190, it started a starboard turn, and Lieutenant Hofer was also turning starboard. I broke to port, coming out behind the Fw 190. He saw me and started down. I gave chase. I made one short deflection shot from about 400 yards and noticed no hits. I held fire until within 100 yards dead astern. I opened fire and immediately saw strikes from tail to nose and his belly tank flew off, missing me very slightly. Several short bursts with slight deflection missed, and then I hit compressability. The ship was buffeting very severely, but I continued to fire and saw two starboard guns put about twenty or thirty rounds directly into the cockpit. The kite immediately straightened out and there was no more evasive action. I pulled aside at 6,000 feet and the Fw 190 went straight in, exploding when it hit. I turned and took a picture of the burning ship. Lieutenant Hofer had been covering me until I pulled up and then he went on another bounce. There were so many Me 109s and Fw 190s that it was impossible to form up for an effective bounce, so after covering and assisting several other friends, I returned to base."[34]

Grover Siems was severely wounded in action on 2 July the same day that Hofer was killed, and he returned to the United States.

The third and last pilot in Red Flight who scored a kill was Maj. Michael G. H. McPharlin. He was a very experienced pilot, who had started flying with the Royal Canadian Air Force and then transferred to 71 Eagle Squadron, when the United States was not yet actively involved in the war. The Eagle Squadrons were disbanded in August 1942 and formed the nucleus of the 4th Fighter Group. McPharlin was assigned to the 339th

Second Lt. Ralph K. Hofer takes a close look to the damage inflicted by German fighters to his P-51B *Salem Representative* (42-106924) over Magdeburg. With this damage, he awed all spectators at Debden by doing a victory roll. He had managed to shoot down a Bf 109 himself for his fifteenth and final air victory. He was killed on 2 July during a "shuttle mission" to Russia. LEROY A. NITSCHKE

Fighter Group, but was influential enough by now to be allowed to fly often with his old Eagle squadronmates, now serving in the 4th Fighter Group. McPharlin, flying P-51B *Wee Ginny* (42-106909), reported: "We had gone down for an attack; at the same time we were attacked by Me 109s and Fw 190s. Thus split up, I joined in with a P-51 making an attack on an Me 109, protecting his tail. The P-51 gave the Me 109 a long burst. I witnessed the strikes, saw the 109 roll on its back and dive. The P-51 broke. As the 109 rolled over, I managed a quick burst and saw strikes in the belly of the enemy aircraft at the intersection of the wing roots and fuselage. It disappeared in the haze and smoke below. I claim one Me 109 damaged.

"Following the first engagement I saw what I thought was an Me 109. I dove on the enemy aircraft which then entered a large cumulus cloud and an area of black smoke and haze directly over Magdeburg. I formated on this aircraft for a complete 360 degrees turn before opening fire.

"The area was so thick I could not determine whether this was an Me 109 or a P-51. On the second orbit, I got close enough to see there were no stripes on the wings and noticed the outlines of the nose. I fired a continuous burst through another approximately 360-degree turn and saw strikes.

Second Lt. Grover C. Siems is pictured in June 1944 with his P-51D *Gloria III* (44-13322). In this aircraft, he was severely wounded in action on 2 July during a "shuttle mission" from Russia. Having been shot in the shoulder, neck, and chin and paralyzed on his left side, he managed to get *Gloria III* back to a base in Italy, trip the landing gear switch with his foot, land, and fire his guns to attract help. He was returned to the United States. TIMOTHY KIRKUP VIA BRUCE ZIGLER

The aircraft reeled about and dove straight for the deck, disappearing in the smoke. On my return to base, Lieutenant Siems stated he witnessed this combat and saw the Me 109 flaming and diving into the deck. I claim one Me 109 destroyed. I pulled up immediately and nearly collided with a spinning, flaming aircraft. A piece of this aircraft (later I learned it was Lieutenant Hewatt's) struck my prop cowling. I banged on bottom rudder and snapped to get away. When I came out I was directly behind two P-51s attacking a 109. When this a/c broke, I saw QP-C make an attack and saw pieces flying off the 109. A few seconds later, the enemy aircraft fell into a dive and crashed into the deck. I confirm one Me 109 destroyed, shared by these two P-51s."[35]

McPharlin also flew with his friends in the 4th Fighter Group on D-Day. It was also to be his last combat flight, as he was killed in action that day, flying his *Wee Ginny*.

In Blue Flight, only Lt. Mark H. Kolter was successful; with 692 rounds, he destroyed a Bf 109 for his one and only air victory. He was shot down and killed in action just two days later. Since Kolter apparently was not debriefed

Maj. Michael G. H. McPharlin
wearing the coveted RAF pilot
wings, denoting those who
had flown in one of the
Eagle Squadrons before the
United States entered the war.
McPharlin was killed in action
on D-Day. CECIL MANNING VIA
BRUCE ZIGLER

on the evening of the twenty-eight, flew another mission on the twenty-ninth, but did not return from the one on the thirtieth, Capt. Thomas E. Joyce submitted a claim for Kolter.

As would later become clear, it was a posthumous claim for Kolter's only air victory: "Lieutenant Kolter [No. 3] and I [No. 4] became separated at 20,000 feet from Cobweb Blue Section in the attack on fifteen plus Me 109s who were coming in high and starboard to middle bunch of bombers. We followed two P-51s who were attacking an enemy aircraft to the deck. After the Me 109 [Hofer's] crashed, we pulled up above haze to 7,000 feet. Three Me 109s were seen some distance at ten o'clock, 5,000 to 6,000 feet, descending through break. We made an orbit above break and then went down through to about 1,500 feet. One Me 109 was seen slightly below us and with advantage of altitude and speed, we closed on unaware Me 109. Blue 3 commenced firing well within range. Strikes were seen on Me 109 which broke 180 degree port. I saw pieces of cowling falling off and nearly hitting them. Lieutenant Kolter closed, firing a long burst. I believe he killed the pilot. The enemy aircraft lost altitude gradually to about 200 feet. The plane turned over on its back, inverted flight, at 150 feet for about ten seconds, then fell off on one wing and crashed. It exploded and burned."[36]

Not a textbook landing, but the aircraft was probably easily repaired. *Unteroffizier* Helmut Riehl of 2./JG 1 and his Fw 190 *Schwarze 4* on 28 May near Schkeuditz. Note the two machine guns in front of the cockpit as well as the JG 1 emblem and the white spiral on the propellor hub. HANS LÄCHLER

Joyce returned to England and landed at Honington minus the top and left side of his canopy, which was torn off during a power dive.

A typical flight of four fighters was 334th Fighter Squadron's Green flight. Its actions are therefore covered in greater detail. Leading the flight in his P-51C 43-24793, coded QP-C, was the veteran 1st Lt. Joseph L. Lang from Boston, Massachusetts. In 1943, he had flown with the RAF, and he had served with the 334th Squadron since 28 December 1943. He was already credited with three and a third enemy fighters destroyed.

According to Fighter Command operational procedure, a less experienced man flew as Green Two, covering the tail of the leader, not yet being responsible for navigation or making any tactical decisions. When a pilot gained enough experience, he was made element leader and, later, flight leader. When he lived long enough and displayed sufficient skill, he might even become squadron leader. This Green Two was 2nd Lt. Richard L. Bopp, flying in P-51B 42-106846, coded QP-H. Bopp, from Revere, Massachusetts, joined the squadron fresh from flying school in the United States on 16 May and had flown only twice on short combat missions to France. This was to be his first escort mission to a German target, and unfortunately, he was to be in the thick of it. Flying Green Three and thus leading the second element of the flight, in P-51C 42-103791, coded QP-N, was 1st Lt. Robert P. Kenyon from Detroit, Michigan. He had been with the squadron since 9 March and had one confirmed air victory.

Up the slot, Green Four, thus covering Kenyon's tail, was a relative freshman, 2nd Lt. Aubrey E. Hewatt, in P-51B 43-6933, coded QP-Y. He had joined the squadron on 17 April. On 21 May he had shared the destruction of a German aircraft with Ralph Hofer. Robert P. Kenyon reported: "Lieutenant Hewatt was flying on my wing when we encountered enemy aircraft at about 14.00 hours, approximately five miles east of Magdeburg. I went down to about 4,000 feet on the tail of an Me 109 and shot it down, pulled up and looked back to see if Lieutenant Hewatt was still with me. He indeed still was in trail with me, but another Me 109 was closing in on him rather fast. I called him on the r/t, telling him to break, but he didn't. I told him twice more, but for some reason or other, he continued to fly as he was. The Me 109 started getting hits, and Lieutenant Hewatt's aircraft burst into flame. As the burning parts fell to about 2,000 feet, I saw his parachute open."[37]

First Lt. Joseph L. Lang of the 4th Fighter Group, 334th Fighter Squadron. He led its Green Flight on 28 May and shot down a Bf 109 and shared one with Lt. Edwin Heller of the 352nd Fighter Group. This brought him ace status. Despite always flying with good luck charms (the baby shoes seen here around his neck), he was killed in action on 14 October. FORREST WILLIAMS

Hewatt himself later recalled: "I was tailing Kenyon. He was doing amazing shooting, 60- and 90-degree deflection. I didn't hear break, so maybe I was too carried away watching him or possibly my radio was out. Anyway, my instrument panel disintegrated and at the same instant I received metal fragments from my left temple down to my left hip. Next, the seat was surrounded by orange flames but I did not receive any burns, flames stopping just inches from my face.

First Lt. Robert P. Kenyon of the 4th Fighter Group prepares for take-off for another escort mission. Pvt. Ben Reizen is ready to close the canopy of the P-51. Kenyon shot down a Bf 109 for his second and last victory on 28 May. He safely finished his tour of operations in October 1944. USAAF

"I had some difficulty getting the canopy off so I could bail out; I had to pull the emergency release lever several times before I could get it off. Then I bailed out. I didn't think I was going to be able to bail out. I know I was fairly low by the time I did because the chute opened and it had time to oscilate just once before I hit the ground. My plane and I hit the ground within a stone's throw of each other. I have no idea why I did it, then or now, but the first thing I did on the ground was to look at my watch—1400 hours exactly. Then I saw four Nazi soldiers with rifles running toward me and I was taken prisoner."[38]

Hewatt and his Mustang came down near the Vogelsang sanatorium, five kilometers south-southeast of Magdeburg. It is possible, although it cannot be verified, that Hewatt was the victim of *Oberleutnant* Rüdiger Kirchmayr, who had also succeeded in shooting down one of the B-17s of the 390th Bomb Group in the vicinity of Magdeburg. Kenyon, now on his own, returned to England and landed at 1720 hours at Steeple Morden, the base of the 355th Fighter Group, since Debden was closed because of haze.

Second Lt. Richard L. Bopp in February 1944 at Hillsborough Army Air Base.
VIRGINIA B. RUSSELL

Every airman had his picture taken in England wearing civilian clothes. If he was shot down and trying to evade back to England, these pictures were to be used on forged papers supplied by the resistance. Richard Bopp didn't need his pictures as he was captured immediately upon landing on French soil.
VIRGINIA B. RUSSELL

In the meantime, the Green Leader, Lt. Joseph Lang, and his number two, Lt. Richard L. Bopp, had seen plenty of action. Lang submitted the following report: "I was leading Cobweb Green Section, with Lieutenant Bopp as my wingman. We were in combat on the deck when he lost me. Later, he called me and asked my position. I told him, but he kept calling. I told him the course and all the necessary information to get him home."[39]

Richard L. Bopp would not return to Debden. On this his very first escort mission over Germany, he had great difficulty in following his leader, the experienced Lang, in his combat maneuvers. When he lost Lang, he apparently lost all sense of direction, not unusual after a hectic combat and quite understandable when it is one's first. Most of the 334th Squadron pilots returned to England individually, since the squadron was scattered around the Magdeburg district and could not form up as an effective fighter squadron again.

They had to leave the luckless Bopp, hearing his desperate calls over the radio. Eventually, Bopp picked up the right direction, but had stayed in the combat area too long, and over France his fuel warning lights began to flicker. Rather than risking ditching or parachuting in the Channel he chose to bail out over France. He and his fighter came down near Aumont, twelve kilometers north of Poix, in northern France. He was immediately picked up and spent the rest of the war as a prisoner of war.

Lang resumes his account of the action: "I was at 29,000 feet near Magdeburg. I had covered Red Section on several bounces. On one of these, I saw Lieutenant Siems destroy an Fw 190. After we were separated, my section joined and covered Blue Section. An Me 109 bounced Blue Leader and his number two. I immediately went down toward him and he dove for the

Lt. Homer R. Mitchell and Lt. Bartholomew G. Tenore shared the destruction of a Bf 109 on 28 May. STEVE BLAKE

Capt. James W. Edwards destroyed
an Fw 190 after a spectacular dive
from 25,000 to 700 feet in which he
lost his canopy. STEVE BLAKE

deck. I fired several times and missed. We finally leveled off and he made a
starboard turn. By this time, I was 200 yards behind. I fired a long burst
and hit him along the right side of the fuselage. The enemy aircraft made
an outside turn down and to the left. I followed him. He leveled off and
bailed out. Lieutenant Monroe, Blue Leader, who was covering me, can
confirm this.

"As I had found the airdrome with hundred plus aircraft on it [believed
to be Magdeburg] that the enemy aircraft were returning to, I orbited and
bounced them as they came home. On the third bounce , I lost my No. 2
(Lieutenant Bopp) in the haze on the deck. At this time Major McPharlin
joined me as No. 2 to me. I was flying with a blue-nosed section of Mustangs.
(This was Lieutenant Heller of the 352nd Fighter Group.) About the same
time, we saw a 109 and went after him. Lieutenant Heller got there first and
fired, obtaining very good strikes. By this time, I was to the right and slightly
behind Lieutenant Heller. The 109 broke right, and I laid off deflection,
fired and hit him. The 109 went under us and crashed. As it was hazy, I
couldn't tell exactly where it crashed. Major McPharlin can confirm this 109
for Lieutenant Heller and myself."[40]

Thus, two experienced pilots in Green Flight, Kenyon and Lang, who
managed to score victories in this combat, had lost their less experienced
wingmen, who apparently had all they could cope with, while simply trying
to follow their element leader in combat maneuvers. For the loss of Bopp
and Hewatt, who both survived, the 334th Fighter Squadron of the 4th
Fighter Group, had shot down seven and a half enemy fighters.

First Lt. Gus W. Allen shot down
yet another Bf 109 during combat in the Neuhaldensleben area.
BARBARA ALLEN

Unfortunately, the combat
reports for most of the 354th
Fighter Group have not survived.
These pictures may serve as a
tribute to some of the successful
pilots of the group. Capt. Wallace
N. Emmer accounted for two Bf
109s and one Fw 190 on 28 May.
He was shot down on 9 August
1944 and succumbed to his
wounds on 15 February 1945.
STEVE BLAKE

Capt. Glenn T. Eagleston ended the war as the highest-scoring ace of the Ninth Air Force, with 18.5 confirmed victories. He obtained two of these on 28 May. STEVE BLAKE

First Lt. William Y. Anderson on the wing of his *Swede's Steed III.* The second of the victories so proudly displayed was a Bf 109 he shot down on 28 May. WILLIAM Y. ANDERSON

P-51D *Swede's Steed III* (44-13383), the aircraft flown by 1st Lt. William Y. Anderson of the 354th Fighter Group, shown here in June 1944 on an improvised airstrip near Isigny in Normandy, France. On 28 May, Anderson flew this aircraft when he shot down a Bf 109. WILLIAM Y. ANDERSON

First Lt. Clayton K. Gross scored his third victory, a Bf 109, over Neuhaldensleben. STEVE BLAKE

Their brothers in arms of the 354th Fighter Group of the Ninth Air Force, who had taken off from Lashenden at 1153 hours with forty-nine Mustangs, would do even better. Unfortunately, only a few pilot encounter reports of the 354th Fighter Group have survived in the archives. One of these is that of 2nd Lt. Homer R. Mitchell, who reported: "I was flying number 4 position in Blue Flight of the 356th Fighter Squadron, at 25,000 feet and about 1405 hours. An Me 109 passed under our flight about 1,000 feet below. I called it in to the flight leader and was told to go after it. I went down on it and immediately it started turning tight to the left. I started turning with it and after a short time I was able to get lead by chopping throttle and fired several short bursts, getting many strikes on the tail and some on wing and fuselage. I snapped out of the turn and Lieutenant Tenore, who was flying number 3 position in our flight, pulled in and fired, getting strikes on the wing. At that time I was behind and covering him. The enemy aircraft did a split-S and started down. Lieutenant Tenore fired more short bursts from dead astern. I observed many strikes on tail and fuselage and many pieces of the cowling came off and black smoke poured out from the fuselage. The enemy aircraft appeared to go into an out-of-control dive, almost straight down, into the low overcast from about 6,000 feet. I claim a destroyed Me 109, shared with Lt. Bartholomew Tenore."[41]

First Lt. Edward E. Hunt claimed a Bf 109, bringing his total to six and a half. This picture was taken in early November 1944, when the 354th Fighter Group switched from the P-51 to the P-47. On 8 November, only days after this picture was taken, Hunt was killed in action over France. USAAF VIA JAMES BOLLINGER

Leading Blue Flight was Capt. James W. Edwards. He was to have a more than exciting action, nearly losing his life in an uncontrollable aircraft and then forcing a Fw 190 into the ground: "My number three and four were attacking an Me 109 and I supported top cover for them. They went into a dive with the enemy aircraft; I followed. I and my number 2 dived too fast and hit compressability. The dive started at 25,000 feet and I pulled out at about 500 to 700 feet, losing my canopy on pull-out. After I regained control, I saw that I was alone so started climbing up. At 4,000 feet, I was jumped by two Fw 190s. I saw them coming and fired two short bursts in their general direction to shake them up a little. I dropped twenty degrees of flaps and started turning, losing altitude at the same time. At 500 feet, I was having no trouble turning inside of them, with my canopy gone and flap damaged by the canopy as it tore loose. We made about two turns at 500 feet and I was about to get deflection on them, when the leader snapped and spun. He hit the ground and flame spread for about 200 yards where he hit. The remaining Fw 190 made a diving turn for the deck, but I didn't follow as I knew I couldn't catch him with the added drag. I climbed back up to 15,000 feet and joined three P-51's from another group."[42]

The pilots of the 354th Fighter Group were credited with no fewer than 17.5 enemy fighters destroyed, with no losses on their side. The highest scorer was Capt. Wallace N. Emmer, who shot down two Bf 109s and one Fw 190.

Oberleutnant Walter Krupinski, *Gruppenkommandeur* of II./JG 11, was shot down by a P-51 over Magdeburg and bailed out of his Bf 109. RUDOLF STROSETZKI

Oberleutnant Eugen Kotiza, the
Austrian *Staffelkapitän* of 3./JG 1,
died when his Fw 190 crashed. He
is still listed as missing in action.
ERIC BAKKER

Gefreiter Josef Körner of 9./JG 1
was injured while belly-landing
his Bf 109 near Sondershausen.
HILDEGUND KÖRNER

Their opponents most probably were pilots from JG 1 and JG 11. Both units lost six pilots killed in action in the Magdeburg area, with several others bailing out or belly-landing their damaged aircraft. One of those bailing out was *Oberleutnant* Walter Krupinski, the *Gruppenkommandeur* of II./JG 11. He was shot down by a Mustang, but got out safely to fight another day. Not so lucky was *Oberleutnant* Eugen Kotiza, the *Staffelkapitän* of 3./JG 1. He died when his aircraft crashed and was another one of the more experienced pilots the *Luftwaffe* was losing at an alarming rate.

After their successful clash with the enemy, the pilots of the 354th Fighter Group were scattered over a wide area. Most of them turned in a westerly direction, to head for England and their base at Lashenden. Of course, most were looking eagerly for more targets, either in the air or on the ground. One of them was 1st Lt. William R. Perkins, who had not succeeded in downing a German aircraft on this day, so far. He was flying alone in the Magdeburg area at about 18,000 feet, when he noticed another P-51 coming from behind and forming on him as wingman, as they each had lost their own in the action several minutes before. The Mustang forming on him was P-51B 43-7195 and was coded FT-X, clearly marking it as a machine of the 353rd Fighter Squadron of the 354th Fighter Group. Its pilot was 1st Lt. Glenn H. Pipes.

William Perkins tells the story: "We let down to 15,000 feet and headed south with the intention of picking up the bombers on their way home to offer them some protection, this being around 1415 hours. Ten minutes

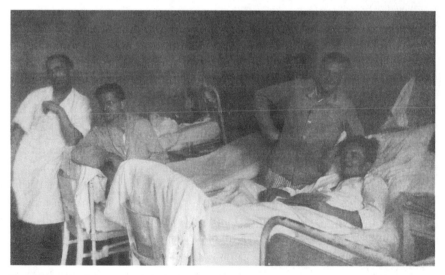

Conditions in the reserve hospital at Sondershausen, where *Gefreiter* Josef Körner was treated for his injuries for several months, were spartan, as this picture testifies.
HILDEGUND KÖRNER

after setting course south, Lieutenant Pipes called in over the radio and said 'there are two aircraft taking off the field off to our right'. I looked but could not see the planes he mentioned, so I told Lieutenant Pipes to go after them and that I would follow him down. We continued south for another minute and then turned around letting down to attack the drome from south to north. I still didn't see the aircraft Lieutenant Pipes had called in that were taking off, so I figured I'd get one on the ground anyway. We approached the field at about 400 miles per hour and at fifty feet. Directly in front of me, I saw a parked aircraft. I opened fire at about 400 yards and kept firing all the way in. When about 300 yards away, I started to get many strikes all over the engine. The aircraft was parked in such a manner that I was attacking it head-on. Almost immediately it burst into flame. The flames shot up about fifteen feet and looked oily for there was black smoke mixed with it. I then identified the plane as a Fw 190.

"I kept firing at it although it was already burning, until I had to pull up to keep from running into it. Another fire off to my right and at the far end of the field attracted my attention then. It was another Fw 190 burning, which Lieutenant Pipes had shot up. Around it were several other parked aircraft. I tried to get my sights on them, but couldn't, so I opened fire on a hangar directly in front of me. I got about a one-and-a-half second burst in the open door. Lieutenant Pipes and I started to climb up again making a wide circle to the right to get back on our course of 180 degrees again. We got on course and were at about 4,000 feet when we sighted a single ship directly in front of us and at the same level. He saw us coming and ducked into a small cloud. But we were then about 800 yards away, so he was out of the cloud again before we were even in range, so we didn't lose sight of him. The bogey then made a steep turn to the right. I pulled up and chopped throttle to cut down my speed, then split-S'ed onto his tail, going down below him and coming up again to do it. I recognized the ship as a Ju 88. It was painted a sort of smoke color with black spots all over it. I got on his tail in the turn and started giving him two-second bursts. I saw no return fire from the rear gunner. My first three bursts whipped short of his tail, so I gave him more deflection and another burst. This time I saw strikes on the right engine and forward part of the Ju 88. The rear part of the 88 was blocked out by my nose.

"As soon as I hit him, he straightened out of his turn and dove down as if he had pushed the stick forward violently. I stayed with him and gave him a long burst at about fifty yards range. I saw strikes all over the aircraft; black and white smoke poured out and pieces flew off. I pulled up and tipped over on my left wing to watch him. His left engine was on fire and he went down weaving, as if he were looking for a field to crash-land. I was at about 1,000 feet then and I watched him fly over a little village and crash-land into

First Lt. Glenn H. Pipes of the 354th Fighter Group was taken prisoner after his P-51 *Pied Piper* was hit by ground fire during a strafing attack. USAAF

First Lt. William R. Perkins destroyed an Fw 190 by strafing and a Ju 88 in the air. These claims were his last, as he was killed in action on 12 June.
STEVE BLAKE

a field on the other side. Immediately on hitting the ground, the 88 blew up. The wings flew off and just seemed to disintegrate into a pall of blackish brown smoke and a ball of flame. I saw no one bail out and believe the pilot was killed on landing."

The unfortunate Ju 88 which had run into both roving pilots of the 354th Fighter Group and was promptly shot down by William Perkins for his second victory was Ju 88C 750400. It was flown by *Feldwebel* Erich Phieler and belonged to *Luftbeobachtungsstaffel 1*, a reconnaissance unit based at Neuruppin and specializing in trailing bomber formations and broadcasting their altitude and course to ground-based fighter controllers. Phieler and his gunner, *Unteroffizier* Frank Hammer, were killed instantly in the fiery crash near Lichtenstein. Radio operator *Unteroffizier* Franz Oertel succumbed to his wounds in a Lichtenstein hospital that same evening.

P-51B *Pied Piper* (43-7195). Its operational life ended in a meadow near Ruppersdorf after a flak hit caused loss of coolant. STEVE BLAKE

William Perkins resumes his story: "After this, we again set course south. It was about 1530 hours then, and we were still between Magdeburg and Dessau. Suddenly, I noticed white smoke trailing from Lieutenant Pipes's ship. Apparently, he had been hit at the unidentified airfield we had strafed previously. I called him over the radio and told him. He said, 'God damn it. They got my coolant.' He then said he would have to get out. I told him to stick with the ship until the last moment. He slowly started losing altitude. When we were at 9,000 feet he called me again saying he would crash-land it and told me to strafe it after he had gotten out of it. Over the radio I directed him to a clear field, as he was already so low he couldn't see any distance. He put it down on the outskirts of a little village; he did a good job, not breaking the plane in half or hitting any obstacles. I circled the area at about 1,000 feet, but I did not see him leaving his cockpit. Within fifteen seconds I was at 1,000 feet over the site where the ship came to rest and saw a man, with a bright colored vest [like a Mae West], standing about thirty feet from the wreck. He then started running away from it, as flames and black smoke started to come out of it. I assumed it was Lieutenant Pipes and set course for home directly, without watching further activities."[43]

Perkins is accurate. Glenn Pipes did set fire to his *Pied Piper* and did try to get away from it. However, the *Volkssturm* of Ruppersdorf, the little village where he landed, quickly captured him and turned him over to the police. Pipes then spend the rest of the war in prison camps. William Perkins was killed in action just two weeks later. Strafing a ground convoy in Normandy, on 12 June, he was apparently hit by light flak, collided with a power line, and then crashed into the line of trucks he was strafing.

The 95th Bomb Group attacked the marshalling yards and industrial area in Dessau after its assigned primary and secondary targets were obscured by clouds. The official report mentions that "The bombs hit in a good pattern in the southern part of Dessau. Bursts cover the railroad line running south as well as the barracks area to the west and industrial area to the east." CROWN COPYRIGHT / PUBLIC RECORD OFFICE

We now return to the two combat wing formations that were turning from their initial point toward the target when the German fighters struck. The 390th Bomb Group, leading the 13th A Combat Wing, bore the brunt of the German attack. It had great difficulties on the bomb run. Lead bombardier Capt. Fred W. Murray reported: "We peeled off at the briefed point and fired redred flares at briefed initial point for bomb bay doors to open. The smoke screen was very effective over the target area due to the wind change and we were unable to pick up the target until we reached a point twenty-five seconds from the bomb release line. I attempted to make a combat run on the target, but was unable to synchronize due to wind change, which affected the pre-set drift. All bombing equipment worked perfectly. Bomb results were unobserved. Had a head-on fighter attack on bombing run, but flak was light."[44]

Later, reconnaissance pictures revealed that the bombing had been very poor, with only four percent of the hits within 2,000 feet of the briefed Aiming Point. The 100th Bomb Group, flying high in this combat wing, encountered similar problems. Here lead bombardier 2nd Lt. John E. Dimel reported: "Medium flak and large swarms of enemy fighters constituted the enemy resistance on the bomb run. Two-tenths cloud cover was observed in the target area and a very effective smoke screen completely obscured the target. The aiming point was never observed and two intersecting roads were used as an alternative aiming point, and no visual results were observed."[45]

Forty percent of the group's bombs landed within 2,000 feet of the briefed aiming point. The composite group, flying low in the combat wing, was the last to bomb. The six aircraft of the 100th Bomb Group, leading this group, fared no better. Lead bombardier, 2nd Lt. Burrough E. Conover, recorded: "Primary target was so obscured by smoke that I could not find an aiming point. We then used the Gera marshalling yards as an aiming point; results are unobserved."[46]

The five B-17s of the 390th Bomb Group in the composite group dropped their bombs on an unknown "target of opportunity" somewhere in Germany. The bombs from the remaining aircraft in this group, seven of the 95th Bomb Group, "hit in fields five miles south east of Magdeburg." By effective use of its smokescreen, and of course greatly assisted by the *Luftwaffe*, which in no small measure distracted the lead bombardiers on their bomb run, the oil refineries in Magdeburg had escaped serious damage so far.

The 13th B Combat Wing, however, was still on its way to the target and could perhaps tilt the scale for the Americans. Only two groups were left in this combat wing becauseo f the mix-up at the rendezvous. The entire 94th Bomb Group formation had returned to England, and only the 95th and 388th Bomb Groups remained. But, in contrast to the 13th A Combat Wing,

The bombs of the 388th Bomb Group straddle the Magdeburg-Rothensee oil refinery, west of the Elbe River. Smoke from the bombs of the 100th and 390th Bomb Groups is visible south of the target area. CROWN COPYRIGHT / PUBLIC RECORD OFFICE

only a few enemy fighters were encountered by these two groups, and no ships were lost before the initial point was reached.

The 95th Bomb Group's bombing was hampered by the same clouds and smokescreen that fouled the bombardiers of the previous groups, and rather than make a second run, the command pilot, Lt. Col. David C. McKnight, elected to attack the assigned secondary target, the aircraft factory at Dessau. Here, only minutes before, the 94th Combat Wing had just been heavily bloodied by the *Luftwaffe*. On the bomb run, B-17G *Worry Bird*

(42-107201), flown by Lt. R. I. Johnson, was hit badly by flak in two engines. Johnson had to jettison his bombs in order to be able to stay in formation. The sixteen remaining ships of the 95th Bomb Group salvoed at 1430 hours from 24,000 feet. The bursts covered a railroad line running south as well as a barracks area to the west and industrial area to the east of the factory.

But the effort of the last group to bomb, the 388th Bomb Group, saved the day for the Americans at Magdeburg. Command pilot was Capt. Leo G. Burkett in B-17G *Gydina* (42-31802), piloted by Capt. George C. Montgomery. Capt. Charles M. Zettek was their lead bombardier. On the way in, no fewer than five B-17s had aborted, four due to mechanical troubles and one because the pilot was sick. But the crews aboard the fifteen remaining aircraft did a good job. At 1423 hours, they released 570 100-pound bombs from 26,000 feet. Photographic reconnaissance later revealed that 3 percent of the identified bombs had landed within 500 feet of the assigned aiming point, 17 percent within 1,000 feet, and 56 percent within 2,000 feet.

The official report states: "The central and western sections of the plant were blanketed by at least ninety-five bursts. Another large pattern was scattered south of the target and covered part of the Magdeburg marshalling yards. Fires were started in the oil storage area. Damage visible included moderate roof damage to the liquid air plant, severe damage to part of the compressors building and to one third of the roof of the injector-circulator house. It is adjudged that after minor repairs the plant would be able to resume operations at 25 to 50 percent capacity."[47]

The bomb group formations returned to England without further mishap, landing at the respective bases around 1800 hours. At interrogation, claims for German fighters destroyed were checked and information gathered from the tired crews for the official reports. In addition to tactical comments, more mundane suggestions were made by the returning crews. This is illustrated in a report by Maj. Marvin S. Bowman, the 100th Bomb Group's intelligence officer: "Such facilities as the P.X., service club, and barber shop should stay open, so that we will be able to use them." "On way back over the enemy coast there were four ships that had no man in the ball turret, one was 695." "We definitely need hot water for showers after a mission. 350th Squadron latrines have no toilet paper. If not available how about newspapers or such. Coffee and sandwiches out on the line this morning was a good thing. The mess sergeant is doing a great job." "Today, for the third time we found guns that had been fired and not cleaned. This is bad business." "Friendly fighters should remain for protection in front of the Group. Didn't see any for fifty-four minutes." "Would like coal for barracks. Would still appreciate sandwiches at interrogation." "Silver ships flying as lead ships should be painted olive drab on the top of fuselage, as it is hard on the eyes." "Want soap in officers club to wash before eating after mission." "Suggest stronger escort from the initial point to the target." "Want place to have dry cleaning done."[48]

Back in his Nissen hut at Framlingham, Robert Munroe, who had flown the mission as navigator on B-17G *Bomboogie* (42-31974), recorded in his diary: "Matthias went straight down and Ingram nearly so. No chutes from either. Both of these crews were in our barracks. On Matthias's crew were Gerards (co-pilot), Jo Freyland (navigator) and Bass (bombardier). They were on their twenty-fourth. Ingram, one of the new boys with lead crew possibilities, had in seven missions . . .

"The roughest mission of all for us and highest losses in history of group. Little difficult to keep from being depressed this evening. This was my thirteenth, or 12B as we prefer to call it. Hermann Goering's boys had a fair day—we a poor one. Things will be different next time!"[49]

CHAPTER 8

Königsborn

Two combat wings, the 45th and the 4th, were scheduled to bomb the army tank ordnance depot in Königsborn, just east of Magdeburg. It was at this depot, the largest of its kind in Germany, that many tanks and half-track vehicles were given a pre-operational inspection. Its destruction would mean a severe blow for the German armament industry, and less armour on the battlefields of Europe.

Leading the 45th Combat Wing was the 96th Bomb Group from Snetterton Heath. A composite group of the 388th Bomb Group from Knettishall and the 452nd Bomb Group from Deopham Green was flying as high group.

The 452nd Bomb Group also put up the entire low group formation. The wing leader was Lt. Col. Stanley I. Hand, flying in PFF-equipped B-17G 42-97666, piloted by Capt. Robert S. Bowman. The groups assembled swiftly, and the combat wing formed without much difficulty. However, between St. Ives and Cambridge, another wing crossed its course, temporarily breaking up the formation, which was then reformed over Bury St. Edmunds. There were only a few aborts. From the lead group, Lieutenant Bond returned to Snetterton Heath with his number three engine out. His place was taken by a scheduled spare flown by Lieutenant MacDaniel in B-17G *Lovely Lady* (42-102633). Both other spares of the group returned to base.

The records of the 452nd Bomb Group indicate that they put up twenty-four aircraft for their own low group, and nine aircraft for the composite group with the 388th Bomb Group, all including spares. Rather mysteriously, the same records show that seven of the B-17s in the low group returned to Deopham Green, all scheduled spares according to the report submitted by group leader Maj. David Rowland. This, however, left only a seventeen-aircraft bomb group, instead of the standard complement of eighteen. In the records a typed page with handwritten corrections gives the clue to the identity of the missing aircraft in the formation. B-17G *Inside Curve* (42-39973) apparently could not take off due to some mechanical troubles, and the crew changed aircraft. Then, because of its consequent late take-off, the crew could not find the group formation and returned to Deopham Green. But why one of the regular scheduled spares did not fill in on the number six position in the high squadron is a mystery, and it consequently stayed vacant for the mission. Also, the three spares of the 452nd Bomb Group for the composite group returned unused. One B-17 of the 388th Bomb Group, which put up the twelve aircraft for the two additional squadrons for this composite group, ran into trouble. Scheduled to fly as number five in the low squadron was B-17G 42-107198, piloted by Lieutenant Barry.

This picture was taken from the left waist windows of B-17G 42-107093, the lead ship of the 452nd Bomb Group, and shows the 96th Bomb Group leading the 45th Combat Wing to Konigsbörn. NATIONAL ARCHIVES

The assistant engineering officer of the group reported later that day: "The pilot was forced to take violent evasive action to avoid hitting another plane. This caused the bombs to be torn loose in the bomb bay. All loose equipment was thrown helter-skelter and the crew was badly shaken up. For all these reasons the pilot brought the plane back to the base. The plane is being checked for structural damage. The right bomb bay door must be changed because two 500-pound bombs fell on it and bent it."[1]

Since the 388th Bomb Group did not send up any spares for this composite group, it now also counted seventeen B-17s. Leading the 4th Combat Wing, the second and last to bomb Königsborn, was the 385th Bomb Group from Great Ashfield. Command pilot and wing leader was Lt. Col. James G. McDonald, in PFF-equipped B-17G 42-97634, piloted by Capt. G. A. West.

Twenty-one aircraft took off, and since there were no aborts, all three spares returned to base.

The low group in the combat wing was a composite group of three squadrons from three different bomb groups. The 94th Bomb Group furnished lead, the 447th Bomb Group low, and the 385th Bomb Group high squadron. Leading this composite group was Capt. John H. Skarren in B-17G 42-107059, piloted by 1st Lt. K. E. Simonds. The three squadrons formed up over their respective home fields, and a good group assembly was made near Bury St. Edmunds.

At Rattlesden, home base for the 447th Bomb Group, which furnished the high group in the wing, 2nd Lt. H. C. Kaye ran into trouble. Scheduled as one of the three spares in brand new B-17G 44-6027, he was taxiing to take off position with the generators off. Suddenly, the electrical system meters began to show excessive readings, and almost immediately the entire electrical system went dead. Consequently, the hydraulic system was inoperative and the aircraft did not have brakes or control. The aircraft came to a stop near the perimeter track. The crew hastily vacated their stranded bomber, which was now blocking passage on the perimeter track, and

High over Germany, some inaccurate flak bursts were photographed by a crewmember of B-17G 42-107093, the lead ship of the 452nd Bomb Group. NATIONAL ARCHIVES

headed for another B-17G, the assigned ground spare. Very quickly all pre-scribed pre-flight checks were done and again an attempt was made to take off. As his first B-17 of the day was blocking the perimeter track, Kaye had to taxi into take-off position along one side of the same runway that was used for take-off.

Kaye, now in B-17G *Scheherazade* (42-31225), apparently was in too much of a hurry and not careful enough. Not having enough clearance, his wing tip collided with old "war weary" B-17 42-3487, which was parked along the runway. Both aircraft were damaged, and Kaye's crew left their second bomber that morning, not trying to take off again and Kaye most probably heading for some harsh words from his Commanding Officer. The rest of the 447th Bomb Group, led by Maj. Clarence L. Elder in B-17G *Piccadilly Ann II* (42-102651), piloted by Captain Leavitt, had a swift group formation. The two remaining spares returned to Rattlesden, and the group arrived at the wing assembly point two minutes before the lead group, the 385th Bomb Group.

Combat wing assembly was then effected from 1134 to 1156 hours. An unidentified formation of Liberators broke up the wing formation by flying on a collision course with it. This peril averted, proper wing assembly again took some time, and the wing left the English coast at 1217 hours, on time, and at 15,000 feet, fifteen miles north of the briefed point, but was able to take its proper position in the division formation. And now, both the 45th

From left to right: Sergeant Walsh, crew chief; Lt. Calvin Samson; and Lt. Milton C. Casebere. On 28 May, Samson was lead pilot and Casebere lead navigator of the Composite Group, flying high in the 45th Combat Wing. This group lost two B-17s of the 388th Bomb Group, piloted by Lt. Arthur M. Codding and Lt. Marquis G. Fjelsted, but had excellent bombing results on Königsborn. JAMES W. GODWIN

and the 4th Combat Wings followed in the long stream, preceded by the Ruhland, Dessau, and Magdeburg-bound Fortress formations.

More than 100 heavily loaded Fortresses of the 45th and 4th Combat Wings flew to a point northeast of Brunswick, where they left the stream, and headed for their primary target, the ordnance depot at Königsborn, at about 1400 hours. At the same time, hundreds of German fighters hit the combat wings just ahead, causing heavy losses. Not one fighter, however, made a serious pass at the Königsborn force, an indication of how local air battles were. Only light and inaccurate flak had been encountered, and the crews began to relax, as they headed to their target, more or less considering it a "milk run" already.

The 45th Combat Wing was led to its target by 1st Lt. Victor Pasetti, lead navigator aboard PFF-equipped B-17G 42-97666 of the 96th Bomb Group. Lead bombardier 1st Lt. James U. Rooker took over the controls after the initial point was passed. No smoke screens, haze, or clouds obscured his view, and at 1415 hours, he signalled the release of all 160 500-pound high-explosive bombs from the group. Results were considered fair, as 13 percent of the identified bombs hit within 500 feet of the assigned aiming point, 38 percent within 1,000 feet, and 89 percent within 2,000 feet. Only five of the groups' B-17s were slightly damaged by flak. The composite group, with eleven aircraft of the 388th Bomb Group and six of the 452nd Bomb Group, would do better, but would pay a higher price for its results. Lead bombardier

This picture was taken through the open bomb bay of B-17G 42-39972 of the 452nd Bomb Group, piloted by 2nd Lt. Thomas R. Dickerson, and shows bombs landing in Königsborn. The B-17 in the picture is *Big Nosie* (42-31358), flown by 2nd Lt. Shirley A. Parvin. This aircraft and crew were lost a day later on a mission to Leipzig. NATIONAL ARCHIVES

was Lt. James W. Godwin, aboard B-17G 42-97289, flown by Lt. Calvin Samson and with command pilot Capt. Ben E. Terry aboard. His bombs, released at 1416 hours from 25,730 feet, created more havoc and smoke on the ground.

No fewer than 21 percent of the 155 500-pound high-explosive bombs landed within 500 feet, 62 percent within 1,000 feet, and 92 percent within 2,000 feet of the assigned aiming point. On the debit side, two aircraft in the formation were hit heavily by flak, and twelve others received slight flak damage. This left only the 452nd Bomb Group, flying low in the 45th Combat Wing, to bomb. Lead bombardier F/O Leon B. Slobodzian dropped at 1417 hours, the 170 500-pound high-explosive bombs of the group exploded in the already smoke-covered target area. No fewer than fifteen of the group's aircraft were slightly damaged by flak, and one crewmember was seriously injured.

One result of the effective bombing by the 45th Combat Wing was that a large cloud of smoke and dust now covered the target area, making it difficult for the trailing 4th Combat Wing to bomb accurately. This wing's lead bombardier, 1st Lt. M. W. Cole of the 385th Bomb Group reported: "The group formation made a seventy-degree left turn at the initial point and opened bomb bay doors. Haze, patchy clouds and smoke made it very difficult to pick up the target. I synchronized short and released bombs with crosshairs on the target. Results unobserved due to smoke. Heavy and accurate flak was encountered over the target area."[2]

Only about 10 percent of this group's 160 500-pound bombs of landed within 2,000 feet of the assigned aiming point. Sixteen B-17s received slight damage, with two crewmembers wounded; one B-17 was hit so badly that it gradually fell behind the formation and was then vacated by its crew, observers in the Group counted ten parachutes. Leading the composite group was a squadron of six B-17s from the 94th Bomb Group, headed by Capt. John H. Skarren in B-17G 42-107059, flown by 1st Lt. K. E. Simonds.

Lead bombardier 2nd Lt. W. C. Wilson reported: "At the initial point, we made a left turn, opened bomb bay doors, and headed for the primary target. At this point, the high group of the wing's turning [447th Bomb Group] put us south of course, and as a result, we had to do a lot of 'S'-sing. Briefed landmarks were not lined up as a result. The area was covered by smoke, it was very hazy and scattered clouds. The target was difficult to pick up and at 1425 hours I released my bombs by my own sighting operation, and the balance of the group salvoed on me as briefed. Results unobserved due to smoke, but reconnaissance revealed poor results. Flak was heavy and accurate on the bomb run, but did not affect our particular run. No enemy fighters were encountered."[3]

The other twelve aircraft in the composite group, six each from the 385th and 447th Bomb Groups, had also salvoed their bombs with Wilson. Results for the entire composite group were marked as a "gross error." The 447th Bomb Group, the last group to bomb Königsborn, dropped its load of 744 100-pound incendiaries into the smoke and haze now fully covering the target area, but the smaller explosions could not be plotted because of the smoke. Only four B-17s of the last two groups were damaged by flak.

Despite the flak and the smoke, the bombing had been generally quite accurate. It was observed that the northern two thirds of the target area was blanketed by a large concentration, and that all six main buildings took direct hits. Numerous other buildings were hit and some destroyed. Also the dispersal area took a beating, several tanks being destroyed.

One of the B-17s of the 385th Bomb Group, flying as number five in its high squadron, was vacated by its crew, after being hit by flak over the target. This was B-17G 42-97847, piloted by F/O Francis J. Hunter and F/O Raymond J. Miller. The latter gives his account of the events: "At the time we dropped our bombs, we were struck by four bursts of flak. Each shell did some damage, but the last one which hit, struck us in the right wing, just back of the outboard engine. It made quite a hole where the lubricating oil tank was located. We immediately tried to feather that engine but there was not enough oil to cause that propeller to stop and as a result it began to windmill. Since there was no oil left the normal 2,400 revolutions per

The officers of the crew of B-17G 42-97847 of the 385th Bomb Group. From left to right: Antero D. Coelho, bombardier; Preston Ray, navigator; Raymond J. Miller, co-pilot; and Francis J. Hunter, pilot. All were made prisoner of war. RAYMOND J. MILLER

minute could not be maintained. The tachometer was built to register up to 4,500 RPMs and the needle on this gauge was right up to this maximum reading and only registered 4,500 RPMs since the needle was stopped by the peg built into the gauge. The windmilling caused a severe vibrating condition which made it impossible to keep ones hands on the flight controls. This vibration was so severe it was straining the airframe and causing rivets to pop out. The navigator's astrodome was torn loose and blew away in the windstream. The hydraulic system located in the cockpit and mounted on the side of the fuselage behind my seat was torn loose and the hydraulic lines ruptured.

"Luckily, we had turned the electric pump off and bled the pressure from the accumulator and the lines. We could stop the vibration by reducing power to the other three engines back to what would be an idle. This then put us into a descending glide which was no good as we were so deep into German territory. We reapplied flight power and put the controls on the automatic flight control equipment. This was working and we continued on course back to England. We had by this time fallen out of formation, but were following the other B-17s on course about 2,000 feet lower altitude. Since the engine had no oil for lubrication, extreme heat in all bearings was generated. This heat was so intense that the magnesium parts of the engines just aft of the propeller began to burn. Flames flowing aft were melting the aluminium cowling. We had high hopes that the propeller would come off or that the vibration would cause the whole engine to separate from the aircraft, but no such good luck. The vibration caused the top turret rotating gears to jam and it was inoperative. This continuing vibration was really tearing the aircraft apart and the billowing smoke was white, which indicated an oil source. But we were noticing some black smoke, from a gasoline source, mingling with the white smoke. Then we decided to abandon the aircraft. We all cleared the ship and all survived the jump, although minor injuries were sustained by most as we hit the ground."[4]

German troops and civilians quickly rounded up nine men, but the engineer, Staff Sgt. Ralph M. Marts, evaded capture for several days and was caught on 6 June in Steudnitz. The vacated aircraft crashed at 1442 hours at Albrechtshain, near Grimmen.

Two other B-17s were also in trouble as a result of flak. One of these was B-17G 42-39845, a 388th Bomb Group aircraft, flying as number five in the lead squadron of the composite group. It was named *Hulcher's Vultures*, after its original pilot, Wendell E. Hulcher, who in the meantime had safely finished his tour of operations. Its pilot for this mission was 2nd Lt. Marquis G. Fjelsted.

Navigator H. Joseph Houlihan later recalled: "After an easy ride to Königsborn, we were hit only seconds after bombs away. The right wing took

B-17G *Hulcher's Vultures* (42-39845) of the 388th Bomb Group. The aircraft was named after its original pilot, Wendell E. Hulcher. He and his crew succesfully completed their tour of operations in it, after which it was used by several crews, until it was belly-landed by Lieutenant Fjelsted on 28 May, near Treysa, some fifty kilometers southwest of Kassel, Germany. WARREN H. WILLIAMS

the main damage, with both engines shot out. Part of the damage was in the control cable section in the bomb bay. The pilot was not able to synchronize the damaged engines with the good ones and we slowly fell out of formation and lost altitude. We feathered number three engine, but number four could not be feathered and created quite a drag problem. We picked up fighter escort, two P-51s, who stayed with us until it was obvious we couldn't make it back. Rather than taking our chances on the chutes, we made a crash landing in the general area of Kassel, where we were all consequently taken prisoner and spent the rest of the war in POW camps."[5]

Fjelsted had crash-landed *Hulcher's Vultures* near Mengsberg, a village some fifty kilometers southwest of Kassel, where the entire crew was captured. The second B-17 hit during the bomb run was also a 388th Bomb Group aircraft in the composite group, flying as number six in its low squadron. B-17G 42-102485 was piloted by 1st Lt. Arthur M. Codding and 2nd Lt. Roger B. Withers.

All crewmembers were flying their thirteenth mission on this day, except radio operator Tech Sgt. Clyde H. Waite, who had missed some missions

The crew of *Hulcher's Vultures*. Back row, left to right: Chester P. Tracewski, bombardier; William C. Hudson, co-pilot; Marquis G. Fjelsted, pilot; Herbert J. Houlihan, navigator; and John R. Shatz, tail gunner. Front row, left to right: Harold S. McCarthy, right waist gunner; John E. McBrien, engineer; John L. Perry, left waist gunner; Edward J. Stringer, radio operator; and George F. Hoover, ball turret gunner. All were made prisoner of war. MRS. JOHN L. PERRY

because of sinusitis, a common illness when flying at great heights. He was flying his seventh mission this day. From his hand comes the following vivid account of the events: "Fortified by the notion that it wouldn't be so bad, we picked up our flying gear after the briefing on our base at Knettishall and headed for the flightline. Daylight was breaking and we could see the outlines of a multitude of big bristling birds that would bear us up and away. The bombs had been loaded, the tanks filled and the ammo to fuel the guns was all on board. It was just a matter of time before warm-up, take-off and flight across the Channel. Our own B-17, *Little Chum*, had been redlined shortly before take-off so we were flying another B-17 that day. After rendezvous over the North Sea, we climbed up on course in the sunshine until we turned at the initial point. Until now, our flight had been uneventful, but flak started to come up.

"Suddenly, number one engine stopped, due to flak damage or mechanical problems. Tech Sgt. Robert C. Berg called in and told us it was a rocker box failure. The pilot immediately feathered number one engine and we dropped our bomb load. We couldn't maintain formation very long and received authorization to drop from high group to low group. We still could

The Germans have tried to camouflage *Hulcher's Vultures* to prevent it from being strafed and destroyed by Allied fighters. KONRAD RUDOLPH

not keep up and again we received permission to leave the group and join it again at the rally point. As we crossed over from the initial point to the rally point some German fighters, who had obviously been hiding in the direction of the sun, came at us. We were sitting ducks and had no alternative but to dive for some sporadic cloud cover, at about 5,000 feet.

"Before making this dive we were hit several times by the fighters which succeeded in rendering inoperative our command and VHF radio equipment. Previous to this, and fortunately for us, we had radioed for fighter cover when we aborted the formation and headed for home. Fortunately for us, the enemy fighters did not follow suit, though they were much better equipped for this action than we were. Our B-17 did survive this power dive from 25,000 to 5,000 feet and leveled out. Flying a crippled bomber at an altitude of 5,000 feet over enemy territory isn't the choice one would opt for on a Sunday afternoon. The cloud coverage soon disappeared and again we were sitting ducks, an easy target for flak-gunners. Again, Codding took the only option he had; he dove to the deck and tree-top level.

"In fact, we were flying so low that on one occasion we had to pull up to go over power lines. In the fortunes of war the best action isn't always enough, as we were soon to discover. At this time we were joined by two of our own fighters and were overjoyed to have their protection. The ball turret gunner, Staff Sgt. Kenneth M. Joye, was ordered out of his turret and he went to the waist gun positions. As we flew over little towns and villages at rapid film speed, the folk dressed in appropriate garb were obviously returning from church. We barely had a chance to take a look at them and they at us, at this altitude. But it was long enough to read the look of surprise and

The crew of B-17G 42-102485 of the 388th Bomb Group was a mixed lot. Arthur Codding's original crew, pictured here in Rapid City, was split up due to illness and other factors. Five of these men were on the fateful 28 May mission, which they all survived as prisoners of war. Back row, left to right: Clyde H. Waite, radio operator; Clyde R. Nash (not on 28 May mission); Albert E. Lynde (not on 28 May mission); Robert C. Berg, engineer; James W. Mulder, tail gunner; and Fred N. McKinley (not on 28 May mission). Front row, left to right: Arthur M. Codding, pilot; Roger B. Withers, co-pilot; L. G. Saum (not on 28 May mission); and L. C. Sacks (not on 28 May mission). CLYDE H. WAITE

fear in their faces. One railroad engineer raced to get his engine under shelter. Robert Berg fired from the top turret and we could see water vapor escaping just as it entered the round-house.

"Up to this point, our substitute *Little Chum* was able to maintain altitude and respond to controls. The pilots had determined to return to Knettishall or failing that, to set down at the nearest available airfield. It involved considerable risk at best. For one thing, evasive action would be non-existent at this altitude with only three engines. There was a strong possibility we would be hit again by ground fire. However, it seemed worth the risk. It seemed that our little friends were overjoyed, and since we had no more radio equipment left, we couldn't ask them why. One would dive in from the left and chandelle up to the left. Then the other would dive in from the right and chandelle up to the right. Too late we realized that our escorts were not exuberant. What they were really doing was trying desperately to tell us, 'Go right' or 'Go left,' but 'Do not go straight ahead.' Not understanding their intentions, we proceeded in our westerly course and then flew squarely over the center of a *Luftwaffe* air base. An enormous amount of light flak came up, and machine-gun and 20mm cannon fire almost immediately blew out our nose section, instantly killing the navigator and bombardier, 2nd Lt. Donald L. Chiles and Staff Sgt. Delmar D. McBeth.* Before we could recover from the first shock and we could clear the air base, we also took heavy damage in the right waist of the ship, resulting in three more casualties. The ball turret gunner, Kenneth Joye, was hit in his left arm; left waist gunner, Lawrence G. Brown, took some flak in his right shoulder. The right waist gunner, Staff Sgt. Thomas L. Roskowick, was hit very badly. Some fragments entered his back, just below his flak suit and came out through his abdomen. He fell down on the floor in the waist of the ship and was attended to as good as anyone could.

Four members of this crew, pictured during training in Rapid City in December 1943, were assigned to Codding to complete his crew. They suffered a heavy loss of life on 28 May. Standing, far left is Staff Sgt. Lawrence G. Brown, left waist gunner (POW); in the center is Staff Sgt. Delmar D. McBeth, togglier (KIA); and far right is Staff Sgt. Thomas L. Roskowick, right waist gunner (KIA). Kneeling in the center is 2nd Lt. Donald L. Chiles, navigator (KIA). LAWRENCE G. BROWN

---

* McBeth was a so-called togglier. These were enlisted men, replacing a bombardier, normally an officer, on bombers where the Norden bombsight was removed. The bombs on these ships were "toggled" at the sight of the bombs dropping from the group lead ship.

"The intercom and all the control cables, except the elevator trim tab were severed. Number three engine was also knocked out. The hole in the right side of the plane was almost big enough to walk through. But the B-17 was a rugged plane, they even wrote a song about her "coming in on a wing and a prayer." Prayer was still to be answered. When the smoke cleared, it became apparent that our ship was doomed. We could see a picture of the frayed ends of wires whipping back and forth against the sky. This was framed by the ragged-edged, gaping hole left by the blast. Our rudder cables to the tail and ailerons were gone. All this, and still our plane flew on, guided, I am sure, by someone bigger than all of us. At one point we barely missed a large brick chimney, and the countdown continued. Our situation was desperate and it was made more difficult that the crew in the rear didn't know anymore what the pilots had decided to do.

"I was determined to find out what was happening. Unlatching the bulk head door to the bomb bay, I was thrust back by a blast of air that entered where the nose used to be, forced its way through the plane and now made an exit through the hole in the waist. The noise was deafening and for all practical purposes the inside air speed was approximately the same as the outside—hurricane speed.

"The good engines must have kept the speed at least 120 miles per hour, though this could not be confirmed. The instruments in the panel had been destroyed by the flak and the blast. Had we flown in our original older-type *Little Chum*, the pilots would have had less armor plating in front of them and would probably have been wounded or killed also. After forcing my way through the bomb bay and the engineer's top turret position I finally reached the pilot's compartment where Arthur Codding and our fine co-pilot, Roger Withers, were doing a supernatural job. I took a long look at the nose area, which was forward and below. It was not a pretty picture. Chiles had been decapitated by the blast and McBeth had also been killed. I could only see their bodies, it would be the last view I would ever have of them. I completed my mission in coming forward and blurting out, 'We'd better get this thing down while it's still in one piece.' Codding yelled back, 'That's exactly what we're going to do.'

"I cautiously made my way back to the radio room and informed the rest of the crew of the decision. Shortly after this Berg came back and ordered us to take our crash-landing position. We had practiced this a dozen times or more in training, now it was paying off. In a sitting position we put our backs against the bulk head in the radio room, and with legs drawn up locked our hands behind our heads to cushion the shock and minimize whiplash. We waited for ground impact. Since both pilots had no way of determining the true air speed, cutting back on the throttle was out of the question. I've often wondered how it felt to be at the controls of a dying ship with dead

The tenth member on 1st Lt. Arthur M. Codding's crew was ball turret gunner Kenneth M. Joye. He was made a Prisoner of War. BETTY H. JOYE

and mortally wounded on board, making a last desperate struggle to land such a ship. Incredibly they were still able to fly it on two engines, using them for turns when absolutely necessary and the elevator trim tab for minor changes in altitude. After some time the number three engine started to windmill and couldn't be feathered. Subsequently it caught fire and kept burning, despite all efforts to extinguish it. Then the remaining elevator cables snapped.

Tech Sgt. Robert C. Berg, engineer of B-17G 42-102485 of the 388th Bomb Group. He was made a prisoner of war with the six other survivors of the crew. ALVIN P. BERG

Second Lt. Donald L. Chiles, navigator of B-17G 42-102485 of the 388th Bomb Group. On his thirteenth combat mission, on 28 May, he was killed, together with togglier Staff Sgt. Delmar D. McBeth by a burst of flak in the nose of the bomber. They were buried on 2 June in Amersfoort, Holland, with the third crewmember who was killed, Staff Sgt. Thomas L. Roskowick. After the war, Chiles's remains were returned to the United States, where they rest at the Rock Island National Cemetery. MRS. DOLORES BANAS

"Fortunately, we had just cleared a forest. In front of us was a pasture, with several irrigation ditches horizontal to our flight path. The shock was real enough when we hit the ground. As a result of the impact the spinning props were immediately pushed under the wings and stopped turning. The jostling was not unlike the scenes in a movie or on a television screen during

Staff Sgt. Thomas L. Roskowick was badly wounded aboard B-17G 42-102485 of the 388th Bomb Group. He died shortly after Lt. Arthur Codding belly-landed the bomber in Groenekan, Holland. After temporary burial in Amersfoort, he now rests in the American Cemetery and Memorial in Margraten, Holland.
THOMAS ROSKOWICK

an accident scene. The ball turret protruded several feet below the aircraft, it fitted nicely in the ditches in the pasture. We hit several of them while coming to a stop. Each time we did it felt like the aft section of the plane would be torn off. But it held, blessed old B-17. She had given the last full measure of devotion."[6]

Arthur Codding made a "textbook" crash-landing near Utrecht in Holland on a pasture belonging to farmer D. E. de Kruyff of Groenekan, a small village northeast of Utrecht. Several people on the ground, either working or enjoying the fine Sunday afternoon, observed the B-17 coming down. Eighteen year-old Willem de Jong was in the adjoining nursery-garden and was alerted by the noise of flak of the nearby Soesterberg air base: "I looked up and saw the B-17 with an engine on fire coming in, very low over a row of trees. It hit the ground and crossed several ditches, just missing some cows grazing in the fields. When it stopped, its nose was resting over a ditch and it immediately started to burn fiercely, some 500 meters away from me. Of course I immediately ran to it, together with several others, including the owner of the field. When we got there the plane was still burning. The crewmembers were hiding in the ditch, and one of them was severely wounded. We helped them out of the ditch, and made a stretcher to move the wounded man, by taking out a fence gate and then carrying it by four men. We went to de Kruyff's farmhouse, where we placed the wounded man in the shade. Just after the arrival of the local fire brigade and a doctor, he died."[7]

Smoke rises from behind the nursery in Groenekan, Holland, where the B-17 of Lt. Arthur M. Codding bellied in and burned. Three of the crew were killed during the flight, AND seven others were made prisoners of war.

Clyde Waite recalls the last moments aboard the B-17: "Waiting for her to stop seemed like an hour. The forward section, the wing and engine section immediately burst into flame. Our driving passion could now be summed up in one word: survival! Chiles and McBeth were dead, and there was no point in risking life and limb to retrieve shattered bodies. There was high octane gasoline in the wing tanks which were ruptured and began to fuel the fire. Although the bombs had been dropped, there was still live .50 armor-piercing ammunition aboard. The plane was obviously a death trap and we had to leave quick, with the two light and one mortally wounded.

"With some effort, we succeeded in opening the escape hatch. Although we had the right use of mind and body we were suffering from shock which rendered us quite weak, almost to the point of immobility. How glad we were when the last man was out. The ammo began to explode. We headed for the only possible shelter in this flat country, the ditch. We dragged Roskowick and ourselves into the waist deep water and it seemed to us quite cold. Even with the buoyancy the water provided, with the shock of our overtaxed nervous system, it took all our efforts to hold Tom Roskowick's head above the water. He was in a coma and never regained consciousness. From our vantage point we could look across the open field and see the condemned plane burning with fury. She made a grim, if not spectacular, sight.

She had served us well. There were still some bursts of ammo, but we felt it was safe to come out—but how?

"Several man came to help us and we were retrieved by warm and friendly hands. We were frustrated by the language barrier but I'm sure they understood how grateful we were. An old pasture gate that was handy was put into service as a stretcher to move Tom. In the plane he had asked me to pray for him, which I did at the time. Now he was carried to a farmhouse, we following him. He was placed in the shade and died peacefully shortly thereafter. The Germans were soon on the spot and took us prisoner of war. The wounded were brought to a hospital and the rest were interrogated in Utrecht. Later that evening our captors took us back to tie up some loose ends and to take a final look at our once 'Flying Fortress.' The gasoline had done its work. The plane was a burnt-out hulk back to the radio room. The engines which had thrust this craft on its mission—what was left of them— were now grotesque, shapeless blobs of charred aluminium. She was not pretty, but she had been a good ship. One cannot help but wonder as our escort viewed the battered plane with its majestic tail section still intact, if they had a premonition that hundreds of these very aircraft would soon be marshalling to complete their defeat."[8]

Sergeant Brown and Sergeant Joye were first treated for their wounds in the *Luftwaffe* hospital in Amsterdam; the five other survivors were sent to Dulag Luft for interrogation. The three crewmembers killed were buried in the Rusthof cemetery in Amersfoort.

For the rest of the Königsborn force, excluding the three unfortunate bomber crews mentioned in this chapter, the return flight was uneventful, and all groups landed at their own base after some seven flying hours.

CHAPTER 9

Zeitz

"On Sunday morning, 28 May 1944, I had the surprise of my life. When I went to the early briefing, since I was a lead navigator now, I could not believe what I heard. We were going to Zeitz again. The very same synthetic oil-refinery twenty miles southwest of Leipzig, Germany that we had left wrecked and burning just sixteen days before on our tenth mission of May 12. My question was: 'What are we going back to Zeitz again for?' I thought we were going on a wild goose chase that made no sense. We all know better now and before the day was out, I was to once more look down on this refinery, to see with my own eyes that it had been rebuild and put back into production."[1]

Thus wrote 44th Bomb Group navigator John W. McClane in his diary after he safely returned from one of the most successful bombing missions of the day. The enormous Braunkohle-Benzin A.G. synthetic oil refinery at Zeitz had indeed suffered a great blow on 12 May, but this would be surpassed by the results of this day's bombing.

The first B-24-equipped units in the bomber stream were the two combat wings assigned to Zeitz. As explained in the chapter 1, these combat wings were divided into an A and a B group, each comprising three squadrons of twelve aircraft each, flying lead, low left, and high right.

In the leading 96th Combat Wing A Group, the 466th Bomb Group from Attlebridge put up the lead and low squadrons, with the 467th Bomb Group from Rackheath furnishing the high squadrons in both the A and B groups. The 458th Bomb Group from Horsham St. Faiths flew in the lead and low position in the B Group.

Following the 96th Combat Wing was the 14th Combat Wing. Its A Group had the lead and low squadrons furnished by the freshman 492nd Bomb Group from North Pickenham. The 392nd Bomb Group from Wendling put up the high squadrons in both the A and B Groups, and finally, the 44th Bomb Group, based at Shipdham, furnished the lead and low squadrons for the B Group.

Penetration support for these combat wings and those following closely behind, heading for Merseburg, was provided by forty-four Thunderbolts of the 353rd Fighter Group from Raydon, led by their commanding officer, Col. Glenn E. Duncan.

The crew of B-24J *The Banana Barge* (42-110045) of the 44th Bomb Group. Back row, left to right: Mort Baumann, bombardier (not on 28 May mission, POW on 7 October); Irving S. Gurman, pilot; Robert F. Jipson, co-pilot; and Andrew J. Kaulbach, navigator. Front row, left to right: Charles D. Williams, tail gunner; James H. McMaster, nose turret gunner; George B. Costello, engineer; Joseph Carson, radio operator; Eino J. Wiitala, left waist gunner; and Theodore D. Willis, right waist gunner. All were made prisoner of war. MRS. THEODORE D. WILLIS

The formation assembly of both wings was without problems, due to the fine weather conditions, and the English coast was left on time, at 1230 hours. The reports of the 467th Bomb Group, however, mention that a group of B-17s flew through its formation when it approached the division assembly line. Most probably this is the same situation, but now seen from the other cockpit, of which we have read in the account of the men of the 4th Combat Wing, heading for Königsborn. Landfall in Holland and the subsequent flight at 20,000 feet over enemy occupied territory was without any serious incidents. At 1306 hours, the 353rd Fighter Group made rendezvous over the Dutch coast near Egmond. Just before the Dümmer Lake area, the wings gradually climbed to 22,000 feet to avoid the infamous Dümmer Lake flak, which was known to be quite accurate. All nine B-17 wings had passed this area without problems, but the second B-24 wing would lose one of its aircraft there, just one example of bad luck. One of the very first victims of the German defenses this day was one of the only three Liberators that the Second Air Division would lose this day. *The Banana Barge*, as B-24J 42-110045 was known, in the 44th Bomb Group was piloted by 2nd Lt. Irving S. Gurman and 2nd Lt. Robert F. Jipson. Near Dümmer Lake several flak bursts appeared, one of which exploded just below the aircraft.

B-24J 42-110045 of the 44th Bomb Group was named after one of the less complimentary nicknames for its type. *The Banana Barge* was shot down by flak on the shores of Dümmer Lake; the nine men of its crew were made prisoners of war.
STEPHEN P. ADAMS

Robert Jipson clearly remembered what happened: "The burst knocked out our number one engine, set fire to number 2 engine and number 3 engine was a run away and couldn't be feathered."[2]

The B-24, heavily loaded with fuel for the long trip to Zeitz and with its bombs still aboard, could not keep up with the formation. Friendly fighters escorted it, as it gradually fell away from the formation, which slowly but surely pushed ahead and out of sight. Gurman and Jipson were convinced that they would never make it back to England on *The Banana Barge*'s single good engine, and with one windmilling propeller. Consequently, the bail-out bell sounded throughout the bomber, and the crew took to their parachutes. *The Banana Barge* crashed near Dümmerlohausen on the shores of Dümmer Lake at 1352 hours. Credit for its destruction was given to four individual batteries of *schwere Flak Abteilungen 137, 273, 306,* and *393.* The nine American crewmembers were all rounded up and taken prisoner of war within a few hours of their arrival on enemy soil.

Only two Liberators in the two combat wings had mechanical trouble. B-24H *Bugs Bunny* (42-52530), piloted by Lieutenant Wescott, of the 467th Bomb Group had a supercharger failure and turned back. Wescott decided not to bring his bombs back to England and selected the airfield at Havelte, five miles north of Meppel in Holland, as a target of opportunity for his ten 500-pound bombs. Lieutenant Harkonen of the same group turned back in B-24H *Slick Chick* (41-29380) as the oxygen line servicing the top turret and radio table was cut when the turret rotated while the servicing hose was in position. The abort was charged to personnel failure, but since the crew was on its very first combat mission, the unfortunate gunner probably escaped a heavy reprimand.

The fighter escort for the B-24s was strengthened by thirty-eight Mustangs of the 361st and forty-three Lightnings of the 20th Fighter Groups arriving near Dümmer Lake at 1343 hours and Sangershausen at 1437 hours, respectively. It is interesting to note that both fighter groups, just like the 353rd providing the penetration escort, were led by their commanding officers, Col. Thomas J. J. Christian Jr. and Lt. Col. Harold J. Rau. Apparently, both had been impressed—and attracted—by the results of the one and only previous mission to oil targets carried out by the Eighth Air Force on 12 May and the way the *Luftwaffe* reacted to this attack. As such, they were hoping for a similar show.

B-24H *Bugs Bunny* (42-52530) and its pilot, Lt. Wells L. Wescott. On 28 May, the aircraft suffered from supercharger troubles and had to abort the mission to Zeitz, bombing the airfield at Havelte on the return route. The aircraft was lost in action on 13 August 1944. WILLIAM WESCOTT

Maj. Kenneth W. Gallup of the 353rd Fighter Group shot down a Bf 109 near Gütersloh on 28 May for the first of his nine air victories. GRAHAM CROSS

The 353rd Fighter Group, which had provided the penetration support, broke off escort at 1445 hours near Sangershausen and returned to England, seeking some action on the homebound trip. Near the airfield at Gütersloh, one enemy aircraft was sighted, a Bf 109, which was shot down by Maj. Kenneth W. Gallup, for his first air victory: "I was leading Red Flight of 351st Squadron and we had been strafing on the deck, when I pulled up to gain altitude to about 5,000 feet. I looked off to my right and saw this silver ship heading 180 degrees from our course about five miles away. I went after him and he apparently didn't see me and I closed in only just before we crossed over the airdrome and started firing at 150 yards. I saw strikes all over the tail and kept on firing, and then there was so much smoke that I was unable to see the aircraft and I pulled up to keep from ramming him. I then cocked my aircraft up on its wing and looked down and saw him bail out and the plane crash just west of the airdrome."[3]

The 353rd Fighter Group eradicated a large amount of German rolling stock. Eighteen locomotives were destroyed, another four damaged. Where these attacks exactly took place is not known, but it is highly probable that at least several occurred in occupied Holland. Unfortunately, a large number of innocent Dutch civilians, most on their way to family gatherings on this Whit Sunday with fine spring weather, were killed in one such strafing attack. Records of the Dutch Railroad Company indicate that no fewer than twenty-one people were killed and twenty-seven wounded during a single attack at 1535 hours near Maarsbergen. In addition, one engine driver was killed and eleven wounded on the seven locomotives the records show as being destroyed or damaged in Holland alone on this day.

Hits register on the engine of a freight train. This picture comes from gun camera film of Lt. Donald Hart of the 78th Fighter Group. He barely missed some telegraph or high-tension poles in this successful strafing attack. DONALD C. HART

A returning pair of fighters ran across a straggling B-17 "with H in square markings and last two numbers 85." It was escorted to the south of the Zuider Zee, where it bellied in. This was the 388th Bomb Group aircraft of 1st Lt. Arthur M. Codding, whose story was told in the previous chapter. The 353rd Fighter Group also lost one aircraft, P-47D 42-75457 of its 351st Fighter Squadron, piloted by 2nd Lt. Joseph R. Farley.

After the squadron left the bombers and while on the way home, they went on a sweep, searching for ground targets while flying at about 1,500 feet, with White and Red Flight line abreast and Blue Flight behind. Lieutenant Farley was the very last man in the squadron—tail end Charlie—flying as Blue 4. Near Bielefeld, the squadron encountered light flak and ground fire. The squadron leader called "to hit the deck" and immediately they took violent evasive action, which resulted in a breakup of the formation. Upon re-forming, Lieutenant Farley was missing and no radio contact could be established with him. Two pilots later reported that they had heard someone say over the radio that his tail was hit, although they were not sure that it was Lieutenant Farley. Lieutenant Farley with his Thunderbolt, crashed on the rails of the freight railway at the edge of the Loddenheide airfield, a little south of Münster, and was killed. He was buried on 30 May at the Haus-Spital cemetery for prisoners of war in Münster, and was reburied after the war at the Ardennes American Cemetery and Memorial in Belgium, where he still rests.

Second Lt. Joseph R. Farley of
the 353rd Fighter Group was
killed in action near Münster.
GROVER MCLAUGHLIN VIA GRAHAM CROSS

In the meantime, the bomb groups had arrived at their initial point and turned for the oil refineries, clearly visible under an almost cloudless sky. Some accurate flak was reported coming from Rehmsdorf, a suburb of Zeitz, but this did not hamper the lead bombardiers, now bent over their Norden bomb sights. In all, only five Liberators of the two combat wings sustained flak damage during the mission. However, in one of the ships of the 392nd Bomb Group, the flak had tragic consequences. Tech Sgt. Elbert E. Gilmore, on his eighteenth mission and flying as engineer on Lt. Charles Bell's crew in B-24H *Tondelayo* (42-50343), was hit by a flak fragment. He died within a few minutes, despite the efforts of other crewmembers to save his life.

Tail gunner Arthur J. Egan recalls: "I do remember our radioman Sgt. Joseph Knight on the intercom say, 'Oh, my God. Gil is hit.' And he cried out, 'His legs are severed from his body! He is hanging by his hands.' At this point, all was quiet. Gilmore and Knight had flown together in anti-submarine patrols off the east coast of the United States and they joined our crew as we were preparing to fly the southern route to England. Gilmore already had a close call on 12 April, when he was almost blown out of the bomb bay without a parachute. On the same mission two of our waist gunners bailed out because they thought the ship was going down. On 20 June, we flew to Pölitz, without Sergeant Knight, who was grounded by the flight surgeon and we were heavily hit by fighters. We then decided to try to make it to Sweden, which we managed to do. Three days later, Tech Sgt. Joseph S. Knight also lost his life while flying as the radioman on Lt. C. J. McCarthy's crew."[4]

Tech Sgt. Elbert E. Gilmore receives a second oak leaf cluster to his Air Medal on 27 May 1944 from Col. Irvine A. Rendle, commander of the 392nd Bomb Group. Just one day later, Gilmore was killed in action by flak over Zeitz, flying as engineer on the crew of Lt. Charles L. Bell in B-24H *Tondelayo* (42-50343).
ARTHUR J. EGAN

However, despite the fine weather conditions, the lead bombardiers of both squadrons of the 466th Bomb Group did a poor job. The thirteen aircraft in the lead squadron hit open fields in a "stringy loose" pattern, and the eleven aircraft of the low left squadron "scattered" their bombs in open fields near the target.

The high squadron of the 467th Bomb Group did far better, but only after very intricate maneuvers in the target area. Its operations officer, Maj. Walter R. Smith, wrote: "The wing turned south as we passed Brunswick, and the low squadron of the 466th Bomb Group fell behind. We then asked Lincoln Leader [wing commander] to let our squadron go over the target second, as it was obvious the low squadron would not catch up. We crossed the sing initial point a little right of course and went over the group initial point about three miles left of course. The lead squadron took up a heading about ten miles north of the briefed course; we followed them in trail as we were to be the second squadron to bomb. The 466th was obviously having trouble locating the target and, as both our command pilot and the pilotage navigator spotted the target, the squadron swung back on a heading of 117 degrees. The bombardier had little trouble synchronizing on the target and was well set up when the 466th apparently saw the target and changed their heading, which put them on a collision course with the 467th. The 466th passed just beneath our squadron and for a few moments we did not know whether or not we would be able to release. The bombardier released as we cleared the other squadron and then observed several large explosions in the target area."[5]

Two B-24s of the 492nd Bomb Group on their way to Zeitz on 28 May.
USAAF

Lead bombardier 1st Lt. Truman D. Simpson reported: "The first squadron apparently had difficulty in finding the target because it swerved off course to the left. I picked up and identified the target from about twenty miles away and proceeded with the bomb-run. I synchronized for deflection and had partially synchronized for range, when my pilot called and said that the first squadron was flying a collision course with us. I left the bomb sight then to watch them and when I knew my bombs would not hit their formation I engaged the trigger. Bombs away was at 1452 hours."[6]

These eleven aircraft in the high squadron of the 96th Combat Wing A Group hit the center of the target with 110 500-pound high-explosive bombs.

Because of interference by their lead squadron, the ten Liberators of the 467th Bomb Group in the high squadron of the 96th Combat Wing B Group had to execute a very tight 360-degree turn to avoid the Leipzig flak and then dropped another 100 500-pound bombs on the target, with results classified as very good. The remaining two squadrons in the 96th B Group belonged to the 458th Bomb Group. The lead squadron's results were poor, those of the low squadron good, with 40 percent of the 558 100-pound bombs hitting within 1,000 feet of the aiming point. As a result of the bombing by the 96th Combat Wing, huge fires were started in the target area, and clouds of black smoke billowed up.

Now it was the turn of the 14th Combat Wing's bombardiers. The lead squadron of the 492nd Bomb Group, in the 14th A Group, dropped its bombs in the northern edge of the target area. The low squadron, furnished by the same group, performed disastrously.

Leading this squadron was Capt. Henry G. Gendreizig in B-24J 44-40163, piloted by 1st Lt. Peter Val Preda. Just before the initial point, bombardier 2nd Lt. Chas M. Lefdahl found that his bomb sight was inoperative, and informed Gendreizig. Then an effort was made to let the deputy lead take over. First Lt. Thomas R. Graham, another pilot in the squadron, remarked at the debriefing: "Lead was changed before initial point from

Cockpit view taken from B-24H 44-40154, piloted by Lt. William V. Prewitte of two other Liberators of the 492nd Bomb Group heading for Zeitz. This squadron encountered many difficulties on the bomb run. The aircraft from which the picture was taken was lost the next day on the mission to Pölitz, all but one of the crew being rescued after bailing out over the North Sea. NATIONAL ARCHIVES

lead ship to deputy Lead. In changing the lead, the formation broke up. From here on it appeared as that the new lead ship was lost."[7]

Second Lt. Charles W. Beard in the same squadron: "Do not let Lieutenant ——— ever lead or deputy lead a squadron again. Deputies should know where they are and be prepared to take over."[8]

Needless to say, the bombs of this squadron were wasted, being dropped at random by Liberators seeking other formations to tag on to. The unlucky deputy lead remarked at debriefing: "Leader of formation moved out 1418, in at 1422, then moved out again at 1435, then I took over. B-17s came through formation on bomb run and our formation scattered."*[9]

Twenty-six Liberators of the 392nd Bomb Group, flying as high squadrons in the A and B Groups, dropped all 1,568 100-pound bombs amidst the smoke that now covered the target, with flames now and then erupting. Then both squadrons of the 44th Bomb Group added another 1,400 bombs to this inferno. Navigator John W. McClane: "The antiaircraft gunners at Zeitz must have been low on ammunition or asleep, because the flak was much less than we expected and our fighter escort was so excellent that we never saw an enemy fighter on the way in or out. Our bombing results were excellent, visibility was unlimited and the black smoke was almost up to our flying altitude before we were out of sight of the target. This time we tore them up badly."[10]

As far as the plan was concerned this should have been the final blow given to the Zeitz oil refineries that day, but no fewer than four squadrons, scheduled to attack Merseburg, dropped their bombs on Zeitz instead.

After extensive photographic coverage, it was noted that a large concentration of bombs had covered almost all of the target area, scoring direct hits on many of the principal installations, and causing oil fires of tremendous size. In addition to the fires in the oil storage area caused by at least twenty-five direct hits, the catalyst plant, one hydrogenation stall, the liquid air plant and the injector house were ablaze from direct hits at the close of the attack. Other important structures affected by direct hits, in most instances by several of them, included the gas generation plant, compressor house, gas purification plant, boiler house, conversion plant and distillation plant.

Reconnaissance photographs taken four hours later showed oil fires still burning fiercely and smoke still rising from the gas purification plants. The following morning additional photo cover revealed two of the oil storage tanks still afire. It was difficult to see what damage was caused exactly by the attack of the previous day, since craters were still visible from the 12 May attack. But as a result of both attacks, it was estimated that oil production at Zeitz would be completely suspended for a considerable period.

---

* The unlucky deputy lead and his crew safely finished their tour of operations.

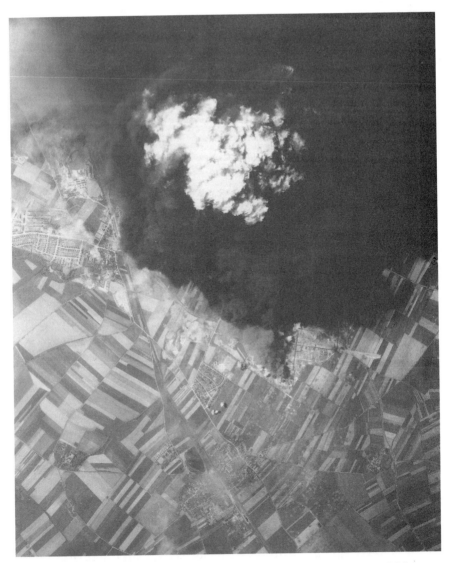

The excellent bombing results at Zeitz are well illustrated in this picture, which was taken from a B-24 of the 446th Bomb Group after it had bombed Zeitz as a target of opportunity some time after two combat wings had bombed Zeitz as their primary target. HAROLD E. JANSEN

CHAPTER 10

Merseburg

In the long bomber stream heading for Germany, the 2nd and 20th Combat Wings followed the wings attacking Zeitz. They were assigned to bomb another industrial target, the huge oil refineries at Merseburg, or Leuna as they were often named. The 445th Bomb Group from Tibenham furnished the lead and low squadrons for the A Group in the 2nd Combat Wing. The 389th Bomb Group from Hethel put up the high squadrons, for both the A and B Groups. The two other squadrons in the B Group were furnished by the 453rd Bomb Group from Old Buckenham.

The 20th Combat Wing A Group had Squadrons of the 448th Bomb Group from Seething, flying lead and low, and a squadron of the 446th Bomb Group from Bungay, flying high. The B Group's low squadron was also provided by the 446th Bomb Group, both other squadrons belonging to the 93rd Bomb Group from Hardwick. Their penetration support was also supplied by Thunderbolts of the 353rd Fighter Group from Raydon.

The assembly of the various groups and wings went generally without trouble; however, the 453rd Bomb Group noted that "During assembly, some difficulty was caused by a group of B-17s flying through our area."[1] Again, this probably refers to either the luckless 94th Combat Wing, heading for Dessau, or the 4th, heading for Königsborn. It is interesting to note that in all reports it is always "the other guy" causing the difficulties!

As with the preceding wings in the bomber stream, it was an easy flight up to the target area, with only a few incidents worth recording. Leading the 446th Bomb Group's high squadron in the 20th Combat Wing A Group, was the experienced crew of Capt. Richard A. Cole, in B-24H *The Shack II* (41-29143). Just after crossing the Dutch coast near Egmond and having passed the Zuider Zee, they had to turn back for mechanical reasons. The deputy lead, Capt. James D. Shannon, in B-24H *Hula Wahine II* (42-52467), took over the lead. Cole, rather than take his bombs back to England or jettison them in the North Sea, bombed the German occupied airfield at Bergen in Holland and then returned safely to Bungay. Three other B-24s of the same group, those of Lieutenant Kent, Lieutenant Morris, and Lieutenant LeRoy, also returned to England, with one of the bomb loads dropped in the North Sea. Two aircraft of the 448th Bomb Group also returned, one bombing the

This picture was taken from the right waist window of the brightly coloured assembly ship of the 448th Bomb Group. It shows the group formation still fairly spread out, heading out over the coast of East Anglia, just north of Great Yarmouth. Clearly visible is one of the many airfields in the countryside, probably Ludham, which had an inactive status at that time. NATIONAL ARCHIVES

airfield at Vechta on the return route. Three Liberators of the 453rd Bomb Group returned to Old Buckenham and reported mechanical trouble. Two of these reports were later attributed to personnel failure.

Only one enemy aircraft was sighted by the bomber crews, and it was promptly destroyed. Flying as tail gunner in B-24H *Becky* (42-95216) of the 453rd Bomb Group, in the low left squadron of the 2nd Combat Wing B Group, was Staff Sgt. Raymond P. Cormier, who reported: "At 1355 hours and 21,500 feet in the Nienburg area, I saw an Me 410 doing 360-degree turns and lazy eights, it came near our plane and made a chandelle. As it started to break away to its left, at four o'clock, at approximately 600 yards, I fired about 150 rounds at it. As it broke off, someone called fighters. I saw none and followed the Me 410 again and observed it hitting a patch of wood and blow up."[2]

It was be the only enemy aircraft claimed shot down that day by a Liberator crewmember. In the German loss listings, two Me 410s of the I./ *Zerstörergeschwader 26* from Königsberg are reported to have been severely damaged or destroyed. It is possible that one of these was the one claimed by Cormier.

Near the target, flak began to increase and was reported later as "intense and accurate." The flak at Merseburg would, later in the war, become even worse and claimed many attacking bombers making it a dreaded target for the bomber crews. This time the flak succeeded in badly hitting three B-24s in the 2nd Combat Wing, two of the 445th Bomb Group, and one of the 389th Bomb Group and slightly damaging another six B-24s in each group. The third and last bomb group that furnished aircraft to the 2nd Combat Wing, the 453rd, came away with only slight damage to three of its Liberators.

First hit was B-24H 42-50346 of the 445th Bomb Group. Its pilot, 1st Lt. John W. Campbell, describes the events: "This was to be our twenty-first mission, and we were beginning to think we might finish our tour. At least, some of us were. Some were thinking our luck was bound to run out. Normally, after each five completed missions, a crew was given a forty-eight-hour leave pass and, at fifteen missions, a seven-day leave. We should have been on a '48,' but due to a shortage of crews, we were scheduled to fly. We had been practicing for several weeks for the D-Day that we knew was coming, but, as had happened three times before, our assigned aircraft had been

B-24H *The Shack II* (41-29143) of the 446th Bomb Group carried the lead crew for this group on 28 May. Over Holland, mechanical trouble forced it to abort the mission and return to England. The crew bombed the airfield at Bergen.
HAROLD E. JANSEN

The bombs of *The Shack II* head for the airfield at Bergen. The airfield, visible at the top center of the picture, was already inactive at the time, after a destructive daylight raid on 4 May. NATIONAL ARCHIVES

flown by a new crew, and didn't return. As a result we were given a new B-24, the first we had flown that was unpainted. No name, and no mission bombs on the nose. As I remember it, there were no problems with the first part of the mission. It was a nice day, and we had felt fortunate not to have been sent to Berlin.

"There were no fighters and I don't recall any great amount of flak, until we got to the initial point. As we began the run to the target area from there, we began to pick up flak from a couple of four-gun batteries, 88mm, firing a diamond pattern. At almost every salvo, it seemed, one of the bursts either hit our ship, or was a near miss that made a very rough ride. I don't recall the order in which all things happened, but number three engine took a burst of flak that knocked it out of commission, and set it afire. We got a burst in or right under the bomb bay, and another amongst the bombs when they were released, and had cleared the ship. Number four engine was out, but not burning, and one of the propellers would not feather, I think it was on number four.

"After the bombs were gone, we made the usual steep turn in formation, to avoid more flak. There was so much gasoline in the bomb bay, falling like rain from the wing tanks, that the engineer, Staff Sgt. Harold Bennett, reopened the doors, to let it run out. Number three was still blaz-

First Lt. John W. Campbell, pilot of B-24H 42-50346 of the 445th Bomb Group. He was made prisoner of war with eight of his crew. One man was killed by a German military police official. The .45 that Campbell wears in the picture caused him anxious moments on 28 May. JOHN W. CAMPBELL

ing, so I slid the plane out of formation, to avoid damaging the rest of the Group, in case we blew up. We got two more hits out there, and I decided we were not going to make it. We could see the black smoke from the bomb strike extending high into the sky by this time, I think we had a very success-ful run. The damage to the airplane wasn't the only problem.

"During the bomb run, the tail gunner, Staff Sgt. Leo J. Vallette, had called over the intercom that he had been hit. I had asked the waist gun-ners to help him out of the turret, and to do what they could for him. Also, though I wasn't aware of it at the time, the engineer had at some point received a deep head wound, and was semi-conscious. In order to hold a straight course, with the two engines gone on the right side, I had to reduce power. It was clear by now that we wouldn't be returning to England. I pressed the bail-out bell, and at the same time yelled in the intercom for the crew to get out. The co-pilot, 2nd Lt. Roger T. Marlin, watching for enemy fighters and with his communication box set on VHF, didn't hear my call, or the bell. When he turned his head and saw my hand on the bell, he leaped up, and dove headlong off the flight deck, through the partially open bomb doors.

"Now, I had always told him that when I said, 'Bail out,' not to wait, just go. He did, and for many years I blamed him for the trouble he didn't assist me with. Unfortunately for me, he was doing what I had told him to do. Not only was I left with the problems of holding the airplane, but I had very stupidly snapped the front half of a flak suit on under my parachute. In addition, I hadn't fastened the leg straps of the chute, so I had a lot to deal with, all while holding a straight course, so that the others could bail out. When I finally had myself put back together, and thinking everyone would be gone, I got out of the seat, and as I got to the flight deck I was shocked to see the radio operator, Tech Sgt. William M. Robinson, sitting on the cat-walk, legs dangling over the edge, his face a sickly green. I yelled, 'For God's sake, Robbie, jump!' and he disappeared. I didn't learn until later, that he had caught his trouser leg in a bomb rack, and had only then got it free. The fuel was still raining down, and when I sat on the catwalk, the slipstream took off my fleece-lined boots.

Some of the crew of B-24H 42-50346 of the 445th Bomb Group waiting for a train to London. Left to right: Cophlin Williams, ball turret gunner; John Bowen (not on 28 May mission); Harold Bennett, engineer; Daniel J. Matheu, bombardier; William M. Robinson, radio operator; and Bernard Wholeben, navigator. All were made prisoner of war. JOHN W. CAMPBELL

"I thought of going back for the combat boots I had left behind my seat. With the engine still burning and the fuel falling, I was afraid to go back. When the boots came off, they took with them the heated booties that were held to the flying suit by electrical connectors. I thought I'd slip them back on after I bailed out, since they were still attached and finally got enough courage, or fright, to roll out of the ship. Instead of waiting to pull the rip-cord, as the training had suggested, I pulled it almost immediately, and as a result, had to watch and listen to the airplane, as it curled its way down, mostly out of my sight, until it finally crashed and exploded, I remember wondering if it would fly into my chute, when I couldn't see it. We had been at about 20,000 feet, so there was a lot of time to think, and to try to put on the booties, on the way down. Each time I tried to raise my leg, either one, to put on a bootie, the straps of my chute, a back-pack type, caused such pains in my groin and testicles, I was unable to get them on, and came to earth in cold, stockinged feet. Fortunately, I landed in a field that had at some time been plowed, and suffered only minor damage to one foot.

"There was no place to hide the parachute, the nearby forest had no undergrowth, and the trees were planted in orderly rows. I carried it over and placed it at the foot of a tree a short distance into the wood, and started walking down a lane. I got out my .45 caliber Army issue automatic, and put a round in the chamber, foolishly, but at twenty years old, I didn't know any better. I was met by a group of villagers and saw behind me another group, carrying my parachute. There were, fortunately, two soldiers and a submariner in the group, and the seaman had a few words of English. He stopped the one civilian, who several times pounded me in the face and nose with his fists, so no irreparable damage was done. They took my gun, and it was with great difficulty that I made them understand it was not only loaded, but there was a shell in the chamber, ready to fire.

Staff Sgt. Leo J. Vallette, tail gunner of B-24H 42-50346 of the 445th Bomb Group. This picture was taken in front of the crew's earlier B-24, *Shoo Shoo Baby*, which was shot down with another crew shortly before the 28 May mission. JOHN W. CAMPBELL

"They had taken me to the local tavern and were drinking beer while waving the .45 around the room, comparing it with their own smaller weapons. I was really frightened of what they would do to me if it fired and one of them was hurt. Eventually, after a short stay in a cell, I was taken out to the main street, where a truck was parked. There were four privates and a corporal as escorts, with a wooden box for me to sit on in the middle of the flatbed. It took a while for them to get it going, and while waiting I smiled at a couple of young women and the corporal knocked me off the box, so I quit. I was driven to a jail and afterwards an airfield, where I met most of the crew. The ball turret gunner, Staff Sgt. Cophlin Williams, had been taken to identify the body of one of my crewmembers, waist gunner Ray M. Wampler. He told us there was blood on the parachute harness and on his chest and that he apparently was shot. Williams had been in the waist with Wampler, and knew he left the ship safely. This was the last time we were to be together until the end of the war in Europe."[3]

The B-24 crashed one kilometer southwest of Stössen, a village ten kilometers southwest of Weissenfels. All nine surviving crewmembers were transported to various prison camps and returned safely to the United States in the summer of 1945. Cophlin Williams was correct in his assumption that Ray Wampler was shot dead. After examining German records, the American authorities found that he was shot "while escaping" by a military police official named Koehler from a village called Unterkaka. Wampler was buried in Kistritz, eleven kilometers south of Weissenfels, and after the war was reburied at the Netherlands American Cemetery and Memorial, where he still rests. The author has been unable to find evidence in American archives that Koehler was ever brought to trial, so the exact circumstances under which Wampler died will remain a mystery.

A small testimony of the rough way in which some fliers were handled is given by the crew's other waist gunner, Staff Sgt. Royce E. Ball, who reported in September 1945: "I bailed out of the plane at about 1520 hours when I hit the ground. I came down in an open field about five kilometers north of Merseburg and about two kilometers north of a small hamlet which is a suburb of Merseburg. It was three or four minutes before anyone came out to where I landed. In landing, I had hurt my leg and broken a foot. I was sitting on the ground examining my foot when the first person came up to me. The first person who came up to me was a photographer who was dressed in uniform, but I am not sure whether he was an army photographer or a newspaper photographer. He searched me and began setting the bone in my foot the best that he could. In another two or three minutes, a farmer and his wife and another woman whom I took to be their daughter arrived on the scene. They just stood around and looked me over, felt my parachute, but made no threatening gestures.

"I was still sitting on the ground and had opened my escape kit and was eating a chocolate bar when a man came up behind me and started kicking me in the back with hob-nail shoes. By that time, forty or fifty civilians had collected around me, but only this man was abusing me. He wore the stationmaster's uniform and was at least sixty years of age. He spoke a few English words and knew quite a few American slang curse words. I would understand very little of what he was trying to say, but I did manage to learn from his tirade that his house had been burned either by bombs dropped in the vicinity of it or by a plane crashing into it. I think the latter was the case. The first I knew of his being around at all was when he kicked me in the back. He kept kicking me around and trying to stomp on me with his hobnail shoes. He was trying to kick me in the face, but I was guarding my face with my hands; he did succeed in bloodying up my face a bit. He broke several of my ribs on the left side. I suppose he would have continued his stomping and beating and kicking of me had he not been stopped by a Gestapo agent. He wore a gray-green uniform with a Nazi swastika armband and seemed to be in a position of authority in that community."[4]

Ball then was transported to Dulag Luft, then to Stalag Luft IV, and ended up in Stalag VII-A, where he was eventually liberated. There is no doubt that several American airmen were not so lucky to be rescued by a Germans who were aware of the Geneva Convention and were kicked to death or shot like Wampler, unwitnessed, the murdered thus never brought to trial.

First Lt. James H. Dobson, who landed his badly damaged B-24 without hydraulic pressure at Tibenham. He used parachutes as brakes to make a safe stop. He was awarded the Distinguished Flying Cross for his coolness in this action.
JAMES H. DOBSON

The second B-24 of the 445th Bomb Group which was hit, B-24H 42-95308, was piloted by 1st Lt. James M. Dobson. He was an experienced pilot on his twenty-sixth mission and relates: "The mission was a long one and the flak over the target area was very heavy. That was where my ship received the heavy hit that destroyed or severely damaged the hydraulic system. After leaving the target area and heading back to England one of the crew called me back to the bomb bay area to assess the damage. I turned the plane over to the co-pilot, 2nd Lt. Keith H. Palmer and went back. I found the bomb bay doors were full of fluid, since they were closed immediately after the bombs were dropped. My first thought was that it was gas, but after further examination I realized that it was hydraulic fluid. Fortunately all four engines were performing okay. I reached the decision that what fluid we might have left in the system must be preserved. Subsequently, upon arriving at Tibenham, the crew manually cranked the landing gear down.

"In the service newspaper *Stars and Stripes*, we had read about a Flying Fortress that had landed using parachutes as brakes. That was what we decided to do. Two parachutes were firmly fastened around the mounts of the waist guns, one on each side, and hung outside the plane. Two crewmembers were stationed at the waist gun windows, ripcords in their hands, waiting for the moment to pull. Since our gasoline supply was adequate, we circled the field until all of our group's planes had landed. This was in case we had an accident on the runway and would block it for use. Needless to say, when I landed, I used every bit of runway and didn't have much wind to help us stop either. The two with the ripcords were ordered to pull at the second we touched the runway. It was a good landing at the first few feet of the runway. I applied the brakes and did have a little pressure, that was shortly exhausted however. But, with help of the huge parachutes out of the waist windows the plane did roll to a stop before we reached the end of the runway, and we also made the *Stars and Stripes* with our story. I finished my missions on 4 June, two days before D-Day."[5]

Third and last to be heavily hit by the Merseburg flak was B-24J *Satan's Mate* (42-110074) of the 389th Bomb Group. The crew of pilot 2nd Lt. Jack Eley was flying a spare aircraft since their own *Fat Mama* was undergoing repairs at Hethel. They flew in the high squadron of the 20th Combat Wing B Group. Over the target, the aircraft received flak damage, causing troubles with several engines. At first, number two engine leaked oil, initially in just small amounts, but the leakage gradually increased to nine gallons an hour.

At 1515 hours, the propeller on this engine had to be feathered, before the oil ran out. There was no other choice but to leave formation and try to return to England alone. Number three engine was also damaged and shortly afterwards its supercharger went out and its propeller had to be feathered as well. From that point on, about twenty kilometers from the

Channel, and still over France, the aircraft lost 700 feet of altitude per minute, gradually going down in the direction of the cold water off the French coast. Still the crew elected to go on, trying to get back to Hethel and doubtlessly with the intention of finishing their only so recently started tour. We can only have the highest respect for their determination to carry on. When it was obvious that *Satan's Mate* could not carry them much farther, an SOS was sent out, and a fateful decision was taken.

The parachutes have done their work. Dobson's B-24 has come to a stop at Tibenham. Some crewmembers, still wearing their parachute harnasses, inspect the makeshift brakes. The aircraft was salvaged in September 1944 after being involved in a midair collision. NATIONAL AIR AND SPACE MUSEUM

Jack Eley recalled: "I ordered the crew to bail out, adding that I would see them in England, and out they went, except the co-pilot, 2nd Lt. Walter L. Tucker and myself. Since the B-24 was a high-wing plane it was very difficult to ditch, as it tended to break near the bomb-bay and sink rapidly. I decided to bail the crew out, then try to ditch the B-24 as close to them as possible, to afford them the safety of the dinghies, if I succeeded. This was not to be; while I was making a circle to ditch, the overstrained number one engine started to act up, the governor ran away and the engine lost its pressure. Since I was then heading into the enemy coast, I couldn't turn the aircraft any more in the direction I wanted, where my crew was. Just off the coast I also ordered Tucker to jump, he declined and told me to fasten my chute first, since he already wore his back-pack and I still had to pick mine up. After some time I assumed flying and out went Tucker. Then I jumped, at about 1,000 to 800 feet, just inside the French coast. I landed on the beach area and was dragged into a gun-emplacement and immediately captured. The plane crashed inland, five kilometers west of Gravelines, near the French-Belgian border.

"The Germans took me to the crash site in a truck and tried to make me get out so they could take pictures of me and my plane. I refused, they threatened, I won. Then they told me that Tucker's chute had fouled up on the tail of the ship and that he was dragged down with the ship and was killed. I can't verify this, since I didn't come out of the truck."[6]

Tucker had indeed been killed in the crash and Eley, the only man captured of his crew, spend the rest of the war in Stalag Luft III and, in 1945, returned to his wife. The seven other crewmembers who parachuted over the Channel all landed in a minefield off the coast. Two P-47s, returning from escort duty observed them, and circled above. Later, they were relieved by Spitfires who circled until a RAF Walrus seaplane of 277 Squadron managed to pick up two of the crew—radio operator Tech Sgt. James C. Tennant and engineer Tech Sgt. Howard E. Crepp. While flying over, a dinghy was dropped near the crewmembers in the water, and one of them was observed to climb aboard and the Walrus, crewed by squadron leader R. W. Wallens,

The crew of B-24J *Satan's Mate* (42-110074) of the 389th Bomb Group. Back row, left to right: James C. Tennant, radio operator (saved by air-sea rescue); Charles E. Osborne, nose turret gunner (MIA); and Howard E. Crepp, left waist gunner (saved by air-sea rescue). Middle row, left to right: Victor Lacourse, tail gunner (MIA); Arthur J. Daly, right waist gunner (KIA); and Robert H. Kaems, engineer (MIA). Front row, left to right: Walter L. Tucker, co-pilot (KIA); Albert Joblonicky, navigator (KIA); Jack Eley, pilot (POW); and Anthony J. Falsone, bombardier (not on 28 May mission) (POW on 25 July). JACK ELEY

Warrant Off. W. L. Butler, and Flight Sgt. J. W. E. Lawrence, alighted and picked up the occupant of the dinghy, who later proved to be Crepp. Then Tennant, still floating around in his Mae West, was found and picked up. Crepp and Tennant were taken to Shoreham in England and made the 504th and 505th rescue by 277 Squadron.

Unfortunately, the high-speed launches of the air-sea rescue were not able to approach, due to the proximity of the enemy coast and its gun batteries, and the fact that the crew went down in a minefield. Although both rescued men thought that their comrades might have made it to the shore or were picked up by the Germans, unfortunately no such thing happened. All five drowned. Four of them remained missing in action, their names being recorded on the walls of the missing at the Ardennes American Cemetery and Memorial in Belgium. Only the body of the navigator, 2nd Lt. Albert Joblonicky, was washed ashore on 28 September 1944, near Knocke in Belgium. He was buried as an "unknown airman." After the war, the American war graves registration unit was able to positively identify the remains, and reburial in the Ardennes cemetery took place. Upon request of his next of kin, Joblonicky was finally reburied in his hometown of Muskegon Heights, Michigan, in 1949.

Squadron Leader Raoul W. Wallens (center) was a very experienced pilot who flew a Spitfire with No. 41 Squadron during the Battle of Britain in 1940. He piloted a Sea Otter of No. 277 Squadron and, with his crew, undoubtly saved the lives of Howard Crepp and James Tennant. NORMAN FRANKS

In 1965, French children were playing on the beach at Malo-les-Bains, near Dunkirk. While digging deeply into the sand they found evidence of a buried body. After the official services had been notified there was little difficulty in identifying the body as that of Staff Sgt. Arthur J. Daly, the right waist gunner of *Satan's Mate*, who had been listed as missing in action for twenty-one years. His body was returned to the United States and buried in Rosemount, Minnesota.

The bombing results of the A Group in the 2nd Combat Wing were not what might have been expected with such good visibility and lack of German resistance. The lead squadron of the 445th Bomb Group had reasonable results, as seven per cent of its bombs struck within 500 feet of the assigned aiming point, 22 percent within 1,000 feet, and 73 percent within 2,000 feet. The low squadron from the same group had no bombs at all within the 2,000 feet radius. The high squadron of the 389th Bomb Group reported that all its bombs had struck the target, but the target picture was so obscured by smoke and dust that individual hits could not be certified.

Then it was the 2nd Combat Wing B Group's turn. Its lead squadron was led by Lt. Col. Robert P. Harris in B-24H *Porky* (42-95111) flown by Captain Warrington of the 453rd Bomb Group; its bombardier, 1st Lt. Orvis G. Martin, reported: "At the initial point, we made a turn to the left to 112

F/Sgt Bill Upperton, a Typhoon pilot in No. 257 Squadron, saw the crew of *Satan's Mate* bail out off the French coast and, after alerting the air-sea rescue unit, circled the area for some ten minutes. BILL UPPERTON

degrees, but we were off course a little to the right. This error was soon corrected. There was very little cloud, but haze and smoke hindered target identification, the target being picked up about one and a half minutes before release. After picking up the target I was able to make a satisfactory bomb run. There was flak at the target, but it did not interfere with the run. Good hits were seen on the target."[7]

In all, 506 100-pound bombs were dropped by the squadron and again the results could not be appraised. Lead bombardier for the low squadron of the same group was 1st Lt. Robert W. Haron in B-24H 42-64452, who reported: "We turned at the group initial point to the left, and started a run on the target. About one half way down I picked up a check point and saw smoke on what I believed was the target. I made a two-minute run and dropped my bombs. After release, I saw that I had bombed the oil refinery at Zeitz instead of Merseburg. I did not see any flak or fighters."[8]

A total of 572 100-pound bombs were on their way to the wrong target. Results were unobserved, which is not surprising if one studies the target pictures, taken over Zeitz during the bombing which show a mass of billowing black and white smoke. The 389th Bomb Group's high squadron ran into violent prop wash on the bomb run, which prevented an accurate bomb-run. Some rail sidings were then chosen as Aiming Point and the bulk of the bombs hit only within 2,000 feet.

The command pilot for the 20th Combat Wing, Major Heber H. Thompson in B-24J *Sky Queen* (42-110026), flown by Capt. E. L. Chapman, who was also assigned to attack the Merseburg plant, in trail of the 2nd Combat Wing, reported: "We flew slightly north of course to avoid prop wash of the wing ahead. At the initial point the wings were already in trail and the Groups began to uncover. Upon reaching the initial point the 448th Bomb Group began to converge with the 92nd Combat Wing [on their way to Lützkendorf] and we were forced to turn to the right instead of the left to avoid hitting them. We finally turned onto the bombing run but the target was obscured by smoke and haze. Also it was necessary to stay right of course on the bombing run to avoid prop wash. The bombardier was unable to make a run on the primary so we turned south and picked up another oil refinery approximately twenty-five miles south of the primary. A run was made and bombs released on this target."[9]

Both squadrons of the 448th Bomb Group had released their loads, in all 480 100-pound and 120 500-pound bombs, on the oil refineries in Zeitz, which already had been the target of two other complete combat wings. Five aircraft in the high squadron, where three of the 446th Bomb Group's aircraft had aborted earlier, made a pass at the primary target, three dropped with the 448th Bomb Group at Zeitz and one found an airdrome near Altenburg for its target.

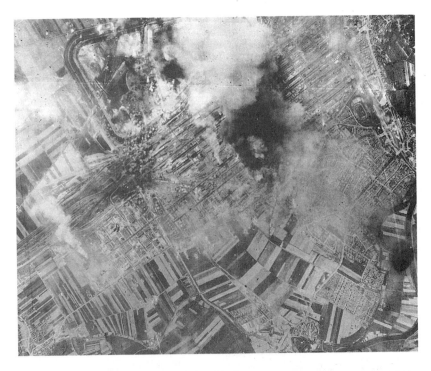

The refinery at Merseburg before and during the attack on 28 May.

This left only the 20th Combat Wing B Group to bomb. The 93rd Bomb Group, putting up the lead and low left squadron, encountered the same difficulties; the official 20th Combat Wing critique remarks: "The 93rd Bomb Group high squadron had trouble bombing target of opportunity due to large number of groups and combat wings on the return route, each time this squadron started to make a run on a target of opportunity it would have to abandon the run because of another formation crowding them out. Squadron finally attempted to bomb a small town; however, bombs landed in an open field."[10]

This small town was Limburg, where 100 500-pound bombs were wasted. The lead squadron of the same group fared no better—its bombs were scattered around on several "last resort" targets, such as Meiningen, Triptis, and Ulzen.

The low squadron, led by Capt. Jack T. Martin in B-24H *Home Breaker* (42-52612) of the 446th Bomb Group, did do better. His bombardier, 1st Lt. Donald A. Michaelson, dropped his load and those of the ten other remaining B-24s in his formation on the oil refinery at Zeitz, with excellent results.

Flown by Capt. Jack T. Martin and his crew, B-24H *Homebreaker* (42-52612) of the 446th Bomb Group led the low squadron of the 20th Combat Wing B Group in a highly successful attack on the oil refinery at Zeitz. MIKE BAILEY

All this, together with the bombs from the two combat wings that had the refinery at Zeitz as primary target (as described in the preceding chapter) caused tremendous fires in the target area. No losses were suffered by the 20th Combat Wing and all B-24s returned to their respective bases. Only three Liberators of the 93rd Bomb Group received slight flak damage and Maj. J. J. Smith was wounded by a flak fragment.

Damage to the Merseburg plant was not as extensive as after the 12 May attack, but additional important installations were seriously damaged, notably one of the carbonizing ovens, a paste preparation building, a boiler house, and several other buildings. In the adjoining railroad yard, tracks were cut in numerous places and several railroad buildings were damaged. The 12 May attack was believed to have cut production by two thirds and it was not thought likely that this day's attack would further reduce the output. Of course, the Germans would now have much more to deal with before normal production could be resumed.

The fighter escort had an easy job, since no enemy fighters made passes at the four combat wings bombing Zeitz and Merseburg. Yellow Flight of the 79th Squadron of the 20th Fighter Group strafed the main railroad line from Liege to Brussels, claiming no fewer than three locomotives destroyed and three tank cars, twelve motor vehicles on flat cars, twenty-three freight cars, and three rail switch houses damaged.

CHAPTER 11

Lützkendorf

The three bomb groups of the Third Air Division that were equipped with B-24s—the 34th from Mendlesham, the 486th from Sudbury, and the 487th from Lavenham—followed at the rear of the bomber stream, making up the 92nd and 93rd Combat Wings. The target for these wings was the Wintershall A.G. oil refinery at Lützkendorf, at that time producing some 300,000 tons of oil per year. These groups had only recently become operational.

The 34th Bomb Group was on its fifth combat mission, the others their tenth. The 487th Bomb Group was the only one of the three which had lost bombers in combat. On 11 May, three of its crews were shot down during an attack on marshalling yards in France. The other two were unbloodied in combat so far. The 34th put up three squadrons of twelve Liberators each, as well as three spares. This force was called the 93rd Combat Wing, although it had only half the usual size for a combat wing. It followed the last wing of the Second Air Division at a three-minute interval. Wing leader was Col. Frank P. Bostrom, who was assigned to become commanding officer of the not yet operational 490th Bomb Group within a month, and therefore, he had to get some operational experience. He was flying in B-24H *Kisco Kid* (42-94930), flown by the crew of 1st Lt. O. Allen Israelsen. The 34th Bomb Group had a smooth take-off from Mendlesham, a normal assembly was made, and course was set for Lützkendorf. The English coast was crossed at 12.42 hours, and when all three spares, piloted by Lieutenants Armstrong, Holmes, and Coupland were not needed, they returned to base. In all, thirty-six Liberators of the group crossed the Dutch coast in good formation.

At a three-minute interval, this small 93rd Combat Wing was followed by three squadrons of the 487th Bomb Group and two squadrons of the 486th Bomb Group, together making up the 92nd Combat Wing. This wing was led by the commanding officer of the 487th Bomb Group, Col. Robert Taylor III, flying with the crew of 1st Lt. Robert G. Reeder in B-24H *Midnight Mistress* (42-52461). The 487th Bomb Group commenced its take-off from Lavenham at 1015 hours. Take-off was normal, and assembly was accomplished over the base at 1058 hours at 2,000 feet. At 1210 hours, Lieutenant Gile returned with severe stomach cramps, and two spares; Lieutenant Wood and Lieutenant Witham returned since they were not needed.

The lead crew for the 93rd Combat Wing. Standing, from left to right: David Ashley, waist gunner; William V. VanBuskirk, radio operator; Seamons J. Jones, bombardier (not on 28 May mission); James R. Reed, navigator; O. Allen Israelsen, lead pilot; Clarence J. Markham, engineer; Charles W. Kleinfall, second navigator; and Wilmer J. Dreher, co-pilot (not on 28 May mission). Sitting, from left to right: William Abraham, ball turret gunner; Charles E. Barclay, waist gunner; and Samuel Baglio, tail gunner (not on 28 May mission). O. ALLEN ISRAELSEN

The 486th Bomb Group experienced more difficulties. Take-off from Sudbury commenced at 1000 hours, but only twenty-three aircraft of the twenty-eight scheduled departed on time. Three Liberators were out of commission even before take-off, and the crews of these craft hurried to other ships and quickly took off, the last one leaving Sudbury as late as 1158 hours. One of these three crews was that of Lt. Alfred M. Sanders, who traded B-24H 42-52682 for B-24H 42-52764. It was a ship of the 833rd Bomb Squadron, while Sanders and his crew belonged to the 832nd. This may be an indication of how the group was scraping the bottom of the barrel to get its full complement of planes in the air. Sanders's new mount was adorned with the nickname *Mike, the Spirit of LSU* and sported a yellow tiger head, the symbol of Louisiana State University. All three spares filled in the formation when needed, as three other B-24s returned with a sick crewmember, supercharger trouble, and engine difficulties, respectively.

After take-off, a climb to 12,000 feet was made individually, and group assembly was completed at 1130 hours. A one-minute-early assembly was made with the 487th Bomb Group. After some shuffling, the 92nd Combat Wing (twenty-five Liberators of the 486th and thirty-six of the 487th Bomb Groups) now followed the 93rd Combat Wing (thirty-six Liberators of the

A typical thirteen-
aircraft lead
squadron of the
34th Bomb Group.
JAMES S. HOLLOWELL

34th Bomb Group) out of England at 1244 hours. At 1312 hours, three minutes after the last spare aircraft left, the first crew of the 487th Bomb Group
aborted. Lieutenant Munson returned with three stuck throttles, and had to
feather an engine to land safely. Then, four minutes later, Lieutenant
Liebert left with superchargers fluctuating in two engines and not enough
power to stay in formation. Nine minutes later, Lieutenant Winters returned
with a broken oil line in his rear turret. Another thirteen minutes later,
Lieutenant Eubank left the formation when his number four engine had a
runaway propeller, and he dropped his bombs in the Zuider Zee. He was followed within two minutes by Lieutenant Spangler, who found that his Liberator used excessive amounts of gas and judged that he could not endure the
long mission. Finally, at 1352 hours, Lieutenant Hatfield left the 487th
Bomb Group with a feathered prop on number two engine and two other
engines that were overheating; he dropped his bombs on barracks somewhere in Holland. Within forty minutes, six Liberators had aborted, leaving
the group with thirty aircraft. The pilot of one of these, Lt. Mike
Volechenisky, remarked cynically at the debriefing in the afternoon that
"large number of aborts do not keep up morale when going in."

Two B-24s of the 486th Bomb had to abort. One with engine trouble,
and the other because of its very late take off. Penetration support was provided by forty-two P-38s of the 479th Fighter Group, which took off from
Wattisham at 1128 hours. Four Lightnings aborted, and rendezvous was
made at 1300 hours at 22,000 feet, some sixty miles east of Great Yarmouth.
At 1355 hours, the next fighter group made rendezvous at 21,000 feet. The
339th Fighter Group had departed Fowlmere at 1225 hours with forty-nine
P-51s, commanded by Maj. Harold W. Scruggs. Six fighters returned for

Second Lt. James S. Hollowell and his crew aborted the mission in *Lucille*. Here they are pictured with B-24H *Misschief* (42-94775). *Misschief* was flown to Lützkendorf by Lt. Walter H. Heath and his crew. JAMES S. HOLLOWELL

various reasons, and now over Lingen, in Germany, forty-three Mustangs took their positions around the Liberators, steadily heading toward Lützkendorf. At 1408 hours, the 479th Fighter Group broke off the escort and returned to Wattisham.

One aircraft in the low squadron of the 34th Bomb Group was experiencing trouble. The supercharger on number three engine of B-24H *Lucille* 42-52759 went out around 1400 hours, and staying in formation, with the full bomb load aboard and flying in thin air, was found to be impossible. Its pilot, Lt. James S. Hollowell decided to jettison his ten 500-pound general-purpose bombs over Germany, in an effort to lighten his ship. This was done at 1405 hours, and *Lucille* and her crew made it safely back to Mendlesham.

For the other crews in both combat wings, the flight to the target area was uneventful, with only some moderate flak and no enemy fighters sighted. At 1447 hours, another fighter group reinforced the escort. The 55th Fighter Group, with thirty-eight Lightnings, under command of Maj. John L. McGinn, had departed Wormingford at 1241 hours and now made contact with the bombers at 22,000 feet.

The initial point was reached, where the formation made its last turn and headed straight for the refineries. During this part of the mission, the flak increased and various ships were hit. Around 1500 hours, the bombs of

Some of the 487th Bomb Group lead personnel were pictured on Lavenham after the group had switched to B-17s. They are in front of B-17G *Paddlefoot* (42-97969). Back row, center is Robert G. Reeder, lead pilot. Second from right is John O. Painter, pilotage lead navigator, and far right is Lee D. Lauren, high squadron lead bombardier. Front row, far left, is Staff Sgt. Harold E. Lassor, and far right is Tech Sgt. Robert W. Huff. JOHN O. PAINTER

the thirty-five ships in the 93rd Combat Wing were dropped. The official reports just state that hits were seen in the target area. Lead pilot O. Allen Israelsen remembers: "It was not a successful mission. The note in my log, 'Bombs dropped over,' was an understatement. As I remember, the bombs missed the target by a long distance—a half mile, a mile, or more. My crew remembers that mission well for that reason. We also flew lead on the first combat mission of the 34th Bomb Group on 23 May. The Lützkendorf mission was the next mission for our crew to fly as lead. The practice was then for lead crews to alternate flying lead crew one mission and deputy lead the next.

"Colonel Bostrom, the wing leader, was a complete stranger to us. As I remember he was very excitable and was on the interphone throughout the mission: telling me how to fly the lead airplane, the navigator how to navigate, and on the bomb run he was continually yelling at the bombardier. We were trained by then that the reason for our existence was to get 'Bombs on the Target' and we were a very disappointed crew. It wasn't a good day."[1]

The 92nd Combat Wing was to follow, and it would mark the end of this day's bombing operations over Germany. First Lt. Robert G. Reeder, flying the 487th Bomb Group's lead ship, *Midnight Mistress*, reported: "A formation from the 2nd Division—Orange diagonal, block OI squadron—ran through our formation. This group turned at the initial point with bomb doors open, apparently with the intention of bombing the same target. In doing so, the

Second Lt. James H. VanCamp and his crew of the 486th Bomb Group, 834th Bomb Squadron, in B-24H 42-52693 Aries over Lützkendorf on 28 May. USAAF

high squadron was forced to give way, and the lead squadron was forced into a flak area over Leipzig. The flak was intense and accurate. Smoke, the result of the bombs dropped by the 34th Bomb Group three minutes earlier, and artificial smoke pots operated by the Germans by then had covered the aiming point and the lead bombardiers of the lead and high squadrons had great difficulty in picking up their assigned target. The lead and high Squadrons dropped their bombs on the primary target at 1504 hours."[2]

Results of the seventeen ships that bombed the primary target were reported as "fair." But the low squadron of the group still had its bombs aboard. The lead bombardier of this squadron, Flight Off. John C. Broom, in B-24H *Solid Sender* (42-52431), flown by 1st Lt. Edgar L. Fuller, recounted what happened: "We approached the initial point, Bad Frankenhausen, and made a left turn to come in on a heading of about 120 degrees. We had some difficulties in flying through the turbulence of the preceding group. Although I knew where the target lay, it was impossible to pick it up because of haze and smoke resulting from smoke pots. The smoke was lying at about our altitude. At this point the interphone in our ship went down and I couldn't communicate with the pilot any more. At the near end of this run, I recognized the target off to the right and gave the pilot a turn indication, but he could not carry it out since we would be carried under the high

The officers of the crew of B-24H *Star Duster* 42-52651 of the 487th Bomb Group. Front row, far left: Ralph S. Burckes, pilot (POW). Middle row left to right: Paul F. Chavez, co-pilot (evaded); Homer A. Weeks, bombardier (POW); and William F. Dunham, navigator (POW). WILLIAM F. DUNHAM

squadron. At this point I decided not to bomb the target. It was now completely covered with smoke and I closed the bomb bay doors. We had now switched to Command on the jackbox for interphone communication. We then followed the lead squadron on out to the rally point and when reaching the initial point to the last resort target, which was recognized by a red-red flare signal, I set up the sight and proceeded down the run, sighting for range only, as briefed. I used the railway marshalling yards for my aiming point and released my bombs upon the target, closed the bomb bay doors and turned off immediately."[3]

In all, ten ships in the squadron had bombed at Wetzlar. Strike pictures established that the pattern achieved by Lieutenant Broom covered a large industrial plant. Ten to twelve hits were scored on a large building and scattered bursts struck smaller buildings in the area. This was probably the optical glass factory, which indeed was the assigned last resort target for the combat wing. Flak defenses along the route had hit several B-24s. Ten ships of the 34th and six of the 487th Bomb Group were damaged. One ship in the latter group would not return to Lavenham. This was B-24H *Star Duster* (42-52651), piloted by 2nd Lt. Ralph S. Burckes and 2nd Lt. Paul F. Chavez.

Left to right: Sgt. Donald W.
Carpenter, nose turret gunner
(POW); Staff Sgt. James M.
Toole, engineer (POW); 2nd Lt.
Ralph S. Burckes, pilot (POW);
Sgt. Rex L. Henze, tail gunner
(evaded); and Sgt. Emil J.
Abadie, waist gunner (evaded).
RALPH S. BURCKES

Navigator was 2nd Lt. William F. Dunham, who recalled: "We were hit by heavy flak while on the bomb run and shortly after leaving the target area we had to drop out of the formation and go it alone. The two inboard engines were stopped and we were losing large amounts of fuel and oil from both wings. Eventually we were down to one engine operating and smoke was coming from one of the inboard engines. The emergency bell to bail out was sounded and I helped the nose turret gunner, Sgt. Donald W. Carpenter, out of the turret while Lt. Homer A. Weeks, the bombardier, opened the escape hatch in the nose of the plane. By the time I got Carpenter out of the turret, Weeks had bailed out. Carpenter didn't want to bail out of the nose and went back to the bomb bay to bail out.

"Shortly after, I bailed out of the nose escape hatch. I landed right in the middle of a small town called Daun in Germany, near the Belgian border. I was captured right away, and a few hours later, Lieutenant Weeks was brought into the same jail and we were in adjoining cells. About 2200 hours, we were taken from the jail by two policemen in a large car and driven for about one and a half hours to a field where a B-24 had crashed and was pretty badly burned up. It was not possible to tell if it was our plane, but I presume it was. We were then taken to a town called Trier and held in the cellar of a large house, chained to large pipes. We were in the cellar for two days and were questioned every few hours. I sprained an ankle very badly when I landed and these men repeatedly kicked me in the ankle to try to get some information. After two days we were turned over to the Wehrmacht and held by them for another day. Then we were turned over to the Luftwaffe and brought to the interrogation center just north of Frankfurt. We were then sent to Stalag Luft III and were finally liberated in Moosburg on 28 April 1945."[4]

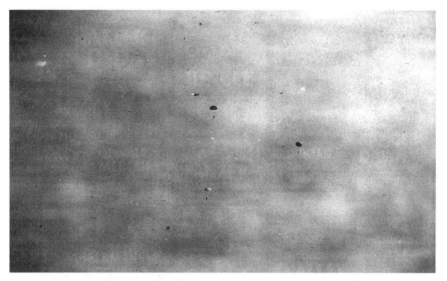

Upon hearing an aircraft in distress over his house, Belgian resistance member Jean Marie Gilles ran out to see what was happening. He then grabbed his box camera and went outside again to snap this picture. It shows three crewmembers of *Star Duster*—Burckes, Henze, and Toole—in the final phase of their descent, being circled by a small German observation aircraft. All three were quickly hidden by Gilles and his friends, although Burckes and Toole were later captured. JEAN MARIE GILLES VIA RALPH S. BURCKES

What Dunham did not know was that the rest of the crew, including Carpenter, had waited for some time before jumping from the stricken *Star Duster*. Where Dunham and Weeks bailed out near Trier, in Germany, the eight others of the crew went out south of Liège, Belgium, and while the first two were captured immediately, seven of the others stayed out of German hands for some time. The one and only crewmember captured almost immediately in Belgium, was ball turret gunner Charles L. Henry, who was caught at 1900 hours near Awan-Chateau, by a traffic patrol. All others, whose events are covered in chapter 13, were hidden by Belgian civilians. Their deserted *Star Duster* had crashed at 1700 hours near Xhoris, twenty-one kilometers south of Liège.

The 486th Bomb Group, with its two squadrons as very last units in the bomber stream, was to suffer its first combat losses of the war. Its lead squadron, twelve aircraft led by Capt. Winfred D. Howell in B-24H *Gemini* (41-29490), piloted by 1st Lt. Howell A. Paynter, released its 528 100-pound general-purpose bombs on the primary target at 1504 hours. Leading the eleven aircraft in the low squadron was 1st Lt. Eugene R. Hicks in B-24H 42-50345. Apart from his normal crew of ten, there was an additional navigator aboard, Capt. James H. Bogert.

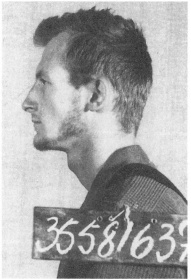

Sgt. Charles L. Henry, the ball turret gunner of *Star Duster*. He bailed out over Belgium and was made a prisoner of war.
CHARLES L. HENRY

What happened next is recounted by 2nd Lt. Richard D. Wolfe, the bombardier in the deputy lead aircraft of the low squadron: "Just before we reached the initial point our lead ship, Number 345, was hit by flak in the number three engine. The lead ship then dropped out of formation after we passed the initial point and my ship, Number 740, took the lead position. We then turned onto the target heading and attempted to find the target. The navigator was forced to make three or four five-degree turns.

"Approximately seven miles away, we could see the target covered with clouds of smoke from previous bombings. The target itself was not visible as we approached for the bomb run. I planned to bomb on the smoke and flames, but the pilot said that no bombs were to be dropped on the primary target. Decision was made to bomb the secondary target. When we reached the initial point for the secondary target, a formation of B-24s was sighted

The last of the many. Leading the last bomb group in action was the crew of 1st Lt. Howell A. Paynter. This photograph was taken in front of B-17G *American Beauty* (42-98008) on 5 October 1944, after the 486th Bomb Group had traded its B-24s for B-17s. Back row, left to right: Howell A. Paynter, pilot; Herbert W. Hitzke, co-pilot; Frank A. Edwards, navigator; Ulysses W. Miller, pinpoint navigator; and Rinehart Zerbel, Mickey operator (not on mission). Front row, left to right: Edward L. Kimball, gunner; Clarence M. Flaig, gunner; Morris D. Robley, gunner (not on mission); William G. Seitz, radio operator; and Ivan R. Hofmeister, engineer. MORRIS D. ROBLEY

between us and the target. This prevented us from making a run on this target. We tried to locate a target of opportunity on the return trip and failing in this we were forced to jettison our bombs due to the lack of fuel. Bombs were jettisoned on the edge of a wooded area and an open field."[5]

With great skill, 1st Lieutenant Hicks and his co-pilot, 2nd Lt. John C. Johnson, managed to keep their damaged Liberator in the air.

Navigator Capt. James Bogert recalled: "We got hit at the initial point and we got hit pretty good. But I don't think anybody on the crew was injured, if so, not appreciably. We had an engine shot out and another engine badly damaged. And so we started losing altitude very fast. Being the lead ship everybody would follow you, and when you cross a target too low it's a massacre. So we had to abort the lead, so number two man could take over. You can't drop your bombs right then or everybody else will also drop. You have to break off and then dump them. And so in that period of time we lost, I think, about 4,000 to 5,000 feet. And then we dropped on a railroad line there, which wasn't much of a target, but we had to get the bombs out because we were losing altitude too fast, had to get the weight out of there. And then we headed on back, still losing a little altitude."[6]

Hicks's aircraft was observed trailing the formation with its number three engine feathered and was last seen by others in the formation thirty miles inland from the Belgian coast, at 8,000 to 10,000 feet. The crew's last radio message gave their position as south of Liège. James Bogert recalled the fateful events: "We got just about five miles out into the North Sea, about to the Channel now, and then we lost another engine. And then we started down pretty fast in a big spiral. We got the bail-out order. We had one-man dinghies, which was a little raft strapped to the back on your parachute. There were three of us in the front of the airplane, the two navigators and Lieutenant Russell, the bombardier. And I had never flown with them before and I didn't know the crew or their capabilities or anything. One of the two that was up there passed me a dinghy, which incidentally I had missed the training on using it. I hadn't really used one or seen one before.

"One of the others, I think it was Lieutenant Russell, snapped the dinghy on the back of my chute and then the bell continued to ring and I was behind everybody else. The pilot was supposed to go out last and was still in his seat. He wanted me to go back and check who was still in the plane. I got back as far as the catwalk in the bomb bay and one guy was there that couldn't make up his mind to get off. I got him to get off and went out myself. I looked back and the pilot got out right after us. I counted the chutes and all were in the air. So everybody got out of the airplane all right. I landed in a rather rough sea and I had a lot of trouble getting into the dinghy because I hadn't been to the courses on how best to get in them. I

Second Lt. David V. Moll, Roberta Sinnock, and 2nd Lt. Eugene R. Hicks posing in January 1944 on the campus of the University of Arizona. Hicks, pilot of B-24H 42-50345 of the 486th Bomb Group, and Moll, his navigator, remain missing in action since 28 May, together with six other crewmembers.
ROBERTA SINNOCK

didn't finally get into the dinghy until almost dark and I got in over the low end. I figured all the time that's the way you must have to get in. The dinghy is high on one end and tapered back along and some straps on there. I finally worked my way up and got in it, belly down. I was afraid to turn over for fear that I would upset again. I'd be back in the water, I was out of strength, I couldn't have gotten in again. So I laid that way all night, and I was sick as a dog from so much sea water.

"The next day, I could see one of the guys, he was the one that was on the catwalk, we'd gone out very close to each other. A little later on, we heard someone calling, and it turned out to be the radio operator. I think that most of the crew either drowned or were gotten by exposure. We got together with the radio operator. We were supposed to have hand fins in the dinghy to propel ourselves. One of the dinghies had two, and the other two had one apiece. It's really hard to paddle with one, the fins weren't very good. They were just little things that fitted over your hands. So we had to paddle with one paddle and one hand, we really made no progress. We were out there three days, it was just starting to get light when we got pretty close to shore. The Germans put a burst of machine-gun fire over our hands, as a sign that they knew we were there. And we paddled in the waves, and they waded out, knee deep and grabbed our dinghies and got us ashore. None of us could even walk."[7]

Formblatt 1
(D Luft 2766/07, Anlage 2)

Nur für den Dienstgebrauch!

KU 2042

Angaben über Gefangennahme oder Bergung von feindlichen Luftwaffenangehörigen

Meldung wird erstattet durch:

Dienststelle: **Kdo. Fl.H.Bereich 8/III**

Ort: **L i l l e**

Zeit: **2. 6. 44**

Verteiler:

Lg. Kdo. Belgien-Nordfrankreich, Ic

Dulag Luft, Oberursel

Kdo. Fl. H. Ber.

Betr.: Abschuß
Notlandung } einer   **L i b e r a t o r**
Absturz

bei   **nördl. Zydcoote auf See**

am   **28. 5. 44**   um **17.30** Uhr.

Personalien des Angehörigen der feindlichen Luftwaffe

Dulag-Luft, Wetzlar

Familienname ("Surname")   **M u n r o**

Vornamen ("Christian Names")   **George Hale**

Dienstrang ("Rank")   **Sgt.**

Erkennungsnummer ("Service Number")   **37 355 832**

Nationalität
(RAF, RCAF, RNZAF, RNAF, Pole, Rhodesier usw. — **USA Air Corps**)

Angaben bei Gefangennahme	Angaben bei Bergung von Toten
Zeitpunkt der Gefangennahme **30.5.44**	Zeitpunkt der Auffindung
Genaue Ortsangabe der Gefangennahme **bei Gravelines am Strand**	Ort der Auffindung
Gefangennahme erfolgte durch **Lw.-Feldeinheit**	Zustand der Leiche
Der Gefangene trug Uniform / Zivilkleidung **Uniform**	Beschriftung der Erkennungsmarke
Etwaige Unterstellung unter Dienststellen der GFP oder des SD zur Ermittlung der Feindbegünstigung	Wodurch wurden die Personalien des Toten festgestellt?
	Funktionsabzeichen:
Lazaretteinlieferung:	Ort und Zeitpunkt der Beisetzung (Grablage):

Zeitpunkt der Überführung zum Dulag Luft, Oberursel **3. 6. 44**

Sonstige Angaben (Fluchtversuch, Besonderheiten im Verhalten des Kgf. usw.):

Rückseite beachten!

The report concerning the capture of George Munro of the 486th Bomb Group on the beach at Gravelines. Munro and the other two survivors of the crew had spent two nights in dinghies in the Channel. NATIONAL ARCHIVES

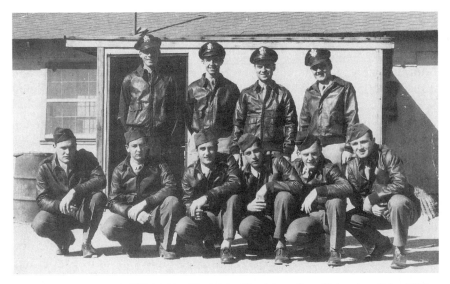

The crew of B-24H 42-52764 *Mike, The Spirit of Louisiana State University*, of the 486th Bomb Group. Back row, left to right: Alfred M. Sanders, pilot (evaded); Daniel M. O'Connell, bombardier (evaded), Thomas J. Zoebelein, navigator (evaded); and Fred A. Morley, co-pilot (POW). Front row, left to right: James R. Sizemore, ball turret gunner (evaded); Autley B. Smith, left waist gunner (evaded); William Kozulak, engineer (POW); Louis Lujan, right waist gunner (POW); John H. Lawrence, radio operator (POW); and Robert C. Swaffield, tail gunner (POW). ALFRED M. SANDERS

Bogert, engineer Staff Sgt. Charles A. Smith, and radio operator Staff Sgt. George H. Munro were the only survivors of the crew. The eight others were never seen again, nor were their remains ever recovered from the sea. They were the first combat casualties of the 486th Bomb Group, and their names are recorded on the walls of missing at three different American cemeteries in Europe. The Germans reported that the bomber had crashed in the Channel off Zuydcoote, north of Dunkirk in France, and that the three survivors had reached the shore near Gravelines.

At 1513 hours, the Mustangs of the 339th Fighter Group broke off their escort to the bombers just south of Zeitz, and returned to England. Captain Routt and Lieutenant Stockman of the 504th Fighter Squadron destroyed a locomotive and a switch house, on the way out. The 55th Fighter Group stayed with the bombers until, at 1530 hours, some fifteen miles east of the River Rhine, the Mustangs from the RAF were seen coming in to take over the escort to both combat wings. Freed from their duties, the thirty-eight Lightnings roamed over the German, French, and Belgian countryside and strafed anything that looked like it might have a military purpose. Locomotives, radar installations, machine-gun emplacements, barges, high-tension towers, and trucks were shot up. Even a "look-out tower in forest with occupant" was destroyed by Captain May. Two Lightnings were hit by ground fire, but all returned safely to Wormingford after a rewarding days work. The RAF had dispatched fifty-six Mustangs, of which eight aborted. They were furnished by the 19th, 65th, 129th, 306th, and 315th Squadrons.

One of these squadrons, the 65th operating from Funtington, noted in the typical British style in its logbook: "Squadron with ten aircraft airborne at 1355 hours. Weather fine, briefing at 1230 hours. Operational withdrawal cover to Libs. Rendezvous twenty-five miles north of Frankfurt. Crossing in over Bolougne at 17,000 feet. About six bursts of flak met us there, but nowhere near enough to cause any panic. After that we proceeded uneventfully as far as Coblenz, where we received an unpleasant reception. Loads of flak came up—very close indeed, but after violent evasive action we came out unscathed, although quite a lot of us had to look carefully at our machines afterwards to believe it. Rendezvous on time and escorted the Libs back to the French coast without further incident. Landed at 1740 hours."[8]

The other squadrons had an uneventful mission and returned safely. There was, however, one more bomber in the Combat Wings assigned to their protection that would not make it back to England. We have seen that the lead ship of the 486th Bomb Group's low squadron, piloted by Lieutenant Hicks was hit by flak on the bomb run and that in the ensuing confusion, the squadron went to the secondary target, and eventually dropped its bombs somewhere in a wooded area. One of the other aircraft in this squadron was B-24H *Mike, the Spirit of LSU* (42-52764), piloted by 2nd Lt. Alfred M. Sanders. Co-pilot was 2nd Lt. Fred A. Morley, who recalls: "We started that morning in our regular aircraft, but it had problems, so we aborted even before take-off. Since our squadron, the 832nd Bomb Squadron, was short on aircraft, we and our gear were moved to a B-24 of another squadron, the 833rd Bomb Squadron. As I recall, the ground crew was still working on it as we arrived. There was no time for a pre-flight inspection. We had engine problems after we left the target. I'm not at all certain of the source of the problems at this point in time. However, the German flak was very heavy in the target area. It became necessary for us to bail out over Belgium."[9]

The tail gunner of the crew, Staff Sgt. Robert C. Swaffield, made this brief statement on his questionnaire, which he filled in somewhere in late 1945: "Would like to know why we were not given time to check ship before take-off on last mission. We were given only ten minutes to change ships and take off."[10]

On 29 May, Lt. Verner K. Davidson flew a bomb-damage assessment flight in his Spitfire XI MB946 of the 7th Photo Group. Over Lützkendorf, one of his camera's recorded some oil storage tanks still burning from the mission a day earlier. USAAF

Pilot Alfred M. Sanders reported: "Ran out of gas on way back, just into Belgium. Got back into formation. Numbers one and two engines cut out. I dropped out of formation. Fuel pressure zero, but gauges read ninety gallons. Switched reserve to number one engine direct, but then numbers three and four engines quit. Switched to number four, now we had numbers one and four engines running. Navigator said we couldn't make it to the coast, so we bailed out. Everyone left the plane. When everyone was out, I set the autopilot and packed a bag and jumped at 2,000 feet. Delayed jump and landed in pasture near Braine-le-Comte, where about 400 people were waiting for me."[11]

Five of the crew, were captured by German troops. Five others, including Sanders, managed to stay out of their hands for the months to come, and were liberated by advancing American ground forces in September 1944. Their abandoned and much despised B-24 crashed near the small village of Charly-des-Bois in southern Belgium.

A close-up view of the "Zoot suit" nose art of B-24H *Solid Sender* (42-52431) of the 487th Bomb Group. On 28 May, while flown by 1st Lt. Edgar L. Fuller, the aircraft bombed Wetzlar instead of the primary target, Lützkendorf. MIKE BAILEY

CHAPTER 12

Cologne

If all went well, 28 May was not to be just "an ordinary mission," but an important milestone in the air war. The staff of the Eighth Air Force had become alarmed by the ever-rising number of bombers shot down by flak, while approaching their targets, committed as the bombers were to course, speed and altitude on their bomb-run. A possible way to avoid the flak surrounding large industrial targets was developed. The result was the GB-1 glide bomb.

It was a standard M34 2,000-pound high-explosive bomb, but with twelve-foot-span glider wings and a tail unit attached. Eleven feet, seven inches long, two of these could be carried underneath a B-17, if the bomber was fitted with special shackles. The idea was to create a "stand-off weapon" and to release the bombs some distance from the target. A gyro system in the bomb was then to take over directional control and glide the bombs into

Glide bombs are stored along a road at Grafton Underwood, base of the 384th Bomb Group. MICHAEL L. GIBSON

the target. If the bombs were dropped by a group formation, an adequate concentration was to be achieved. The modified bombs were delivered to the three bomb groups of the 41st Combat Wing, the 303rd, 379th, and 384th, and were stored on their bases. Some smaller practice runs over England were made and an earlier attempt for an operational debut was scrubbed, due to the weather. Since the weather forecast for 28 May predicted CAVU (ceiling and visibility unlimited), it was decided to give the glide bomb its first operational test. The code name for the operation was "Grapefruit," and the target was the marshalling yards at Cologne. Cologne had the ideal combination of being well within range for B-17s fitted with cumbersome bombs under their wings, and with its huge marshalling yards big enough to have a good chance of being hit.

Upon receiving the field order detailing the mission, frantic activities started. The three bomb groups concerned not only had to carry out the Grapefruit mission with around twenty aircraft each, including spares, but also had to put up an ordinary combat wing for the mission to Dessau, thus needing an additional twenty-one aircraft and their crews from each group. At Grafton Underwood, the 384th Bomb Group even put up two B-17s of the F-type, rarely used in combat at that time. Both of these ships had arrived in England in August 1943 and had already seen plenty of action, during their nine months service.

To keep it from interfering with the assembly of the normal combat wings flying deep into Germany, the Grapefruit force was scheduled to depart earlier. At Molesworth, base for the 303rd Bomb Group, breakfast was at 0430 hours, with briefing one hour later. Leonard Raterman, ball turret gunner on B-17G *Bonnie B* (42-31483), recalls: "The briefing was differ-

Second Lt. Theodore R. Beiser takes a close look at the glide bombs hanging below his B-17G *Betty Jane* (42-32027) of the 303rd Bomb Group. RICHARD R. JOHNSON

ent. Instead of flying through the flak guns protecting Cologne, we would turn away from the target miles before the city even knew it was to be bombed. I have to admit it took a big worry off our minds. On our previous missions it was necessary to fly straight as an arrow for some miles before bomb release. If a city has 200 88s shooting, some gunners on the ground had to make a hit. It seemed they were just shooting at you!"[1]

Engineer Tech Sgt. Lennie J. Buchanan posing next to *Betty Jane* shortly before take-off on the glide bomb mission. *Betty Jane* was lost on 13 September.
RICHARD R. JOHNSON

The crew of *Betty Jane* suiting up for the glide bomb mission in the morning of 28 May. In the center is engineer Lennie J. Buchanan, and at the right is ball turret gunner Charles W. Latta. The tent was "home" for the ground crew of *Betty Jane*.
RICHARD R. JOHNSON

Leading the combat wing was the 303rd Bomb Group from Molesworth. Gen. Robert F. Travis, commanding officer of the 41st Combat Wing, took the opportunity of leading this, hopefully, historic mission and flew in the group's lead ship, B-17G 42-102432. The commanding officer of the 303rd Bomb Group, Col. Kermit D. Stevens, decided to go along too and claimed a seat in another B-17 of his group. The 379th Bomb Group from Kimbolton, flying low in the wing, was also led by its commanding officer, Col. Maurice A. Preston. The 384th Bomb Group from Grafton Underwood, flying high in the wing, was led by Lt. Col. Alfred C. Nuttall.

The crews arrived at their aircraft at 0810 hours and took a close, and sometimes doubtful, look at the glide bombs under each wing of their aircraft. Engines were started at 0900 hours, and take-off was begun at 0925 hours. Take-off at the three bases concerned—Molesworth, Kimbolton, and Grafton Underwood—was without difficulty, and the groups assembled at 18,000, 17,000, and 19,000 feet, respectively, over Molesworth. Wing formation went smoothly, General Travis in the lead aircraft, no doubt pleased with this fine display of airmanship. In all, fifty-nine Fortresses were dispatched, nineteen by the 303rd Bomb Group, and twenty each by the 379th

Getting ready for the glide bomb mission. From right to left: pilot Theodore R. Beiser, engineer Lennie J. Buchanan, ball turret gunner Charles W. Latta, and tail gunner Carrol H. Brackey. RICHARD R. JOHNSON

and 384th Bomb Group. While still over England B-17G 42-31394 of the 379th Bomb Group, piloted by Lt. Thomas D. Butcher, aborted, and returned to Kimbolton, with problems in its number two engine. The combat wing formation, now with fifty-eight Fortresses, climbed to an altitude of 19,500 feet and left the English coast near Clacton at almost exactly the briefed time—11.36 hours.

Forty-nine P-38s of the 364th Fighter Group, scheduled to provide penetration support for the Grapefruit wing, took off from their base at Honington, led by group commanding officer Col. Roy W. Osborn, at 1053 hours. Rendezvous was made at 1150 hours over the Channel, and the briefed course was followed closely. Landfall was two miles south of Nieuport, Belgium, at 1205 hours, and fifty-one minutes later, the initial point was reached and a complicated sequence of events ensued. Just before reaching the initial point, the combat wing uncovered to have an unobstructed approach to Cologne.

The groups spread out, with the low group assuming the lead position, followed by the lead and high groups. During this process, three bombs were accidentally dropped, two from the same ship, because of a blown fuse, and one from another, when its bombardier accidentally put the bomb switch in "select" position. At the initial point, the three groups started a dive to pick up additional air speed.

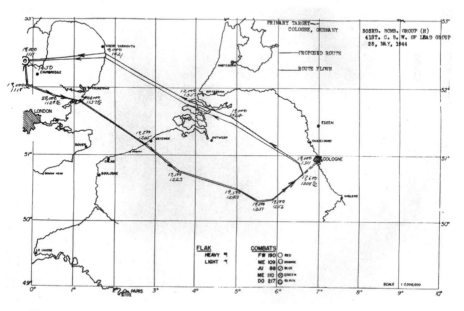

The track chart for the combat wing dropping the glide bombs on Cologne. The chart shows that the course was followed nearly as briefed and also shows some significant times and altitudes for the mission. NATIONAL ARCHIVES

Before this dive commenced, speed was 140 miles per hour, flying at approximately 19,000 feet. The 303rd and 379th Bomb Groups dived at a rate of 1,500 feet per minute, the 384th Bomb Group at 1,200 feet per minute. It was a spectacular sight, and not without risk for the crews. After about two minutes, the air speed of the B-17s had increased to 195 miles per hour. Then level flight was assumed for ten to twenty seconds, to stabilize the gyroscopes on the glide-bombs. Finally, the code word "Scatterbrain" was sent over VHF, and the lead ships fired Red and Green flares signalling the bomb release. The glide bombs were then released, at a heading of approximately sixty degrees, under conditions of excellent visibility, at a distance of twenty miles southwest of Cologne. The 379th and 384th Bomb Groups each had two bombs released late, but eventually 113 2,000-pound glide bombs were on their way to the Eifeltor marshalling yards in Cologne. What happened then can best be described by some anxious spectators in the Flying Fortresses, as they recalled events forty-five years after the mission.

Capt. Hobart H. Steely, lead navigator of the 303rd Bomb Group: "Some of the bombs were caused to go into all sorts of manoeuvres [climbs, dives,

On the left is 1st Lt. William M. Kirkpatrick in B-17G 42-97573 JD-Q, and on the right is 2nd Lt. Ralph M. Dean in B-17F *Patches II* (42-3441 SO-E), both of the 384th Bomb Group. Dean has just released his glide bombs toward Cologne. The picture was taken from the number six ship in the squadron, piloted by Lt. Walter T. Peterson. Kirkpatrick's aircraft was lost a day later, its crew becoming POWs. USAAF

turns, spins, etc]. In some respects it was almost comical to watch the gyrations of a few of the bombs."[2] Unfortunately, Steely did not describe the reactions of General Travis aboard the same B-17.

Second Lt. Ed G. Cooper was the bombardier on *Betty Jane*, B-17G 42-32027, of the 303rd Bomb Group: "I would say we were about ten miles from Cologne when bombs were released. I imagine that it was quite a surprise to see the bombers turn away from Cologne, and a short time later have the glide-bombs drop in their midst. Probably the reason for not using them again was the result. I estimated only one-fourth to one-third reached the target. Some spun out on release, and if they were not dropped when planes were at needed speed, they fell short."[3]

Sgt. Leonard Raterman, *Bonnie B*'s ball turret gunner: "As I recall, our two bombs did sail to the target. I did see a couple of bomb blasts in Cologne. Most of what I saw was the field below the bombers, with dozens of bombs exploding. I don't know how many planes took part in the raid, but I

Upon returning from their glide-bomb mission, the lead crew was pictured on Molesworth in front of their B-17G *Tiny Angel* (42-102432). Standing, left to right: 2nd Lt. Robert S. McCall co-pilot and formation observer in tail; Capt. George T. Orvis, bombardier; Capt. Hobart H. Steely, navigator; Brig. Gen. Robert F. Travis, command pilot; Maj. Alexander C. Strickland, pilot; and 1st Lt. Albert B. Skarsten, navigator. Kneeling, left to right: Staff Sgt. John R. Chancellor, ball turret gunner; Staff Sgt. Clifford B. Underwood, right waist gunner; Tech Sgt. Fred T. Kuehl, radio operator; Tech Sgt. Willie T. Sparks, engineer; and Staff Sgt. Craig W. Winters, left waist gunner. *Tiny Angel* was one of the nine B-17s lost by the 303rd Bomb Group on 15 August 1944. ROBERT S. MCCALL

do know that ninety-five percent of the bombs fell straight down below, and a few exploded in Cologne. My view from the ball turret was limited so I did not see the whole pattern except by rotating the turret back and forth. All I know is the idea was good, if it only had worked."[4]

John A. Thurmon was the navigator of B-17G *Pogue Ma Hone* (42-31060) of the 303rd Bomb Group: "Theoretically, the bombs were to glide in the direction they were aimed, with the aid of a gyroscope to stabilize their flight. The experiment was anything but successful. Some of the bombs went into a flat spin immediately, and dropped almost straight down. Others turned and flew various directions away from the target. A few of them did glide straight, as intended, and hit the city. I never did learn what the percentage of success was, but I am sure it was not high."[5]

After releasing their bombs, the bombers turned to the left and took up course for England, flying out over the south of Holland. Fighter escort for this part of the flight was provided by the 406th Fighter Group of the Ninth Air Force with thirty-nine P-47s. Nothing untoward happened, however, and the combat wing returned, unmolested by fighters, with only nine B-17s slightly damaged by flak which was encountered en route.

Strike picture taken by a camera aboard B-17G *Thunderbird* (42-38050) of the 303rd Bomb Group and clearly showing two glide bombs diving out of control toward the countryside near Cologne, with only one bomb heading for Cologne itself.

It is interesting to note the comments made at the debriefing at the three bases concerned. The mission had been free of fighters and almost free of flak, and there was obviously nothing the combat crews liked better. We have just read how some of them still remember the results of the mission forty-five years after it took place. Now we turn back the clock and go to the interrogation room at Kimbolton, the base of the 379th Bomb Group. This is how various crews, identified by pilots name, viewed the day. Lieutenant Berwind: "like this system." Lieutenant Day: "more of these missions." Lieutenant Ross: "liked this mission very much, more of them, think very successful." Lieutenant Bridwell: "more trips with glide bombs." Lieutenant Vickers: "more Grapefruit." Lieutenant Smith: "results very good—request more raids of same type." Lieutenant Middleton: "more missions like today." Unfortunately for these crewmembers, many aircraft had carried cameras. Even a movie had been made, and four F-5s (the photographic configuration of the P-38) of the 7th Photo Group were dispatched to take pictures of Cologne. Experts immediately started evaluating the pictures and largely disregarded the enthusiastic comments of the crews.

It was established that eighty-one bombs were released successfully, as twenty-eight spun in immediately because of prop wash or imperfect adjustments, and the four late releases missed completely. Approximately forty-four bursts were scattered throughout Cologne, and about fifteen bursts were seen seventeen miles southwest of the city. Although the assigned aiming point, the Eifeltor marshalling yard, was identified and used by the lead bombardiers, none of the bursts was within these yards. The bursts seen in and near Cologne were distributed as follows:

1. one hit within the plant limits of the Gotfried Hagen A.G. accumulator factory, which produced submarine batteries
2. one hit on the southbound reception side of the Kalk-Nord marshalling yards
3. one hit within a railway junction just off the Gereon goods yard, probably not on the tracks, and another on the tracks at the southwest entrance to the yards
4. one hit in an industrial area north of the goods yard
5. six hits in the solidly built central portion of the city, mostly in areas already bombed out
6. one hit on a small warehouse on the quays at the north edge of the city
7. one probable hit on a railway in the northeast part of the city
8. seven hits in residential areas throughout the city, including some sparsely built up and some already bombed out
9. at least twenty-five bursts in open areas, parks, rivers, etcetera in the vicinity of the city.[6]

Strike pictures taken by B-17G *Mairsy Doats* (42-31484) of the 384th Bomb Group, showing the bombs (circled in pencil) heading for Cologne. Three of the bombs hit in a close pattern in some open fields. This B-17G was the lead ship for the group. It was piloted by Capt. Lloyd R. Armstrong and carried Lt. Col. Alfred C. Nuttall, the command pilot. MICHAEL L. GIBSON

It is evident that no one at Eighth Air Force Headquarters was very pleased with these results, despite the crews' enthusiasm. Results appeared similar to the indiscriminate "area bombing" concept—something they had always tried to avoid. Records in the Cologne city archive reveal that the suburbs on the right bank of the Rhine River had been particularly hit. In all, 82 civilians were killed, and 145 were wounded; 1,161 people were evacuated from 137 damaged apartment buildings.

This picture was taken by F-5B 42-68235 of the 7th Photographic Group. The aircraft was flown by Maj. Robert R. Smith over Cologne during the impacts of glide bombs in the city. In the top right corner is the Rhine River with the Hohenzollern railway bridge and main station. The large building close to the station is the famous Cologne cathedral. The picture also shows the extensive damage in the city already inflicted by previous bombings by the Royal Air Force. Several hits by glide bombs can be seen throughout the city. The impact at the top of the picture, in the Thürmchenswall, claimed many civilian lives. CROWN COPYRIGHT/PUBLIC RECORD OFFICE

Jack Thurmon: "I recall the debriefing officer after the mission almost gleefully describing his impression of the bombs skidding down the streets of the city as families were going home from church. He seemed to take great delight in this aspect. It had the opposite effect on me. We knew that cities were sometimes bombed indiscriminately, but I always convinced myself that a military target was involved."[7]

Leonard Raterman: "The idea was good and I even think, sometimes, that maybe the planners of the missions had the safety of the crews in mind, instead of the airplanes."[8]

The GB-1 glide bombs were never used again. Richard R. Johnson, co-pilot of *Betty Jane*: "My first impression of the 303rd Bomb Group, when arriving in late April was the large stacks of glide-bombs along the taxi-ways. When I left in mid-August, most of the bombs were still there. I understand that our ground crews later dismantled the flight controls, and used the bombs in the traditional manner. They were always carried externally, since a 2,000 pounder wouldn't fit inside the bomb bay."[9]

Research, however, continued and some progress was in the development of "stand-off weapons." But other experiments, such as radio-controlled war-weary bombers filled with explosives (the Aphrodite project) and the radio-controlled Azon bombs, simply did not work. These new techniques could not yet replace the formations of manned bombers, visually sighting their targets, making appropriate adjustments, and dropping their bombs. It is only in recent years that technology has made a reality of the concept that was already dreamed of in 1944.

Ground crew pose for the camera and pretend to add another mission marker to the nose of B-17G *Betty Jane* (42-32027) of the 303rd Bomb Group, 427th Bomb Squadron, one of the glide bomb carriers that attacked Cologne unsuccessfully.

CHAPTER 13

Aftermath

After the bombers and their fighter escort had returned to England in the early evening of 28 May, the reckoning could be made. In all, the Eighth Air Force had lost thirty-two bombers, twenty-six B-17s and six B-24s. Together with these thirty-two bombers, 302 crewmembers were listed as missing in action. Eleven crewmembers from two different bombers had been picked up during the day by air-sea rescue units and returned to their bases. Four crewmembers were brought back dead aboard returning bombers. In addition, there were nine seriously and thirteen slightly wounded airmen admitted to hospitals. In all, 210 bombers were damaged, with damage ranging from single flak holes requiring brief attention from sheet metal workers on the base, to extensive damage that would put the aircraft out of commission for weeks.

The fighter escort, provided by both the Eighth and Ninth Air Forces, had lost four P-47s and ten P-51s, leaving fourteen pilots missing in action. One fighter pilot was slightly injured during a take-off crash at Martlesham Heath. Ten P-47s and three P-51s were classified as seriously damaged.

The actions of the Ninth Air Force Marauder-equipped bomb groups on targets in France and Belgium had not been without loss either. The 344th Bomb Group lost six aircraft, and the 391st Bomb Group lost two; all losses were attributed to very accurate flak in the target area. Unfortunately, it was not possible to cover the many missions by the Marauders and other aircraft types on 28 May. However, the sacrifices of their crews were as great as those of their brothers-in-arms in the heavy bombers, and should be remembered as well.

After various photographic reconnaissance aircraft had made runs over the targets of the day, damage was assessed and presented to Headquarters, Eighth Air Force. The results have been mentioned in the various chapters of this book. That same evening, five B-17s of the Night Leaflet Squadron, which operated under command of Eighth Air Force, dropped leaflets in Norway, and France, and all returned safely.

During the night of 28 May, the 801st Bomb Group, flying from Harrington, had twenty-two B-24s on secret "Carpetbagger" missions over the continent, mainly dropping supplies and agents for various resistance

Gen. Carl Spaatz, commander of U.S. Strategic Air Forces in Europe, in a pensive mood at the Cambridge American Cemetery and Memorial on 30 May 1944 after the Memorial Day services. Several men killed in action on 28 May were buried in this cemetery around this time. IMPERIAL WAR MUSEUM

groups in occupied Europe. One of its bombers, B-24D *Charlie* (42-40550), piloted by 1st Lt. Henry Wolcott III, was shot down by a German night-fighter over Belgium, killing one of the nine crewmembers. At about the time this was taking place, the teletypes on the bases of the regular Eighth Air Force bomb and fighter groups began to rattle again. A new field order was coming out with details of Mission 379 on 29 May. For this mission, the targets were located even deeper in Germany than those on the 28th. Again, aircraft plants and an oil refinery were to be attacked, this time in Pölitz, Tutow, Leipzig, Krzesinski, Posen, Sorau, and Cottbus. Many crews flying on the mission also flew on the 29 May mission, and some of them were shot down. Again there was an aggressive response from the *Luftwaffe*, and this time, losses were thirty-four bombers and ten fighters. But, no fewer than eight of these bombers were able to seek sanctuary in neutral Sweden.

THE EVADERS

When these events occurred, several crewmembers shot down on the twenty-eighth were still at large, either in Germany or Belgium. Some of them were captured within a couple of days, but in all, 11 men of the 316 who went missing in action that day, managed to stay out of German hands. Two of them managed to escape from Germany to France and were finally liberated by Allied ground forces in September 1944. These two men were Sgt. Daniel

E. Dunbar and Sgt. Benjamin R. Norris, both waist gunners of *War Eagle*, the B-17G of the 305th Bomb Group that didn't make it back from Ruhland. The former recalled: "After our B-17 crashed in Germany, Ben and I left the other members of the crew with the remains of the ship. The two of us used the cover of the forest to wait until dark to start our trip out of Germany. The last we saw of the remaining crew members, they were walking the sky line for all to see. Being part Indian, even living in the city, I knew this wasn't healthy. There were days after using our escape kit to start this trip, that the only food found was potatoes planted as seed potatoes. These, when dug up by hand, were more than half rotten. I can taste these rotten potatoes even now. With this food and the fresh cool water found on the way to France, is how Ben and I got strength to push on each day."[1]

Norris recounted of the journey to France: "We traveled in flying suits and GI shoes. We crossed the Siegfried line just before we came to the Saar river, but it was just pill boxes and concrete block houses at that point and entirely deserted. We walked through a village and crossed the Saar river on a main highway bridge. The bridge was unguarded. There were several people in the streets of the village though it was midnight, but we were not recognized. All villages and towns were completely blacked out and so were the farmhouses. We crossed the Maginot Line just before we came to the Moselle River. It too, was deserted, but it was much more heavily fortified than the Siegfried. The big guns were all gone, though. The Moselle Valley from Thionville to Metz is quite an industrial district and people were on

Sgt. Daniel E. Dunbar of the 305th Bomb Group managed to evade from Germany to France, where he was liberated by advancing Allied ground troops. DESMA DUNBAR

the streets all night, but we weren't bothered. We stole a boat and crossed the Moselle River about halfway between Thionville and Metz. Thionville was pretty well bombed and filled with German soldiers. After we crossed the Moselle River, we headed due west and were in France the next morning. The section of the frontier that we crossed was not patrolled. The first village we came to was Avril. After we had reached France, people took care of us until we were picked up by the 25th Cavalry, of the 4th Armored Division, twenty kilometers west of Toul, France on 1 September 1944."[2]

Daniel E. Dunbar remembers the last days of their hide-and-seek adventure: "It was from a camp in the woods, that we first saw the half-tracks, jeeps and trucks with the American flags on them. The night before, the German tanks were retreating away from Paris, and we could hear the firing of big guns for days before the scout unit rolled through. We were dressed in the clothes of the outlaw French and met the scout unit at some highway. When the officer in charge of this unit stopped, he asked what we wanted. I spoke to him and told him we were B-17 flyers that had been shot down, and that we had fought with the French underground. We then were moved to the American camp for a few days, and afterwards to Paris. There Ben and I had a chance to see some of the city. From there, the air force flew us over to England."[3]

Staff Sgt. Ralph M. Marts of the 385th Bomb Group had little to smile about after having been captured on 6 June. He had been on the run for a remarkable ten days. RALPH M. MARTS

Dunbar and Norris arrived in England on 5 September, the only two of their crew to successfully evade capture. Another example of an attempt to evade the Germans is that of Staff Sgt. Ralph M. Marts, the engineer of Flight Off. Hunter's crew of the 385th Bomb Group. The difference between the stories is that Marts's attempt did not succeed. He had landed much deeper into Germany, thus his route to freedom was even more difficult. Marts recalls: "As I was floating down in my chute I checked my watch and it was 1510 hours. I landed in some tall pine trees. I pulled the chute down from the trees and hid it. Also, I changed from flying boots to my GI shoes, which I held in one hand when I bailed out. I moved out to another area and hid out until dark. Then after dark I started walking in hopes of getting away without capture. I evaded this for ten days by hiding in fields and timber by day and walking by night. I crossed a large river the first night over a railroad bridge.

"After getting across the river, I slept a while and was awakened by some troops talking nearby. I think it was a manned antiaircraft emplacement protecting the bridge. I moved from this area some distance before hiding again for the day. I survived the next few days on food tablets and digging up potatoes, which had been recently planted. I lost my compass and was guided by the North Star as I headed west. I evaded capture one morning after being chased by a German with a hoe. It had been a wet and chilly night walk. I hid in a deep gully surrounded by timber and started a fire to roast some potatoes. As I looked up, there was two men with hoes watching me, so I took off the other side. Seeing people working in the field, I recrossed the gully. As I looked back, I saw that one of them had fallen on the rocks, but the other one came across after me. After running several miles I got far enough ahead of him, so that I could hide in a field until dark.

"The day of my capture, I had hidden in a stack of baled hay, as it had been another night of wet chilly rain. I removed bales of hay to make room to lay down between them and covering myself with bales on top. I was awakened the next morning by talking around the stack. After some time a young man removed the bale covering me. I motioned for him to recover me and he did, but removed and replaced it again a few minutes later. It is my belief now that these were Polish laborers working on farms as prisoners. Anyway as they gathered on one side of the stack I slipped out of the other side and took off. As it was still daylight I met up with a civilian and soldier and was locked up for the night. Then I was turned over to the Gestapo for questioning and then transported to the interrogation center in Frankfurt."[4]

Marts was captured on 6 June in Steudnitz and had been at large alone in Germany for ten days—a remarkable feat. There were several other attempts by airmen shot down in Germany to evade capture, but in the end, only that of Norris and Dunbar was successful. The other successful evaders

Evaders. Ralph S. Burckes and Rex L. Henze, pilot and tail gunner of *Star Duster* of the 487th Bomb Group, are shown here with Belgian resistance member Robert Martin (center). Burckes was captured in early September while Henze manage to remain in hiding until advancing Allied troops liberated the area. RALPH S. BURCKES

all had come down in Belgium. No fewer than seven crewmembers of *Star Duster* of the 487th Bomb Group were hiding at various locations in the south of the country after they parachuted there. One of them, top turret gunner Emil J. Abadie, reported: "I was picked up right away, and met the co-pilot, Paul Chavez. Two days later radio man Howard A. Witherow and nose gunner Donald W. Carpenter came. Moved to Aywaille, then to Florze, where we were taken care of for one month by people by the name of Hanzel. Then we moved to Ayeneux, where I stayed with people named Fastre for one month. Moved to their relatives in Forest [probably Forêt] where I was met by the 3rd Armored Division."[5]

In addition to the three men mentioned by Abadie, pilot Ralph S. Burckes, engineer James M. Toole, and tail gunner Rex L. Henze were also hiding in the area. On 22 July, Carpenter was captured in Liège by the Germans and was questioned for almost a month before finally being sent to Germany. On 7 September, shortly before the arrival of the Allied troops in the area, Burckes and Toole were also captured. In all, four of the crew were liberated by advancing Allied ground forces.

Four crewmembers of Lieutenant Sanders's B-24H of the 486th Bomb Group—Daniel M. O'Connell, James R. Sizemore, Autley B. Smith, and

The crewmembers of B-24D 42-40550 Charlie of the 801st Bomb Group, 406th Bomb Squadron. They were shot down by a German night-fighter during the night of 28 May while on a supply drop for the Belgian resistance. Standing, left to right: William G. Ryckman, navigator; Henry W. Wolcott III, pilot; Robert F. Auda, co-pilot; and Wallis O. Cozzens, bombardier. Kneeling, left to right: Dirvin D. Deihl, engineer; Richard G. Hawkins, tail gunner; Frederick A. Tuttle, gunner; and Dale S. Loucks, radio operator. A ninth crewmember on board was Carmen J. Vozzella, a navigator on a familiarization flight. Hawkins was found dead near the aircraft with his parachute unopened. All others managed to bail out safely and evade. Wolcott spent much of this time with Lt. Alfred Sanders of the 486th Bomb Group. HENRY W. WOLCOTT

Thomas J. Zoebelein—had also landed with their parachutes in Belgium and were hiding at various farms close to each other, near the village of Gosselies. They were regularly moved from place to place and were also liberated in early September. Their pilot, 2nd Lt. Alfred M. Sanders, had an even more adventurous escape. Fortunately, the archives still contain the details of his escape: "Lieutenant Sanders landed on 28 May near Braine-le-Comte in Belgium. He was met at once by Melchior Deseau, who hid him in a field and returned to him there in a 1940 Ford station wagon driven by a man called 'Roland.' There was a girl riding in this station wagon also, and three men armed with Tommy-guns guarded the road while Sanders was put into the automobile and driven away. He was given civilian clothes in the automobile, while they drove to a farm south west of Brussels. There Deseau and 'Roland' left Sanders with a man named Alfred. Arms were brought to them by another man called Bernard and the three of them then proceeded to a neighbouring farm where Sanders was put to bed. This farm was deserted, but presently, the man from the adjoining farm, a handsome man of forty-five years, square faced with greyish hair and side-burns, brought food and the next day brought a doctor who bandaged Sanders's injured foot. The following day, the chief of the organization, Alex, a chemical student about twenty years old, came in and told Sanders that he was bringing some comrades to the farm.

"The day after that two lorries drove up. In them rode eighteen Russians who had been forced into the German army and had deserted; they still wore German uniforms. Several days later the man from the adjoining farm brought in Lt. Henry Wolcott III, whose home is in Royal Oak, Michigan [he was the pilot of the Carpetbagger Liberator shot down in the night of 28–29 May]. The whole group remained here for several days helping Alex making mines and fortifying the place. Then a fifteen-year-old-girl arrived and said that the Germans had killed the man at the adjoining farm and were on their way to the evaders' hiding place. The whole party set out in their lorries at once and went to the farm of Georges Tondeur where Sanders, Wolcott, three Russians and a Belgian lived until June 18.

"That afternoon, German troops raided the farm and took Tondeur and his servants prisoner but the evaders, deserters and the Belgian refractor, who were hiding in a cachette under the floor escaped notice. When the Germans had left after tearing up the interior of the house, the whole party was gathered together and went by lorry to Rebecq. On a farm near this town, the two Americans and five of the Russians lived for four days. Then the mayor of Rebecq warned the farmer that the Germans planned to raid his place. Sanders and Wolcott were taken at once to Clabecq to the hill-top mansion of an iron manufacturer. They spent a night and a day there, were then taken by a Belgian to an empty house for one day, and then a party of the White Army [the Belgian resistance] took them to the house of Jean Howart in Rebecq. After living in this house for several days, Sanders and Wolcott were moved from farm to farm for four nights and were finally taken to the ship of Maurice F—— on the outskirts of Trop. There they lived until August 10. On that day Deseau and a man named Claude, came and told them that they were to leave for Switzerland. The following day Deseau returned in his automobile with a young woman about twenty-three years old, short, thin, and flat chested, who spoke both French and German. He left this woman with the Americans after telling them that another car would come to take them and her to Brussels.

"Shortly afterwards, an automobile arrived driven by a very dark, pock-marked man of forty years whose jaws were sunken as if he had no teeth and who wore a black cloth over the thumb of his right hand. In this car, the two Americans and the young woman were taken to Brussels, though they were stopped by a German soldier at a barrier and went to a German Headquarter where they waited some forty-five minutes while the driver went inside to argue about his papers. In Brussels the driver and the young woman led Sanders and Wolcott into a house where they were greeted by an elderly man with greyish hair, who wore thick, horn-rimmed spectacles and seemed to be about 5 feet, 8 inches tall, though, since he never stood straight, he may have been taller. Sanders had a list of seven evaders who Deseau had helped, and this man took that list 'to check against his books.' In this house Sanders also saw the following people: a woman about thirty years old with coal-black hair and a 'fine figure' who spoke German and English in a high-pitched voice, then a maidservant who wore spectacles, and two boys, one six or seven years old, and the other about fourteen. When Sanders and Wolcott arrived, there were about four other American evaders in the house. Later six more Americans and two Russians were brought in. Sanders and Wolcott were in this house two nights.

"On the third morning, the driver who had brought them to the house returned to take three Americans 'to Switzerland.' Sanders overheard the elderly man coaching the driver to say, '*Je suis Belge.*' That afternoon, a short, blonde man arrived in an automobile and took Smith, a Thunderbolt pilot,

Second Lt. Alfred M Sanders, who had an adventurous escape from the Germans in the summer of 1944.
ALFRED M. SANDERS

Sanders and Wolcott, after having first taken their identification tags away, around the city of Brussels, down an alley and into a courtyard. There he turned them over to several other men who were waiting and left at once. These men led the Americans on to a glassed-in porch, had them sit down, and gave them drinks. The man in charge, a tall blond blue-eyed chap, gave them some forms to fill up and looked at their identity cards. These he said were no good and he would have to take them to get different ones. He led them through the house and into a waiting lorry in which they were driven to a large building. The blonde man led them up into this building and into an office where there sat a man in a German officer's uniform. The blonde man then laid a pistol on the desk and said: 'I suppose you now know that you are prisoners of the German intelligence.' When Sanders offered to take him with them to Switzerland, the blonde man became very angry. The Americans were made to strip naked. After they had been searched and everything had been taken from them, they were interrogated and threatened with execution as spies because they had no identity tags. They were then taken to St Gilles prison where they spent fourteen days in separate cells. After that the same blond German tried to interrogate Sanders again but simply returned him to his cell when he refused to talk.

"On 2 September at 0800, the British and American prisoners in St Gilles were taken to the railway station and put into a box car. Three times the Germans attempted to move this train out of Brussels and failed. At the third attempt, the cars carrying the prisoners were derailed and the Ger-

Sanders was liberated in Brussels, hiding himself in the front cabin of the Dutch barge *Irwin*. BEN WIJS

mans cut them loose. Sanders left the car with several other prisoners. He made his way to a canal and there took refuge on a barge when a German patrol came along the bank. The barge captain put him into a cabin for the night. The next morning the British entered Brussels and Sanders made his way to the palace where he reported to an American Colonel. He and other evaders were put up in a hotel that night and sent to Amiens the next day. There Sanders found a pilot who offered him a ride to the U.K. He arrived on 6 September and reported to 63 Brook Street for interrogation."[6]

Sanders and the other ten evaders were lucky. The rest of the 316 men reported as missing on the evening of 28 May were either killed or made prisoner of war.

MISSING IN ACTION

A total of 316 telegrams was sent to families in the United States, in which the Secretary of War expressed "his deep regret that your [son, husband, or brother] has been reported missing in action" and that "if further details or other information are received the next of kin will be promptly notified." The families of the four men who were brought back dead aboard their B-17 were notified by telegram as well.

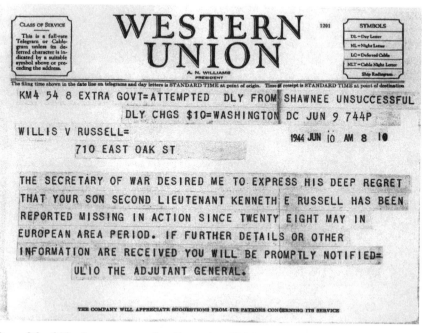

One of the 316 telegrams sent after Operation 376. Kenneth Russell, a bombardier in the 486th Bomb Group, and the rest of his crew had bailed out over the Channel.
LINDA CAMP

For 316 families, an agonizing period of uncertainty had arrived. There is no more appropriate description of this than the letter that Marie Scharff, mother of Lt. Paul Scharff of the 401st Bomb Group, wrote to a friend on 12 December 1944: "I have been waiting for news about Paul and the time goes on and no information of any kind. It soon will be seven months since Paul is missing and it seems a year to me. The shock was terrible. I will never forget when Fred came with a telegram in his hand. It cast such a gloom over the entire community and our home was like a funeral home, friends came from far and near, letters from different states.

"The HQ Army Air Forces sent us as complete list of the names of the crewmembers who were serving with our son at the time he was reported missing, also the names and addresses of the next of kin of the men, so if we desire to correspond we may do so. Fred and I got busy at once to write letters, and letters flocked in with plenty information. 28 May, thirty planes left England on a mission over Dessau, Germany. B-17 Flying Fortress left the formation in the vicinity of the target and was last seen at 2:55 PM. That was the plane, Paul was the pilot, and the letter stated thirty left England and two crews returned to the base.

"Twenty-eight planes went down, then I wept bitterly as I knew my boy was the pilot on one of the twenty-eight air ships. Then after a few days a letter came that the Government notified the parent that wrote to us that B-17 was under control, came down slowly and did not catch on fire. This was big news and I thanked my Heavenly Father that he guided Paul's hand at the controls and Paul and his gallant crew of men did not burn up alive. Then letters kept coming in with news from parents that their boys were prisoners of war in Germany and gave their addresses, they had plenty to eat, conditions were liveable and clean. Three officers are still missing, names are not listed in any prisons and no clue to be had any where.

"May God hasten the day that will bring good news of these three fine young officers. It's such bitter pain not to know where our dear ones are. I will never ceasing praying for Paul and his crew of men. Paul spoke very highly of them all and loved all the boys. We heard through the navigator's mother that Paul was a wonderful pilot, and he certainly could handle his plane well after what happened to it. We people are like one large family now, we all got the same sad news when the telegrams came our sons were missing over Germany 28 May, 44. I will never forget and still feel the effects of it."[7]

Though Paul Scharff and the two other officers were killed in action, it had been impossible to identify them at that time. From the above letter, it is obvious that not all information that the next of kin obtained was correct. With no other means of communication available to the next of kin than exchanging these letters, they express all the anxiety, hope, despair, and love that nowadays is so easily conveyed in a telephone conversation. Every rumor was a shimmer of hope, unfortunately in most instances only to prove false in the end. When we read these letters, with our present knowledge of the ultimate fate of the men, they are a forceful reminder of the human side of war, not only touching the airmen, but also their loved ones. As one example of the correspondence between the families of the crews, excerpts are included from letters that were written to the parents of Lt Kenneth E. Russell of the 486th Bomb Group.8 He and the rest of the crew of Eugene Hicks had bailed out over the North Sea.

From the wife of one of Kenneth's best friends, 19 June 1944: "The co-pilot, Lt. Johnson, is the one that was married while stationed here—he married a girl from Phoenix. I do not know her name at present but am fairly sure I can get it. Her father is one of the leading physicians of Phoenix. Norma will look his name & address up thru the Telephone Co. We can write to him & maybe his daughter, Mrs. Johnson, will have more news—or the addresses of the rest of the crew. I'm sure she'll be more than glad to help . . .

"We received two letters from him & one was written enroute—he was stationed in England & if he's missing over the channel—well, there's lots of hope. This is purely speculation—but I think that the ship Fords Folly was damaged & it made it out of the main-land o.k. but they had to crash-land or bail out, & either one would take time to report to their outfit—especially if they were quite a ways from their base. As far as anything happening to the pilot—well—Ken could always take the plane over because he's as good a pilot as any & he could easily bring a plane in."

From the 486th Bomb Group Chaplain in England, 30 June 1944: "I know you both are more than anxious to hear from your son Kenneth, and I wish as his chaplain and good friend that I could give you some definite facts of his status.

"Therefore I beg of you to be patient and keep your faith in the good promises of God to care for his own. You can rest assured that the Red Cross or War Department will give you the best and latest information as soon as it is available.

"In my own heart I feel that God has a plan for Ken's life, and I have faith enough to believe that the purposes of God are never brushed aside. I will join you in prayer that God will bring your son and his friends through no matter what the conditions may be."

From the wife of the co-pilot, 14 July 1944: "Received your letter this morning. You and Thomas E. Drake are the only ones of the crew whom I write to who have been notified that the boys were over the English Channel. Was very sorry to hear it. We had all assumed they landed in France or bailed out. We do have good reason to believe the boys are safe because

Chaplain Costner wrote me that they were well on the way home and that their chances were very good. Please acknowledge receipt of my letter.—The chaplain married Johnny and me and all the boys liked him immensely."

From the wife of the co-pilot, 17 July 1944: "The pilot's fiancée received the following letter from Lt. Garland H. Hendricks of the 833rd Sqdn: 'There is not much information I can give you—just my opinion. No one seems to know exactly what happened to Hicks. He was hit over the target and lost an engine. Someone called him over the radio and asked him if he was O.K. He said that none of the crew was hurt but he would have to drop out of formation and try to get home alone. We could see him practically all the way out but lost him just before we reached the Channel but a few minutes later we saw him again and the crew was bailing out. It was about one mile out over the Channel so I feel sure he was able to get back to land. I really don't think you have anything to worry about, because I am pretty sure everyone got out O.K. and are either prisoners of war or evading. If they are evading, you may not hear from him for some time, but when he does come back, he will be sent to the States and will not have to fly any more operational missions.'

"This is very encouraging. I imagine they all had on life-savers and merely paddled ashore. They were probably picked up by the German patrol. It has been one month and eight days since they were reported missing, and they have been missing since Sunday, 28 May, so we really shouldn't expect to hear they are prisoners of war for a couple more months. As busy as the Germans are, we might not hear for six months. It they are evading it may be more, or less."

From the mother of the radio operator, 20 July 1944: "Mrs. Johnson sent your name to me, seems your son was on the plane my son was on & is reported missing. This morning I had some good news, should I say good news, at least I know where my boy is. A wire from the Adjutant General telling me George ('Torchy' as he is know) is a German prisoner. I hope and pray you have had news as to the same, and also hope our boys are together & that they will not be mistreated. For surely our boys did not wish this, they surely hated to leave home. I hope & pray your son is with mine. At least we have the feeling we have some chance of seeing them again. The wire stated that a letter would follow with information. We hope & pray that this will soon be over & our boys home again. Will you kindly let me know if you hear any different."

From the mother of the navigator, 22 July 1944: "It certainly is terrible sad news to hear that our boys are missing in action. It is almost more that I can stand just waiting from day to day. Hoping to receive some word from our precious sons. But I know that even though I don't know where David is at tonight. But one thing I do know, God is with him and is able to take care of them, where ever they are. David's father has been dead eleven years and

2nd. Lt. Kenneth Russell
Very tall- 6ft. 4 inches.
Light Brown Wavy hair.
Greenish blue eyes.
Age 24.
Missing as of May 28th 1944
with crew of 11 , of which 3
are reported prisoners at
Stalagluft No. 3 , they are -:
Capt. James/3/4/5/Bogert of
N. Jersey---Sgt George Munro
of Colorado, and Sgt Chas. Smith
Of Georgia.

Missing with Kenneth on
B-24 Liberator are---
M/Sgt.James Todd- of Tennessee.
2nd. Lt Eugene Hicks ofNebraska.
Sgt. Olin Bundrick ofSo. Carolina.
Sgt Murray Moscowitz of Florida.
2nd. Lt John Johnson of So. Carolina
2nd.LtDavid Moll of California.
S/Sgt Robert Drake of N.York.

William V. Russell
710 East Oak Cushing. Okla.

On 12 March 1945, Mr. and Mrs. Russell travelled to Tulsa, Oklahoma, for a meeting with former POWs. They took this card with them, hoping that one of these men would recognize their son, but no one did. LINDA CAMP

it is wonderful how God has always helped me care for my children. My youngest child is now eighteen years old. I'm earnestly praying for all the boys and I'm expecting to hear from David before long and I know some day before so terrible long he will be at home again with us. We received word June 11 that the boys were missing in action. The last letter I received from David was written May 24."

From the wife of the co-pilot, 25 July 1944: "You know, you and I should be sort of special friends because Russ and Johnny bunk together and are very good friends. They are closer to each other than to anyone else in the crew. In Johnny's last letter he spoke of proudly showing Russ a button I had sewed on! We were only together a month, you know, and had little time for anything but a honeymoon, so anything domestic Johnny would notice especially. My degree is nearly finished and I go back home the 18th of August where I will remain until Johnny comes home or I have my child. I hope Johnny gets home first. Do you think he'll make it by November 11th?"

From the mother of the navigator, 14 August 1944: "I received a nice letter from Mrs. Johnson last week, saying that Mrs. Smith had received official word that her son Charles was a prisoner. That makes two of the crew that are safe, we are sure of. I feel sure that the other boys are safe. They are probably somewhere with the underground. I don't believe they are prisoners or we would surely have heard by this time.

"Well, Mrs. Russell all we can do is just keep our faith up, and pray that God will take care of our Darling Sons, wherever they may be.

"The day and nights are certainly awful long to me and I know they are for all the other Dear ones. I would have written you before now, but I just kept thinking I would surely get some word from David every day. I will let you know just as soon as I receive any news at all from my Son, and if you hear anything be sure & send me word right away."

From the wife of the co-pilot, 15 August 1944: "Today they invaded France from the South. Do you realize what that means to us? If the boys are evading there, all they will have to do is to come back to England and straight home. They are through with this man's war and will be ours again. You don't know how I look forward to my husband's return, and how I pray it will, by some miracle of God be before my baby comes. I'm very optimistic from the way the war is turning out, and I know you must be the same.

"Always glad to hear from you. When do you think they will be home now?

"P.S. Received a letter today from Thomas E. Drake that his son, Robert is officially reported a prisoner. Mr. Drake has been corresponding with a boy named Scotty Keenan and his (Scotty's) mother called up Mr. Drake and said that Scotty had heard on the field, Scotty is in the 834th, that Robert was officially a prisoner. So that makes three out of the ten that have been reported prisoners. I am sure we will hear soon."

From the father of the pilot, 21 August 1944: "Mr. Drake informed us he had received reliable information all the boys except the co-pilot were German prisoners. No doubt he has given you the same information. This morning we also received the information from a friend of Gene's, a lieutenant in England, saying it was hard for them to find out anything, that they tried to keep all the information from them but he wanted to tell us all—the boys were German prisoners but the copilot who is not reported. We feel quite badly about this as Mrs. Johnson has been very down in the dumps ever since they were reported missing, however, I have been told that the Germans don't report prisoners who are in hospitals until they are moved to a concentration camp, this may be the case.

"It is tough to be a prisoner but at the same time the boys are out of a hellish mess and it is a relief to know they are safe. However, we did know none of them were hurt when the engines were shot out over the target and they were almost home when they parachuted out but we were still in suspense. I am sure you feel as good as we do. Mrs. Hicks and I pray they will all be returned to us soon."

From the wife of the pinpoint navigator, 21 August 1944: "We received a wire a month ago informing us that he is interned in a German prison camp. The government promised us a follow up letter with his camp number and address which we haven't received as yet. Chances are that the whole crew are there together, it sometimes takes quite a while for them to notify you. Hoping you hear some good new soon. If so I'd appreciate hearing."

From the father of the ball turret gunner, 24 August: "The following information was received from Sgt. George S. Keenan, attached to the 486 Bombardment Group on Aug. 17—under date of Aug. 9 he writes me that my son and the rest of the crew of his plane with the exception of the co-pilot (Lt. Johnson) have been officially reported prisoners of war—This report came from their base in England. Backing up the news I have just had word from Mr. Hicks that he has received a letter from the base in England from a Lieut. friend of his son's, that his son, Gene, is a prisoner and that the crew (with the one exception) are prisoners too. Perhaps you are already in receipt of this news. If so it has no doubt eased the suspense involved since the report of missing in action was received. If not, I hope the aforesaid information will gladden your heart once again and ease matters considerably until your boy eventually comes home."

From the grandmother of the co-pilot, 7 September 1944: "I have heard that your son Lt. Kenneth Russell were on Lt. John C. Johnson's plane when it were damaged Lt. John C. Johnson is my grandson, I reared him, his mother is dead . . .

"I love him more than anything in the world and I am the only person that he loves, I miss him so much. I have worried myself sick about him, I can't find out anything . . .

"I don't know what to believe, I am so worried, Johnnie were all I had in the world to live for. If he's gone I don't want to live. I know if he's living he's worried about me he knows I have a weak heart and can't stand too much trouble. I have more then a hundred letters that he has wrote me since he has been in service."

From the wife of the co-pilot, 16 September 1944: "Have been ill and unable to write. Have heard that all the crew was safe except my husband— that is, that they are prisoners of war. The chaplain wrote me day before yesterday that Russell was a prisoner. I suppose you have heard by now that Russ is well and safe. I'm glad for you. I can't reconcile myself to Johnny's not being all right so now I have just made up my mind that he was separated from the crew and that he is evading. He's just got to be all right.

"My baby comes November 11, or is supposed to. Perhaps we will all have heard something definite by then. I hope and pray so, anyway. I seem to be having trouble with my baby, (I spoke of being ill in this letter.) Perhaps it will all come out all right, though.

"I was interested to know about your daughter and son-in-law. Did she stay at home? I am at home now, you know. I shall stay here until my baby is born and I can travel. Then I am going to Tucson and finish my degree, I have a position teaching school in February. All this is of course in case Johnny isn't found. I'm hoping he will be found and then he will be able to join me just after I have finished my degree. Perhaps by the end of January. This is my hope right now.

"I surely did and have enjoyed all your letters. They have been such a consolation to me, especially to hear from Russ's mother. Johnny likes Russ so much. He really thinks he is a fine young man, and so did I. I do hope so that they are together somewhere. I feel that they will each take care of each other. If Johnny is gone I will hate it because we had such a short time and my baby will need him so much. We were together only a month you know. I know there are many others in the same position, but of course my case seems particularly 'tough going' to me. But I am so glad I have understanding parents and a good education, almost completed."

From the wife of the right waist gunner, 19 September 1944: "After hearing all were prisoners but one through Mr. Drake and then getting this other letter from the War Department puts me to wondering more, looks like the War Department would know since these two from England wrote that, then again I don't believe they would notify us unless they were absolutely sure, do you?

"Mrs. Smith had two letters from her son, (Sept. 15th) one was dated June 27 and the other July 27 he wrote he stayed in English Channel two days before being picked up by the 'Jerries'. He has a garden and a potato patch by his barracks and had a real nice 4th July. I don't suppose he would be allowed to mention the rest of the crew, do you?"

From the father of the ball turret gunner, 19 September 1944: "From my boy Bob's buddy in England I received a letter dated the 3rd of September and in it he says 'I assure you that Bob is a P. W. You see the Group has released a list of P. W.'s and Bob is one of them'—'You asked me thru what sources the group was informed of Bob's P. W. status. I have no idea how they found out. But I do know it's official'—'M/Sgt Todd is also a P. W. and so are the rest of the crew except for Lt. Johnson he is still unheard of.'

"I haven't heard anything different from the Army other than that letter we all received a week or so ago containing the list of the crew members. Soon I know we will get word from our boys."

June 25, 1945.

My dear Mr. Russell:

The President has requested me to inform you that the Purple Heart has been awarded posthumously to your son, Second Lieutenant Kenneth E. Russell, Air Corps, who sacrificed his life in defense of his country.

The medal, which you will receive shortly, is of slight intrinsic value, but rich with the tradition for which Americans are so gallantly giving their lives. The Father of our country, whose profile and coat of arms adorn the medal, speaks from it across the centuries to the men who fight today for the proud freedom he founded.

Nothing the War Department can do or say will in any sense repair the loss of your loved one. He has gone, however, in honor and the goodly company of patriots. Let me, in communicating to you the country's deep sympathy, also express to you its gratitude for his valor and devotion.

Please believe me,

Sincerely yours,

Henry L. Stimson

Mr. Willis V. Russell,
710 East Oak Street,
Cushing, Oklahoma.

A year and a day after being reported missing in action, Kenneth Russell and the other missing crewmembers were officially declared dead. Purple Hearts were awarded posthumously. LINDA CAMP

From the grandmother of the co-pilot, 26 September 1944: "Have you heard anything more about them, they could be on an island somewhere and no way of getting out or they could be with the underground. I talked with a Lt. yesterday that had just come from Europe and he said they would be finding missing boys over there for the next three or four years. He said he believe they were alive, he said if they had been killed in the water they would have floated in the water and would have been picked up and identified and their people would have been notified. I surely hope they are all alive somewhere. I shall keep praying them and I know you will join me in prayer for our Dear loved ones please write me real soon."

But the prayers of these families were not answered. Also the rumours about the crew being reported as prisoners turned out to be false. Only three of the crew had made it to the coast of France; none of the other eight was ever found and a year and a day after they went missing, they were officially declared dead. Mrs. Johnson had her baby—a boy, one of so many war orphans, children that would never know their father.

For some families, there was relief when a telegram brought the news that their family member was a prisoner of war. But for others that telegram confirmed their worst fears, as death was announced. In all, 107 American airmen, including the four brought back by returning bombers, paid the supreme price for their effort to liberate the countries of Europe. Of these 107, the bodies of 24 men were either never recovered, or not positively identified, and these men remain missing in action until the present day. This leaves 202 airmen who were sooner or later captured by the Germans.*

THE PRISONERS OF WAR

A typical account of the events that most of these men experienced after their landing in enemy territory is given here by one of these men, 2nd Lt. Henry J. Gerards, co-pilot of Lieutenant Matthias's *Mountaineer* of the 390th Bomb Group: "I felt good, wonderful, to be out of that hell upstairs. But the enjoyment of my solitude and quiet was short lived, for I was in the heart of Germany. I knew that if I was to escape, I'd have to cover as much distance as rapidly as possible.

"First I cut a piece of silk from the chute for mosquito netting and then buried the rest of it and other equipment not needed, under the pine nee-

---

* A statistical breakdown of the personnel losses: bomber crewmen lost on mission, 313; fighter pilots lost on mission, 14; crewmembers killed in action in bombers, 4; crewmembers picked up by air-sea rescue, 11; crewmembers dead on arrival at base, 4; personnel reported missing in action, 316; evading personnel, returning to England before VE-Day, 11; personnel made prisoner of war by Germans, 202; personnel killed in action, 79; personnel remaining missing in action, 24.

dles. I walked to the end of the row of trees. Here I found a dirt road which hadn't been used for some time. Standing here for a moment, I pondered whether to go right or left. I turned and looked back. Suddenly, I heard a noise. Turning my head, I saw a German civilian about thirty feet from me, riding a bicycle.

"Trying to swallow my heart again, I stood motionless as he rode by, not fifteen feet behind me, his head bent down as if he were concentrating on the difficulty of riding through the loose dirt. He did not see me for that reason, or perhaps he was as scared as I and would rather be elsewhere. For a moment I thought I should have taken his bicycle and clothes and posed as a German civilian while escaping. But if caught, they could have me shot for a spy, and besides, what would a young guy be doing as a civilian in Germany. They were all in the army. It was time to get moving, I found north on my compass, the direction of Sweden and started walking. Meanwhile I hoped to find some of my crew members. Being alone was a little discouraging. Walking for a couple of hours, I came to an open field. On the other side was a car parked with some people walking around. So I remained hidden in the forest. This was my first chance to open my escape kit and look at the map to see just where I should go to make good my escape. In the kit were Halizone tablets for purifying water, a plastic water bag, a razor, gum, morphine for cases of serious pain, two small compasses, a saw blade, a few pieces of concentrated food and other items including a silk map about eighteen inches square.

"I pondered some time over the map, and finally decided to go in the same direction of Sweden, since it was closer than either France or Switzerland. The distance measured about 175 miles, part of it across water. Walking alone 175 miles through enemy territory without being seen would be next to impossible. But the decision to try was easy, since the other choice was to give up. The car and people had disappeared from the other side of the field. So I decided to cross and try to keep hidden by crawling along a drainage ditch. A German Fw 190 flew low overhead as I left the protection of the trees. But he was gone in a second and I made my way along the ditch. Not a cupful of water was to be found in the ditch, and since it was a warm afternoon, I was getting thirsty.

"On the other side of the field, I felt safer, walking through forest again. I walked in this forest for about three hours until I came to a highway. To cross it in daylight would be too much of a risk. So I sat down behind a tree and smoked one of my three remaining cigarettes. I tried to sleep till dark, but sleep wouldn't come, not even rest. I could hardly bear to sit still. Finally I got up and walked through the trees along the highway, hoping to find some way to cross. It wasn't long till I came to a culvert under the road. My hopes soared as I thought of finding water and a crossing at the same time.

"For you the war is over!" More than 200 American airmen were captured on 28 May and experienced situations like these. Under guard of military personnel or home guard (note the old rifles), airmen are marched into custody. One, who has obviously sprained an ankle, is helped along by a fellow prisoner. They are all wearing their combat outfits; the cords for the electrically heated flying suits are clearly visible. After being searched, some were lucky enough to be granted a smoke before their journey to Dulag Luft commenced. These pictures were probably all taken on 12 May 1944 at Merzhausen, where II./JG 27 was stationed; they show crewmembers of three different B-17s of the 96th and 452nd Bomb Groups. FRIEDRICH KELLER VIA JEAN LOUIS ROBA

The only obstacle was the clearing from the trees to the culvert, about twenty-five yards.

"Several people walked and rode bicycles by as I watched from my hiding spot. It was still daylight when I decided to make a break for the culvert. When I was almost there, I saw a German soldier on a bicycle coming around the corner. I stopped and ran back to the trees, but it was too late. He had seen me and was shouting 'Halt! Halt!' He took his rifle off his shoulder. I halted. The soldier sent one of three boys who came by, after help. Soon an officer in a German jeep drove up. They searched me and motioned me to get into the car. We drove along the highway three or four miles, then onto a side road a short distance, and there was our plane. She was scattered all over, gas tanks hanging in trees, engines a hundred yards from each other and bits of metal everywhere. The largest piece was the cockpit. I knew it was my plane by the serial number and also by my helmet lying nearby. I was not allowed to leave the jeep where the soldier kept guard over me. We left in a few minutes.

"From there, we drove to a small village, where I was given a glass of water. I had no idea what we were waiting for, and when I saw a group walking toward us, I thought I might be mobbed and beaten. As they came closer, I recognized Charlie Oliver, the ball turret gunner of my crew, in the lead. It was sure good to see someone I knew. They loaded Charlie into the jeep, and as we left the village, I gave him one of my cigarettes. We decided to save them awhile. About a ten mile drive took us through the city of Magdeburg, and to an airfield, where we were searched again and relieved of all our belongings, including the cigarettes. We should have smoked them. At the airfield we were locked in a room with about twenty-five other American airmen, some badly wounded. Three more of my crew were there. We sat around the floor and tried to sleep that night, but no one could. The wounded's cries of pain strung our nerves tight as a wire. Next day, we left for Frankfurt and after interrogation there, I spent the rest of the war in various Stalags."[9]

It is also worthwhile including an account from a German. *Feldwebel* Johannes Wagner was serving in the *Wehrmacht* on the Eastern Front and was on leave in his home village: "On one of the last days of my leave, my fiancée and I were biking from Treysa to Mengsberg. On the return trip, I suddenly saw a low flying heavy bomber, coming from the direction of Fritzlar. I recognized the bomber as a B-17 and we took cover in a ditch. Just before a small forest, the plane pulled up and disappeared out of sight. Just afterward, we saw a pile of dust and assumed it had crashed. I left my fiancée, took my bike, and headed for the plane. I saw it lying in a field and went inside, finding no one. As I knew that the B-17 had a ten-man crew, I went to the small forest some 500 meters from the plane. Slowly, I walked along the

Feldwebel Johannes Wagner from Mengsberg was on leave from the Russian front and captured eight crewmembers of *Hulcher's Vultures* on 28 May. KONRAD RUDOLPH

small road that leads through the forest, when I noticed one or two airmen. I raised my pistol and told them to come near and to surrender, which they did. There were four of them and I left them on the road, guarded by a man who just arrived.

"I went into the woods again, and after 300 meters, I found the rest, who also surrendered to me. With the crew I went back to the plane and asked them if any bombs were left aboard, which they denied. Then we went in the direction of Mengsberg and lots of spectators followed us. I had to protect the airmen from an angry man from Kassel, who had been bombed out. I wanted to put the fliers in the school and hand them over to the police, which happened indeed. Later, I was questioned by an officer of the Fritzlar airbase, who stated that they had shot the bomber down."[10]

The B-17 was *Hulcher's Vultures* of the 388th Bomb Group, piloted by Lieutenant Fjelsted. However, not all crewmembers were captured by Johannes Wagner. Two men, co-pilot William C. Hudson and bombardier Chester Tracewski, still hid in the woods, trying to make their way to safer surroundings. However, the next day they were also captured and joined the rest of their crew.

Usually held in different types of accommodations during their first night in Germany, prisoners were soon transported to the huge interrogation center for Air Force personnel, *Durchgangslager der Luftwaffe*—Dulag Luft for short—at Oberursel, a suburb of Frankfurt. Here, all personnel were interrogated by specialized *Luftwaffe* personnel and confronted with

Change of status from
Nicholas D. Furrie to
prisoner of war number
1889. These dog tags
were worn by Furrie
during his stay at Glatton
and then in Stalag Luft
IV. NICHOLAS D. FURRIE VIA
TOM KRACKER

material found on him, or on other crewmembers, in an effort to obtain more useful information for the Germans. After interrogation, most of the enlisted men were sent to Stalag Luft IV near Grosstychow, close to the former Polish border. Most officers were transported to Stalag Luft III, near Sagan, southeast of Berlin. At the end of January 1945, Russians troops were advancing rapidly in the East, and German headquarters decided to move the prisoners of war from this camp, probably to keep them for bargaining purposes when necessary.

One of the American officers in Stalag Luft III was Leon Lobdell, the navigator of *War Eagle* of the 305th Bomb Group. Ironically, the only two men to evade out of Germany itself were also from this crew. He recalls: "On 27 January 1945, we were sitting around listening to a show given for our block (169, room 5). Suddenly, someone rushed in with the latest news. We were to prepare to move in an hour! All was in confusion. Most of us weren't expecting to move; consequently we didn't hardly know what to do. However, Captain Moss came around with a good idea for a pack and rescued us. After we had prepared our packs, we made strong coffee and ate sandwiches.

"We split up the food amongst us for we didn't know whether we would receive any Red Cross parcels. Then we were called out and waited for about half an hour in the snow and cold. Later we were allowed to fall back in, ate some more, and took stock of things. Everyone hoped that we had been cut off by the Russians and wouldn't be able to move. But then our hopes were shattered by the call to fall out. Musical instruments from the show were broken in the rush. Hundreds of cartons of cigarettes and tobacco together with much food were left; we just weren't able to carry them. The Germans looted through the barracks together with quite a bunch of the kriegies.

"We were rushed at double time out the gate and past the Vorlager where a full parcel was shoved in our hands. We were then double-timed for two more kilometers. Many, being in poor shape, were forced to throw away their parcels or parts of them. German civilians ran sleds up to the side of the road and carried a lot of the food away. We marched all that night, arriving at the town of Freywalden, about thirty kilometers from Sagan, at 1330 hours. We rested for over six hours; over 2,000 men froze outside in the bitter cold with no way of keeping warm. We were allowed twenty minutes in, out of the cold and snow—no sleep.

"About 1900 hours that evening (28 January), it was decided to move on, and on we went! We marched quite a way to the next town, where we were supposed to be put up for the night. On the way, a scare sent the bunch into the snow while the guards fired over our heads. One kriegie had a bullet through one of his food cans. At the town a number of hospital cases, about fifty, were taken out and the rest of us slowly started to freeze. After stopping for an hour, we were told that we'd have to go on and started out. Many, including myself, were going to sleep on their feet. Three stops had to be made in which approximately 200 men each who couldn't go on were bedded down in barns. Others fell out by the wayside and were taken in by civilians. On the last few kilometers the whole bunch was staggering. Again packs and food were thrown away. I kept going by eating a few lumps of sugar at each stop. Towards the end, my pack came apart and I kept losing food, but didn't know when it dropped.

"Finally, we arrived in the square at Muskau around 0700 hours on 29 January, having marched forty-five kilometers farther. Most of us were half crazy that night; I know I was. We were promised rooms in various factories, but it took an hour to arrange for them and men were freezing and going crazy in the square. I saw two men actually going out of their minds. One of the medical officers said that he hit a man, nearly gone, full in the face to get him angry and bring him back. I remember being marched past a row of troops with machine guns and wondering if this was it. Finally, we were taken to a pottery works where we spent the night and part of the next day, dirty but warm.

"On Tuesday, 30 January, I left at noon with 300 volunteers to join the south camp; we were judged to be in good enough condition to resume the march. That night we slept in a barn after doing 18 kilometers. On Wednesday, 31 January, we arrived in Spremberg at 1100 hours; good soup was issued us on arrival. The next day, we left in regular boxcars, with fifty men in each car. We had anxious moments on a siding in Chemnitz with our

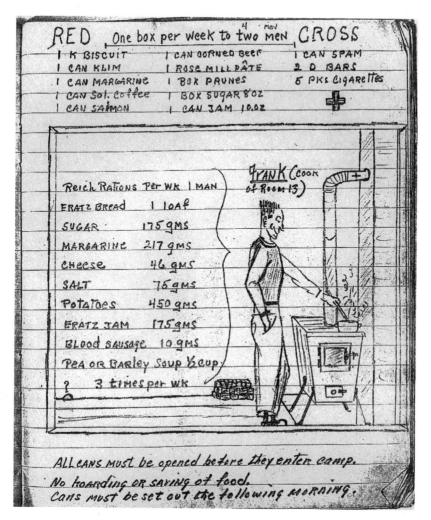

RED, One box per week to two men CROSS

I K BISCUIT	I CAN CORNED BEEF	I CAN SPAM
I CAN KLIM	I ROSE MILL PÂTÉ	2 D BARS
I CAN MARGARINE	I BOX PRUNES	5 PKS CigAReTTes
I CAN SOl. Coffee	I BOX SUGAR 8OZ	
I CAN SALMON	I CAN JAM 10.OZ	

Reich Rations Per WK I MAN

FrANK (cook of Room 13)

ERATZ BREAD	1 loAf
SUGAR	175 gMS
MARGARINE	217 gMS
cheese	46 gMS
SALT	75 gMS
PotaToes	450 gMS
ERATZ JAM	175 gMS
BLood sausage	10 gMS
Pea or BarLey soup	½ cup
3 times per wk	

ALL cans must be opened before they enter camp.
No hoarding or saving of food.
Cans must be set out the following morning.

Food was an all important matter for "kriegies." This is reflected in Richard Bopp's scrapbook, in which many pages are dedicated to the subject. One page shows the German and Red Cross rations in Stalag Luft III, accompanied by a drawing of the cook in barracks 161, room 13. He was Frank Lawn, a co-pilot in the 389th Bomb Group, shot down on 27 May. Irving Gurman, the pilot of *The Banana Barge* of the 44th Bomb Group, shot down on 28 May, was in the same room. VIRGINIA B. RUSSELL

train parked next to an SS train, the air raid sirens sounded and bombers droned overhead. Luckily, they were headed for another target and we breathed easier. On Saturday, 3 February, we arrived at Stalag VII A in Moosburg, and were housed in an old stable. Two days later, we were deloused and given a shower, then moved to a flea-infested barracks."[11]

Lobdell was lucky, since he and the others in his compound were sent directly to Moosburg. Many more ended up in Stalag XIIID near Nuremberg first and were to march again for another 145 kilometers, early in April 1945.

With this huge contingent of prisoners in one place, the situation grew worse. Fortunately, the ordeal was over when, on 29 April, the camp, and its occupants were liberated by General Patton's 14th Armored Division. Then, as soon as possible, the prisoners were flown to France and housed in Camp Lucky Strike, to await their return home. Also arriving here were the former prisoners from Stalag Luft I in Barth and Stalag Luft IV in Grosstychow, who had been liberated by advancing Russian armies. Most ex-prisoners were shipped out at the end of May and returned to the United States early in June.

Since it is United States' policy not to let its dead rest in hostile soil, immediately after the war, the mortal remains of men buried in Germany were reinterred in American military cemeteries in France, the Netherlands, and Belgium. When this major operation was completed in 1948, the next of kin were given the option to have the body returned to the United States for reburial or to let it rest in the military cemetery.

Now thirty-five headstones on five cemeteries in Europe mark the final resting place of an American airmen killed on "an ordinary mission" on 28 May 1944. Also twenty-four names of men whose mortal remains were never recovered or positively identified are engraved on the various walls or tablets of the missing at these cemeteries.

CHAPTER 14

War Crimes

Several chapters of this book briefly mention how airmen who had bailed out of their disabled bombers or fighters were treated after landing by the German military and civilian population. Some were treated well, wounds were bandaged and some were even given food or a drink, before being sent to the collection points. Others were beaten by civilians and often barely rescued by military officials before a worse fate awaited them. One typical case, that of Staff Sgt. Royce E. Ball of the 445th Bomb Group, is already covered in the Merseburg chapter. Another case is that of the crew of 1st Lt. Rudolph Stohl of the 457th Bomb Group, flying *Black Puff Polly*. An interesting account of the crash is given by then twenty-one-year-old Leen Stolk, a Dutchman. He had been summoned by the Germans for forced labor in Germany after they effectively closed down Verenigde Touwfabrieken, the Dutch factory where Stolk worked. He had to leave Maassluis, close to Rotterdam, in October 1942 and was put to work in the Borgward factory in Bremen, where half-track armoured personnel carriers for the German Army were built. During his stay in Bremen, Stolk kept a diary, in which he freely and quite understandably somewhat biased, voiced his opinion about his experiences. This is an excerpt of his notes for Sunday 28 May.

Whit Sunday was a day off from work in the factory: "Got up at ten o'clock and went to the Weser river to swim. Beautiful warm weather. At one o'clock air raid alarm. Dressed and went to the bunker until two o'clock. Then on to the Bremer Kampfbahn [soccer fields], but the soccer match is called off, as there still is an air raid alarm. All of a sudden there is heavy flak fire, a big bomber dives down and keeps circling around. It keeps circling, then suddenly it drops three men with parachutes, then another three and finally two, that makes eight. The flak fires like mad, they put a crossfire on that plane. But apparently it is looking for a place to land, has to make a crash-landing, then drops two bombs. We saw another man jump out, but he was too close to the ground for his chute to open and he fell to his death. We saw the plane disappear and a few moments later a big black cloud. At four o'clock, the 'all clear' was sounded.

A group of Dutch forced laborers at the banks of the Weser River in Bremen. Leen Stolk, bottom right, was an eyewitness to the final moments of *Black Puff Polly*. Just visible to the left of the head of the third man in the top row is a flak tower that had several light guns on top of it. This tower and several others put up crossfire during the final moments of the B-17. The barracks for the flak crews and an antenna for their communication equipment are visible to the left of the man seen at top left.
G. L. HAMMER

"At 5:30 PM, we went to Camp Weserlust. There we spoke some other boys, among them Leen Ditmars. They were in Osterholz, visiting the grave of a friend from the work camp who recently died. As they were there, the firing began. Behind the graves some airmen came down. A German came towards the boys on a bike and said: 'Help to search for those pigs.' The boys made off, not wanting to help to search for our friends. And behind the grave they saw one, with his hands up, but he was shot from behind by a German, the dirty dog. The airman then undid something that apparently chafed on the wound on his hip. He regularly wiped the blood away, which gushed out. His legs were tied up, and he was thrown on a cart. The boys said he was a handsome guy with black hair, a Canadian. He looked at them with wide eyes. What would have gone on inside this poor guy's head, he surrendered and still they shot him and threw him on a cart despite his wounds. The boys wanted to speak some English with him, but others stopped them. A German who spoke English said something like: 'You will never get back to England.'

"Other airmen had surrendered and stood with their hands raised; Germans came out with rifles and rubber sticks and hit the airmen in their faces with these, dirty dogs these Germans. They were tied up, loaded in a sidecar of a motorcycle, a leg which dangled out was kicked in and when they drove off, they were still hit on their heads with sticks, it was horrible! An officer stood aside and watched and said: 'Calm down people, soon three more of these dogs will arrive.' Some airmen were hit in the face by a little woman, one warded off the blows and was immediately beaten up. It really drove you mad, according to the boys. The aircraft has burned out behind the Borgward works in Sebaldsbrück. The brave pilot continued to fly straight through the crossfire from the flak until all his men had left. As the boys walked back, they passed several Russian women, who said: 'There lies a dead Tommy.' That was the man who bailed out last and who fell to his death. Some Germans stood near the dead airman; on his belt was a pistol and a leather case with compass, maps, chocolate, chewing gum, and rolls of candy.

"The next day, I met Wassilie [a Russian also working in the Borgward factory] and he told me that the chute of the pilot opened just in time, just above some trees. After he landed he shot at some Hitler Jugend and NSKK-people [National Socialist Motor Corps], as they were shooting at him with small-caliber rifles."[1]

The wounded man who landed in the cemetery was waist gunner Sgt. William Bemus, who had received his wound while bailing out of the stricken aircraft, as extensively described in Bemus's own words in the chapter concerning the Dessau mission. The man whose parachute apparently did not open was radio operator Walter Wagoner. He was killed aboard the aircraft and his body fell out of the aircraft in its final spins, through the hole in the bottom that presented itself after the ball turret had been dropped earlier. However, Stolk's observations about the rough treatment of the surviving crewmembers is backed up by facts. In 1947, two men, Otto Rueger, a forty-three-year-old baker, and Wilhelm Schroeder, a fifty-six-year-old police sergeant, were sentenced to three and two and a half years' imprisonment, respectively, for "deliberately and wrongfully encourage, aid, abet and participate in commencing assaults upon members of the United States Army, who were then and there surrendered and unarmed prisoners of war in the custody of the then German Reich."[2]

In this instance, the flyers came away with bruises and dog bites. However, in a number of cases, there is little doubt that a luckless American flier was killed on the ground before anyone could come to his rescue. Since many of these instances were not witnessed by others than those directly involved in the crime, there was no trial for war crimes in these cases after the war. We have read about Ray Wampler, of the 445th Bomb Group, who was "shot while escaping" by a military policeman. And about James Singleton, of the 351st Bomb Group, who was shot while still floating down in his parachute. About Forest L. Knight, of the 390th Bomb Group, who was seen alive in his parachute by fellow crewmembers and who inexplicably died on the ground. These are some of the known events. But how many airmen really died on a foreign field, beaten, stabbed or shot to death, will forever remain unknown.

The single instance in which I have been able to trace the trial and actual conviction of the German responsible for the death of a helpless American airman shot down on 28 May is that of Richard Wegmann. He was accused and later found guilty of the murder of LeRoy D. Cruse, the tail gunner of Lt. Clyde W. McClelland's B-17 of the 351st Bomb Group. This one case is presented here in great detail to sketch the tragic events. It shows how bad luck with a landing place could mean a cruel death instead of a prisoner of war camp and eventual return to families and friends in the United States after the war.

Staff Sgt. LeRoy D. Cruse was the tail gunner of B-17G *Black Magic* (42-31721), piloted by Lt. Clyde W. McClelland. This picture was taken during stateside training. LARRY L. TUEL

LeRoy Desmond Cruse was born on 26 April 1915 in Terril, a small village of a few hundred inhabitants in northwest Iowa. He graduated in 1933 from the local Community High School. LeRoy entered the service on 4 August 1941, more than three months before the attack at Pearl Harbor. Initially, he was sent to Camp Grant, Illinois, where he served in the Medical department. In April 1942 he was able to join the Air Force. Cruse became a gunner and his crew, after Stateside training, was assigned as a replacement crew to the Eighth Air Force. On 17 August 1943, the day of the big Schweinfurt-Regensburg mission, the crew arrived in England and finally ended up at Polebrook, in the 510th Bomb Squadron of the 351st Bomb Group. LeRoy Cruse's first combat operation was on 4 October 1943, it was a rough mission to Frankfurt, with heavy enemy opposition. On only his second mission, to Münster on 10 October, Cruse was wounded in action at his tail guns. He was awarded a Purple Heart and was not back on operations until 3 November.

The original crew had by then been split up, due to injuries that several crewmembers had sustained. From that time on he had to fly as a spare gunner for crews who were short of a gunner for a mission. Slowly, but surely, LeRoy Cruse flew his combat missions, working towards that magic number required—twenty-five. Kassel, Knaben, Emden, Frankfurt, Brunswick, Stettin, Schweinfurt, Cherbourg, Pölitz, and Berlin were among the targets that he bombed. But he too was caught by the unexpected raise of the required number of combat missions from twenty-five to thirty.

With twenty-six missions to his credit—flown in nearly eight months from Polebrook—he boarded Lieutenant McClelland's *Black Magic* on 28 May and headed for Dessau. Cruse had already flown with McClelland on several earlier missions, as McClelland's original crew was also split up due to injured crewmembers. But, sadly, Cruse was not to complete his thirty missions and return to his family in Iowa. *Black Magic* was struck by flak and fighters over Dessau and was finally abandoned by its crew about fifty miles northeast of Frankfurt.

Tech Sgt. Marcel Copt, who was a member of Cruse's original crew and had flown the mission as engineer on the group's lead ship, wrote to the parents of LeRoy "Bud" Cruse on 9 June: "First let me tell you that Bud was one of our best friends and I hope and pray to see him again some day. We have taken the liberty of taking care of a few of his personal things and we will send them to you in the near future. Now I will relate to you just what I saw happen. Everything went along fine till we got to the target, then we were hit by fighters. They came in from the front and they got two engines on Bud's ship. Their was no fire or smoke. They kept up with us till the target and dropped their bombs. Then with only two engines left to do the pulling, they started to drop back and lose altitude. When they dropped out

Three buddies at Polebrook. Marcel Copt (left) was flying as engineer on *Linda Ball II*, the group's lead ship on 28 May, and watched the deputy lead ship, *Black Magic*, with his friend LeRoy Cruse (right) at the tail guns, go down. Gerard Devlin (center) did not fly on this mission. LARRY L. TUEL

of sight they were still under control and had several of our friendly fighters escorting them. I feel sure the whole crew parachuted to safety. Kriesky, our radio-operator, was also in the same ship. I hope that you hear from him very soon, and if you do hear something we would appreciate you letting us know. We will say good bye for now and we are all pulling for the boys."[3]

The letter was also signed by Gerard Devlin, another member of Cruse's original crew. Copt was quite accurate in his reassuring remarks, as all crewmembers indeed managed to leave the doomed ship by parachute in the vicinity of Frankfurt.

However, things on the ground turned out for the worse for LeRoy Cruse. What happened is related by Eva Weitzel, a thirty-nine-year-old housewife from Elm, who stated in September 1945: "I was standing at my kitchen window, looking out, when I saw a plane come down low from a wave of planes. As I was looking I saw somebody jump and I said: 'My God! Somebody jumped out!' and while I looked I saw three people jump out. They went out in all directions. I took my child and was standing in the yard. I then saw a crowd coming down from the direction of Kirschenkubel, escorting an American flier. Well, I had never seen a parachute in my life before and I took my child and I went over in the direction they were coming from.

"When I got there, I saw the parachute was being carried by the pilot and it had just fallen apart on him, on the ground; he was just kneeling down, putting it back together again. I heard Dollefeld say: 'Hurry up, get that stuff together, so we can get going.' By that time, two men came down from a little side road. They came up running. One was Wegmann, as I was later told; in fact, he said himself who he was. The other one was just a short distance behind Wegmann; he was limping. And when they got near the crowd, in fact, they were running quite fast, then I saw Wegmann take a weapon that he was carrying off his shoulder. He just pushed his way into the crowd, and I just held on to my child, I don't know why, it all happened so fast, and I heard a shot.

"That was just as the American flyer was going to cross the road. Then the American ran across the road into the field approximately three or four meters; he broke down with his hands raised up and letting out cries and saying something, I don't know what. I don't understand English. And then I heard the second shot; I think he shot him then. The American then was rolling on the ground, crying and hollering from pain; it was something terrible; I can still hear it. Maybe I was dazed by it, I don't know. I ran up to Wegmann and said: 'Why did you shoot that man? He gave no resistance

A seasoned combat veteran in the spring of 1944, Cruse is proudly wearing his gunner's wings with a blue patch denoting combat service. He has already received a Purple Heart for being wounded in action and an Air Medal with a number of oak leaf clusters for missions completed. LARRY L. TUEL

whatsoever.' And Wegmann looked like he was crazy, and he was sputtering something. I turned around, grabbed my child, wanted to get away from it all, and he ran up to me, and he, Wegmann, said: 'Are you a German woman? How can you have sympathy with an air-gangster?'

"I turned around, grabbed my child, and ran toward home. I was very excited, the child was crying, and everybody seemed to be in an uproar and I heard, as I left, somebody say: 'Why don't you finish that poor man?' I don't know what person said that, and then I heard another shot. I ran back again and looked at him, I don't know why I did it, but I was so excited that I did not know what I was doing. I grabbed my child again and ran toward home, and for some reason or other, I came back again and looked at the body, and I'm sure that Wegmann fired the last shot. He had a great big gun in his hand. When I came back, I looked on the ground, and I saw a car-tridge case. I picked it up and I said, 'I'll keep that as remembrance; I'll never forget it anyway to my dying day.'

"Then a car pulled up, and I saw two men come out of it; one was Lutz. Later on, I heard that the other was Geschwindner. And I saw that Lutz shook hands with Wegmann and said something, but I don't know what he said to him. Then I heard Wegmann say, 'Let's go, we'll get another one,' and he and another man that limped left the crowd. They went up the hill called Kalkwerk, and then I heard when Lutz and Geschwindner called over Moller, who had come down the hill at the time and said: 'What, you are afraid that an American will shoot you? You're just a coward'—or something to that effect. And then they were going, from the way it looked, to bury the American on the place where he was shot, but by that time, my husband came along and he said, 'No, don't you bury that man in front of my wife and my child's eyes; we have to live nearby. Take him where he belongs, to the cemetery.' By that time, the police came out, and policeman Kahler said: 'That's a soldier, and he is going to be buried where the rest of them are buried, and that's in the cemetery,' and they picked the dead soldier up and went away with him. And then I left and went home and I was all excited for some time to come."[4]

The body of luckless LeRoy D. Cruse was buried in Elm cemetery on 29 May. The burgomaster of Elm, no doubt trying to cover up the murder, reported that Cruse was killed "by parachuting." The news that LeRoy Cruse was killed in action and would not return to Terril shattered his parents' hopes in late September 1944.

When American ground forces occupied the Elm area in February 1945, his body was exhumed and brought to the recently established military cemetery in St. Avold, France. Here he was buried in plot QQQ, row 2, grave 18. However, just a few months later, doubts arose about the way that LeRoy had died.

One of the men who suspected that something was not right was Leonard Kriesky, the crew's radio operator and also one of LeRoy's original crewmembers in October 1943. Kriesky wrote to LeRoy's parents on 13 July 1945: "I am rather late in writing you this letter, but I thought I'd get home first and see if there was additional information I could get hold of. The only news I can give of Bud is that day of 28 May 1944, he was not injured in the plane. We were given orders to bail out, we shook hands and said we should see each other on the ground. Bud left second, while I jumped fourth. That was the last I saw of him. The ball gunner saw him on the ground, but didn't get to talk to him as they were about a half a mile apart—however, he did see Bud hide his chute and take off. That is the reason I did not want to betray him should he be making his way out. It was distressing news to learn that the government informed you that he was killed in action. This was the first I'd heard of it, you see information of that type doesn't reach us. It's hard for me to realize it and I know it's trying for you. The only possible explanation of his death could be that the Jerry had shot at him in making his attempt to escape. I know that sentence seems coarse—but we have to look at the facts and possibilities. He was one that would not give in easily and I know if it happened this way the Jerry had a fight and I mean a good fight on their hands.

In February 1945, LeRoy Cruse was buried in the Lorraine American cemetery in St. Avold, France. In December 1948, his remains where exhumed and returned to the United States. LARRY L. TUEL

"Cruse was a very good buddy of mine and the rest of the crew, we loved him so easy going, refreshing and always eager for the battle—he was the tops with us. I know your loss is a great thing but perhaps you can find a little solace in the fact that we too share it—the loss of a grand son, a great soldier and a best buddy."[5]

He and the other crewmembers made similar statements during the official investigations that would find their way in the missing air crew report that was compiled for their aircraft and crew. The evidence for a possible atrocity was strong enough to have Cruse's body disinterred and have an autopsy performed on 5 September 1945. The autopsy clearly showed that Cruse was killed by a shot in the head, that there was another bullet wound in the abdomen, and, most important, that the range of firing had been very close.

Investigations in Elm soon led to Richard Wegmann, who was arrested and interrogated on 28 September. It appeared that he was a twenty-four-year-old farmer at the time of the crime. He had served in the *Wehrmacht* from 1938 until he was wounded in action during the invasion in Poland in September 1939. He was discharged from the *Wehrmacht* in 1941, and since that time, he had been working on his parents' farm. His only brother had been killed during an air raid by the RAF on Frankfurt in 1941.

During his trial the reason for his discharge from the *Wehrmacht* became clear. The wound he had received in Poland had been a steel splinter in his head. This resulted in spells of unconsciousness, temporary loss of memory, and a tendency to become very nervous and excitable. The family doctor, who was one of the witnesses for the defense of the accused, summarized his behavior in the period between 1940 and 1944 as "Serious weaknesses as far as the brain's capacity to work is concerned, with effective aberrations, extreme irritation, excitability and typical sensibility to weather."[6]

A further medical examination showed that the steel splinter was still lodged in Wegmann's brain. It was removed easily in the Internee Hospital 2 in Karlsruhe on 7 March 1946. The final trial took place in Dachau on 10 and 11 June 1946, and despite all efforts by Wegmann's advocate, the General Military Government Court sentenced him to death by hanging.

However, after a petition for clemency, which claimed insanity at the moment of the crime, the judge advocate recommended the commutation to thirty years' imprisonment on 23 December 1946. Later, the sentence was reduced to twenty-five years. Wegmann behaved well in prison, and when his father was killed in an accident on his farm in 1954, the sentence was reduced to ten years of imprisonment beginning 13 May 1945, and thus he was released shortly thereafter.

LeRoy Cruse's final resting place is in the family plot in the Fairview Cemetery, Terril, Iowa. JERRY D. NELSON

By that time, LeRoy Cruse was already back in Iowa. When given the opportunity by the government, his parents had his body disinterred from the Lorraine cemetery at the end of 1948. After a long sea and rail journey, the casket with his body arrived in Terril. On 31 January 1949, LeRoy was buried in the Fairview Cemetery in Dickinson County. His final resting place is barely two miles outside Terril, from which he had departed in 1941 to serve his country.

Appendix 1: USAAF Losses

B-24J 42-110045 GJ-K 44 Bomb Group, 506 Bomb Squadron
Shot down by flak, crashed in Dümmerlohausen, Germany

Gurman, Irving S.	2/Lt	Pilot	POW
Jipson, Robert F.	2/Lt	Co-pilot	POW
Kaulbach Jr., Andrew J.	2/Lt	Navigator	POW
McMaster, James H.	Sgt	Bombardier	POW
Costello, George B.	S/Sgt	Engineer	POW
Carson, Joseph	S/Sgt	Radio operator	POW
Wiitala, Eino J.	Sgt	Left waist gunner	POW
Willis, Theodore D.	Sgt	Right waist gunner	POW
Williams, Charles D.	Sgt	Tail gunner	POW

B-17G 42-31389 EP-J 100 Bomb Group, 351 Bomb Squadron
Shot down by fighters, crashed in Barleben, Germany

Lacy, Lucius G.	1/Lt	Pilot	POW
Schindler, Claude E.	1/Lt	Co-pilot	KIA
Rossman, Raymond E.	2/Lt	Navigator	POW
Greenberg, Herbert	1/Lt	Bombardier	POW
Cary, Sidney A.	T/Sgt	Engineer	POW
Wood Jr., Clarence H.	T/Sgt	Radio operator	POW
Powell Jr., Chester L.	S/Sgt	Ball turret gunner	KIA
Mitchell, Raymond J.	S/Sgt	Left waist gunner	POW
Folsom, Joe S.	S/Sgt	Right waist gunner	KIA
Rotz, Michael	S/Sgt	Tail gunner	POW

B-17G 42-107028 VK-I 303 Bomb Group, 358 Bomb Squadron
Shot down by flak, crashed in Albrechtshain, Germany

Determan, Alvin G.	2/Lt	Pilot	POW
Pfahler, Ervin J.	2/Lt	Co-pilot	KIA
Palmer Jr., Jackson	2/Lt	Navigator	KIA
McCamy, James A.	2/Lt	Bombardier	KIA
Hendrickson, Milton C.	T/Sgt	Engineer	KIA
Asman, Robert H.	T/Sgt	Radio operator	POW
Vasquez, Manuel	Sgt	Ball turret gunner	KIA
Livingston, Acel E.	Sgt	Left waist gunner	KIA
Cope, Wayne E.	Sgt	Right waist gunner	POW
Carroccia, Albert R.	Sgt	Tail gunner	KIA

B-17G 42-39878 XK-S 305 Bomb Group, 365 Bomb Squadron
Mechanical troubles, belly-landed in Zerf, Germany

Herrick, Julius F.	2/Lt	Pilot	POW
Saunders Jr., Lloyd H.	2/Lt	Co-pilot	POW
Lobdell, Leon W.	2/Lt	Navigator	POW
Boraz, Herbert	2/Lt	Bombardier	POW
Gillespie, Charlie	T/Sgt	Engineer	POW
Schwartz, William S.	S/Sgt	Radio operator	POW
Busby, Orval R.	Sgt	Ball turret gunner	POW
Dunbar, Daniel E.	Sgt	Left waist gunner	EVD
Norris, Benjamin R.	Sgt	Right waist gunner	EVD
Napier, John C.	S/Sgt	Tail gunner	POW

B-17G 42-31721 TU-S 351 Bomb Group, 510 Bomb Squadron
Shot down by flak, crashed in Mernes, Germany

McClelland, Clyde W.	1/Lt	Pilot	POW
Francis, Richard E.	1/Lt	Co-pilot	POW
Duncan, John B.	1/Lt	Navigator	POW
Kiely, George F.	1/Lt	Bombardier	POW
Poole, Louis E.	T/Sgt	Engineer	POW
Kriesky, Leonard J.	T/Sgt	Radio operator	POW
Williams, Nathan L.	S/Sgt	Ball turret gunner	POW
Edwards, Junior H.	S/Sgt	Waist gunner	POW
Cruse, LeRoy D.	S/Sgt	Tail gunner	KIA

B-17G 42-31757 YB-G 351 Bomb Group, 508 Bomb Squadron
Shot down by fighters, crashed in Waldau, Germany

Condon, William J.	2/Lt	Pilot	KIA
Kolceski, Joseph P.	2/Lt	Co-pilot	KIA
Zindar, Laddie J.	2/Lt	Navigator	KIA
Onken, Edwin S.	2/Lt	Bombardier	POW
Jackson, Junny O.	S/Sgt	Engineer	KIA
Morris, William H.	S/Sgt	Radio operator	POW
Jenkins, Charles G.	Sgt	Ball turret gunner	KIA
Norris, Harry M.	Sgt	Waist gunner	KIA
Jackson, John J.	Sgt	Tail gunner	POW

B-17G 42-39987 DS-D 351 Bomb Group, 511 Bomb Squadron
Shot down by fighters, crashed in Lönnewitz, Germany

Probasco, Robert E. L.	F/O	Pilot	POW
Lewellyn, Stephen B.	2/Lt	Co-pilot	POW
Bragg, William P.	2/Lt	Navigator	POW
Branch, Bruno	2/Lt	Bombardier	POW
Ulreich, Herman T.	S/Sgt	Engineer	POW
Moore, Arlie W.	S/Sgt	Radio operator	KIA
Ringstmeyer, Norman W.	Sgt	Ball turret gunner	KIA
Seaman, Raymond G.	Sgt	Left waist gunner	KIA
Frankowski, Edward J.	Sgt	Right waist gunner	POW
Singleton, James D.	Sgt	Tail gunner	KIA

B-17G 42-97191 DS-X 351 Bomb Group, 511 Bomb Squadron
Shot down by fighters, crashed between Deetz and Nedlitz, Germany

Miller, Carl F.	2/Lt	Pilot	KIA
Fikes, Maurice G.	2/Lt	Co-pilot	POW
Brown, Russell A.	2/Lt	Navigator	POW
Lemcke, Ernest A.	S/Sgt	Togglier	POW
Avry, Frank	T/Sgt	Engineer	POW
McCann, James D.	T/Sgt	Radio operator	POW
Kaplowitz, Isidor P.	S/Sgt	Ball turret gunner	KIA
Lien, Albert L.	Sgt	Left waist gunner	POW
Bushlow, Anthony J.	Sgt	Right waist gunner	POW
Stafford, George A.	S/Sgt	Tail gunner	POW

B-17G 42-97472 DS-H 351 Bomb Group, 511 Bomb Squadron
Shot down by fighters, crashed in Westdorf, near Aschersleben, Germany

Anderson, Charles F.	2/Lt	Pilot	POW
McFetridge, Robert L.	F/O	Co-pilot	POW
Ryan, Robert E.	2/Lt	Navigator	POW
Baird, William H.	2/Lt	Bombardier	POW
Williams, Neal W.	Sgt	Engineer	POW
Vecchione, Casper	S/Sgt	Radio operator	POW
Nitzberg, George P.	Sgt	Ball turret gunner	POW
Matzke, Bernard J.	S/Sgt	Waist gunner	POW
Vanhorn, Edward E.	Sgt	Tail gunner	POW

B-17G 42-97847 Q 385 Bomb Group, 569 Bomb Squadron
Shot down by flak, crashed in Albrechtshain, Germany

Hunter, Francis J.	F/O	Pilot	POW
Miller, Raymond J.	F/O	Co-pilot	POW
Ray, Preston	2/Lt	Navigator	POW
Coelho, Antero D.	2/Lt	Bombardier	POW
Marts, Ralph M.	S/Sgt	Engineer	POW
Schrotter, Jerome H.	S/Sgt	Radio operator	POW
Scott, Richard E.	Sgt	Ball turret gunner	POW
Kowalski, Edward J.	S/Sgt	Left waist gunner	POW
Sheehan, Kenneth E.	Sgt	Right waist gunner	POW
Pruner, Maurice J.	Sgt	Tail gunner	POW

B-17G 42-39845 B 388 Bomb Group, 563 Bomb Squadron
Shot down by flak, belly-landed in Mengsberg, Germany

Fjelsted, Marquis G.	2/Lt	Pilot	POW
Hudson, William C.	2/Lt	Co-pilot	POW
Houlihan, H. Joseph	2/Lt	Navigator	POW
Tracewski, Chester P.	2/Lt	Bombardier	POW
McBrien, John E.	S/Sgt	Engineer	POW
Hoover, George F.	Sgt	Radio operator	POW
Perry, John L.	Sgt	Ball turret gunner	POW
Stringer, Edward J.	Sgt	Left waist gunner	POW
McCarty, Harold S.	Sgt	Right waist gunner	POW
Shatz, John R.	S/Sgt	Tail gunner	POW

B-17G 42-102485 R 388 Bomb Group, 562 Bomb Squadron
Shot down by flak, belly-landed in Groenekan, Holland

Codding, Arthur M.	1/Lt	Pilot	POW
Withers, Roger B.	2/Lt	Co-pilot	POW
Chiles, Donald L.	2/Lt	Navigator	KIA
McBeth, Delmar D.	S/Sgt	Togglier	KIA
Berg, Robert C.	T/Sgt	Engineer	POW
Waite, Clyde H.	T/Sgt	Radio operator	POW
Joye, Kenneth M.	S/Sgt	Ball turret gunner	POW
Brown, Lawrence G.	S/Sgt	Left waist gunner	POW
Roskowick, Thomas L.	S/Sgt	Right waist gunner	KIA
Mulder, James W.	S/Sgt	Tail gunner	POW

B-24J 42-110074 HP-Pilot 389 Bomb Group, 567 Bomb Squadron
Mechanical troubles, crashed west of Gravelines, France

Eley, Jack	2/Lt	Pilot	POW
Tucker, Walter L.	2/Lt	Co-pilot	KIA
Joblonicky, Albert	2/Lt	Navigator	KIA
Osborne, Charles E.	S/Sgt	NTG	MIA
Kaems, Robert H.	S/Sgt	Engineer	MIA
Tennant, James C.	S/Sgt	Radio operator	RTD
Crepp, Howard E.	T/Sgt	Left waist gunner	RTD
Daly, Arthur J.	S/Sgt	Right waist gunner	KIA
LaCourse, Victor	S/Sgt	Tail gunner	MIA

B-17G 42-31651 FC-G 390 Bomb Group, 571 Bomb Squadron
Shot down by fighters, crashed in Ebendorf, Germany

Strate, Herbert V.	2/Lt	Pilot	KIA
Elliott, Samuel R.	2/Lt	Co-pilot	KIA
Brown, Richard C.	2/Lt	Navigator	KIA
Woolfolk, Robert L.	2/Lt	Bombardier	KIA
Stoy, Edward C.	S/Sgt	Engineer	POW
Mamula Jr., Nick	S/Sgt	Radio operator	KIA
Reed, Arthur E.	Sgt	Ball turret gunner	KIA
Bolton, Harold B.	Sgt	Left waist gunner	POW
Smart, Robert B.	Sgt	Right waist gunner	KIA
Molenock, Edward D.	Sgt	Tail gunner	POW

B-17G 42-31985 DI-Pilot 390 Bomb Group, 570 Bomb Squadron
Shot down by fighters, crashed in Lostau, Germany

Ingram, John H.	2/Lt	Pilot	KIA
Banks, Douglas C.	2/Lt	Co-pilot	KIA
Tabeling, Robert G.	2/Lt	Navigator	KIA
Cosgrove, Daniel J.B.	2/Lt	Bombardier	POW
Buntin Jr., William C.	S/Sgt	Engineer	POW
Czerpak, Henry	S/Sgt	Radio operator	KIA
Lewis, James J.	Sgt	Ball turret gunner	MIA
Czyz, Edward J.	Sgt	Left waist gunner	POW
McKee, Arnold	S/Sgt	Right waist gunner	MIA
Salmons, Kenneth A.	Sgt	Tail gunner	KIA

B-17G 42-32089 DI-W 390 Bomb Group, 570 Bomb Squadron
Shot down by fighters, crashed near Colbitz, Germany

Matthias Jr., Adolph J.	1/Lt	Pilot	POW
Gerards, Henry J.	2/Lt	Co-pilot	POW
Freyland, Joseph P.	2/Lt	Navigator	POW
Bass, Quentin R.	2/Lt	Bombardier	POW
Wolf, Jerry	T/Sgt	Engineer	POW
Abbot, Charles N.	T/Sgt	Radio operator	POW
Oliver, Charles M.	S/Sgt	Ball turret gunner	POW
Veale, Roy E.	Sgt	Left waist gunner	POW
Spencer, Laurene W.	S/Sgt	Right waist gunner	POW
Walker, Leon C.	S/Sgt	Tail gunner	POW

B-17G 42-37806 FC-Z 390 Bomb Group, 571 Bomb Squadron
Shot down by fighters, crashed in Walternienburg, Germany

Holmes, Henry C.	1/Lt	Pilot	POW
Kruger, Charles B.	2/Lt	Co-pilot	POW
Steck, Walter	2/Lt	Navigator	POW
Thompson, Oral G.	2/Lt	Bombardier	POW
Baccaro, Victor L.	T/Sgt	Engineer	POW
Knight, Forest L.	T/Sgt	Radio operator	KIA
Watson, Frank R.	S/Sgt	Ball turret gunner	POW
Roock, Harold R.	S/Sgt	Left waist gunner	POW
Sanders, Soldier	S/Sgt	Right waist gunner	POW
Kast Jr., Paul A.	S/Sgt	Tail gunner	POW

B-17G 42-102440 BI-K 390 Bomb Group, 568 Bomb Squadron
Shot down by fighters, crashed near Burg, Germany

Weigle, Walter P.	2/Lt	Pilot	POW
Richardson, Charles A.	F/O	Co-pilot	POW
Preusser, Herman H.	2/Lt	Navigator	POW
Severson, Elmer D.	2/Lt	Bombardier	POW
Curiston, Thomas J.	S/Sgt	Engineer	POW
Rudolph, Donald F.	S/Sgt	Radio operator	POW
Mniszewski, Irvin T.	Sgt	Ball turret gunner	POW
Becker, Joseph M.	Sgt	Left waist gunner	POW
Minor, Gale W.	Sgt	Right waist gunner	POW
Spotanski, Alexander	Sgt	Tail gunner	POW

B-17G 42-31034 SC-G 401 Bomb Group, 612 Bomb Squadron
Shot down by fighters, crashed between Otterwisch and Pomssen, Germany

West, George E.	1/Lt	Pilot	KIA
McKinnon, Douglas H.	1/Lt	Co-pilot	POW
Nutter, Lloyd A.	1/Lt	Navigator	POW
Montgomery, Thomas B.	1/Lt	Bombardier	POW
Russell, Francis L.	T/Sgt	Engineer	POW
Andrus, Robert L.	T/Sgt	Radio operator	POW
Womble, Johnnie L.	S/Sgt	Ball turret gunner	POW
Russell, Hugh D.	S/Sgt	Left waist gunner	KIA
Morini, Alfred J.	S/Sgt	Right waist gunner	POW
Lefkin, Michael	S/Sgt	Tail gunner	KIA

B-17G 42-31557 IN-R 401 Bomb Group, 613 Bomb Squadron
Shot down by fighters, crashed 8 km southeast of Belzig, Germany

Keith, Walter B.	1/Lt	Pilot	POW
Maloney, John J.	2/Lt	Co-pilot	KIA
Priest, Jack B.	1/Lt	Navigator	KIA
Weiss, Norman	2/Lt	B	POW
Wells, James E.	S/Sgt	E	POW
Mahler, Arthur P.	Cpl	Radio operator	POW
Beckowitz, Peter	Sgt	Ball turret gunner	KIA
Barnes, Merle E.	Sgt	Left waist gunner	POW
Cass, Leo C.	Sgt	Right waist gunner	KIA
D'Agostino, Victor	Sgt	Tail gunner	POW

B-17G 42-39837 SC-L 401 Bomb Group, 612 Bomb Squadron
Mechanical troubles, ditched in the North Sea

Carter, Gerald F.	2/Lt	Pilot	RTD
Johnston, Clayton A.	1/Lt	Co-pilot	RTD
Locklear, Willard O.	F/O	Navigator	RTD
Deaton, Lloyd G.	F/O	Bombardier	RTD
Truax, Floyd A.	Sgt	Engineer	RTD
Heinlon, John N.	S/Sgt	Radio operator	RTD
Hardister, Stanford M.	Sgt	Ball turret gunner	RTD
Miller, Carl J.	S/Sgt	Waist gunner	RTD
Hafko, John	Sgt	Waist gunner	RTD
Wepner, John L.	Sgt	Tail gunner	RTD

B-17G 42-97073 IY-Navigator 401 Bomb Group, 615 Bomb Squadron
Shot down by fighters, crashed in Mühro, Germany.

Kaminski, Vincent J.	1/Lt	Pilot	KIA
Enstad, Robert J.	2/Lt	Co-pilot	POW
Black, J. Dee	1/Lt	Navigator	KIA
Manning, Charles H.	2/Lt	Bombardier	POW
Agee, Jack D.	T/Sgt	Engineer	KIA
Cooper, Larry R.	T/Sgt	Radio operator	KIA
Johnson, Joe R.	Sgt	Ball turret gunner	KIA
May, William M.	S/Sgt	Left waist gunner	KIA
Bushendorf, Everett M.	S/Sgt	Right waist gunner	KIA
Hertzan, Harold	S/Sgt	Tail gunner	KIA

B-17G 42-102580 IN-Q 401 Bomb Group, 613 Bomb Squadron
Shot down by fighters, crashed between Aken and Dessau, Germany

Protz, William F.	1/Lt	Pilot	POW
Barnett, Richard S.	2/Lt	Co-pilot	KIA
Bennett, Sam B.	2/Lt	Navigator	KIA
Stiegel, Alvin J.	F/O	Bombardier	KIA
Morrow, Jim K.	T/Sgt	Engineer	KIA
Wicks, Wayne W.	T/Sgt	Radio operator	KIA
Bartak, Frank S.	S/Sgt	Ball turret gunner	POW
Reinhardt, Albert P.	Sgt	Left waist gunner	POW
Cliff, Glenn I.	S/Sgt	Right waist gunner	POW
Appleby, James C.	S/Sgt	Tail gunner	POW

B-17G 42-102581 IN-L 401 Bomb Group, 613 Bomb Squadron
Shot down by fighters, crashed in Glienicke, Germany

Scharff, Paul F.	1/Lt	Pilot	KIA
Eckert, Charles A.	2/Lt	Co-pilot	KIA
Schwartz, Bernard	1/Lt	Navigator	POW
Hoover, Robert E.	2/Lt	Bombardier	KIA
Karl, Richard X.	T/Sgt	Engineer	POW
Strong, Robert C.	Sgt	Radio operator	POW
Bedell, Charles H.	S/Sgt	Ball turret gunner	POW
Tomlinson, Roscoe D.	S/Sgt	Left waist gunner	KIA
Pynigar, Frederick G.	Sgt	Right waist gunner	POW
Smallin, James M.	S/Sgt	Tail gunner	POW

B-17G 42-102647 IN-G 401 Bomb Group, 613 Bomb Squadron
Shot down by fighters, crashed in Niemegk, Germany

Windham, Frederick H.	2/Lt	Pilot	POW
Ferguson, Donald P.	2/Lt	Co-pilot	KIA
Floto, Carl T.	2/Lt	Navigator	POW
Melito, Angelo J.	2/Lt	Bombardier	POW
Rittmaier, Robert W.	S/Sgt	Engineer	POW
Johnson, Dana B.	S/Sgt	Radio operator	KIA
Mihalich, Leonard A.	S/Sgt	Ball turret gunner	KIA
Garcia, Jose G.	Sgt	Left waist gunner	KIA
Irelan, Clyde E.	Sgt	Right waist gunner	POW
Miller, Floyd O.	S/Sgt	Tail gunner	KIA

B-24H 42-50346 ? 445 Bomb Group, 703 Bomb Squadron
Shot down by flak, crashed in Stössen, Germany

Campbell, John W.	1/Lt	Pilot	POW
Marlin, Roger T.	2/Lt	Co-pilot	POW
Wholeben, Bernard E.	1/Lt	Navigator	POW
Matheu, Daniel J.	1/Lt	Bombardier	POW
Bennett, Harold	S/Sgt	Engineer	POW
Robinson, William M.	T/Sgt	Radio operator	POW
Williams, Cophlin	S/Sgt	Ball turret gunner	POW
Ball, Royce E.	S/Sgt	Waist gunner	POW
Wampler, Ray M.	S/Sgt	Waist gunner	KIA
Vallette, Leo J.	S/Sgt	Tail gunner	POW

B-17G 42-31520 A 457 Bomb Group, 751 Bomb Squadron
Shot down by fighters, crashed in Döllbach, Germany

Knipfer, Clyde B.	1/Lt	Pilot	POW
Bruha, Richard H.	2/Lt	Co-pilot	POW
Derdzinski, George R.	2/Lt	Navigator	POW
Gray, Stanley V.	2/Lt	Bombardier	POW
Voit, Stephen T.	T/Sgt	Engineer	POW
Bendino, Nicholas F.	T/Sgt	Radio operator	POW
Furrie, Nicholas D.	S/Sgt	Ball turret gunner	POW
Waltho, Percy	S/Sgt	Waist gunner	POW
Goldstein, Joshua	S/Sgt	Tail gunner	POW

B-17G 42-97067 Y 457 Bomb Group, 749 Bomb Squadron
Shot down by fighters and flak, crashed in Osterholz, Germany

Stohl, Rudolph M.	1/Lt	Pilot	POW
Schellenger, David W.	2/Lt	Co-pilot	POW
Millham, John O.	2/Lt	Navigator	POW
Thomas, James E.	2/Lt	Bombardier	POW
Kriete, Robert C.	M/Sgt	Engineer	POW
Wagoner, Walter W.	T/Sgt	Radio operator	KIA
Moore, Sheldon E.	Sgt	Ball turret gunner	POW
Welling, Irwin A.	S/Sgt	Left waist gunner	POW
Bemus, William F.	Sgt	Right waist gunner	POW
Stewart, Charles L.	S/Sgt	Tail gunner	POW

B-17G 42-97452 L 457 Bomb Group, 751 Bomb Squadron
Shot down by fighters, crashed in the North Sea

Hauf, Emanuel	1/Lt	Pilot	MIA
Swain, Donald V.	2/Lt	Co-pilot	MIA
Hawley, William R.	2/Lt	Navigator	MIA
Jaqua, Richard E.	2/Lt	Bombardier	MIA
Johnson, Willis H.	T/Sgt	Engineer	MIA
Kilroy, James J.	T/Sgt	Radio operator	MIA
Furtta, Walter	S/Sgt	Ball turret gunner	MIA
Moore, Paul R.	S/Sgt	Waist gunner	MIA
Gascon, Oscar A.	S/Sgt	Tail gunner	MIA

B-24H 42-50345 3R-B 486 Bomb Group, 832 Bomb Squadron
Shot down by flak, crashed in the English Channel, off Zuydcoote, France

Hicks, Eugene R.	1/Lt	Pilot	MIA
Johnson, John C.	2/Lt	Co-pilot	MIA
Bogert, James H.	Capt	Navigator	POW
Moll, David V.	2/Lt	Navigator	MIA
Russell, Kenneth E.	2/Lt	Bombardier	MIA
Smith, Charles A.	S/Sgt	Engineer	POW
Munro, George H.	S/Sgt	Radio operator	POW
Drake, Robert E.	S/Sgt	Ball turret gunner	MIA
Bundrick, Olin L.	Sgt	Left waist gunner	MIA
Todd, James R.	M/Sgt	Right waist gunner	MIA
Moskowitz, Murray	Sgt	Tail gunner	MIA

B-24H 42-52764 4N-O 486 Bomb Group, 832 Bomb Squadron
Shot down by flak, crashed in Charly des Bois, Belgium

Sanders, Alfred M.	2/Lt	Pilot	EVD
Morley, Fred A.	2/Lt	Co-pilot	POW
Zoebelein, Thomas J.	2/Lt	Navigator	EVD
O'Connell, Daniel M.	F/O	Bombardier	EVD
Kozulak, William	Sgt	Engineer	POW
Lawrence, John H.	Sgt	Radio operator	POW
Sizemore, James R.	S/Sgt	Ball turret gunner	EVD
Smith, Autley B.	Sgt	Left waist gunner	EVD
Lujan, Louis	S/Sgt	Right waist gunner	POW
Swaffield, Robert C.	Sgt	Tail gunner	POW

B-24H 42-52651 4F-R 487 Bomb Group, 838 Bomb Squadron
Shot down by flak, crashed in Xhoris, Belgium

Burckes, Ralph S.	2/Lt	Pilot	POW
Chavez, Paul F.	2/Lt	Co-pilot	EVD
Dunham, William F.	2/Lt	Navigator	POW
Weeks, Homer A.	2/Lt	Bombardier	POW
Toole, James M.	S/Sgt	Engineer	POW
Witherow, Howard A.	S/Sgt	Radio operator	EVD
Henry, Charles L.	Sgt	Ball turret gunner	POW
Carpenter, Donald W.	Sgt	Gunner	POW
Abadie Jr., Emil J.	Sgt	Gunner	EVD
Henze, Rex L.	Sgt	Tail gunner	EVD

P-51B 42-106846 QP-H 4 Fighter Group, 334 Fighter Squadron
Ran out of fuel, crashed in Aumont, France

Bopp, Richard L.	2/Lt	Pilot	POW

P-51B 43-6933 QP-Y 4 Fighter Group, 334 Fighter Squadron
Shot down by fighters, crashed in Vogelsang, Germany

Hewatt, Aubrey E.	2/Lt	Pilot	POW

P-47D 42-26016 HL-A 78 Fighter Group, 83 Fighter Squadron
Collided with P-51, crashed in Jeggau, Germany

Juchheim, Alvin M.	Capt	Pilot	POW

P-47D 42-26064 MX-M 78 Fighter Group, 82 Fighter Squadron
Shot down by flak, crashed in Gildehaus, Germany

Hazelett, Philip H.	1/Lt	Pilot	KIA

P-47D 42-76318 MX-W 78 Fighter Group, 82 Fighter Squadron
Shot down by flak, crashed in Elbergen, Germany

Orvis Jr., William S.	2/Lt	Pilot	KIA

P-51B 42-106635 PZ-A 352 Fighter Group, 486 Fighter Squadron
Shot down by fighters, probably crashed in Achersleben, Germany

Anderson, Woodrow W.	Capt	Pilot	MIA

P-47D 42-75457 YJ-A 353 Fighter Group, 351 Fighter Squadron
Shot down by flak, crashed in Loddenheide, Germany

Farley, Joseph R.	2/Lt	Pilot	KIA

P-51B 42-106712 FT-I 354 Fighter Group, 353 Fighter Squadron
Mechanical troubles, crashed in North Sea

McDowell, Don	1/Lt	Pilot	KIA

P-51B 43-7195 FT-X 354 Fighter Group, 353 Fighter Squadron
Shot down by flak, belly-landed in Ruppersdorf, Germany

Pipes, Glenn H.	1/Lt	Pilot	POW

P-51B 43-6631 WR-T 355 Fighter Group, 354 Fighter Squadron
Shot down by fighters, probably crashed in Zerbst, Germany
Barger, Clarence R.   1/Lt   Pilot   MIA

P-51B 43-6983 WR-O 355 Fighter Group, 354 Fighter Squadron
Shot down by fighters, crashed in Buhlendorf, Germany
Christensen, Walter M.   2/Lt   Pilot   KIA

P-51C 42-103004 ? 363 Fighter Group, 380 Fighter Squadron
Shot down by fighters, crashed in Schackensleben, Germany
Clemovitz, Feodor   2/Lt   Pilot   POW

P-51B 42-106481 ? 363 Fighter Group, 382 Fighter Squadron
Shot down by fighters, crashed in Bennstedt, Germany
Wilson, Curry P.   2/Lt   Pilot   POW

P-51B 42-106486 C3-A 363 Fighter Group, 382 Fighter Squadron
Collided with P-47, crashed in Sichau, Germany
Ladas, Anthony E.   2/Lt   Pilot   KIA

Appendix 2: *Luftwaffe* Aircraft and Personnel Losses

Unit	Name	Rank	Fate	Type, W.Nr., and Fuselage code	Crash Location
2./JG 1	Riehl, Helmut	Uffz	Safe	Fw 190A-8, unknown, Black 4	Schkeuditz, one wheel landing
3./JG 1	Kotiza, Eugen	Oblt	KIA	Fw 190A-8, 730483, Yellow 1	Crash near Hannover
3./JG 1	Schmidt, Karl-Heinz	Gefr	KIA	Fw 190A-8, 680153, Yellow 3	Crash near Helmstedt
3./JG 1	Knoll, Gustav	Ofhnr	WIA	Fw 190A-7, 430688, Yellow 18	Bailed out near Wolmirsleben
I./JG 1	Unknown pilot		Safe	Fw 190	Combat loss, unknown
I./JG 1	Unknown pilot		Safe	Fw 190	Combat loss, unknown
6./JG 1	Golinger, Bernhard	Uffz	WIA	Fw 190A-8, 730388, Yellow 12	Bailed out near Magdeburg
6./JG 1	Brodbeck, Kurt	Fw	Safe	Fw 190	Goslar, belly-landing
III./JG 1	Halbey, Hans	Lt	WIA	Bf 109G-6, unknown, Black 13	Bailed out near Mölln/Marburg
9./JG 1	Körner, Josef	Gefr	WIA	Bf 109G-6, 440939, White 4	Sondershausen, emergency landing
9./JG 1	Timm, Fritz	Ofw	KIA	Bf 109G-6, 440700, Yellow 3	Crash near Ebsdorf/ Mölln
2./JG 3	Herdy, Hans	Uffz	KIA	Bf 109G-6, 440703, Black 4	Crash near Dreileben
2./JG 3	Petzschler, Horst	Uffz	Safe	Bf 109G-6, unknown, Black 14	Bailed out near Dreileben
2./JG 3	Tiepner, Karl	Gefr	WIA	Bf 109G-6, 110231, Black 1	Bailed out near Gommern
3./JG 3	Witt, Ernst-Eduard	Ofhnr	WIA	Bf 109G-6, 410859, Yellow 6	Bailed out south of Magdeburg
3./JG 3	Sandweg, Kurt	Fw	WIA	Bf 109G-6, 440541, Yellow 5	Bailed out near Calbe/Saale

Unit	Name	Rank	Fate	Type, W.Nr., and Fuselage code	Crash Location
5./JG 3	Schneider, Rudolf	Uffz	WIA	Bf 109G-6, 412422, Black 7	Bailed out near Halberstadt
7./JG 3	Spittler, Georg	Uffz	KIA	Bf 109G-6, 410452, White 4	Crash near Papenrode
8./JG 3	Molitor, Wilhelm	Ofw	WIA	Bf 109G-6, 163753, Black 8	Destroyed in Belly-landing at Werferlingen
9./JG 3	Grunendahl, Hans	Uffz	WIA	Bf 109G-6, 20090, Yellow 9	Bailed out near Salzwedel
11./JG 3	Käding, Horst	Uffz	KIA	Fw 190A-8, 170369	Salzwedel, collision w/Savoia during takeoff
1./JG 5	Englert, Ludwig	Fw	KIA	Bf 109G-6, 440535, White 9	Crash near Tangeln/ Salzwedel
3./JG 5	Doll, Otto	Uffz	KIA	Bf 109G-6, 162299, Green 1	Crash southwest of Gardelegen
3./JG 5	Klein, Erich	Ofw	WIA	Bf 109G-6, 440302, Green 3	Bailed out near Salzwedel
1./JG 11	Hasenmajer, Rainer	Uffz	KIA	Fw 190A-8, 680180, Black 7	Crash in Magdeburg area
3./JG 11	Rosenkranz, Karl	Ofw	KIA	Fw 190A-7, 642540, Yellow 13	Crash in Magdeburg area
I./JG 11	Unknown pilot		Safe	Fw 190	Combat loss, unknown
I./JG 11	Unknown pilot		Safe	Fw 190	Combat loss, unknown
I./JG 11	Unknown pilot		Safe	Fw 190	Operational flight, unknown
II./JG 11	Krupinski, Walter	Oblt	Safe	Bf 109G-6	Bailed out near Magdeburg
4./JG 11	Heger, Alfred	Fw	Safe	Bf 109G-6, unknown, White 10	Schönebeck, belly-landing
6./JG 11	Kunz, Heinz	Uffz	KIA	Bf 109G-6, 412163, Black <	Crash in Magdeburg area
6./JG 11	Strosetzki, Rudolf	Uffz	Safe	Bf 109G-6	Schönhausen, emergency landing
8./JG 11	Brandes, Heinz-Helmut	Oblt	KIA	Fw 190	Gross-Börnecke
III./JG 11	Unknown pilot		Safe	Fw 190	Operational flight, unknown
III./JG 11	Unknown pilot		Safe	Fw 190	unknown
III./JG 11	Unknown pilot		Safe	Fw 190	unknown

Unit	Name	Rank	Fate	Type, W.Nr., and Fuselage code	Crash Location
1./JG 27	Jansen, Josef	Hptm	WIA	Bf 109G-6, 440973	Combat over Halle, died of wounds on 31 May
2./JG 27	Büsing, Heinz	Uffz	KIA	Bf 109G-6, 440181	Crash near Baalberge, southwest of Bernburg
4./JG 27	Wunnike, Gerhard	Lt	KIA	Bf 109G-6, 441319, White 3	Crash near Lockstieg, near Ebersfelde
4./JG 27	Franke, Gerhard	Uffz	KIA	Bf 109G-6, 162893, White 8	Crash near Zethlingen/ Salzwedel
5./JG 27	Bock, Eberhard	Hptm	KIA	Bf 109G-6, 441324, Black 6	Crash near Helmstedt
7./JG 27	Weth, Günther	Uffz	KIA	Bf 109G-6, 441403, White 1	Crash near Dessau
8./JG 27	Ottnad, Alexander	Lt	Safe	Bf 109G-6	Bailed out southwest of Zerbst
8./JG 27	Mühlbauer, Otto	Uffz	Safe	Bf 109G-6	Belly-landed at Leipzig, slight damage to aircraft
8./JG 27	Curth, Herbert	Gefr	WIA	Bf 109G-6, 160813, Red 2	Crash near Zerbst
12./JG 27	Döring, Werner	Fw	KIA	Bf 109G-6, 165068	Crash near Leipzig/ Gross Zschocher
4./JG 53	Kellinger, Friedrich	Uffz	WIA	Bf 109G-6, 412447, White 8	Emergency landing at Helmstedt/Mariental
5./JG 302	Breuers, Hans	Uffz	WIA	Bf 109 G-6, 440757, Red 1	Bailed out north of Koethen
4./ZG 26	Kubetzki, Johann	Uffz	KIA	Me 410A-1	Died in a/c, a/c belly-landed at Königsberg
Luftbeobachtungsstaffel 1					
	Phieler, Erich	Fw	KIA	Ju 88C 750400	Crash near Lichtenstein/ Thüringen
	Hammer, Frank	Uffz	KIA		
	Oertel, Fritz	Uffz	KIA		
I./KG 1				He 177 A-3 332476	Destroyed by bombs at Brandis/Polenz

Unit	Name	Rank	Fate	Type, W.Nr., and Fuselage code	Crash Location
Flugzeugführerschule B 31				Ju 88S, unknown, White 20 (probably six other aircraft)	Destroyed by bombs at Brandis/Polenz
Flugzeugführerschule B 31					
	Lenski, Werner	Uffz	KIA		KIA/WIA by bombing at Brandis/Polenz
	Schröter, Siegfried	Obgfr	KIA		
	Stölting, Kurt	Uffz	WIA		
	Haack, Otto	Gefr	WIA		
	Scheiblberger, Heinrich	Gefr	WIA		
	Willenbrink, Heinrich	Gefr	WIA		
Flugzeugführerschule A 72					
	Schulze, Heinz	Obgfr	KIA		Killed by bombing at Gera

Appendix 3: U.S. Fighter Pilot Air-to-Air Victory Credits

4 FG/334 FS	2/Lt Hofer, Ralph K.	1 Me 109
4 FG/334 FS	1/Lt Kenyon, Robert P.	1 Me 109
4 FG/334 FS	2/Lt Kolter, Mark H.	1 Me 109
4 FG/334 FS	1/Lt Lang, Joseph L.	1.5 Me 109
4 FG/334 FS	Maj McPharlin, Michael G. H.	1 Me 109
4 FG/334 FS	2/Lt Siems, Grover C. Jr	1 Fw 190
4 FG/334 FS	Capt Sobanski, Winslow M.	1 Me 109
78 FG/83 FS	1/Lt McDermott, William M.	0.5 Me 109
78 FG/83 FS	2/Lt White, Frederick	0.5 Me 109
352 FG/328 FS	1/Lt Thornell, John F. Jr	1 Me 109
352 FG/328 FS	1/Lt White, Henry W. Jr	1 Fw 190
352 FG/486 FS	Capt Anderson, Woodrow W.	1 Me 109
352 FG/486 FS	Maj Andrew, Stephen W.	1 Me 109
352 FG/486 FS	1/Lt Heller, Edwin L.	1.5 Me 109
352 FG/486 FS	2/Lt Howell, Lester L.	1 Me 109
352 FG/486 FS	1/Lt Barnes, Harry H.	1 Me 109
353 FG/Hq	Maj Gallup, Kenneth W.	1 Me 109
354 FG/353 FS	1/Lt Anderson, William Y.	1 Me 109
354 FG/353 FS	Maj Bradley, Jack T.	2 Me 109
354 FG/353 FS	Capt Eagleston, Glenn T.	1 Me 109
354 FG/353 FS	Capt Eagleston, Glenn T.	1 Fw 190
354 FG/353 FS	Capt Emmer, Wallace N.	2 Me 109
354 FG/353 FS	Capt Emmer, Wallace N.	1 Fw 190
354 FG/353 FS	1/Lt Frantz, Carl M.	1 Me 109
354 FG/353 FS	1/Lt Hunt, Edward E.	1 Me 109
354 FG/355 FS	1/Lt Allen, Gus W.	1 Me 109
354 FG/355 FS	1/Lt Gross, Clayton K.	1 Me 109
354 FG/355 FS	Capt Lasko, Charles W.	1.5 Me 109
354 FG/355 FS	2/Lt Moran, Patrick E.	1 Me 109
354 FG/356 FS	Capt Edwards, James W.	1 Fw 190
354 FG/356 FS	2/Lt Mitchell, Homer R.	0.5 Me 109
354 FG/356 FS	1/Lt Perkins, William R.	1 Ju 88
354 FG/356 FS	1/Lt Tenore, Bartholomew G.	0.5 Me 109
355 FG/357 FS	2/Lt Eshelman, Francis L.	1 Me 109
355 FG/357 FS	1/Lt MacFarlane, Walter E.	1 Me 109
357 FG/Hq	LtCol Hayes, Thomas L. Jr	1 Me 109
357 FG/362 FS	Maj Broadhead, Joseph E.	1 Fw 190

357 FG/362 FS	1/Lt Carson, Leonard K.	1 Fw 190
357 FG/363 FS	1/Lt Peters, Charles K.	1 Me 109
357 FG/364 FS	1/Lt Howell, John C.	1 Me 109
357 FG/364 FS	Capt Peterson, Richard A.	1 Me 109
357 FG/364 FS	1/Lt Ruder, Leroy A.	1 Me 109
363 FG/Hq	Maj McWherter, Robert C.	1 Me 109
363 FG/380 FS	1/Lt Clough, Gerald C.	1 Me 410
363 FG/380 FS	2/Lt Hill, James E.	1 Fw 190
363 FG/380 FS	1/Lt Kammerlohr, Morton A.	1 Me 109
363 FG/380 FS	1/Lt McEachron, Gordon T.	1 Me 109
363 FG/380 FS	2/Lt Ray, Donald W.	1 Fw 190
363 FG/380 FS	2/Lt Steiner, Walter H. Jr.	1 Fw 190
363 FG/380 FS	2/Lt Turner, Bruce W.	1 Fw 190
363 FG/380 FS	1/Lt Vance, Edwin E.	2 Me 109
363 FG/380 FS	1/Lt Williams, Burl R.	1 Fw 190
363 FG/382 FS	1/Lt Robertson, John	1 Me 109

Appendix 4: Roll of Honor

THOSE KILLED IN ACTION ON 28 MAY 1944

The burial locations at the American military cemeteries are the individual grave numbers (plot-row-grave). WOM stands for Walls or Tablets of the Missing.

Agee, Jack. D.	T/Sgt	Engineer	401 BG, 615 BS	Lorraine, C-11-83
Anderson, Woodrow W.	Capt	Pilot	352 FG, 486 FS	Henri-Chapelle, WOM
Banks, Douglas C.	2/Lt	Co-pilot	390 BG, 570 BS	Lorraine, K-26-09
Barger, Clarence R.	1/Lt	Pilot	355 FG, 354 FS	Henri-Chapelle, WOM
Barnett, Richard S.	2/Lt	Co-pilot	401 BG, 613 BS	USA
Beckowitz, Peter	Sgt	Ball turret gunner	401 BG, 613 BS	USA
Bennett, Sam B.	2/Lt	Bombardier	401 BG, 613 BS	USA
Bernstein, Harry	S/Sgt	Engineer	457 BG, 751 BS	USA
Black, J. Dee	1/Lt	Bombardier	401 BG, 615 BS	Lorraine, K-24-35
Brown, Richard C.	F/O	Navigator	390 BG, 571 BS	USA
Bundrick, Olin L.	Sgt	Left waist gunner	486 BG, 832 BS	Henri-Chapelle, WOM
Bushendorf, Everett M.	S/Sgt	Right waist gunner	401 BG, 615 BS	USA
Carroccia, Albert R.	Sgt	Tail gunner	303 BG, 358 BS	USA
Cass, Leo C.	Sgt	Right waist gunner	401 BG, 613 BS	USA
Chiles, Donald L.	2/Lt	Navigator	388 BG, 562 BS	USA
Christensen, Walter M.	2/Lt	Pilot	355 FG, 354 FS	Lorraine, E-36-23
Condon, William J.	2/Lt	Pilot	351 BG, 508 BS	Margraten, M-21-12
Cooper, Larry R.	S/Sgt	Radio operator	401 BG, 615 BS	Lorraine, D-20-25
Cruse, LeRoy D.	S/Sgt	Tail gunner	351 BG, 510 BS	USA
Czerpak, Henry	S/Sgt	Radio operator	390 BG, 570 BS	Ardennes, C-34-15
Daly, Arthur J.	S/Sgt	Right waist gunner	389 BG, 567 BS	USA & Ardennes, WOM
Drake, Robert E.	S/Sgt	Ball turret gunner	486 BG, 832 BS	Cambridge, WOM
Eckert, Charles A.	2/Lt	Co-pilot	401 BG, 613 BS	Lorraine, D-20-22
Elliott, Samuel R.	2/Lt	Co-pilot	390 BG, 571 BS	Lorraine, E-37-18
Farley, Joseph R.	2/Lt	Pilot	353 FG, 351 FS	Ardennes, D-01-43
Ferguson, Donald P.	2/Lt	Co-pilot	401 BG, 613 BS	USA
Folsom, Joe S.	S/Sgt	Right waist gunner	100 BG, 351 BS	USA
Furtta, Walter	S/Sgt	Ball turret gunner	457 BG, 751 BS	Ardennes, WOM
Garcia, Jose G.	Sgt	Left waist gunner	401 BG, 613 BS	Ardennes, C-03-12
Gascon, Oscar A.	S/Sgt	Tail gunner	457 BG, 751 BS	Cambridge, WOM
Gilmore, Elbert E.	T/Sgt	Engineer	392 BG, 577 BS	USA
Hauf, Emanuel	1/Lt	Pilot	457 BG, 751 BS	Ardennes, WOM

Hawley, William R.	2/Lt	Navigator	457 BG, 751 BS	Ardennes, WOM
Hazelett, Philip H.	1/Lt	Pilot	78 FG, 82 FS	Ardennes, D-14-30
Hendrickson, Milton C.	S/Sgt	Right waist gunner	303 BG, 358 BS	Margraten, Pilot-05-01
Hertzan, Harold	S/Sgt	Tail gunner	401 BG, 615 BS	USA
Hicks, Eugene R.	1/Lt	Pilot	486 BG, 832 BS	Henri-Chapelle, WOM
Hoover, Robert E.	2/Lt	Bombardier	401 BG, 613 BS	Ardennes, C-25-01
Ingram, John H.	2/Lt	Pilot ,	390 BG, 570 BS	USA
Jackson, Junny O.	S/Sgt	Engineer	351 BG, 508 BS	USA
Jaqua, Richard E.	2/Lt	Bombardier	457 BG, 751 BS	Ardennes, WOM
Jenkins, Charles G.	Sgt	Ball turret gunner	351 BG, 508 BS	USA
Joblonicky, Albert	2/Lt	Navigator	389 BG, 567 BS	USA
Johnson, Dana B.	S/Sgt	Radio operator	401 BG, 613 BS	USA
Johnson, Joe R.	Sgt	Ball turret gunner	401 BG, 615 BS	Lorraine, A-28-41
Johnson, John C.	2/Lt	Co-pilot	486 BG, 832 BS	Cambridge, WOM
Johnson, Willis H.	T/Sgt	Engineer	457 BG, 751 BS	Ardennes, WOM
Kaems, Robert H.	S/Sgt	Engineer	389 BG, 567 BS	Ardennes, WOM
Kaminski, Vincent J.	1/Lt	Pilot	401 BG, 615 BS	Lorraine, D-22-42
Kaplowitz, Isidor P.	S/Sgt	Ball turret gunner	351 BG, 511 BS	USA
Kilroy, James J.	T/Sgt	Radio operator	457 BG, 751 BS	Cambridge, WOM
Knight, Forest L.	T/Sgt	Radio operator	390 BG, 571 BS	Lorraine, A-15-21
Kolceski, Joseph P.	2/Lt	Co-pilot	351 BG, 508 BS	USA
Lacourse, Victor	S/Sgt	Tail gunner	389 BG, 567 BS	Ardennes, WOM
Ladas, Anthony E.	2/Lt	Pilot	363 FG, 382 FS	Ardennes, A-22-03
Lefkin, Michael	S/Sgt	Tail gunner	401 BG, 612 BS	USA
Lewis, James J.	Sgt	Ball turret gunner	390 BG, 570 BS	Margraten, WOM
Livingston, Acel E.	Sgt	Left waist gunner	303 BG, 358 BS	USA
Lutzi, Frank R.	S/Sgt	Ball turret gunner	401 BG, 615 BS	Cambridge, E-04-18
Maloney, John J.	2/Lt	Co-pilot	401 BG, 613 BS	Ardennes, B-12-09
Mamula Jr., Nick	S/Sgt	Radio operator	390 BG, 571 BS	Lorraine, K-48-29
May, William M.	S/Sgt	Left waist gunner	401 BG, 615 BS	Lorraine, E-42-26
McBeth, Delmar D.	S/Sgt	Bombardier	388 BG, 562 BS	USA
McCamy, James A.	2/Lt	Bombardier	303 BG, 358 BS	USA
McDowell, Don	1/Lt	Pilot	354 FG, 353 FS	Cambridge, D-02-11
McKee, Arnold	S/Sgt	Right waist gunner	390 BG, 570 BS	Margraten, WOM
Mihalich, Leonard A.	S/Sgt	Ball turret gunner	401 BG, 613 BS	Ardennes, C-18-06
Miller, Carl F.	2/Lt	Pilot	351 BG, 511 BS	USA
Miller, Floyd O.	S/Sgt	Tail gunner	401 BG, 613 BS	USA
Moll, David V.	2/Lt	Navigator	486 BG, 832 BS	Ardennes, WOM
Moore, Arlie W.	S/Sgt	Radio operator	351 BG, 511 BS	USA
Moore, Paul R.	S/Sgt	Waist gunner	457 BG, 751 BS	Cambridge, WOM
Morrow, Jim K.	T/Sgt	Engineer	401 BG, 613 BS	USA
Moskowitz, Murray	Sgt	Tail gunner	486 BG, 832 BS	Cambridge, WOM
Norris, Harry M.	Sgt	Waist gunner	351 BG, 508 BS	USA
Osborne, Charles E.	S/Sgt	NTG	389 BG, 567 BS	Ardennes, WOM
Orvis Jr., William S.	2/Lt	Pilot	78 FG, 82 FS	USA
Palmer Jr., Jackson	2/Lt	Navigator	303 BG, 358 BS	Margraten, N-22-14
Pfahler, Ervin J.	2/Lt	Co-pilot	303 BG, 358 BS	Margraten, B-07-20
Powell Jr., Chester L.	S/Sgt	Ball turret gunner	100 BG, 351 BS	USA
Priest, Jack B.	1/Lt	Bombardier	401 BG, 613 BS	USA
Reed, Arthur E.	Sgt	Ball turret gunner	390 BG, 571 BS	Lorraine, D-37-35
Ringstmeyer, Norman W.	Sgt	Ball turret gunner	351 BG, 511 BS	USA
Roskowick, Thomas L.	S/Sgt	Right waist gunner	388 BG, 562 BS	Margraten, P-08-11
Russell, Hugh D.	S/Sgt	Left waist gunner	401 BG, 612 BS	Lorraine, C-24-75

Russell, Kenneth E.	2/Lt	Bombardier	486 BG, 832 BS	Henri-Chapelle, WOM
Salmons, Kenneth A.	Sgt	Tail gunner	390 BG, 570 BS	USA
Samuelian, George	Sgt	Tail gunner	381 BG, 532 BS	Cambridge, F-07-132
Scharff, Paul F.	1/Lt	Pilot	401 BG, 613 BS	USA
Schindler, Claude E.	1/Lt	Co-pilot	100 BG, 351 BS	USA
Seaman, Raymond G.	Sgt	Left waist gunner	351 BG, 511 BS	Ardennes, A-22-03
Singleton, James D.	Sgt	Tail gunner	351 BG, 511 BS	USA
Smart, Robert B.	Sgt	Right waist gunner	390 BG, 571 BS	USA
Strate, Herbert V.	2/Lt	Pilot	390 BG, 571 BS	Lorraine, D-29-35
Stiegel, Alvin J.	F/O	Navigator	401 BG, 613 BS	USA
Swain, Donald V.	2/Lt	Co-pilot	457 BG, 751 BS	Ardennes, WOM
Tabeling, Robert G.	2/Lt	Navigator	390 BG, 570 BS	USA
Todd, James R.	M/Sgt	Right waist gunner	486 BG, 832 BS	Henri-Chapelle, WOM
Tomlinson, Roscoe D.	S/Sgt	Left waist gunner	401 BG, 613 BS	USA
Tucker, Walter L.	2/Lt	Co-pilot	389 BG, 567 BS	USA
Vasquez, Manuel	Sgt	Ball turret gunner	303 BG, 358 BS	USA
Wagoner, Walter W.	T/Sgt	Radio operator	457 BG, 749 BS	USA
Wampler, Ray M.	S/Sgt	Waist gunner	445 BG, 703 BS	Margraten, E-21-10
West, George E.	1/Lt	Pilot	401 BG, 612 BS	USA
Wicks, Wayne W.	T/Sgt	Radio operator	401 BG, 613 BS	Margraten, D-03-03
Woolfolk, Robert L.	2/Lt	Bombardier	390 BG, 571 BS	Ardennes, C-30-03
Zindar, Laddie J.	2/Lt	Navigator	351 BG, 508 BS	USA

Notes

CHAPTER 2: THE PLAN FOR A MISSION
1. Letter to author, 22 September 1982.
2. Quoted from Lowell Thomas and Edward Jablonski, *Bomber Commander* (London: Sidgwick and Jackson, 1977), 266.
3. 401st Bomb Group Mission Report, 28 May 1944; Record Group 18, Washington National Records Center.
4. Letter to author, 2 April 1993.

CHAPTER 3:THE GERMAN DEFENSES
1. Information based on Ernst Obermaier, *Die Ritterkreuzträger der Luftwaffe*, vol. 1, 61.
2. Telephone conversations, March 1988; and letter to author, 27 May 1988.
3. Author's interview with Strosetzki on 3 September 1999; and letters to author 9 July and 10 December 1999.
4. Information based on Schade interview in the unpublished manuscript *25 Milk Runs (and a Few Others)* by Richard R. Johnson, co-pilot in the 303rd Bomb Group.

CHAPTER 4: RUHLAND
1. Letter to author, 10 January 1987.
2. 201 File André R. Brousseau, through Catherine Brousseau, September 1999.
3. Letter to author, 4 July 1988.
4. Pilot encounter report; USAF Historical Research Center, Maxwell AFB, Alabama.
5. Statement in MACR 5138; Record Group 92, Washington National Records Center.
6. Letter to author, 23 December 1989.
7. Letter to author, 4 July 1988.
8. Statement in MACR 5026; Record Group 92, Washington National Record Center.
9. Pilot encounter report; USAF Historical Research Center, Maxwell AFB, Alabama.

CHAPTER 5: THE FIRST TWO COMBAT WINGS STRIKE DESSAU
1. Letter to author, 9 January 1999.
2. RL 2/1638, page 101; Bundesarchiv, Freiburg and interpretation report K2303; AIR 40/638 Public Record Office, London.
3. Public Relations Report 381st Bomb Group, through David R. Osborne.
4. Letter to author, 29 October 1997.

5. Letter to author, 15 November 1990.
6. Public Relations Report 381st Bomb Group, through David R. Osborne.
7. Pilot encounter report; USAF Historical Research Center, Maxwell AFB, Alabama.
8. Ibid.
9. Letter to author, 16 October 2000.
10. Letter to author, 15 November 1990.
11. 379th Bomb Group Mission Report; Record Group 18, Washington National Records Center.
12. Ibid.
13. Diary John B. Pratt, through Raymond R. Stevens, 4 October 1999.
14. Letter to author, 22 September 1982.
15. Statement by Tech Sgt. Francis H. Stender in MACR 5340; Record Group 92, Washington National Records Center.
16. 303rd Bomb Group Mission Report; Record Group 18, Washington National Records Center.
17. E-mail to author, 30 December 2000.

CHAPTER 6: THE 94TH COMBAT WING OVER DESSAU
1. Letter to author, 16 November 1992.
2. Letter to author, 19 July 1981.
3. Letter to author, 25 February 1991.
4. Letter to author, 16 November 1992.
5. Letter to author, 29 October 1990.
6. 351st Bomb Group Mission Report; Record Group 18, Washington National Records Center.
7. Letter to author, 9 July 1999.
8. Pilot encounter report, in "JG 1 und 11," by Prien and Rodeike.
9. 354th Fighter Squadron History, through Ray L. Shewfelt, September 17, 2000.
10. Pilot encounter report; USAF Historical Research Center, Maxwell AFB, Alabama.
11. Ibid.
12. Ibid.
13. Ibid.
14. Ibid.
15. Statement in MACR 5099; Record Group 92, Washington National Records Center.
16. Pilot encounter report; Washington National Records Center.
17. Statement in MACR 5136; Record Group 92, Washington National Records Center.
18. Letter to author, 31 October 1996.
19. Letters to author, 6 March and 29 March 1998.
20. Statement in MACR 5134; Record Group 92, Washington National Records Center.
21. DFC citation, Lt. Gordon McEachron; letter to author, 30 November 1989.
22. Quoted from "Fighter pilots in aerial combat," winter 1983 issue. With permission from author Steve Blake.
23. Letter to author, 25 February 1991.
24. Letter to author, 16 March 1981.
25. Letter to author, 8 January 1993.
26. Pilot encounter report; Washington National Records Center.

27. Pilot encounter report; Washington National Records Center.
28. Letter to author, 31 October 1987.
29. Statement in MACR 5328; Record Group 92, Washington National Records Center.
30. Letter to author, 11 November 1987.
31. Letter to author, 4 February 1993.
32. Letter to author, 16 November 1992.
33. Pilot encounter report; Washington National Records Center.
34. Letter to author, 12 August 1991.
35. Statement in MACR 5311; Record Group 92, Washington National Records Center.
36. Letter to author, 28 May 1981.
37. Letter to author.
38. Letter to author, 27 March 1990.
39. Letter to author, 16 May 1990.
40. Statements by Sgt Karl and Lt Schwartz in MACR 5306; Record Group 92, Washington National Records Center.
41. Letter to author, 12 February 1990.
42. Letter to author, 4 February 1993.
43. Statement in MACR 5305; Record Group 92, Washington National Records Center.
44. Pilot encounter report, Washington National Records Center.
45. Letter to author, 4 February 1993.
46. Letter to author, 29 November 1990.
47. diary; through Harold E. Jansen.
48. Letter to author, 26 February 1991.
49. Mrs. Brackley, letter to author, 1 September 1997.
50. Audio tape, February 1991.
51. Letter to author, 2 February 2000.
52. Audio tape, June 1982.
53. Letter to author, 19 January 1991.
54. Letter to author, 12 January 1991.
55. Dupont diary; through Harold E. Jansen.
56. Statement in MACR 5334; Record Group 92, Washington National Records Center.
57. Letter to author, 19 July 1981.
58. Letter to author, 25 December 1981.
59. Letter to author, 19 May 1988.
60. Letter to author, 1 November 1990.
61. Letter to author, 11 October 1990.
62. Letter to author, 4 February 1993.
63. Letter to author, 29 November 1990.
64. 401st Bomb Group Mission Report, Record Group 18, Washington National Records Center.

CHAPTER 7: MAGDEBURG

1. 94th Bomb Group Mission Report; Record Group 18, Washington National Records Center.
2. 95th Bomb Group Mission Report; Record Group 18, Washington National Records Center.

3. Letter to author, 8 April 1992.
4. Pilot encounter report; RL 10/483, Militärarchiv Freiburg.
5. Letters to author, 14 August 1989 and 21 May 1990.
6. Pilot encounter report; RL 10/483, Militärarchiv Freiburg.
7. Telephone conversation with author, 27 August 2000.
8. Diary of Charles N. Baker, given to author 3 May 2000.
9. Pilot encounter report; RL 10/483, Militärarchiv Freiburg.
10. Ibid.
11. Ibid.
12. Ibid.
13. Letter to author, 2 May 1990.
14. Pilot encounter report; RL 10/483, Militärarchiv Freiburg.
15. Letter to author, 11 October 1987.
16. Diary William E. Hill, through Gary L. Hill, March 2000.
17. Pilot encounter report; RL 10/483, Militärarchiv Freiburg.
18. Statement in MACR 5382; Record Group 92, Washington National Records Center.
19. Letter to author, 14 March 1990.
20. Telephone conversations with author, December 1999 and October 2000.
21. 100th Bomb Group Mission Report; Record Group 18, Washington National Records Center.
22. Ibid.
23. Ibid.
24. Ibid.
25. Pilot encounter report; USAF Historical Research Center, Maxwell AFB, Alabama.
26. Ibid.
27. Ibid.
28. Ibid.
29. Ibid.
30. Ibid.
31. Ibid.
32. Ibid.
33. Ibid.
34. Ibid.
35. Ibid.
36. Ibid.
37. Statement in MACR 5397; Record Group 92, Washington National Records Center.
38. Letter to author, 29 March, 1988.
39. Statement in MACR 5726; Record Group 92, Washington National Records Center.
40. Pilot encounter report; USAF Historical Research Center, Maxwell AFB, Alabama.
41. Pilot encounter report; through Steve Blake.
42. Pilot encounter report; through Steve Blake.
43. Statement in MACR 5137; Record Group 92, Washington National Records Center and pilot encounter report, through Steve Blake.
44. 390th Bomb Group Mission Report; Record Group 18, Washington National Records Center.

45. 100th Bomb Group Mission Report; Record Group 18, Washington National Records Center.
46. Ibid.
47. Statement in G-2 Target Intelligence Report 28 May 1944; Record Group 243, Washington National Records Center.
48. 100th Bomb Group Mission Report; Record Group 18, Washington National Records Center.
49. Diary of Robert A. Munroe, given to author 3 May 2000.

CHAPTER 8: KÖNIGSBORN
1. 388th Bomb Group Mission Report; Record Group 18, Washington National Records Center.
2. 385th Bomb Group Mission Report; Record Group 18, Washington National Records Center.
3. 94th Bomb Group Mission Report; Record Group 18, Washington National Records Center.
4. Letter to author, 21 April 1988.
5. Letter to author, 11 August 1981.
6. Letter to author, 15 January 1981.
7. Interview by author, June 1981.
8. Letter to author, 15 January 1981.

CHAPTER 9: ZEITZ
1. McClane diary, through Will Lundy.
2. Letter to author, 16 March 1981.
3. Pilot encounter report; USAF Historical Research Center, Maxwell AFB, Alabama.
4. Letter to author, 11 May 1990.
5. 467th Bomb Group Mission Report; Record Group 18, Washington National Records Center.
6. Ibid.
7. 492nd Bomb Group Mission Report; Record Group 18, Washington National Records Center.
8. Ibid.
9. Ibid.
10. McClane diary, through Will Lundy.

CHAPTER 10: MERSEBURG
1. 453rd Bomb Group Mission Report; Record Group 18, Washington National Records Center.
2. Ibid.
3. Letter to author, 10 December 1989.
4. Statement in trial 12-2564; Record Group 153, Washington National Records Center.
5. Letter to author, 13 December 1989.
6. Letter to author, 1 December 1987.
7. 453rd Bomb Group Mission Report; Record Group 18, Washington National Records Center.
8. Ibid.

9. 448th Bomb Group Mission Report; Record Group 18, Washington National Records Center.
10. 20th Combat Wing Mission Report; Record Group 18, Washington National Records Center.

CHAPTER 11: LÜTZKENDORF
1. Letter to author, 8 March 1992.
2. 487th Bomb Group Mission Report; Record Group 18, Washington National Records Center.
3. Ibid.
4. Letter to author, 14 November 1989.
5. 486th Bomb Group Mission Report; Record Group 18, Washington National Records Center.
6. Interview with James Bogert, by Linda and Ed Camp, 28 November 1993.
7. Interview with James Bogert, by Linda and Ed Camp, 28 November 1993. German records indicate that Smith reached the shore already on 28 May near Zuydcoote, and that Bogert and Munro reached the shore on 30 May near Gravelines. However, the date on Smith could well be an error of the clerk or interrogator who noted the date that the crash occurred. I do not have a suitable explanation for the difference in location where the men reportedly came ashore.
8. Operational Record Book 65 Squadron; Air 27, Public Record Office, London.
9. Letter to author, 24 September 1987.
10. Statement in MACR 5390; Record Group 92, Washington National Records Center.
11. Escape and evasion report 1595; Record Group 332, Washington National Records Center.

CHAPTER 12: COLOGNE
1. Letter to author, 8 May 1990.
2. Letter to author, 5 April 1990.
3. Letter to author, 2 April 1990.
4. Letter to author, 6 April 1990.
5. Letter to author, 11 April 1990.
6. Information in AIR 40/638, Public Record Office, London.
7. Letter to author, 11 April 1990.
8. Letter to author, 8 May 1990.
9. Letter to author, 6 August 1990.

CHAPTER 13: AFTERMATH
1. Letter to author, 30 November 1989.
2. Escape and evasion report 1504; Record Group 332, Washington National Records Center.
3. Letter to author, 30 November 1989.
4. Letter to author, 19 August 1997.
5. Escape and evasion report 2048; Record Group 332, Washington National Records Center.
6. Escape and evasion report 1595; Record Group 332, Washington National Records Center.
7. Letter provided by Wade Scharff, 1 January 2001.

8. These letters were kindly provided by Linda Camp, a niece of Lt. Kenneth Russell. She has also devoted a fine website to the crew, www.geocities.com/llcamp_to/index.html.

9. Letters to author, 14 August 1989 and 21 May 1990.

10. Statement by Johannes Wagner, through Konrad Rudolph.

11. Letter to author, 1 October 1987.

CHAPTER 14: WAR CRIMES

1. Diary Leen Stolk, through G.L. Hammer, 22 November 1998.

2. Trial 12-57, Record Group 153, Washington National Records Center.

3. 9 June 1944 letter, through Larry L. Tuel, February 5, 2001.

4. Trial 12-1967: Record Group 153, Washington National Records Center.

5. 13 July 1945 letter, through Larry L. Tuel, 5 February 2001.

6. Trial 12-1967: Record Group 153, Washington National Records Center.

Acknowledgments

This book is based on historical records that are brought to life by the stories and pictures of participants. The book could not have been written without the help of many people, worldwide.

First, I would like to thank the late Clyde H. Waite; his enthusiasm in the early days of my research really influenced me and made me feel I was doing something worthwhile. Had it not been for his enthusiasm, I may never have embarked on this endeavour. Unfortunately, Clyde did not see the completion of this book, as he passed away in October 1994.

I thank my father, for starting me off on this project with his stories. I feel very fortunate that I am able to turn his wartime memory into a book.

My dear friends Richard and Marjorie Johnson greatly facilitated my two visits to the National Archives and did everything to make my visit successful.

Many people in the United States kindly answered my letters of inquiry and supplied me with photographs and other material. They are the people who really made this story of 28 May 1944 and to all of them I convey my sincere thanks: Barbara Allen, Marjorie Anderson, William Y. Anderson, Paul M. Andrews, Teri Babcock, Victor L. Baccaro, Charles N. Baker, Dolores Banas, Quentin R. Bass, William F. Bemus, Mrs. Nicholas F. Bendino, Alvin P. Berg, Walter Bergstrom, Steve Blake, Harold W. Bowman, Juanita and Jim Brackley, Bruno Branch, Edward J. Brazinski, George L. Brice, Donald W. Brooman, Catherine Brousseau, James R. Brown, John R. Brown, Lawrence G. Brown, Russell A. Brown, Ralph S. Burckes, Donald L. Caldwell, Linda Camp, John W. Campbell, William Carleton, Lorraine Caron, Bruce W. Carr, Ray Cary, Lawrence R. Casey, Franklin D. Cass, Fred Clemovitz, Arthur M. Codding, Philip D. Cohen, Thomas W. Colby, Clinton Combs, Robert W. Condon, Ed G. Cooper, Marcel Copt, Walter F. Creigh, John B. Dann, James Derk, Alvin G. Determan, Charles W. Dewitt, James R. Dobson, John R. Duchesneau, Daniel E. and Desma Dunbar, John B. Duncan, William F. Dunham, Arthur J. Egan, Jack Eley, Robert J. Enstad, Norman A. Erbe, Doris Freyland, Gary L. Fry, Henry J. Gerards, John J. Gides, Elmer C. Gillespie, James W. Godwin, Harry Goland, Thomas W. Gougarty, Stanley V. Gray, Herbert R. Greene, Clayton K. Gross, Robert A. Hadley, Wardlaw M. Hammond,

Charles E. Harris, Thomas L. Hayes, Edwin L. Heller, Charles L. Henry, Patrick W. Henry, Aubrey E. Hewatt, Gary L. Hill, James E. Hill, James S. Hollowell, H. Joseph Houlihan, John C. and Michael Howell, Winfred D. Howell, O. Allen Israelsen, Tom Ivie, Robert F. Jipson, Donald M. Johnston, Betty and Kenneth Joye, Robert V. Kerr, James H. Kincaid, Dan C. Knight, Lawrence Kofoed, Claude M. Kolb, Thomas L. Kracker, Leonard J. Kriesky Jr., Lucius G. Lacy, Gene Lamar, Charles W. Latta, Stephen LeBailly, Irving Lewis, Leon W. Lobdell, Willard O. Locklear, Walter E. MacFarlane, Ralph M. Marts, Jackie Matthias, Edgar C. Miller, Gale W. Minor, Robert S. McCall, Clyde W. McClelland, Gordon T. McEachron, Doris M. McFetridge, Clem B. and Jo Nell McKennon, Kent D. Miller, Raymond J. Miller, George C. Montgomery, Fred A. Morley, William H. Morris, Julius J. Moseley, Fred W. Murray, Stephen G. Nason, Jerry D. Nelson, John W. Norton, Lloyd A. Nutter, Helen Ochsenhirt, Peter L.M. Packard, John O. Painter, Edward T. Pawlak, Bonnie Perry, Green B. Poore, Marcia Prather, John B. Pratt, William F. Protz, Fred G. Pynigar, Leonard Raterman, Richard Ray, Lynn W. Rice, Mrs. Robert W. Rittmaier, John Robertson, Morris D. Robley, Thomas Roskowick, Frank J. Rowe, Perry Rudd, Virginia B. Russell, Robert E. Ryan, Alfred M. Sanders, William E. Satterwhite, Wade Scharff, David W. Schellenger, O. Dean Settles, Charles D. Shebell, Roberta Sinnock, Jane Sipp, James M. Smallin, Talbert E. Spenhoff, Paul Spiers, Flo F. Stafford, Hobart H. Steely, Kermit D. Stevens, Raymond R. Stevens, Donald K. Stewart, Rudolph M. Stohl, Edward C. Stoy, Raymond E. Strate, Walter R. Subora, Jack Sutherlin, Murray Swerdlove, Roscoe L. Taylor, John A. Thurmon, Larry L. Tuel, Margaret Ulreich, Dale L. Vance, Casper Vecchione, Gil Villalpando, Harold Walker, Kale S. Warren, Kevin Welch, James E. Wells, Vera Wepner, Bill Wescott, Samuel H. Whitehead, Forrest Williams, Warren H. Williams, Carolyn Willis, Craig W. Winters, Henry W. Wolcott, Max J. Woolley, Charles M. Zettek, Bruce Zigler, and Ann M. Zuravic.

I am much indebted to Charles Harris and, again, Richard Johnson for proofreading the first version of the manuscript and their valuable comments and advise.

The following representatives of various bomb or fighter group associations were great help during the long research period, and provided help in many ways: John M. Balason [353 FG], Rom Blaylock [452 BG], James E. Bollinger [354th FG], Chris Brassfield [466 BG], Homer L. Briggs [457 BG], Francis O. Brown [486 BG], Al Buehler [390 BG], Carl M. Christ [344 BG], Joseph B. DeShay [357 FG], Francis J. DiMola [445 BG], Michael P. Faley [100 BG], Fred Fehsenfeld [354 FG], Carl Fyler [303 BG], Harry D. Gobrecht [303 BG], Marc Hamel [352 FG], H. C. "Pete" Henry [44 BG], Ed J. Huntzinger [388 BG], Sheldon W. Kirsner [92 BG], Will Lundy [44 BG], Leroy A. Nitschke [4 FG], Merle C. Olmsted [357 FG], Marc Poole [384

BG], George A. Reynolds [458 BG], Jan Riddling [100 BG], Robert J. Robinson [352 FG], Ben Schohan [351 BG], Arthur W. Silva [487 BG], Terri Staton [354 FG], Sam Sox [352 FG], Ray L. Summa [34 BG], Ralph W. Trout [401 BG], Horace L. Varian [100 BG], Joseph Vieira [303 BG], Charles L. Walker [445 BG], John S. Warner [390th BG], Leroy C. Wilcox [381 BG], and Earl Zimmerman [389 BG].

Researching and writing this book was a labor of love, and I had to do it in my spare time, balancing my family and my military career. I am truly sorry that the long time it took me to complete this book also meant that some of the fine contributors I mentioned above, passed away before it was finished. I sincerely hope that this book is a fitting tribute to their service for their country and their cooperation in my research.

My visits to the National Archives in Washington D.C. were highlights in my research. In the person of Mr. Richard Boylan I thank his staff of the Military Branch and the employees in the reading room. I would especially like to mention the help that Holly Reed from the Still Picture Reference Team at the National Archives gave me. Other U.S. officials who assisted me in various ways were Mr. John R. Bolton at Randolph Air Force Base, Mr. James H. Kitchens and Captain Joe T. Reams at Maxwell Air Force Base and Mr. John F. Manning of the Mortuary Division of the Department of the Army in Alexandria. Artists Robert Bailey and Troy White kindly permitted me to use their fine work in the colour section in the book.

In Germany, help was given by Herr Nilges at the Bundesarchiv in Koblenz, Herr Dahl from the archive in Cologne and the Militärarchiv in Freiburg and Deutsche Dienststelle in Berlin. Others who provided help were Wilfried Brandes, Rudolph Gloeckner, Hans Halbey, Hans Höhler, Rüdiger Kirchmayr, Frau Hildegund Körner, Hans Lächler, Stephen Ransom, Konrad Rudolph, Rudolph Strosetzki, Herbert Treppe, and Hans Schuffenhauer. Former *Luftwaffe* pilot Horst Petzschler, now living in the United States, also kindly answered my letters of inquiry.

My thanks also go to the staff of the Public Record Office in England and the following British amateur historians, many of which I was priviliged to meet in person, and spent many pleasant hours with: John W. Archer, Stephen P. Adams, the late Bernard W. Bains, Tom Brittan, Peter Claydon, Graham Cross, Stewart P. Evans, Ken Everett, Norman Franks, Roger A. Freeman, Michael L. Gibson, Chris Goss, Ken Harbour, Mike Harris, the late Vic Maslen, Robert B. Mynn, David R. Osborne, John Walker, Ken Wells and John B. Wilson. Also Bill Upperton, a Typhoon pilot, and Jim Hammond and George Seeley, both members of an Air Sea Rescue launch, who were in action on 28 May contributed to this book.

In Belgium, help was provided by Robert Cotyle, Eric Mombeek, and Jean Louis Roba.

In Holland, I would like to thank Eric Bakker, G. L. Hammer, Jan A. Hey, Marcel Hogenhuis, Ab A. Jansen, Harold E. Jansen, Arie P. de Jong, Johan Manrho, Johan Schuurman, L. Stolk, and Bernard G. Wijs.

But all of the help that the people mentioned above provided would have been in vain had it not been for my wife, Hester. She supported me almost from day one of my research. She rarely complained about the countless hours I spent writing letters to the veterans and working on my manuscript; she wandered around deserted former Eighth Air Force fields in East Anglia with me; visited many American War Cemeteries in Europe; it was she in the first place who persuaded me to go to the National Archives for research and finally ended up spending a day of her honeymoon in those same archives, viewing exciting unedited combat film shot on 28 May 1944. Without her continual endurance and support for more than twenty years, this book could never have been written.

Index

419

Stackpole Military History Series

Real battles. Real soldiers. Real stories.

Stackpole Military History Series

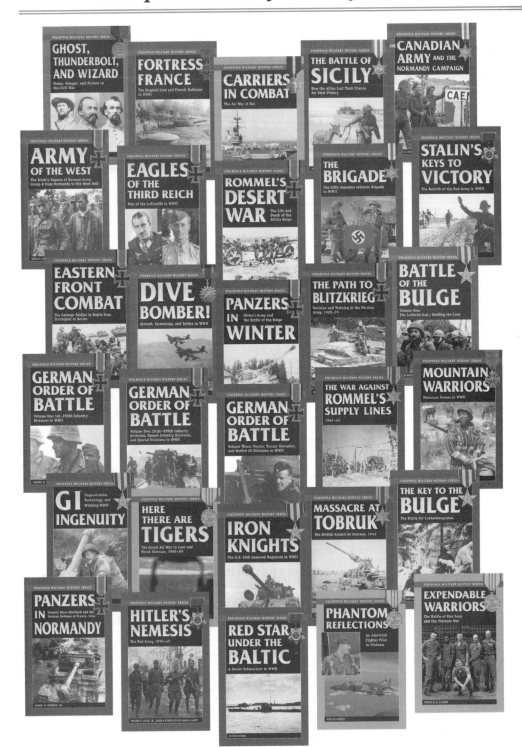

Real battles. Real soldiers. Real stories.

Stackpole Military History Series

Real battles. Real soldiers. Real stories.

STACKPOLE MILITARY HISTORY SERIES

TWO ONE PONY
An American Soldier's Year in Vietnam, 1969

STACKPOLE MILITARY HISTORY SERIES

JAPANESE ARMY FIGHTER ACES
1931–45

NEW for Spring 2012

STACKPOLE MILITARY HISTORY SERIES

JG 26 LUFTWAFFE FIGHTER WING WAR DIARY
Volume Two: 1943–45

DONALD CAL

STACKPOLE MILITARY HISTORY SERIES

PANZER WEDGE
The 3rd Panzer Division's Drive on Moscow, 1941

STACKPOLE MILITARY HISTORY SERIES

THE SPARTAN ARMY

J.F. LAZENBY

STACKPOLE MILITARY HISTORY SERIES

WAR OF THE WHITE DEATH
Finland against the Soviet Union, 1939–40

BAIR IRINCHEEV

STACKPOLE MILITARY HISTORY SERIES

WINTER STORM
The Battle for Stalingrad and the Operation to Rescue 6th Army

HANS WIJERS

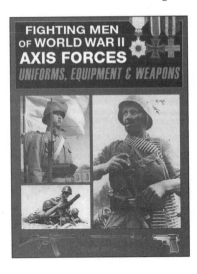
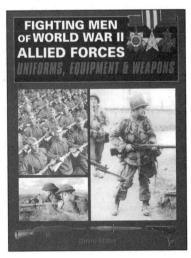